THE ZULU KINGS

THE ZULU KINGS

BRIAN ROBERTS

BARNES
&NOBLE
BOOKS
NEW YORK

This edition published by Barnes & Noble, Inc.,
by arrangement with Brandt & Brandt Literary Agents, Inc.

1994 Barnes & Noble Books

ISBN 1-56619-683-3

Printed and bound in the United States of America

M 9 8 7 6 5 4 3 2 1

FOR
KEITH KILLBY

CONTENTS

CONTENTS

III Downfall

ILLUSTRATIONS

ACKNOWLEDGEMENTS

This book is based largely on unpublished and primary sources and is the result of several years of research. As this research dates back to the writing of my first book, *Ladies in the Veld* (published in 1965) it is impossible to thank by name all those who have assisted me. On my various journeys through Zululand I have been helped in countless ways by people of all races: complete strangers have gone out of their way to offer aid, advice and hospitality. I have drawn on the reminiscences and knowledge of those well versed in Zulu history as well as the encouragement of local enthusiasts. Without the help of all these people the writing of this book would have been a far more difficult, if not impossible, task; while my thanks to them cannot be specific they are none the less sincere.

It would, however, be a serious omission if I failed to acknowledge the very real debt of gratitude I owe to Mr Theo Aronson whose unstinting assistance and encouragement have, as always, proved invaluable to the writing, research and revision of my manuscript. I am grateful also for the assistance I have received from the staff of the Cape Archives; particularly for the most helpful co-operation of Mr J. Smalberger who directed me to several unpublished sources. I am greatly indebted to Mrs Daphne Strutt of the Old House and Local History Museums in Durban whose timely assistance proved most helpful in locating illustrations and to Miss Norah Henshilwood for her usual generosity in lending me many urgently required books. I would like to thank those members of the staffs of the South African Library in Cape Town, the Killie Campbell Africana Library in Durban and the Public Record Office in London, whose patience in answering my many queries is greatly appreciated.

My final thanks are due to Howard B. Timmins of Cape Town,

publisher of *Zulu Horizons*, for permission to quote B. W. Vilakazi's poem *üshaka KaSenzangakhona* and to the Van Riebeeck Society of Cape Town to quote extracts from their various publications listed in the Bibliography.

PART ONE

SHAKA

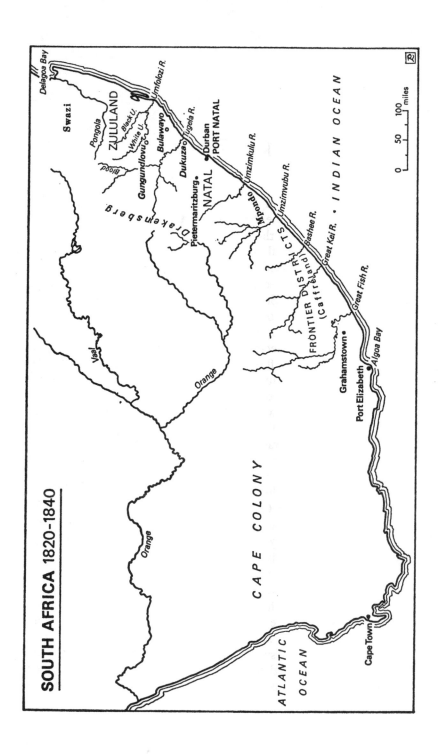

SOUTH AFRICA 1820-1840

Delagoa Bay

Swazi

ZULULAND

Pongola

Umfolozi R.

Black U.

White U.

Blood

Bulawayo

Gungundlovu

Dukuza

Tugela R.

Durban

PORT NATAL

Pietermaritzburg

NATAL

Drakensberg

Umzimkulu R.

Umzimvubu R.

Mpondo

Bashee R.

Great Kei R.

FRONTIER DISTRICTS
(Caffreland)

INDIAN OCEAN

Great Fish R.

Grahamstown

Algoa Bay

Port Elizabeth

Vaal

Orange

Orange

CAPE COLONY

ATLANTIC
OCEAN

Cape Town

0   50   100
miles

THE FORBIDDING COAST

OF ALL THE coasts of the Dark Continent, few were more mysterious than this one. Stretching for hundreds of miles, along south-east Africa, from the scrappy British settlement at Algoa Bay to the hardly better established Portuguese base at Delagoa Bay, it remained unexplored and uncharted until well into the nineteenth century. Many had sailed past it but few had set foot on it. Yet it looked benign enough. Seen from the tilting deck of one of the ships that plied between Europe and the East, its appearance was anything but forbidding. Long lines of waves unfurled onto sunlit beaches; luxuriant vegetation spread almost to the water's edge; wide, tree-lined rivers flowed into placid lagoons; gentle hillocks melted away into a blue-hazed distance. There was something peaceful, almost park-like, about it all. Such greenery, claimed one enthusiastic observer, 'would have been the glory of some gentleman's estate in England'.

But the appearance was deceptive. This apparently idyllic stretch of coast was known to be extremely treacherous.

First sighted by the Portuguese explorer, Vasco da Gama, on Christmas Day, 1479, the coast had been named Natal to mark the day of its discovery. Da Gama was rounding the tip of Africa on his epic voyage to India and his association with the coast went little further than the naming of it. Other sailors were not so fortunate. Once the sea-route to the East was open, the ill-constructed, often badly navigated, and invariably overladen merchant ships of Portugal battled their way along the coast, lashed by the ferocious gales for which the southern African littoral soon became notorious. By the end of the sixteenth century, the history of the Natal coast was largely a history of shipwrecks and disaster.

Stories told by the survivors of ships wrecked off Natal were awesome. The few, pathetically small, groups of emaciated sailors and passengers who succeeded in making their way along the coast

SHAKA

to Portuguese East Africa kept themselves alive by remarkable feats of endurance. Starvation, thirst, disease and attacks by hostile tribes claimed the majority; some gave up along the way, overcome by exhaustion or despair.

Survival was not always a matter of fortitude; sometimes it was the result of luck or temperament. Occasionally a passing ship would arrive in time to rescue the remnants of a shipwrecked party, or a friendly coastal tribe would succour, and even assimilate, a band of castaways. It was by no means unusual for the survivors of later shipwrecks to stumble upon Europeans—scarcely recognisable and forgetful of their past—living as tribesmen in the African kraals along the coast.

But survivors were few, the death toll enormous. The fate of the crew and passengers of the *Saó João*, one of the first ships to be wrecked off this grim coast, was to become typical of those who followed. When the *Saó João* foundered and eventually sank, some three hundred miles north-east of Algoa Bay, in June 1552, more than a hundred of those on board were drowned. Of the five hundred people who reached the shore, only twenty-odd survived the gruelling march to Portuguese East Africa.

Throughout the seventeenth and eighteenth centuries the list of ships wrecked on the southern African coast continued to alarm merchant seamen. The Portuguese were followed by the Dutch and the British, but improvements in shipbuilding and seamanship did little to offset the dangers of the treacherous coast. From time to time attempts were made to explore it from the sea, but the results were far from encouraging. Neither merchants nor slavers were sufficiently impressed by reports of Natal to brave the dangers of trading with the coastal Africans.

Of the tribes of the interior, little or nothing was known. The only recorded attempt of white men trying to reach Portuguese East Africa from the Cape by an overland route was that made by Dr Robert Cowan in 1807. Accompanied by an army officer and twenty Hottentot soldiers, Cowan, a military surgeon, had been despatched on his mission by the then Governor of the Cape, Lord Caledon. The little party had made its way north before branching off to the east. They were never seen again. Quite obviously, the interior of south-east Africa was, if anything, even more frightening and mysterious than its seaboard.

Not until 1821 was serious consideration given to making a scientific survey of the Natal coast. Two years earlier the Cape authorities had decided to strengthen the eastern frontier—then the boundary between white and black South Africa—by granting land to British immigrants who wished to settle there. The arrival of some five thousand of these settlers at Algoa Bay, in 1820, had sparked off new interest in the neglected coast line. The British Admiralty, wanting employment for naval officers sitting idle after the long drawn-out Napoleonic wars, turned their attention to an extensive survey of the eastern coast of Africa.

A surveying expedition, under the command of Captain William Fitzwilliam Owen, was instructed to explore and chart the African coast from the Cape of Good Hope to Cape Guardafui, north of Portuguese East Africa. Where possible, a report was to be made on the hinterland and its inhabitants. Two ships, the *Leven* and the *Barracouta*, were fitted out for the expedition. They sailed from England in February 1822 and arrived at the Cape on 7 July.

At Cape Town there was some delay while Captain Owen collected additional equipment and arranged for the Cape authorities to supply him with interpreters to communicate with the coastal Africans. When they arrived, these interpreters included six convicts from the off-shore penal settlement, Robben Island. They were a sorry looking lot these convicts—dressed in filthy skins, their hands tied—and appeared somewhat apprehensive about their new assignment. 'Kaffirs,' remarked one of the naval officers with fine British superiority, 'have an unaccountable dread of water.'

One of them, however, towered above the others. Known as Jacob (although the sailors called him Jakot) he was said to be very handsome, strong and tall and possessed of a commanding figure. Jacob was thought to be a chief of one of the frontier tribes, but his claims to chieftainship were dubious. For years he had been in conflict with the Boers on the eastern border of the Cape Colony and had finally been captured while leading a cattle raid on a frontier farm. Sent to Robben Island for an unspecified term of imprisonment, Jacob, like his companions, had been promised his freedom as a reward for assisting Owen's surveying expedition. Captain Owen considered ex-convict Jacob to be 'excellent and trustworthy' and before long he had become a favourite with the crew of the *Leven*.

By the end of August, Owen, commanding the *Leven*, was ready to start out on his surveying operations. The *Barracouta* had left earlier to make a running survey of the south-eastern coast. Its mission had hardly been a spectacular success. Bad weather had prevented it touching at many points beyond Algoa Bay and what little contact the officers of the *Barracouta* had been able to make with the coastal tribes had not impressed them. They found them 'a composition of cunning, treachery, drunkenness and gluttony'. A less damning, and certainly more interesting, observation was that these apparently deplorable tribesmen were not the 'aboriginal inhabitants' of the coastal strip. They were merely refugees of a fierce warrior race which occupied the interior.

'At the time,' it was recorded, 'the work of depopulation was carried on with savage rapidity by the merciless and destructive conquests of a tyrannical monster named Chaka, whose bloody proceedings promised soon to leave the whole of the beautiful country . . . totally desolate.' It was an early mention of a name about which a great deal was to be heard.

In October, Owen in the *Leven*, having made his way slowly along the coast, was joined by the *Barracouta* at Delagoa Bay, in Portuguese East Africa. Here the detailed survey began in earnest.

Efforts were made to explore the river mouths and parties of sailors were sent ashore to investigate the surrounding country. They found it singularly uninviting: hot, swampy, infested by mosquitoes and teeming with hippos. Human habitation was confined to the lethargic Portuguese garrison at Delagoa Bay and a few clans of the miserable looking Africans common to the coastal areas. Information about the powerful interior tribe was as confusing as it was vague. If the Portuguese knew little about the people of the coast, they knew even less about those of the hinterland.

'To the southward . . .' reported one of the officers of the *Leven*, 'there exists a tribe of warlike Kaffers, called Zoolos, but by the Portuguese Vatwas, being the same as the ancient term Batwa, or Butwah: the people of Delagoa call them Hollentontes, doubtless a corruption from Hottentots, as they come from the south, which is considered their country.' The only thing certain about this many-named tribe was its reputation for ferocity.

Owen was forced to cut short his survey of Delagoa Bay. The entire area was blighted by malaria which soon struck the surveying ships. By the end of November so many officers and men had died that Owen had no alternative but to put to sea again. Setting course southwards, he resumed the running survey of the coast; this time with greater success. But the fever-stricken men continued to die and many of the headlands and creeks charted were named, not only after the leaders of the surveying teams, but in memory of sailors buried at sea. It was a gruesome voyage. More than half the seamen and two-thirds of the officers were stricken by the fever; few of them survived.

Closer aquaintance with the miserable inhabitants of the coastal strip merely confirmed Owen's earlier findings. On one occasion the redoubtable Jacob was able to give the naval officers a telling demonstration of his contempt for the tribesmen. An exploring party from the *Leven* rowed ashore and were approached by a band of Africans who challenged Jacob to a trial of skill. One of them selected a small tree and, retreating some forty yards, threw his assegai (spear). He missed his target. Jacob picked up the assegai, walked a further twenty yards off and, with 'a tremendous motion in his hand, threw the spear with such force and dexterity that it entered the centre of the tree so deep as to be with difficulty extracted'. Leaving the assegai quivering in the tree and the Africans gaping with astonishment, Jacob strolled off 'without altering a muscle of his features, apparently conscious of his superiority over them'. That the sailors accepted Jacob's claim to be a chief of some renown is hardly surprising.

Bad weather again prevented Owen from completing his survey. After a few weeks he abandoned the coast and sailed back to Cape Town. Here, despite the disasters of their voyage, the crews of the *Leven* and the *Barracouta* were feted. Everyone was eager to know more about the coast and considerable interest was shown in a new African interpreter whom Owen had acquired at Delagoa Bay. Known as 'English Bill', this somewhat garrulous linguist not only spoke the dialects of the coast but was reasonably proficient in English, Dutch, Portuguese and Hindustani. The fact that he was known to have seven wives and a good knowledge of Delagoa Bay added to his fascinations. He was much in demand. At the Greenpoint races, at a ball held aboard the *Leven*, and even at Government House, English Bill was trailed by a crowd of curious admirers. Captain Owen was so taken with his protégé that he often sat up talking to him far into the night. Jacob, for all his admirable spear throwing, could not begin to compete with his sophisticated rival.

But English Bill was not Owen's only acquisition in Portuguese East Africa. A Cape merchant named John Robert Thompson had been recovering from a bout of fever at Delagoa Bay when the *Leven* and the *Barracouta* began operations there. Excited by stories of ivory, and rumours of gold, in the Natal interior, Thompson, on his return to Cape Town, decided to finance a joint stock company 'for the purpose of trading with the natives on the coast of Natal'. The company was duly formed. Responsible for its formation was a naval officer who had recently settled at the Cape—Lieutenant Farewell.

[2]

Lieutenant Francis George Farewell was then a young man in his late twenties. He looked very much what he was: the son of an English country parson, who had spent most of his life at sea; fresh-faced and forthright.

Details of Farewell's early career are scrappy. It is known, however, that he was born at Holbrook House, in Wincanton, Somerset, and that his father was the Reverend Samuel Farewell, rector of the Church of St Peter and Paul. His father died when Francis was young and his family moved to Tiverton, in Devon, where, in March 1802, he was enrolled as a day-boy at the well-known Blundell's School. Five years later he left school and, at the age of thirteen, joined the Royal Navy as a midshipman. During the Napoleonic wars, he served with distinction: in a naval action at Lissa, he is reported to have taken charge of a gun after the midshipman manning it had been killed and, on another occasion, he was himself badly wounded. His promotion to lieutenant with seniority was gazetted in February 1815. The next few years of his life are something of a mystery.

Like a great many other naval officers, Farewell was reduced to half pay when the war against Napoleon ended. Still drawn to the sea, he made his way to India where he eventually became the managing owner of a trading ship. Nothing is known of his career in India but a later acquaintance was to hint that he had disgraced himself there. For all that, Farewell appears to have been an amusing and enterprising young man. His reputation as an adventurer gave him a certain dash; his bluff charm won him many friends.

It was probably while serving in the Indian merchant service that Farewell first became attracted to the Cape. For years Cape Town had been recognised as a victualling station for ships travelling to the East. The strictly commercial policies of the Dutch East India Company had prevented it developing into anything more. Territorial expansion in southern Africa was frowned upon in Holland and it was not until some years after the British occupied the Cape permanently, in 1806, that the character of the isolated settlement showed signs of change. Even then it was a slow business.

When Farewell first came to know it, Cape Town was still a leisurely seaport, set against the flat-topped grandeur of Table Mountain. Its low, beautifully proportioned houses, with their whitewashed walls and vine-covered pergolas, typified the graceful ease of the late eighteenth century. As the only sizeable town in southern Africa, up-country visitors imagined it to be a metropolis and it was often compared with the cities of Europe. But, although its broad tree-lined streets, open spaces, and Grand Parade gave the impression of spacious elegance, the comparison was more romantic than real. Colourful and lively during the day—crowded with red-turbanned Malays, water-carrying slaves, hawkers, hand-carts and ox-wagons—it took on at night the atmosphere of a small provincial town.

Nevertheless, the potential of the Cape was gradually coming to be recognised. The trickle of British immigrants, which had started in 1817, had been considerably increased by the arrival of the settlers of 1820. Merchants, tradesmen, retired military and naval officers, and an ever-growing army of civil servants helped to give a metropolitan flavour to the established community at the Cape. 'In respect to society,' wrote a traveller in 1823, 'this Colony is fortunate above most others in possessing a variety suited to all classes. . . . Though it would be absurd to compare the society of Cape Town with that of an European metropolis for extent and variety, it is not too much to state, that there are few men either of rank or talent so exalted as not to find appropriate companions in the principal official persons of the Colony, (many of them relations and connexions of families of rank in England) and in the officers of His Majesty's military and naval services, and visitors from India.'

As one of the welcome visitors from India, Francis Farewell had found Cape Town very much to his taste. Its attractions had been heightened for him when he met Elizabeth Catherine Schmidt, a pretty girl of Dutch descent whom he married by special licence in the English Church on 17 August 1822. Marriage, however, had presented the roving Farewell with problems. By deciding to settle down he had fallen into the ranks of ex-naval officers who, with families to support, were finding their qualifications inadequate for civilian life. Officers on half-pay were becoming all too familiar at the Cape and outlet for their limited talents were by no means plentiful.

Farewell's only business experience had been as a merchant sailor in India and it may well have been the excitement created by the return of Owen's surveying expedition from Delagoa Bay that gave him the idea of forming a trading company to try his luck along the Natal coast. Whatever its inspiration, the Farewell Trading Company was launched at the beginning of 1823.

As a partner in this new venture, Farewell chose James Saunders King, commander of a small merchant brig called the *Salisbury*. The two men had much in common. King, also, was a former officer in the Royal Navy. Born in Halifax, Nova Scotia, in 1795, he had joined the British navy as a ship's boy at the age of eleven and had resigned as a midshipman some ten years later. For the next eight years he had served, in various capacities, in the merchant service. In 1822 he had been successful in obtaining command of the *Salisbury*, an ancient sailing ship employed, for the most part, in transporting troops between Cape Town and Algoa Bay. But King, like Farewell, was on the lookout for something better. He was not going to spend the rest of his days ferrying troops to and fro.

From the little that is known of his early activities at the Cape, it is obvious that James Saunders King was a man with an eye to the main chance. Generally referred to as Lieutenant King, he had not only managed to pass himself off as an experienced sea captain but had quickly become a popular Cape Town personality. Few, if any, of his many acquaintances were aware that he had left the Royal

Navy as a midshipman. He was seen simply as an 'amiable and enterprising individual' who, like his fellow officers, was struggling to make the best of civilian life. Unfortunately, his efforts had so far brought him little reward.

On one of his early visits to Algoa Bay in the *Salisbury*, King had explored two small off-shore islands and found them 'uninhabited but abounding with Seals, Fish etc.'. With hopes of starting a trade in seal oil and fish, he had landed ten Hottentots on the islands and hurried back to Cape Town to apply for trading rights. His application had been turned down. Aggrieved at this refusal, his disappointment had turned to anger when, on returning to the islands, he had found that his men had been turned off and that a merchant from the Cape had not only taken possession of the 3000 seals they had caught but claimed to have been granted exclusive rights to the islands.

King was still nursing his resentment when Farewell offered to charter the *Salisbury* for the Natal venture. The proposition seemed too good to miss.

With the financial backing of John Thompson's mercantile firm, Farewell hoped to establish a depot on the coast which would handle the shipment of ivory from the Natal interior. Quick to recognise the possibilities of such a scheme, King agreed to act as navigator to the expedition. Their first voyage was to be exploratory: contact was to be made with the coastal tribes and a suitable location selected for a trading settlement. Beyond this their plans were vague.

On one point, however, Lieutenant Farewell was clear. It was he, he maintained, who chartered the *Salisbury* and first interested its skipper, James Saunders King, in the venture. He was to claim that he was solely responsible for providing 'Mr King [with] the opportunity of acquainting himself with that part of the world, which we all then thought offered a fine opening for mercantile profit.' King told another story. But that was later. As the *Salisbury*, with King and Farewell aboard, ploughed its way along the coast, in June 1823, the two naval officers were in full accord.

The *Salisbury* reached Algoa Bay on 27 June 1823. Here a small British settlement, recently named Port Elizabeth, formed the last link with civilisation for ships venturing further. It was a desolate spot, far removed from the mellowness of Cape Town. When the

1820 Settlers had landed there, they had found little to comfort them as they waited for the frontier Boers to convey them up-country. 'The aspect of the whole was impressive, but sombre . . .' remarked one of them, 'and there was likewise that air of *lonesomeness* and dreary *wildness*, which a country unmarked by traces of human industry or of human residence seldom fails to exhibit to the view of civilised man.' Even now, three years later, traces of human industry were few and human residence was confined to a stone fort and a scattering of rough huts set amid the windswept sandhills. To travel beyond this frontier outpost was a daunting prospect.

On the day the *Salisbury* arrived at Port Elizabeth, it was joined by H.M.S. *Leven*. Captain Owen, having made good his losses at Cape Town, was again setting off for Portuguese East Africa. Farewell and King went aboard the *Leven* to discuss their project with Owen and to gather what information they could about the coast. Owen was most helpful. Not only did he put his charts at their disposal, but agreed to persuade one of his interpreters to accompany them. The man they selected was the brawny Jacob, whom Owen—still captivated by English Bill—had intended to release at Algoa Bay. King already knew Jacob. Some months earlier, when the *Salisbury* was acting as a troop carrier, he had transported Jacob to Cape Town where he had been imprisoned on Robben Island. According to the story King told later, his treatment of his African prisoner at that time had been so considerate that Jacob had readily agreed to forgo his freedom and join the crew of the *Salisbury*. But, happy as this reunion appears to have been, it was not to last long.

After leaving Algoa Bay, at the beginning of July, the *Salisbury* nosed its way along the coast, searching for a suitable landing spot. Inevitably it ran into heavy weather: several times the ship was buffeted off-course, often losing sight of land for days at a time. When they were able to approach the shore they found it inhospitable. 'I was fully expecting to meet with several Rivers that would afford us shelter,' reported King, '[but] after trying every part of these shores, we found our hope in vain, and at length attempted to land on the open Beach.' This proved no easy matter. The beach was at St Lucia Bay and Farewell's attempt to land there in a small boat ended in disaster. The boat capsized in the raging surf, drowning three of its crew. Farewell would have been drowned himself had he not been dragged ashore, 'considerably bruised', by Jacob, who proved to be a powerful swimmer. A few days later a second boat from the *Salisbury* overturned while endeavouring to rescue Farewell's stranded party; another man was drowned and the rest of the crew had to swim almost a mile before they gained the shore.

With Farewell and the only other experienced European member of the *Salisbury*'s crew, Alex Thomson, cast ashore, King could make no further rescue bids. 'It then blowing hard with an increasing gale,' he explained, 'we parted our cables and left our people amongst the natives for five weeks, we were apprehensive of their safety.'

King's fears, however, were unfounded. The local tribesmen proved to be prosperous and friendly. They allowed Farewell and his party to wander about without interference and, apart from a natural curiosity, showed little interest in their activities. When King finally succeeded in rescuing the castaways, he found them all well and, for the most part, happy. The only unpleasantness had been a quarrel between Alex Thomson and Jacob. Sometime during their five weeks ashore, the hot-headed Thomson had attacked Jacob and threatened to have him lashed when King arrived. Not wanting to risk a second term in gaol, Jacob bolted. The reason for this quarrel is obscure, but Jacob had apparently vanished for good. When the *Salisbury* finally left St Lucia, both King and Farewell were convinced that they had seen the last of the interpreter.

Supplies were now running low. They had been at sea for some weeks and their failure to find a suitable harbour had badly upset their plans. But they had no intention of giving up. Encouraged by their peaceful reception at St Lucia, they returned to Algoa Bay for provisions, determined to make another attempt on the coast.

[3]

The arrival of the *Salisbury* at Port Elizabeth created some excitement. Despite their many misfortunes, King and Farewell were able to give a favourable report. On the voyage southwards they had kept close to the coast and passed several rivers which, from a distance, appeared to be spacious. Most of the river mouths were blocked by sand-bars but the surrounding country looked promising. It had confirmed Farewell's belief that it was possible to establish a settlement in Natal, and King had become obsessed with 'an idea that Gold might be procured about these Rivers'. Such was their enthusiasm that, when the time came for them to set off again, several of the inhabitants of Port Elizabeth—including a well-known 1820 Settler, Daniel Hockly—clamoured to go with them. The *Salisbury* left Algoa Bay on 11 September, accompanied this time by a small sloop, the *Julia*, commanded by Captain J. Garrott.

They started this second voyage in more favourable weather. For a long stretch they were able to hug the coast, but the chances of finding a landing place seemed as remote as ever. River after river was found to be sealed off by a sand-bar. Not until they were caught in a sudden squall, while anchored off-shore, did King decide to risk crossing one of these bars. Then, cutting his cables, he headed the *Salisbury* towards an inlet of what proved to be a land-locked bay. Very much at the mercy of the wind, the ship successfully scraped across the shallow entrance. The *Julia* followed and, being smaller and lighter, crossed the bar easily.

Once the storm had subsided, they were able to take stock of their refuge. At first sight it was enchanting. On three sides the bay was encompassed by gently rising bush country, fringed by a tangle of tropical vegetation; to the south a narrow, thickly wooded, headland shielded the lagoon from the pounding surf. There was an almost uncanny silence about the place. Apart from the distant roar of the sea, the only sound to be heard was the chattering of monkeys, the squawk of waterfowl, and the occasional rustling of hippos wallowing in the reeds at the water's edge. Further investigation convinced them that they had, by accident, found the ideal spot for a settlement: a natural haven, sheltered and lush enough to provide for their immediate needs.

'The Harbour,' reported King, 'though small (being the only one on this extensive coast) is very easy of access for vessels of a certain draft. It abounds with Hippopotamus & fish of various sorts & the soil in the vicinity, in my opinion, is particularly productive; at present Indian corn is the only produce grown which is large and in great abundance. The Plains are very extensive & the pasture for cattle, rich . . . this country, as far as I can venture to speak of (say a distance of about 40 miles) is beautiful and blest with a salubrious air & a productive soil. Likewise within that short distance are several extensive winding Rivers which add greatly to its importance.'

The local tribesmen were, at first, far from friendly. For days they remained hidden and when they did appear they came armed with assegais and shields. But their hostility proved to be born of suspicion rather than aggression. Like most of the coastal Africans they were easily cowed. Once they discovered that they had no real cause for fear, they were quick to seek the traders' protection. 'When we became better acquainted,' says King, 'they were extremely well disposed & expressed a particular desire for us to remain among them.'

Both Farewell and King had every intention of remaining among them. The harbour—soon to be known as Port Natal—met all their requirements. Having made an extensive survey of the surrounding country and collected a quantity of ivory, they were in no doubt as to the bay's potential. First, however, it was necessary for them to return to Cape Town. Enticing as were their prospects, they were by no means equipped to start trading. They needed extra provisions, merchandise, and some reliable recruits to assist them. What was equally important, neither of them—whether they admitted it to each other or not—intended to work in partnership. Their joint venture had proved successful: now each had his own plans.

When they arrived back at Cape Town, on 3 December 1823, King and Farewell parted. Farewell immediately set about organising his next expedition. King resigned his command of the *Salisbury* and left for London. They went their separate ways, never doubting that they had overcome the jinx which, for years, had kept men in fear of the Natal coast.

What seems not to have bothered either of them (or if they were bothered they did not admit to it) was the mysterious nature of the Natal interior and the formidable reputation of its inhabitants. If their trading venture was to be successful, they would have to travel inland to obtain large quantities of ivory. This would inevitably place them at the mercy of the warrior tribe from whom the coastal Africans had fled. As yet they knew little about that tribe; what they did know was hardly reassuring. From the reports they had gathered, it must have been obvious that it would require more than commercial enterprise to deal with the people whom the Portuguese called Vatwas or Hollentontes and whom others referred to vaguely as Zooloos, Zulos or Zoolahs.

A TRADING MISSION

FROM THE TIME of his appointment as Governor of the Cape, Lord Charles Somerset had been embroiled in financial wrangles with the authorities in Britain. High born and high handed as this second son of the fifth Duke of Beaufort undoubtedly was, his aristocratic influence and autocratic manner had made little impression on the bureaucrats of Whitehall. The times were against him. Somerset had taken up his appointment in April 1814. A year later, the defeat of Napoleon at Waterloo had brought the long and expensive struggle between England and France to an end. The retrenchment policies of Britain after the war had seriously affected the economy of the Cape. Lord Charles, a man of great energy and dedication, had done his best to balance the Cape's hard-pressed budget by encouraging local industries but he had been fighting an uphill battle. Inevitably the needs of the isolated colony outweighed its underdeveloped assets.

Even the arrival of the 1820 Settlers had proved a mixed blessing. Badly as their presence was needed on the frontier, they had been unable to contribute much to the Cape's material prosperity. A series of natural disasters—crop diseases and drought—had undermined their initial efforts to establish a productive settlement. There seemed precious little hope of their assisting in the development of a much needed export trade.

That the Cape authorities should welcome the idea of a trading mission to Natal with open arms was only to be expected. When Lieutenant Farewell first approached Lord Charles Somerset with his scheme, he was assured that if he put his proposal in writing it would receive sympathetic attention. He did not have to be told twice. On 1 May 1824, he submitted a memorandum to the Governor explaining how he had discovered Port Natal and outlining his plans for a settlement.

'My intentions are,' he said, 'to keep a vessel constantly laying in port and to have a small party on shore for the purpose of communicating with the Interior and carrying on the Trade—the natives have already requested that we would come and traffic with them and probably by a constant intercourse we shall eventually lead to a commerce of importance to the Colony and advantageous to ourselves.'

The trading expedition was to be much larger than the exploratory one had been. Farewell estimated that it would require at least twenty-five men, including servants and crew, to establish the settlement he planned. Not wanting the venture to appear too crassly mercantile, he ended his memorandum on a note of high endeavour. 'I hope Your Lordship will conceive,' he wrote, 'that our present undertaking is entitled to every encouragement being one of much hazard, and if successful likely to lead to important advantages to the Colony in furnishing articles of Export as well as new Sources of Trade and tending to the Civilisation of many populace nations hitherto unknown to Europeans.'

Lord Charles was quick to reply. In a short letter, dictated to his secretary three days later, he gave the expedition his qualified blessing. He had no objection to Farewell establishing a commercial settlement in Natal and taking a small party with him. He also approved of Farewell's desire to assist the spread of civilisation in South Africa. Nevertheless, His Lordship made it quite clear that any dealings with the Africans in Natal would be subject to very definite stipulations. 'H.E. begs,' concluded the secretary, 'that you will clearly understand that all your intercourse with the natives must be conducted in a conciliatory manner and upon fair terms of Barter, and that he cannot sanction the acquisition of any territorial possessions without a full communication being made to him of the circumstances under which they may be offered & be intended to be received.'

Forwarding copies of this correspondence to London, Lord Charles assured Earl Bathurst, the Secretary of State for War and Colonies, that: 'Mr F. G. Farewell is represented to me as a Person of respectability and I understand possesses some capital.'

Most of Farewell's capital came, of course, from the Cape Town merchant, John Thompson. However, he had also acquired the backing of his wife's step-father, Johann Peterssen, and another colonial trader, Josias Hoffman. Farewell's glowing reports of Natal had persuaded both these men to support the venture. He had even convinced his backers that the territory was so rich in ivory that the cattle kraals of the interior tribe were made entirely of elephant tusks. Similar inducements had been used to attract volunteers for the expedition. Would-be recruits were not only tempted by stories of untapped riches but were assured that the speculation would be completed within six months. Natal was represented as a land where enterprising young men could make a quick and easy fortune.

Of all Farewell's recruits, the most remarkable was undoubtedly Henry Francis Fynn. Then twenty-one years of age, Fynn was more attracted to the expedition by the prospect of adventure than by thoughts of money making. He was a young man of many talents. Born in England in 1803, he had been educated at Christ's Hospital in London where he had acquired, among other things, an elementary knowledge of medicine. At the age of fifteen he had been sent to join his father and brothers at the Cape but, instead of entering the family trading business, had spent his first four years in the Colony at a Government farm on the eastern frontier. Farming evidently did not appeal to him and in 1822 Fynn returned to Cape Town in search of more suitable employment. Here he was offered the position of supercargo on the *Jane*, a trading brig sailing to Delagoa Bay. His voyage to Portuguese East Africa coincided with King and Farewell's venture along the Natal coast and was almost as eventful. The captain of the *Jane* proved to be an incompetent drunk who ran the ship aground in Delagoa Bay and was finally forced to abandon his command to the mate.

None of this appears to have daunted young Fynn. Regardless of the antics of his superiors, he kept himself busy exploring the surrounding country and learning all he could about the prospects of trade with the interior. By the time he returned to Cape Town, at the end of 1823, Fynn considered himself sufficiently experienced to embark on a more serious trading mission. The Farewell expedition provided him with the opportunity.

According to Fynn, Farewell offered to put him in charge of trading transactions in Natal. Instead of a salary, he was to receive 'a handsome percentage to be decided upon after being one month in port'. This rather vague arrangement was accepted by Fynn who, at that stage, regarded the expedition as little more than a diverting

experience. Despite some misgivings as to the competence of his
employers, he set about preparing for the voyage to Port Natal with
great enthusiasm.

By the time Lord Charles Somerset gave his consent to the
enterprise, Fynn was already at sea. During April he had left
Cape Town in the sloop *Julia* with an advance party to prepare the
settlement for the main body of the expedition. Included in this
party were three 'mechanics': an Englishman named Henry Ogle,
a Frenchman and a Prussian. It was intended that these three men
should set to work on the buildings while Fynn tried to contact the
interior tribe. An African interpreter, Frederick, and a Hottentot
servant, Michael, had been detailed to assist Fynn. Farewell and
his partners were to follow later in a chartered brig.

In many ways it was a bizarre arrangement. Not only was Fynn
relatively inexperienced but none of the men had previously set
foot in Natal. Considering Farewell's difficulties in locating Port
Natal, he was expecting a great deal from the twenty-one-year-old
Fynn.

[2]

On a calm morning in May 1824 the *Julia*, taking advantage of
half-tide, successfully crossed the bar at Port Natal and anchored in
the bay. The voyage along the coast had been uneventful. Apart
from the overcrowded conditions on board the sloop—it carried
twenty-six persons as well as cargo—the advance party had little
cause for complaint. They found the bay very much as Farewell
had described it: hushed and beautiful.

That same afternoon, Fynn and the three mechanics rowed
ashore and, after sending their boat back, explored the beach.
Other than the tracks of hippos, they could detect no signs of life.
Not until they had settled down for the night did they become
aware of the dangers of Port Natal. At midnight they were awakened
by a storm, which not only drenched them and their bedding, but
flooded the hollow in which they were sleeping. Scrambling up to
higher ground, they managed to start a fire and sat huddled in
their wet blankets, waiting for the dawn.

However, long before it broke, the sudden howling of what Fynn called 'troops of wolves', but what was probably a pack of hyenas or wild dogs, jerked them into action. Hoping to scare the animals away, they stoked up their fire. It did not help. The howling came closer; soon they were surrounded by the snarling beasts. Standing back to back, waving firebrands and yelling, they tried to keep the vicious intruders at bay. They were only partly successful. In rushing to take up a position by the fire, they had left their bedding undefended. One of the 'wolves' darted in and seized a pair of leather trousers from Ogle's sleeping place. It was not the trousers, but the thought of a sixty-dollar note in one of the pockets, that alarmed Ogle. 'This,' says Fynn, 'he was determined to defend. He rushed forward, caught hold of the band of the trousers as the wolf was dragging them, and succeeded in recovering them with the loss of only one of the legs. Although all of us had rushed to his assistance in the dark we succeeded only in beating the wind with our firebrands, though that had the effect of scaring the wolves away.'

The attacks continued periodically throughout the night. Fynn and his companions sat back to back, talking and singing, to keep up their spirits. Fortunately—with the exception of the Prussian mechanic, whose toe was bitten when he crawled to secure his bedding—they emerged unscathed.

The following day they collected a mainsail from the *Julia* to serve as a tent and selected a spot further inland for their camp. Here they hacked away the bush and built a strong fence. This was to become the first European settlement in Natal. Work on a twelve-foot square, wattle and mud, house was started the next day.

Fynn explored the bay, searching for the local tribesmen. They were as evasive as ever. Footprints invariably petered out in the dense bush; there was no other indication of human activity. Not until three days after his arrival did Fynn catch his first glimpse of the bay's inhabitants. Then, from the deck of the *Julia*, he saw a group of Africans paddling off a beach on the narrow headland. Immediately he ordered a boat to be lowered and rowed to the beach, but, as he appeared, the Africans fled. One of them, however, was not fast enough and Fynn caught up with him. His name was Mahamba. By bribing him with beads, Fynn was able to persuade the apprehensive African to accompany him back to the *Julia* and then on to the newly established camp.

Mahamba seems to have been typical of the puny, half-starved coastal tribesmen. Fynn's interpreter, Frederick, had great difficulty in communicating with him. His dialect was difficult to understand and he was nervous about answering questions. Nor was the information he gave particularly helpful. He and his companions, like all the refugees from the hinterland, seemed to be motivated entirely by fear. They lived in perpetual dread of the conqueror of Natal, the ruler of the interior tribe, of whose exploits the Europeans had already heard—Shaka.

'My enquiries as to where Shaka resided,' says Fynn, 'were unsatisfactorily replied to. All I could learn was that their nation had been destroyed by Shaka and that he was a powerful chief living to the northwards and I would have to travel 30 days before I reached him . . . such was their fear of him that they durst not accompany us or leave the bush at low tide to get fish, their only sustenance.'

Fynn doubted whether it would take him thirty days to reach the mysterious Shaka's kraal. While at sea he had noticed smoke from encampments much closer to Port Natal. He was undeterred by Mahamba's fear and determined to make contact with Shaka's warriors as soon as possible. What is more, he intended to persuade Mahamba to act as his guide. And, strangely enough, he succeeded. While the rest of his party busied themselves in putting up the first house, Fynn cultivated the local tribesmen. He coaxed them from their hideouts in the bush and soon they were supplying his workmen with fish. Exactly how he overcame Mahamba's reluctance to leave Port Natal, he does not say. But overcome it he did. When Fynn left on his first exploratory journey northwards, he was accompanied by his interpreter, Frederick, his Hottentot servant, Michael, and the far from confident Mahamba.

Fynn expected to be away for two or three days. He reckoned that Shaka's tribe could not be more than ten or twelve miles away. By an odd coincidence, he was proved right. His first meeting with the inhabitants of the interior occurred some twelve miles from Port Natal. However, it was a very different meeting from the one he had expected.

Having marched along the coast for the best part of a day, Fynn decided to rest. Mahamba started a fire and Michael set about making coffee. Fynn sat on the beach listening to the sounds of the bush and watching the tumbling surf. It was when he happened to look back in the direction of Port Natal that he first became aware of an extraordinary sight. A huge army of men, like some great black sea, was moving towards him. So dense was the mass that, from a distance, it was impossible to make out where it ended. Fynn's first thought was that the party at the bay had been destroyed and that their attackers had come after him. This same thought, apparently, had occurred to Mahamba. He promptly disappeared into the bush.

Deciding that he had been spotted and that flight would be useless, Fynn remained where he was. His decision, he later admitted, was taken through ignorance rather than defiance. Not knowing what to expect, he took the only course open to him. Even so it called for immense courage. The closer the army loomed the more terrifying it appeared. Armed with shields and assegais, the warriors were quite obviously a very different breed from the coastal Africans. Tall, powerfully built men, with gleaming bodies and an unmistakable arrogance, there was no doubt as to their superiority. Both Frederick and Michael pleaded with Fynn to hide. But by then it was too late.

The leaders of the army were no less surprised at Fynn's appearance than he was at theirs. They approached him cautiously. Determined to put on a brave front, Fynn stood up and told Frederick to tell them that he had come from across the sea and was anxious to meet Shaka. But, as he spoke, one of the men stepped forward and drew his hand across his throat. This sign, as far as Frederick and Michael were concerned, was crystal clear. Leaving Fynn to be hung, or have his throat cut, they bolted.

But they were wrong. The man wanted beads, not blood. He pointed to a necklace worn by one of his companions and made his intentions clear. There was nothing Fynn could do about it. Without Frederick to interpret for him he was unable to make himself understood. He tried to pantomime friendship; pointing in the direction from which he had come and that in which he wished to go. This only confused matters more. Nor did his repeated attempts to invoke the magic name of Shaka meet with any recognisable response. Puzzled, the men stared at him, spoke among themselves, and trudged off. The army resumed its march.

Fynn stood watching the warriors stream past as the sun set. There were at least 20,000 of them, but he was no longer afraid of their stares. So disciplined were they that, having satisfied their leaders, he knew he was safe. Later he learned that they were part of an army returning from a campaign in southern Natal. Only then did he appreciate the danger he had faced. 'My life evidently was saved on this occasion,' he said, 'by that wonderful talisman of this country, the name of Shaka.'

When the last of the warriors' dust had settled, Frederick, Michael and Mahamba crawled out of the bush. They were astonished to find Fynn alive. Frederick and Michael tried sheepishly to excuse their cowardice, but Mahamba was past pretending. That night he deserted and returned to the bush at Port Natal.

By following the army's well-beaten track, Fynn made good progress the next day. He continued along the coast for another twelve miles until he came to a small kraal. Here his reception was somewhat mixed. Never having seen a white man before, the women and children fled screaming into the bush; the men eyed him suspiciously. By throwing bunches of beads to the men, Fynn was able to overcome their distrust, and once he had convinced them that he intended no harm, they became extremely friendly. The women were brought back from the bush, the headman, Siyingila, presented Fynn with one of his only two cows, and when Fynn explained that he was on a mission to Shaka all doubt vanished. He was treated as an honoured guest.

It was just as well. For while Fynn was talking to Siyingila another dense column of warriors appeared on the horizon. Once again the women and children disappeared into the bush. They were speedily followed by Frederick and Michael. The leaders of the column immediately tackled Siyingila about the presence of a white man at his kraal. Fynn now understood enough of the language to follow the headman's explanation of his guest's intended visit to Shaka and the effect this had on the warriors. The name of Shaka, as always, worked like a charm. After accepting Fynn's offer to share Siyingila's cow with them, the men marched off, leaving Fynn in no doubt as to the size of Shaka's army and the almost mystic sway of his authority.

Detachments of the army continued to pour past the kraal until well into the night. With each new arrival Siyingila was called to account for the stranger sleeping in one of his huts. Not until early morning did the women return to the kraal to report that five of the children had been snatched by 'wolves' while they were hiding. Fynn had good reason to be grateful for the protection of his host. While Fynn slept, Siyingila had sent messengers to Shaka to announce his arrival. He advised Fynn to proceed no further until word was received from the royal kraal. Three days later Shaka's ambassador arrived. Announcing himself as Mbikwane, Shaka's uncle, he delivered a long harangue in praise of his nephew and presented Fynn with four oxen. Fynn, impressed by the old man's dignity, accepted the oxen—two of which he was allowed to send to his companions at Port Natal—and agreed to accompany Mbikwane to his kraal to await further instructions from Shaka.

At Mbikwane's kraal Fynn was treated like royalty. A petty chieftain was appointed to act as his *induna* (headman) and his personal retinue was increased by five servants. Every day Mbikwane presented him with an ox. This enabled Fynn to ingratiate himself with the tribesmen. Having more meat than he could possibly eat, he distributed it freely among the stream of visitors to his hut: he became more popular by the day. His greatest triumph came, however, three days after his arrival. He was told that one of the women of the kraal was suffering from a violent fever. So hopeless was her condition that there was talk of removing her from the kraal and leaving her, as was the custom, to die in the veld. Fynn, who had brought a medicine chest with him, offered to see what he could do for the woman.

His elementary medical training stood him in good stead. At first his peculiar method of treating the patient—feeling her pulse and looking at her tongue—was openly ridiculed; but when the woman began to recover the ridicule turned to amazement. 'The most exaggerated reports were circulated as to my ability as a doctor,' says Fynn. 'The woman was said to be positively dead when restored by me to life. This rumour soon reached Shaka.' In six days the woman was fully recovered. From that time on Fynn was showered with requests for treatment for every type of disease. Often his would-be patients appeared to be in perfect health, but nothing he said could persuade them that he was unable to cure their imaginary pains. The myth of the white man's magic was to take a great deal of discrediting.

Fynn had been at Mbikwane's kraal for two weeks when a deputation arrived from Shaka. They brought with them forty head of cattle and seven large elephant tusks. Shaka, they informed Fynn, was honoured to have such an important visitor in his country but required him to wait a little longer before proceeding to the royal kraal. The army had just returned from an exhausting campaign; it was necessary for them to rest before he could be received with fitting ceremony. This suited Fynn very well. He had just received news that Lieutenant Farewell and the rest of the party had arrived at Port Natal. Telling Mbikwane that he would wait for Shaka's summons at the bay, he immediately set off to rejoin his companions. With a large herd of cattle and seven elephant tusks to his credit, he was all agog to make a report.

[3]

Lieutenant Farewell and his party arrived at Port Natal in a chartered brig, the *Antelope*, in July 1824. Included in this mixed party of Europeans, Africans and Hottentots were two of Farewell's partners—his wife's stepfather, Peterssen, and the Cape Town merchant, Hoffman. They brought with them a fresh supply of provisions, two small cannon, a few horses and some cattle. As soon as the *Antelope* had off-loaded, she returned to the Cape, leaving the now large party entirely dependent on the little sloop, *Julia*, for contact with the outside world. Although Farewell had informed the Governor of the Cape that his undertaking would be one of 'much hazard' he obviously did not intend evacuating Port Natal in a hurry.

The greatest hazard was wild beasts. Not only were the 'wolves' proving a constant threat to the party's livestock—they had already taken three calves—but leopard spoors had been found close to the settlement. For their first few days on shore, Farewell, Peterssen and Hoffman were kept busy reinforcing the stockade around the camp. They also instituted a system of night watches.

Fynn's return to the bay—all flush with tusks and cattle—was an occasion for high rejoicing. His friendly treatment at the hands of Shaka's intermediaries gave Farewell all the encouragement he needed. All work was stopped, a holiday declared, and, in defiance of Lord Charles Somerset's specific instructions, the party took

formal possession of Port Natal. The Union Jack was run up on a
pole, the two cannon were bravely fired and Farewell, with the
high-handedness of all nineteenth-century explorers in Africa,
solemnly declared the bay and its surroundings to be British
territory.

Shortly after this unauthorised display of imperialism, a large
party of Africans, headed by Fynn's friend, Mbikwane, arrived at
the port with news from Shaka. Preparations to receive the traders
at the royal kraal were now under way; Mbikwane was to escort
them upcountry. They left immediately. Arrangements were made
for Hoffman to take charge of the settlement while Farewell, Fynn,
Peterssen and some other Europeans set off with Mbikwane. With
them they took their interpreter, Frederick, an assortment of
presents for Shaka and two or three horses. Farewell, alive to the
significance of the occasion, wore his impressive (if somewhat
uncomfortable) naval dress uniform, topped by a plumed hat.

The only existing details of this first European visit to Shaka, are
those given by Fynn. Unfortunately his memory was not altogether
reliable. Over the years his accounts tended not only to differ but to
contradict each other. However, a few of the more important
features of the journey to Shaka's kraal appear to be reasonably
authentic.

Shaka was evidently determined to impress his visitors. Mbikwane
had instructions to guide the Europeans upcountry by a roundabout
route which would enable them to appreciate the power and extent
of Shaka's kingdom. Their progress was extremely slow. They were
conducted to the kraals of various minor chiefs—where cattle were
slaughtered in their honour—and, more importantly, shown over a
number of regimental barracks. The strength of Shaka's army was
very much in evidence. For Fynn, the sight of these highly trained
warriors was no novelty, but Farewell and the rest of the party must
have been overawed by the size and organisation of the army.
Everything about the country reflected a discipline quite beyond
anything they could have expected.

Fynn was particularly impressed by the neatness and order of the
kraals. These groups of hive-shaped huts, surrounding a central
cattle-pen, were usually situated on sloping ground close to a river.
They formed the basic living unit of the people. Ruled over by a
chieftain or induna, they varied in size according to the status of their

occupants. An important chief might rule an extensive establishment which included a harem and military barracks, while the kraal of a poor man, with two or three wives, would consist of little more than a handful of huts and an enclosure for his goats. Cattle represented wealth and the central cattle-pen was an area of both hierarchical and ritual significance. It housed the kraal's herd at night, winter grain was stored beneath it in flask-shaped pits, and all important administrative and religious ceremonies were conducted within its boundaries. The huts were ten-feet in diameter, built of wattle and thatch, and were entered by crawling through a single low door; they housed the family of one or other of the chief's wives. The floor of these huts was a highly polished mixture of clay and cow-dung and, apart from an assortment of cooking pots, was usually bare. The grass mats on which the family slept were rolled up during the day and hung from the walls on hooks.

'Cleanliness,' remarked Fynn, 'was a prevailing custom and this not only inside their huts, but outside, for there were considerable spaces where neither dirt nor ashes were to be seen.'

Other aspects of kraal life were not quite so reassuring. At some of the larger establishments, the Europeans witnessed a ceremony which, in time, was to become all too familiar. 'We saw large parties seated with grotesquely dressed men apparently lecturing in their midst,' says Fynn, 'and on several occasions saw individuals seized and carried off and instantly put to death. The grotesque characters we learned were "witch finders" whilst those singled out and put to death were said to be "evil doers".'

The manner in which these 'evil doers' were killed varied according to their crimes. For the more fortunate death came quickly: either their necks were broken by experienced executioners or they were clubbed to death. Those denounced as *abaThakathi* (wizards), however, were subjected to a ghastly form of torture. The executioners would drag their victim to a selected spot outside the kraal—usually a nearby hillock—hammer sharpened stakes up his rectum and leave him to the mercy of the ever-present hyenas. The 'smelling out' of *abaThakathi* was probably the most gruesome ceremony of tribal life. By staging demonstrations of this ritual slaughter, Shaka undoubtedly hoped to impress his visitors with his power. He could hardly have chosen a more effective method.

Fynn has very few comments to make about his companions.

How they reacted to their, by no means encouraging, introduction to Shaka's country remains, for the most part, a matter for speculation. The only member of the party to emerge from Fynn's account with any semblance of personality is Farewell's relation by marriage, Johann Peterssen. Then in his sixties, fat, bad tempered, and far from robust, Peterssen did not take kindly to Natal. Indeed, from the moment he landed, he seems to have done nothing but complain. According to Fynn, he seldom spoke without swearing and on the journey to Shaka's kraal he found plenty to swear about.

At the first river they reached, Farewell insisted on searching for gold. He and James Saunders King had been convinced that Natal's rivers were rich with gold deposits; now he was determined to try his luck. Accompanied by Fynn, Peterssen and some other members of the party he began scouring the river bed, only to find that what looked like gold was nothing more than mica. The search took them some way upstream and, when they finally gave up, they decided to make their way back to the beach by following a hippo track. The path was considerably overgrown and they had not gone far before the bulky Peterssen was hopelessly entangled in monkey ropes. Struggling to free himself, he let loose such a string of oaths that the African bearers were left gaping. When Fynn and Farewell burst out laughing, the old man lost his temper completely. Puffing, sweating and cursing, he threatened to return to Port Natal there and then. Only on eventually disentangling himself could he be soothed down. The thought of Shaka's cattle kraals, which he firmly believed to be constructed of elephant tusks, encouraged him to continue. But he did so with loudly voiced misgivings.

Hardly a day passed without Peterssen causing a scene. While crossing yet another river, his horse faltered and he was pitched into the mud. That night he kept the camp awake for hours with a hysterical tirade against Farewell, whom he accused of intending to kill him by bringing him to such a God-forsaken country. Shortly afterwards he was overcome by sickness and the party was held up for an entire day waiting for him to recover. By the time they neared Shaka's kraal, he and Farewell were scarcely on speaking terms.

Shaka was kept well informed about the party's progress. A team of messengers was employed to carry daily instructions to Mbikwane and to report on the activities of the Europeans. The

discipline which characterised Shaka's army was equally evident
among his spies and ambassadors. Nothing that was said or done
by the white men—including, it seems, Peterssen's tantrums—
passed unnoticed.

The journey lasted thirteen days. On the eve of their arrival at the
royal kraal, the party became aware of the elaborate preparations
being made for their reception. Throughout the night they were
conscious of endless commotion. 'Troops of cattle were being driven
in advance,' says Fynn; 'regiments were passing near by and on
distant hills, interspersed with regiments of girls, decorated in
beads and brass with regimental uniformity, carrying on their heads
large pitchers of native beer, milk and cooked food. The approaching
scene we anticipated witnessing cheered us considerably that
evening. Farewell and Peterssen expressed extreme affection for one
another, with mutual apologies for past small differences.'

At ten o'clock the following morning, the white men struck camp
and proceeded on the last stage of their journey. After a two-mile
march they halted on a ridge overlooking an extensive, picturesque
valley. The sight ahead of them was breathtaking. On the gently
sloping hills of the opposite side of the valley, a distance of a mile
or so away, lay Shaka's great kraal. It was quite unlike anything they
could possibly have imagined. On their journey upcountry they
had visited the kraals of several minor chiefs but, impressive and
extensive as some of these were, they bore little resemblance to
Shaka's royal residence. Centred on an enormous circular cattle-pen,
a mass of huts radiated over an area of two or three square miles,
giving the impression of a closely-packed town. The vastness of the
establishment was emphasised by the dense mass of people gathered
in the centre. Even from a distance, there was no mistaking the
size and animation of the crowd; the muffled sound of chanting
voices and stamping feet drifted across the valley, adding a savage
resonance to the bellowing of Shaka's huge herds of cattle. No other
white men had witnessed such a scene: it was awesome.

The party rested under a euphorbia tree, while messengers
hurried to and from the kraal. Eventually word came for Fynn and
Farewell to advance alone. The irascible Peterssen, not surprisingly,
was instructed to remain on the ridge with the rest of the group
until he was sent for. Shaka was evidently well informed about the
leadership of the party. Escorted by Mbikwane and twenty of his

followers, Fynn and Farewell led their horses down into the valley and then rode slowly towards the royal kraal. They took no arms or presents; they trusted entirely in Shaka's goodwill.

The great cattle kraal—over a mile in diameter was black with people. More than 12,000 warriors in battle-dress and countless women and servants were lined up to greet the visitors. Fynn, in a quick reckoning, estimated that fully 80,000 men, women and children were present. So dense was the crowd that it was impossible to distinguish any sort of order among the shield-carrying regiments. Of Shaka there was no sign.

Mbikwane had his instructions ready. As soon as the white men entered the kraal, Fynn was told to mount his horse and gallop round the cattle-pen. This performance produced an outburst from the crowd. Raising their sticks and pointing them at Fynn, they cheered him on with shouts which, he learned later, likened him to a brave and sharp species of finch. Few, if any, had seen a trained horse before; none had witnessed the incredible sight of a white man riding such an animal. No doubt Shaka was aware of the effect this spectacle would produce, for he seems to have arranged it for the sole purpose of impressing his subjects. The white men appeared exceptional beings indeed.

More dramatic still was the introduction of Fynn and Farewell to Shaka. As soon as Fynn had done circling the cattle-pen, he and Farewell were guided by Mbikwane to a spot where the crowd was thickest. Here the old man embarked on a long speech, evidently addressing some hidden member of the assembly. Every so often he would stop and call upon the white men to answer '*Yebo*' to confirm that he spoke the truth. Only too willing to oblige, the uncomprehending Fynn and Farewell did as they were told. As Mbikwane droned on, Fynn's gaze wandered. He began to examine the crowd. Soon his attention was caught by a tall, powerfully built man who—dressed in a kilt of monkey tails, with circlets of white oxtail fringes on his arms and legs—looked much like the other warriors, except that, in his headband, he wore a long tail feather of a blue crane. Fynn recognised him immediately. Turning to Farewell, he pointed to the man. 'Farewell,' he whispered, 'there is Shaka.' The near-sighted Farewell screwed his monocle into his eye and stared blankly into the crowd. But the man, having heard, wagged a knowing finger at Fynn.

By this time Mbikwane had finally finished speaking. From out of the crowd came bearers carrying two elephant tusks. One of these tusks was laid before Farewell, the other before Fynn. Then, with a great leap, the man whom Fynn had singled out sprang forward. Brandishing a stick, he struck to the right and left. The crowd fell back.

Any doubts that Fynn might have had vanished. Standing before his people in solitary splendour, there was no mistaking the man with the quivering blue crane feather. Shaka it was, indeed.

3

THE RISE OF SHAKA

EARLY TRAVELLERS IN South Africa spelt Shaka's name—Chaka. This spelling was an attempt to convey the fricative sound at the beginning of his name, for which there is no alphabetical equivalent. Others have tried to render this sound with the spelling—Tshaka. But this is also unsatisfactory: it omits the almost indistinguishable hum which should precede the name and which has given it the grammatical variation—uShaka. But despite the alternative spellings, some of which are still used, the name is widely recognised and accepted as Shaka. It is a curious name: curious for more than its spelling.

Much of Shaka's early life reads like a fairy tale. This, in a way, is understandable. For the stories told about his birth, his childhood, and his early career depend almost entirely on oral tradition. Told in a poetic African language, these stories have been reduced to the simple narrative of myths and legends and embellished with the heroic romanticism of folk lore. The account given of Shaka's conception and the origin of his name is an excellent example of African story-telling and is doubtless based on a long remembered occurrence.

One day, it is said, a young maiden was bathing in a forest stream. She was seen by a handsome warrior who was immediately attracted by her nude beauty. The girl's name was Nandi; she was the daughter of a chieftain and belonged to the Langeni clan. The warrior was Senzangakhona, chieftain of the relatively small Zulu clan. Now a prevailing, strictly enforced, code of morality forbade full sexual intercourse between unmarried youngsters. Any single girl discovered pregnant was immediately discarded by her parents. However, there was a way in which adolescents were allowed to make love and rid themselves of sexual tension. This was the custom known as *ukuHlobonga* which permitted a wide range of sexual play and culminated in the young man 'satisfying the ideas [aroused] by following the act of cohabitation on the outward parts of the girl between the limbs.' Casual encounters resulting in this type of love making were recognised, rather delightfully, as 'the fun of the roads'. They were by no means uncommon. When, therefore, Senzangakhona approached Nandi she had no hesitation in encouraging him. Indeed, she was an extremely purposeful young woman and, it is said, deliberately contrived the meeting in the hopes of seducing the young chief. Certainly she succeeded. The scenes of passion which followed left the limits of *ukuHlobonga* far behind.

Young as he was, Senzangakhona had already married twice and while this did not prohibit him from taking another bride, the selection of his third wife was subject to tribal politics, not wayside dalliance. Quite obviously he could never have intended his frolic with Nandi to go as far as it did. Nevertheless, he could not escape the consequences. As soon as Nandi was found to be pregnant, a messenger was sent to Senzangakhona's kraal to demand that the young Zulu chief meet his responsibilities. The news was not well received by the Zulu elders. It was unthinkable that Senzangakhona could have disgraced himself with a woman of the Langeni clan. The messenger was sent packing. Nandi, declared the elders, was not pregnant but merely harbouring *iShaka*—an intestinal beetle thought to be responsible for menstrual irregularities.

But the beetle grew: in due course it manifested itself as a boy child. Again a messenger was sent to the Zulu kraal. This time he insisted that Senzangakhona fetch Nandi and her *iShaka*. None too pleased, the easy-going Senzangakhona was forced to obey. Defying the prejudices of his elders, he unceremoniously installed Nandi at his kraal as his third wife. Precisely when these embarrassing events—the birth of Shaka and the marriage of his parents—took place is uncertain. The date usually given is 1787.

Shaka's early childhood was far from happy. As Senzangakhona's third, unwanted wife—a member, moreover, of the despised Langeni clan—Nandi's position at the Zulu kraal was that of an inferior. The elders resented her; the others ignored her. Nor did her temperament add to her popularity. Her name, Nandi, meant 'the Sweet One' but she hardly lived up to it. Self-willed and sharp tongued, she has been described as 'a masculine and savage woman'. Of that seductive creature with whom Senzangakhona had once enjoyed somewhat more than 'the fun of the roads', there remained hardly a trace: although she bore her husband one more child—a daughter named Nomcoba—the couple quarrelled continually. Her husband's first wife, Mkabi, did what she could to ease the marital unpleasantness, but nothing she could say or do succeeded in off-setting the widespread resentment of Nandi and her undesired son. The father's hostility, however, did have the effect of drawing mother and son together. Shaka adored Nandi.

A crisis came when Shaka was about six years old. At this early age he, like other Zulu youngsters, became a herdboy. His failure to carry out his task properly resulted in a decisive break between his parents. One of Senzangakhona's pet animals—some say a sheep, some a goat—was attacked and killed by a dog and little Shaka was blamed for being lackadaisical. In the inevitable parental row which followed, the irate Senzangakhona banished Nandi and her children from his kraal. They were obliged to throw themselves on the mercy of Nandi's kinsmen, the Langeni.

Shaka's unhappiness at his father's kraal was nothing compared with the misery of his life with his mother's people. Nandi's return was not welcomed by her family. A discarded wife was looked upon as a fallen woman. She had no rightful claim to recognition in the hierarchical structure of tribal life. Lowly as had been her position at the Zulu kraal, Nandi, for all her assertiveness, was now little more than an object of her family's charity.

Shaka was made to feel the full force of his mother's humiliation. Moody and rebellious by nature, he was bullied unmercifully by the boys of the kraal who not only took advantage of his lowly status, but resented his obvious intelligence. As a herdboy among the Langeni, he was subjected to endless torment and ridicule. Both his poverty and his person were openly jeered at. For, added to his other disadvantages, Shaka suffered the youthful shame of an apparently stunted penis. Not until he reached puberty did his genitalia develop and, in the nakedness of his childhood, he was exposed to the crude taunts of his more impressively equipped companions.

How true all this is one does not know, but it is said that the effect of this callous persecution helped shape both his personality and his career. He grew up lonely and revengeful; ambitious, ruthless and determined to overcome all opposition. Only to his mother did he show affection. Her dependence upon him was as passionate as his upon her. Certainly the bond between the outcast mother and the ridiculed son produced shattering results.

Invidious as was her position, Nandi managed to make some sort of life for herself among the Langeni until Shaka was about fifteen. Then, in 1802, came disaster. A calamitous drought made it impossible for all but the prosperous to survive in a famine-stricken area. Boasting neither husband nor cattle, Nandi could no longer be supported by the Langeni. She was turned out to fend for herself. Taking her children, she sought refuge with a man who lived some miles away and to whom, it is said, she had already borne a son named Ngwadi. Little is told about Shaka's life with his mother and her lover, but it is thought to have been one of the few tranquil periods in his turbulent childhood. But, like his childhood, it soon came to an end.

By all reports Shaka had grown into a strapping adolescent. Suddenly both the Langeni and the Zulu began to recognise his potential as a warrior and to press for his return. They were, it seems, willing to overlook his mother's shortcomings and to admit him as a recruit in their undersized armies. Neither Nandi nor Shaka was prepared, however, to acknowledge the claims of their persecutors. They hated the Langeni and were suspicious of the Zulu. There was good reason for them to act warily.

By this time Senzangakhona had taken more wives, fathered other sons. As was the custom, one of these sons had been nominated his heir. The exiled Nandi and Shaka had grounds for suspecting that Senzangakhona's renewed interest in his unwanted eldest son was prompted by his determination to rid himself of a possible threat to the Zulu chieftainship. For on the one occasion that Shaka had met his father since his expulsion from the Zulu kraal—at the ritual celebration of the boy's puberty—Shaka's arrogance had caused them to quarrel bitterly. In accordance with tradition, Senzangakhona had presented his son with his first *umuTsha* (a skin loin covering) and the boy had refused to accept it. This refusal was no doubt inspired by Shaka's desire to remain unclothed in order to display his now generously developed manhood, but it was also seen as a defiance of his unloved father. The enmity between father and son had become too apparent to be ignored.

To safeguard her son, Nandi sent him to her father's sister at a kraal near the coast. This move, undertaken as a precautionary measure, was to decide the course of Shaka's career. Nandi's aunt lived among the Mthethwa clan: one of the most powerful Bantu clans then occupying south-east Africa. By growing up among the Mthethwa, Shaka received a military training that was to test his courage and fashion his thinking. Not only did it allow him to develop his undoubted gifts as a warrior but, in time, it brought him under the protection of a remarkable leader—Dingiswayo.

Whatever doubts there might be about Shaka's childhood, there is little doubt about the importance of the Mthethwa or about the influence of Dingiswayo. The marrying of Shaka's warlike propensities to Dingiswayo's statesmanship gave birth to a mighty African nation.

[2]

No one knows when the Bantu first arrived in southern Africa, or precisely where they came from. They are known at one time to have inhabited the region of the Great Lakes of central Africa (although they did not originate there) and to have migrated slowly southwards. 'Though the lateness of their arrival has been much exaggerated,' says Professor Omer-Cooper, 'it is unlikely that they were south of the Limpopo in any considerable numbers before the twelfth century A.D. at the earliest.'

Much has been learned of early Bantu culture from the findings of archaeologists and anthropologists, but there is no documentary evidence of Bantu life in southern Africa before the Portuguese rounded the Cape in 1486. Even after that date, recorded history was sparse and unsatisfactory for almost three centuries. This is particularly true of the south-eastern coastal sector: the wide, grassy, well-watered and temperate region that stretches from the Drakensberg mountains to the sea. The only recorded information about this region is in the reports and journals of shipwrecked travellers and, although the experiences of these castaways were interesting and often instructive, they contain little more than disconnected glimpses of tribal life at, or near, the coast. Consequently the early history of the south-eastern Bantu clans has become largely a matter of hindsight and deduction. It relies heavily on oral tradition which, when recorded, is often contradictory and confusing. Nevertheless, there appears to be a rough consensus of opinion about certain basic facts.

The clans of south-east Africa were part of a Bantu language group known as the Nguni. These Nguni-speaking people occupied not only the Drakensberg coastal sector, but the entire coastal corridor of southern Africa: from an area close to Delagoa Bay to the frontier of the Cape Colony. Speculation as to when the Nguni first settled so far south is endless and inconclusive, but it is certain that—while they probably arrived much earlier—Nguni-speaking clans were established in what later became their homelands towards the end of the sixteenth century. Divisions among the Nguni were as manifold as they were complex; a real distinction, however, exists between the southern Nguni—those living between Natal and Cape Colony, in what was known as 'Caffreland'—and the northern Nguni, who occupied the region from Delagoa Bay to Natal. Shaka, of course, belonged to the northern Nguni and it is the history of these people that remained unrecorded for so long.

Indications are that, until the end of the eighteenth century, the organisation of the northern Nguni tribes was similar to that of the southern Nguni in 'Caffreland'. They were a pastoral people, growing a few crops, and were subdivided into clans which usually claimed descent from a common ancestor. These family units were often wide-ranging—their lineage sometimes spanned several generations—and their ramifications were extensive. Cleavages occurred when a son left home and gained followers of his own and politically inspired marriages could spread the influence of a powerful clan (marriage within a clan was strictly forbidden, but married women retained strong ritual ties with their own people). Moreover, the political claims of a chieftain were not confined to his own clan: a forceful local leader could, and often did, command the allegiance of several neighbouring clans. There were, in fact, distinct differences as well as affinities between family and political groupings.

Rivalry between neighbouring chieftains was, more often than not, reflected in disputes over the ownership of cattle and grazing rights. Cattle represented wealth and cattle ownership was of economic, dietary and, to a certain extent, ritual significance. Men bought their wives with cattle. The sale was provisional and should the wife be returned to her parents, her purchase price (*lobola*) had to be returned; nevertheless the exchange of cattle was essential to the marriage contract. Cattle raiding was frequently the cause of inter-clan warfare and, in battle, triumph was enhanced by the victors plundering the herds of their opponents. On occasion, highly prized oxen were demanded as ransom for captives. The possession of cattle was thus of vital importance to the structure of Nguni society: both the substance and status of individual chiefs was estimated in terms of cattle ownership.

Consequently there existed within the tribal system the means and the incentive for an ambitious leader to establish his supremacy. But, as far as is known, the aspirations of the Nguni chieftains remained for many years surprisingly limited. Not until the advent of Dingiswayo does any clan ruler appear to have made a bid for anything more than local dominance. Precisely what inspired Dingiswayo's attempt to ensure the paramountcy of the Mthethwa is something of a mystery.

Many theories have been advanced. One of the first came from Henry Francis Fynn who, in later years, recorded many of the Nguni oral traditions. According to Fynn, Dingiswayo's real name was Godongwana and he was the eldest son of Jobe, the ageing chief of the Mthethwa. As a young man, having quarrelled with his father, Godongwana became a fugitive, travelling from clan to clan in an attempt to escape his father's vengeance. He is credited with many adventures which his superior intelligence and great courage enabled him to survive.

In the course of these escapades, Godongwana encountered a white man, whom Fynn believed to be Dr Cowan—the army surgeon who had so mysteriously disappeared in the unexplored territory in 1808. Cowan befriended Godongwana and the two of them travelled together to the coast. Here they parted and went their separate ways: Cowan to meet his death at the hands of a hostile tribe and Godongwana to claim the chieftainship of the Mthethwa. For by this time his father had died and his younger brother ruled in his place.

The association with Dr Cowan stood Godongwana in good stead. Not only is Cowan supposed to have instructed him in the superior ways of the white men but the doctor's formidable reputa-tion—his bizarre dress, his horse and his gun had terrified the tribesmen—somehow transferred itself to his protégé. 'The idea of Godongwana riding on a strange animal like a horse, as well as being in possession of a weapon of thunder (a gun),' says Fynn, 'both of which were said to have been brought by him from some distant country, caused a feeling in the minds of the Mthethwa people similar to that which pervaded the different tribes through which the European had passed.' Helped by this legend, Godongwana succeeded in defeating his brother, assumed the chieftainship, and set about reforming the Mthethwa in accordance with the teachings of Dr Cowan. From then on, he was known as Dingiswayo —'the distressed one'—in acknowledgement of his early sufferings. That, at least, is how Fynn tells it.

Another version of this story was given by Theophilus Shepstone in 1875. While agreeing that Dingiswayo fled his father's wrath, Shepstone claimed that, as a fugitive, he made his way to the Cape Colony and was employed there as a servant. His duties were evidently light and left him plenty of time for useful observation. 'He learned the strength of standing armies, the value of discipline and training, as compared with the mobs, called armies, in his own country,' claimed Shepstone. 'He saw that if he could gain possession of his tribe he could gratify his ambition. He had heard of or seen bodies of civilised soldiers. He had ascertained that they were divided into regiments and companies, with regularly appointed officers, and he thought that all soldiers were bachelors. He had no sooner got possession of power than he set to work to organise his tribe in accordance with these ideas.'

The authority for either version is vague; the explanation they offer is not altogether convincing. To imagine that Dingiswayo's rapid and efficient organisation of the Mthethwa resulted from nothing more than such casual instruction is, to say the least, to accept an obvious oversimplification. Fynn was very hazy about his dates. In the first account he gave of Dingiswayo's exile, he put his meeting with Dr Cowan some twenty years before the doctor embarked on his expedition. Admittedly Nguni oral tradition took no account of the Gregorian calendar but means of dating events did exist and an error of over twenty years for such an important happening as that of Dingiswayo's assumption of power which, when Fynn first heard of it, was within living memory, is considerable. The fact that Fynn later changed his dating to fit in with known facts makes his story even more suspect. And Shepstone's unsubstantiated theory seems to be little more than imaginative hindsight.

What both versions have in common is the supposition that any change in the structure of northern Nguni society must have resulted from contact with the white man. This fallacy, as Professor Leonard Thompson has pointed out, is typical of nineteenth-century thinking on events in Africa. Similar theories have been effectively refuted and there appears to be no reason why either of these largely imaginative and contradictory accounts by men who had no personal knowledge of Dingiswayo should be accepted. 'In either version the white-inspiration theory seems to be a white man's concoction,' says Professor Thompson. Certainly there is no way of knowing precisely what happened to Dingiswayo in exile; he might or he might not have met Dr Cowan, he might or he might not have visited the Cape. Modern scholars are inclined to look elsewhere for an explanation of Dingiswayo's ascendancy.

Pressures within the south-eastern region of Africa are thought to have made the attempt at domination by a single ruler inevitable. Dingiswayo is reported to have traded in ivory and cattle with the Portuguese at Delagoa Bay and it has been suggested that this may well have led him to establish a monopoly in such trade. It is also probable that he was influenced by the overcrowded conditions then being experienced by the northern Nguni. The effect of white pressure on the frontier of the Cape Colony had, by the end of the eighteenth century, made expansion in a westerly direction impossible. This created a population problem which required an aggressive and purposeful solution. While both these theories—that of economic motivation and that of a population explosion—are, in turn, typical of twentieth-century thinking, they do, taken together, provide a feasible explanation of widespread social upheaval.

For the reforms introduced by Dingiswayo were to prove cataclysmic. However he achieved power, and whatever his inspiration, once Dingiswayo was installed as chief of the Mthethwa he set about transforming the traditional tribal system.

He started by reorganising the army. In place of the undisciplined 'mobs' referred to by Shepstone, he instituted a regimental system (thus giving rise to the supposition that he was following an outside example). Young Mthethwa warriors were conscripted into regiments of a disciplined force—each regiment distinguished by its dress and the colour of its shields—and became part of what, in effect, was a standing army. The regiments were made up of men of roughly the same age and, for youngsters, enrolment in a regiment served an initiatory purpose, similar to that of the circumcision schools which Dingiswayo abolished. It is doubtful whether Dingiswayo's army was then the all-embracing, efficient machine it later became, but it did provide the means for him to further his political ambitions.

A mixture of war and diplomacy enabled Dingiswayo to achieve mastery over a wide area. His conquests went much further than those of any other Nguni chieftain. And as his influence extended, so his army grew. Young men of the clans he overpowered were conscripted into the Mthethwa age regiments and their traditional clan ties were consequently weakened: adherence to the regimental system gave rise to a new concept of loyalty. But Dingiswayo did not rely entirely upon the allegiance of the new recruits to his army. As a conqueror he was both merciful and judicious; in battle he spared women and children, in victory he sought allies. It was rarely necessary for him to destroy his enemies; those clans willing to acknowledge the Mthethwa's supremacy were allowed to retain their own chiefs or ruling families. In this way Dingiswayo established, not a dictatorship, but a confederacy of chiefdoms which recognised the paramountcy of the Mthethwa and surmounted the traditional bonds of kinship and local allegiance.

Shaka's residence among the Mthethwa began before Dingiswayo assumed chieftainship. He therefore witnessed the inauguration of this novel experiment in Nguni military and political tactics. There was much to be learned from the remarkable achievements of Dingiswayo and Shaka proved an apt pupil. Dingiswayo's innovations were to provide him with both the knowledge and the organisation he required to realise his own, more bloody ambitions.

[3]

As far as is known, Shaka was conscripted into the Mthethwa army when he was in his early twenties. He was then, by all accounts, a magnificent looking young man; six foot three, loose limbed and solidly muscled. Life as a herdboy had done much to develop his physique and his natural abilities: he had learned to handle an assegai, to track and tackle wild animals, to rely on his wits. All this contributed to his rapid advancement as a warrior. He was recognised as a brave and resourceful leader and was soon promoted to command his regiment.

Not only his courage but his ingenuity singled him out as an exceptional soldier. He had his own ideas about how battles should be fought. To Dingiswayo's military reforms, he added some valuable innovations of his own.

He was quick to recognise the disadvantage of going into battle armed solely with the traditional throwing assegai. This long-shafted spear, thrown from a distance, was useless in hand-to-hand combat; it was too flimsy to be used as a thrusting weapon and once it had been hurled a warrior was left defenceless. Shaka devised a new weapon: a short broad-bladed stabbing spear, which he called *iKlwa*—a unique word, said to be an onomatopoeic term imitating the sucking sound made when it was withdrawn from a body thrust. There were obvious advantages to be gained from such a weapon. Once the preliminary rain of flung assegais was over, the Mthethwa could charge their enemy and use their stabbing spears to deadly effect at close quarters.

Simple as this break with tradition appears, it required Shaka to initiate it. He also advocated relinquishing ox-hide sandals to ensure greater speed and mobility: a suggestion which is said to have met with opposition until its effectiveness was shown in battle.

Tradition has it that Shaka demonstrated his new fighting methods in a clash with the Butelezi. The initial stages of this battle followed the usual pattern of inter-clan conflicts. Dingiswayo advanced a Mthethwa regiment to within a hundred yards of the Butelezi and then despatched a messenger to demand an immediate surrender. The Butelezi replied with a stream of shouted abuse. This was the traditional signal for outstanding warriors on either side to engage in single combat before the battle began in earnest. It was the accepted test of champions.

A Butelezi warrior quickly stepped forward with a challenge. He was answered by Shaka. To everyone's astonishment, Shaka strode towards the enemy ranks without stopping to hurl an assegai. He was a mere thirty-five yards from the Butelezi before his opponent, recovering from his surprise, flung the first spear. It glanced harmlessly off Shaka's shield. At that Shaka, tilting his shield so that he could see ahead, broke into a run. Deftly warding off a second spear with his shield, he continued his charge until he was close against the startled warrior. Instantly hooking his shield into his opponent's, he wrenched both shields to the left. With this one movement he was protecting himself from the last spear in his opponent's right hand and, at the same time, exposing the man's left armpit to the thrust of his stabbing spear. So powerful was this thrust that it passed through the warrior's heart and lung and burst out on the other side. As the man dropped, Shaka leaped over his body and rushed at the bewildered Butelezi alone. Only then did his own regiment realise what was happening. They joined in the charge. The Butelezi broke ranks and fled.

This spectacular performance is said to have resulted in Shaka's immediate promotion. Dingiswayo had witnessed the young man's extraordinary feat and from that time on paid particular attention to Nandi's remarkable son. The fact that Shaka was an outcast might also have endeared him to Dingiswayo; he, too, knew what it was to be disinherited by a jealous father. Dingiswayo's patronage was undoubtedly a decisive factor in Shaka's early career. The defeat of the Butelezi was responsible for another important development. One of Shaka's Zulu half-brothers, Bakuza—the son whom Senzangakhona had nominated as his heir—had fought with the Butelezi and had been killed in the battle. Why Bakuza should have allied himself with the Butelezi is not clear, for the Zulu and the Butelezi were old enemies. However, Dingiswayo's victory appears to have had a chastening effect on Senzangakhona. He lost no time in making his submission to the Mthethwa overlord. All the same, Shaka's new found glory did nothing to soften his father's heart. When Senzangakhona named a new heir it was not Nandi's son but Sigujana, son of his eighth wife. Shaka, hero of the Mthethwa, was still a Zulu outcast.

Dingiswayo continued his drive for supremacy; conquering some chieftains, frightening others into submission. Shaka played a major part in all the Mthethwa campaigns. As his renown as a regimental commander blossomed, so too did his reputation as a military tactician. Having instituted new fighting methods, Shaka turned his attention to the all-important question of strategy. The order of attack which he evolved was to become recognised as the tactical advance of his, and his descendants', armies. As with his fighting methods, his strategical innovations were as simple as they were inspired.

He divided his force into three parts. The main body constituting the centre, or chest, of the force, was supported by a reserve regiment. Two other regiments were deployed as flanks, or horns, which advanced and encircled the enemy. In attack, the 'chest' was the strongest contingent which closed with the enemy and held them fast, while the two 'horns' performed their enveloping movement. Ideally, when the tips of the horns met, they combined to attack from the rear. By providing the 'chest' with reserves—who sat with their backs to the fight until they were wanted and were known as the 'loins'—Shaka could call on fresh troops to replace his wounded or battle weary warriors when the occasion demanded. As a further relief measure, he conscripted young boys to act as baggage carriers and employed doctors to tend the wounded. These tactics, together with the use he made of spies, smoke signals and informers, were to make his surprise attacks as ingenious as they were deadly.

It took some time for Shaka to perfect his military system. While he was with the Mthethwa the system was still in its infancy. Nevertheless, his improvisations in battle earned him the continuing support and respect of Dingiswayo. When the time came for him to make a bid for the Zulu chieftainship, he received every encouragement from his admiring patron.

Senzangakhona is thought to have died in 1816. Shaka was then twenty-nine. He had no rightful claim as his father's heir; for succession to the leadership of a clan depended on the known wishes of a dying chief and Senzangakhona had twice disinherited his eldest son. Neither this nor the fact that both he and his mother had been banished from the Zulu clan carried any weight with Shaka. His determination to assume the Zulu chieftainship took no cognizance of tribal traditions and prejudices. It was enough that he was Senzangakhona's son. The chieftainship was vital to his future plans and nothing, certainly not the pretensions of a younger brother, would be allowed to stand in his way.

There is some difference of opinion about the manner in which Shaka seized power. A widely accepted version of this episode has it that, as soon as Shaka heard that his father's nominee, Sigujana, had been installed as the Zulu leader, he sent his uterine brother, Ngwadi (Nandi's son by her lover) to assassinate Sigujana. This seems the most probable explanation of Sigujana's timely death. However, others claim that Ngwadi was merely sent to negotiate with Sigujana and that Sigujana's obstinacy caused them to fight while bathing in a river. The fight ended in Sigujana being drowned. Precisely what there was to negotiate and what Shaka intended to do if the negotiations failed is not clear. In either case, the end result was the same. Sigujana was quickly disposed of and Shaka claimed the chieftainship.

Dingiswayo released Shaka from service with the Mthethwa and provided him with a strong escort to counter any possible opposition on his arrival at the Zulu kraals. This display of Mthethwa approval had the desired effect. Shaka marched into his father's kraal un-opposed. Dressed in a kilt of blue-grey monkey furs and wearing his distinctive blue crane feathers in his head circlet, he was unmistakably master of the situation. 'His regal, dignified bearing,' it is said, 'the easy grace of all his movements, his piercing eyes set in a strong face, and the general look of authority, made it plain to all that here was a warrior-king indeed.'

He needed to act both swiftly and decisively. Others had eyes on the Zulu chieftainship: not the least being another of Senzanga-khona's sons, Dingane, who had been away from home when his father died. By the time Dingane returned, Sigujana was dead and Shaka was the undisputed ruler. One look at the new chieftain was enough to make Dingane abandon all thoughts of insubordination. He was courteously received by Shaka and, for the time being, gave every sign of submitting to the *fait accompli*. By accepting this show of good faith, Shaka made a grave mistake.

One of Shaka's first acts as the Zulu chief was to build himself a new kraal. He called this kraal *kwaBulawayo* (at the place of the killing) in memory of his sufferings as a child. That painful memory was to play a part in more than the building of his kraal. It was responsible for the horrifying vengeance which Shaka now took on those who had once persecuted Nandi and himself.

Seated beneath a euphorbia tree and surrounded by his indunas, this superbly proportioned, gleaming black figure, grimly pro-nounced judgement on his former tormentors. One by one, those who had slighted his mother or shown signs of opposing him, were dragged before him. After a brief questioning they were sentenced to die. The questioning was a mere formality; none was spared. A wave of his hand was the signal for a band of executioners to seize the victims and club them to death.

Later, the same procedure was carried out at the Langeni kraal where, among his mother's people, he and Nandi had suffered even greater humiliations. Here the punishment was more sadistic. The victims were made to wait until final judgement had been passed and then impaled, sitting upright, on sharpened poles, until Shaka relented and 'sent orders to the slayers to end the death agonies of the victims by placing bundles of grass under them and firing them'.

Once his great kraal had been built, Shaka set about organising his army. He used the Mthethwa military system—to which he had contributed so much—as his guide. It is estimated that he had less than 400 adult Zulu males at his disposal at this time. From this small and by no means proficient force, he formed four regiments. All the older, married men, under the age of forty, he banded into a regiment known as the *amaWombe* (battlers). They were allowed to keep their wives, but were housed in a new kraal under the supervision of his father's unmarried sister, Mkabayi. Two other regiments were formed from men in their twenties and thirties. The first of these regiments was made up of men old enough to have acquired the *isiCoco* (a fibre headring, plastered into the hair with beeswax, which symbolised maturity and was worn by males immediately prior to their first marriage). These men now had to relinquish their headrings and were forbidden to marry. Men of a similar age who had not yet donned the headring were recruited into a separate regiment. Together, these two regiments were known as the *izimPohlo* (the Bachelors' Brigade). Finally there was a regiment of Zulu youths which Shaka named the *uFasimba* (the Haze). These youngsters were of an age to be trained in Shaka's methods from the outset of their military career and consequently promised to be a model regiment; they were quickly recognised as Shaka's favourites.

Shaka was now free to shape an army to his own ideas. The fighting methods he had conceived while serving under Dingiswayo could be perfected. His warriors were subjected to rigorous training:

each regiment was conditioned to its particular function in battle, to respond to silent commands and to undertake exhausting marches, living off the country and plundering wayside kraals. They were armed with Shaka's specially designed stabbing spear and their un-shod feet were toughened at compulsory dances in a field of thorns; the fact that any warrior not concentrating solely on the dance was immediately executed tended to keep their eyes—if not their minds —off their feet. Following the Mthethwa pattern, the Zulu regiments were distinguished by the colour of their ox-hide shields—Shaka's own shield being pure white with a single black spot—and each group had its own song and war cry. They formed the nucleus of a formidable force; a force which was to expand rapidly once they went into action.

While Dingiswayo lived, Shaka remained his vassal and as such his military activities were limited. He was not strong enough, or foolish enough, to challenge the Mthethwa paramountcy. This, however, did not prevent his subjugating the smaller clans in his immediate vicinity. He started with the Langeni. In a surprise attack, he surrounded the main kraal of his mother's people and closed in to revenge himself on those who had tyrannised him as a child.

The Langeni offered no resistance but the Butelezi, whom he next attacked, put up a fight. This is said to have been the first real test for the new Zulu army; there is no doubt about its success. The long standing enmity between the Zulu and the Butelezi clans was decisively ended by Shaka's disciplined army. Instructing his warriors to carry their shields at a tilt, in order to make their numbers seem smaller, Shaka sent the horns of his force to encircle the Butelezi. On completing this unexpected move, each warrior turned his shield towards the enemy and immediately the Zulu army appeared to double. The effect was shattering. As the Butelezi started to panic, Shaka's men swept upon them, creating havoc with their stabbing spears and practically butchering the entire force— including the women and children watching from a nearby hillock. Among the few survivors was the Butelezi chieftain, Pungashe, who fled north and sought refuge with Zwide, ruler of the powerful Ndwandwe.

That Pungashe should have fled to Zwide for protection is significant. As leader of the Ndwandwe, Zwide posed a considerable threat to Dingiswayo's paramountcy and, indirectly, to Shaka's ambitions. The spread of Mthethwa influence had thus far been confined to an area south of the Mfolozi river. To the north of that river, Zwide had established a confederacy similar in size and importance to that ruled over by Dingiswayo. The northern Nguni, in fact, were rapidly coalescing into two rival, mutually hostile, groups. A struggle between the Mthethwa and the Ndwandwe for ultimate supremacy was inevitable. They had already clashed twice and each time the Mthethwa had emerged victorious. On these occasions Dingiswayo, true to his conciliatory policies, had magnanimously released Zwide in the hopes of winning an ally. He seriously underestimated his enemy.

Strange accounts are given of Zwide, the Ndwandwe chieftain. He is said to have been dominated by a hag-like mother who collected the skulls of his enemies to decorate her hut. Zwide himself had a reputation for treachery and cruelty which, if it is believed, makes his political accomplishments all the more remarkable. Certainly he commanded a wide allegiance and his army, although smaller than Dingiswayo's, was a powerful force. He was undoubtedly a man to be reckoned with.

Shaka, having defeated the Butelezi, went on to mop up other neighbouring clans. He showed none of Dingiswayo's statesmanship. As a conqueror his main concern was to destroy the possibility of future opposition. His enemies were ruthlessly suppressed; only those whom he could absorb into his own fighting force were spared. The new recruits incorporated into the Zulu regiments rapidly increased the army's size and effectiveness. It is estimated that by the beginning of 1817—the year following Shaka's assumption of the chieftainship—Zulu territories were four times their original size. Shaka's army then numbered 2000 warriors; the *uFasimba* alone accounting for 800 trained youths—more than twice the number included in the entire Zulu force when Shaka took over. These figures are, of necessity, conjectural, but they can be taken as reflecting a rough assessment of Shaka's growing power.

Dingiswayo was quick to recognise his protégé's aggrandisement. The Zulu army was called upon to assist the Mthethwa in some of its major campaigns. In the winter of 1817, for instance, Shaka's troops provided an effective wing to Dingiswayo's army when the Mthethwa attacked and defeated Matiwane of the emaNgwaneni clan. Shortly after this there was a further mobilisation of the Mthethwa for a campaign in which the Zulu regiments were expected to play a prominent part. This time Dingiswayo was moving against his old enemy Zwide, with the intention of disposing of the Ndwandwe trouble-maker once and for all. The disastrous outcome of this expedition was to have far-reaching results.

Exactly what happened has long been a matter of contention. It is known that Dingiswayo made elaborate preparations for the campaign and arranged for Shaka's troops to join him at a specified time and place. Whether or not his instructions were obeyed is not certain. Some maintain that the Zulu contingent was inexplicably delayed and that while waiting for Shaka, Dingiswayo was killed. He is said to have been lured across the Ndwandwe border, escorted only by a band of girls, and captured by one of Zwide's patrols. After entertaining Dingiswayo for a couple of days, Zwide is reported to have cut off his head and presented it to his skull-collecting mother.

Fynn, however, claims that the Zulu and Mthethwa forces had already been united and that Shaka deliberately betrayed Dingiswayo. 'Knowing the spot where Dingiswayo would post himself to observe the battle,' says Fynn, 'Shaka secretly communicated this knowledge to the enemy, who sent a force and took him prisoner.'

Others have attributed Zwide's *coup* to witchcraft. It is said that, sometime earlier, Zwide had sent a beautiful Ndwandwe girl to procure a smear of Dingiswayo's semen. Her mission accomplished, this very personal secretion had been used to concoct a medicine to ensure the Mthethwa chief's downfall. Dingiswayo's semen must, indeed, have been potent.

But be it by secrecy or seduction, Dingiswayo was undoubtedly killed. The Mthethwa were left leaderless and forced to retire under Shaka's guidance. This loss of both face and leadership quickly reduced the Mthethwa confederacy to a state of confusion. Dingiswayo was succeeded by a half-brother whose incompetent rule created divisions among the subject chiefdoms.

Many of the disaffected Mthethwa attached themselves to Shaka and this schism enabled Shaka to assert his own claims. He later attacked and killed Dingiswayo's heir, replacing him with a loyal follower of his own. In any case, the days of Mthethwa supremacy had died with Dingiswayo. It quickly became apparent that the Zulu and their ambitious leader were now in the ascendant.

[4]

But if Shaka had donned Dingiswayo's mantle, he had also inherited his problems. Not the least of these was the threat of Zwide and the Ndwandwe. As it happened, this particular difficulty was overcome by the rashness of the Ndwandwe chieftain. Seriously underestimating his new rival, Zwide invaded Shaka's territories a year after Dingiswayo's death. He did not catch the Zulu unprepared.

The Zulu and the Ndwandwe forces met at Gqokli Hill, just south of the swiftly flowing Mfolozi river. The battle area had been chosen by Shaka, who concentrated his main force in a strong defensive position on the upper slopes of the hill. His reserves, both men and supplies, were hidden in a deep depression at the summit, completely encircled by the other troops. A smaller force was sent to detain the Ndwandwe at the Mfolozi river. Although greatly outnumbered, this force was able to hold the enemy by lining the river banks and clubbing the Ndwandwe warriors as they struggled against a fast and treacherous current. It was late afternoon before Zwide's exhausted and somewhat depleted army gained the southern bank and trudged towards the foot of Gqokli Hill, where they encamped for the night.

When the Ndwandwe attempted to storm Gqokli the following morning they found themselves at a distinct disadvantage. The conical shape of the hill counted against them. The higher they climbed the narrower became their front; by the time they reached the wall of Zulu their advanced troops were so tightly bunched together that their movements were severely restricted. Armed only with throwing assegais and forced on by the press from below, they were neither prepared nor positioned to withstand a frontal attack. When Shaka's men descended on them, bellowing their war cries and flashing their deadly stabbing spears, the Ndwandwe put up a brave fight but could not prevent the inevitable massacre. The entire Ndwandwe force was thrust relentlessly downhill until Shaka—commanding from a convenient height—called a halt.

Slowly the Zulu warriors retired to their original lines, sending their wounded ahead to be tended at the summit, and pausing only to collect assegais from the hundreds of dead Ndwandwe littering the hillside.

This strategic placing of his men enabled Shaka to counter several more Ndwandwe assaults. Time and again Zwide's force charged up the hill but, no matter how much they varied their tactics or what ruses they employed, each charge was effectively thrown back. Moreover, as both sides became progressively more exhausted and parched with thirst, Shaka was able to call on his hidden reserves while the enemy ranks were seriously depleted by Ndwandwe warriors deserting to refresh themselves at the distant Mfolozi river.

For all that, the Zulu victory was by no means decisive. Earlier Shaka had created a diversion by ordering a contingent of his army to drive away the Zulu cattle, in full sight of the enemy, in the hopes of enticing a portion of Zwide's force to pursue them. Successful as this strategem was, it resulted in heavy cattle losses. By the time the Ndwandwe finally retreated, they had acquired some considerable Zulu herds. This was the one comfort to be derived from the day-long battle: on all other counts they were the losers. Not only had their attack been repelled, but numbered among their losses were no less than five of Zwide's sons, including the Ndwandwe heir.

Zwide, who never accompanied his forces, was furious when his commanders came dragging back to report defeat. Having eliminated the powerful Dingiswayo, he had no intention of yielding to a Zulu upstart. He was determined to crush Shaka. At the beginning of 1819, he regrouped and strengthened his army and again sent it into Zulu territory.

This time Shaka adopted elusive tactics. Instructing his people to drive their cattle into the forests, to empty the grain pits in their kraals and to hide themselves, he marched his army ahead of the invaders, luring them further and further away from their base. Elementary as this 'scorched earth' device appears, it was novel to tribal warfare and proved remarkably effective. The Zulu army was well catered for by food-carrying herdboys, but the Ndwandwe ran dangerously short of rations as they advanced deeper and deeper into the deserted territory. For almost a week Shaka led the enemy a frustrating chase; occasionally allowing his troops to be glimpsed but never pausing long enough to be attacked. Finally the Ndwandwe gave up. Famished and exhausted, they camped in a dense forest and decided to retreat. Even then they were allowed no rest. Small parties of Zulu warriors, taking advantage of the darkness, crept into the camp and created havoc among their sleep-bemused enemy. Unable to distinguish friend from foe, the Ndwandwe attacked each other in the confused night fighting and as they did so the Zulu invaders slipped away practically unharmed. Very few of Zwide's men were marching-fit when their retreat began the following morning.

Shaka shadowed the weary Ndwandwe for several miles and then launched his attack. In a battle which raged for two days, along the banks of the Mhlatuze river, the Ndwandwe were utterly defeated. Drooping from hunger and fatigue, they were easy prey for the disciplined Zulu warriors who, by repeated charges, reduced them to a state of panic. Once the army had been destroyed, Shaka despatched two regiments to the Ndwandwe capital with orders to capture Zwide and slaughter his women and children.

It was dark when these regiments arrived at Zwide's kraal. They signalled their approach by singing a Ndwandwe victory chant. The population, expecting the return of a triumphant army, rushed out to meet them and thus placed themselves at their mercy. But, of course, no mercy was shown. Obeying orders, Shaka's men destroyed the inhabitants of Zwide's great kraal and then went on to plunder Zwide's territory. 'By next dawn,' it is said, 'the rest of the Zulu army was sweeping through Ndwandwe-land, destroying without mercy every human being and dog, and capturing all the cattle, sheep and goats, and thereafter burning every hut.'

But they failed in their principal objective. Zwide himself escaped. He is said to have hidden in a river-bed before fleeing northwards with a scattering of his once powerful clan. His infamous mother was not so fortunate: she was captured. Tradition has it that Shaka subjected her to a terrible death. Hyenas were reputed to be the accomplices of witches and Shaka ordered this particular witch to be locked in her notorious skull museum in the company of a ravenous hyena. Only when her limbs were being ripped from her body did he show a semblance of pity and allow her gaolers to set fire to the old woman's hut.

The defeat of the Ndwandwe marked a turning point in Shaka's career. He was now master of an area far larger than that over which

Dingiswayo had ruled. His domain stretched from the Pongola river in the north to the Tugela in the south, and from the Buffalo river in the west to the eastern seaboard: a territory of some 11,500 square miles. It was a singularly beautiful stretch of country. From the massive Drakensberg range on its far western horizon, the grassy, undulating landscape sloped down to the shores of the Indian ocean. In all southern Africa, there were few fresher, greener, more fertile areas than this.

The forces under Shaka's command had likewise increased. Precise figures are difficult to arrive at but, with all fit men being conscripted into the Zulu regiments, Shaka could probably muster a fighting force of anything up to 40,000 warriors. Added to this force were the non-combatant regiments of Zulu girls which were organised along parallel lines to those of the men. Sexual intercourse was strictly forbidden to these male and female regiments. They were expected to sublimate their natural instincts in military activities, exercises and dances. Occasionally they were allowed to indulge in the customary *ukuHlobonga*, but any accidental pregnancies resulting from the misuse of this indulgence cost the offending parties dear, often their lives. Not until a warrior was forty was he given permission to marry.

The rule of Shaka was unique: he established an extensive African kingdom, governed by an army of enforced celibates, dedicated to war, and owing sole allegiance to an all-powerful monarch.

For monarch he was. His authority went far beyond that of all previous chiefs; his rule was that of a tyrant king. Dingiswayo's confederacy was a thing of the past: in its place there arose a single nation, a Zulu nation.

The semi-autonomous chiefdoms were now welded into a Zulu feudal state. Some hereditary chiefs and headmen were permitted to administer their own regions, others were appointed with similar powers, but above them all Shaka reigned supreme. In deference to Nguni custom he retained a small advisory council but its members were his own appointees and, although he consulted them freely, their influence was minimal. No important decisions were taken contrary to Shaka's wishes. 'He was the senior executive,' says Professor Thompson, 'the ultimate court of appeal, the sole source of laws, the commander-in-chief and the high priest . . . The traditions of the Zulu royal lineage became the traditions of the nation; the

Zulu dialect became the language of the nation; and every inhabitant, whatever his origins, became a Zulu, owing allegiance to Shaka.'

But like other military despots, Shaka was both the master and the victim of his regime. His system had been born in aggression and it required continued belligerency to keep alive. Shaka needed enemies, not only to satisfy his war-like propensities, but to keep his warriors employed and thus ensure his own, undisputed leadership.

Such enemies were, at first, not difficult to find. He quickly attacked and subdued all neighbouring chiefdoms, scattering the clans south of the Tugela and laying waste the territories on his immediate borders. In this way he perpetuated the widespread disruption—known as the *Mfecane* (the crushing)—which had resulted from Dingiswayo's attempts at aggrandisement. For the tribes displaced by the Mthethwa (and later the Zulu) fled northwards, attacking others in their flight, and thus disrupted the tightly-knit pattern of African settlement. The effects of this tremendous upheaval were to be felt throughout the southern part of the continent, reaching as far north as Lake Tanganyika.

Equally important were the pressures which the *Mfecane* created on the frontier of the Cape Colony. The rise of a formidable black power to the north-east inevitably had repercussions on the eastern borders of the Cape. Hostility between black and white, manifesting itself in cattle raids and reprisals, was not so much a matter of unavoidable racial conflict as the result—in part, at least—of the pressurised conditions imposed upon the frontier tribesmen, or 'Caffres' ('Kaffirs') as they were called. It is not without significance that the 1820 Settlers arrived at the Cape at the very time that Shaka was busy driving his enemies out of Natal. For those clans in 'Caffreland', wedged between these two formidable power blocs there was little hope of peaceful expansion: expansion which became more and more necessary with the influx of refugees into their territory.

In 1824 the situation was further aggravated when the Zulu army embarked on a raiding expedition against one of the more powerful chiefdoms beyond the southern Natal border. By attacking Faku, the Mpondo chief, Shaka undoubtedly added to the existing tensions among those clans established between his domains and the Cape Colony. It was the return of this expedition that had so alarmed

Henry Francis Fynn during his first attempt to reach Shaka's kraal. Although Shaka had not by that time met any white men, he was fully aware of their existence. He also knew something of their strength.

Whether Shaka was engineering a direct confrontation with the Cape colonists, however, is another matter. What policy Shaka can be said to have had was capricious; resulting more from cause and effect than from deliberate planning. He was a despot who saw no further than immediate threats to his supremacy, real or imaginary. This was apparent, not only in his campaigns but in his domestic life. Basing his rule on fear, he tyrannised his subjects as ruthlessly as he fought his enemies.

All this meant that life at Bulawayo was very much of a gamble. It depended largely on Shaka's whims. His executioners, always close at hand, daily clubbed the skulls or twisted the necks of those who displeased their master. Often the offence was trivial: an untimely sneeze or a misplaced joke was sufficient to warrant a flick of Shaka's hand—the signal for immediate death. To say that he was sadistic—motivated by a desire to inflict pain—is, as Donald Morris has pointed out, somewhat misleading. His regime was rather characterised by a complete and contemptuous disregard for human life. This did not make Shaka unique among tyrants, but it made a visit to his court a perilous venture.

To this court had come Lieutenant Francis George Farewell and his party in search of ivory.

4

kwaBULAWAYO

THE GREAT KRAAL in which Shaka received Farewell and Fynn in 1824, was not the kraal he had built when he first seized the Zulu chieftainship. Some time after the death of Dingiswayo, he had moved his capital to the lower Mhlatuze valley, building a much larger kraal in the heartland of his new domain. This second capital, like the first, was named kwaBulawayo (at the place of the killing) in memory of his tragic childhood; soon, however, his sanguinary practices were to give a new meaning to this choice of name. Those who came to Bulawayo in later years could be forgiven for imagining that the name of the Zulu capital signified the tone of Shaka's reign, rather than the miseries of Shaka's childhood.

A few miles south-west of Bulawayo was the somewhat smaller establishment of the once-despised Nandi, who now enjoyed the status of a queen-mother.

Shaka appears to have moved his capital for administrative reasons. Being more accessible, the Mhlatuze valley provided a convenient focal point for his enlarged kingdom. The new Bulawayo became the centre for all important events in Zululand. Disputes were settled there, religious rites were observed there, and preparations for war were conducted within the palisades of Shaka's great cattle arena. Once a year the entire army assembled at the royal barracks for a harvest celebration at which Shaka ritually tasted the first fruits of the season and gave permission for the corn to be gathered (the eating of grain before this ceremony was punishable, as was so much else, by death). Before and after every military expedition the Zulu warriors were tended by the royal witch doctors whose magic was used to fortify the army and to cultivate a national morale. All these events were organised with painstaking efficiency. Both as a stage manager and a performer, Shaka knew the value of carefully planned dramatic effects.

He had no precedent for receiving the Europeans but his

inventiveness and attention to detail ensured that their welcome would be impressive.

There can be no doubt about the thoroughness of Shaka's preparations to fete his unusual guests. He delayed their arrival at his capital to fit in with his own arrangements. He saw to it that they were fully aware of his power before they reached Bulawayo. He kept himself informed about their movements and reactions. By the end of their journey, he was sufficiently apprised of their relative importance to single out Farewell and Fynn as the men with whom he would have to deal. Farewell's full dress uniform and Fynn's reputation as a doctor might have had something to do with this selection, but it was obviously a matter to which Shaka had given a good deal of thought. By demanding that Farewell and Fynn advance alone, he isolated the leaders of the party and thus safe-guarded himself against any possible trickery. He was, as the Europeans soon discovered, well advised about the unpredictable ways of white adventurers.

Shaka's meeting with the white men was staged at an opportune time. It coincided with the return of the Zulu army from their expedition against Faku, the Mpondo chief. This meant that the fighting regiments were already assembled at the Bulawayo kraal for the doctoring ritual which accompanied the return of the army from a military campaign. No doubt this obligatory ceremony accounted, in part, for Shaka's delaying tactics. Had the fighting regiments not been present they would certainly have been summoned in the same way that Shaka had called upon his regiments of girls to assist at the welcome of the strangers. But had Farewell's party arrived earlier they would have had a longer wait before being admitted to the royal presence. Supreme as he was, Shaka never exposed himself to unnecessary risks. He relied upon his army to impose his authority and to ensure his protection.

By first hiding himself among his bodyguard, then leaping from their midst, Shaka effectively presented himself to Farewell and Fynn as a warrior king. This, however, was only part of a more elaborate ceremony. No sooner had he revealed himself than he rushed to the other end of the kraal where, surrounded by a band of followers, he broke into an energetic and noisy dance. At the same time the mass of warriors formed themselves into regiments, and groups were sent rushing to the river and surrounding hills.

'It was a most exciting scene,' enthused Fynn, 'surprising to us, who could not have imagined that a nation termed "savages" could be so disciplined and kept in order.'

The two astonished Europeans were left standing in the middle of the kraal. Only one man remained at their side. Until that moment this man had been hidden by the crowd. Now when Farewell turned to glance at him, he received a further shock. It was Jacob, his former convict-interpreter. The encounter was, to say the least, unexpected.

The last time that Farewell had seen Jacob had been at St Lucia Bay, where he and other crew members of the *Salisbury* had been stranded. At that time Jacob had fled into the bush to escape punishment by the rescuing party under James Saunders King. Jacob had evidently followed the Mhlatuze river inland, eventually reaching Bulawayo. His arrival at the Zulu capital had created considerable uneasiness. Having appeared, as it were, from out of the sea, he had been given the name Hlambamanzi (which denotes a strong swimmer) but had been regarded with suspicion. However, it is said that he soon 'found out Chaka's weak side, saw his disposition, and how to flatter his desires. He devised many plans which pleased the despot exceedingly, by which he was elevated above the ordinary warriors'.

In time, Shaka placed Jacob in charge of his personal bodyguard, provided him with ten wives and a large herd of cattle and allowed him to build himself a kraal. To all intents and purposes, the former convict was raised to the position of a minor chief; as such he became one of Shaka's advisers. He certainly had no cause to regret his switch from a white to a black master.

From Jacob the Zulu monarch had learned much about the white people of the Cape Colony. 'The king,' it is said, 'found him an amusing fellow, with whom to pass an hour or two at night, when all his attendants had retired. Chaka, ignorant of Europeans, and never before having had intercourse with any one who had known them, found what [Jacob] related exceedingly interesting; particularly as their manners and appearance were so different to anything the savage mind could fancy. The king had always thought there was no other land but that which himself and his people inhabited, and that he was the only great king in the world.'

Whether Jacob was in fact the only person with whom Shaka had discussed the white people is debatable—visitors from Zululand were reported at the Cape long before Jacob reached Bulawayo—but he was undoubtedly Shaka's main source of information concerning European ways and achievements. Now he was able to interpret Zulu customs for Farewell and Fynn.

The dance, started by Shaka, lasted two hours. Once it was under way, the entire army joined in: each regiment advancing and receding in formation with marvellous precision. As the male and female regiments stamped, kicked and chanted, groups of girls from Shaka's seraglio—each group wearing black head-feathers, but distinguished from each other by the colour of their beads—wended their way into the centre of the kraal and performed specially arranged dances of their own. Jacob explained the significance of every move, every gesture.

From time to time, Shaka left the dance to speak to Farewell and Fynn. With Jacob acting as interpreter, he assured the white men that they had nothing to fear from his people. He wanted to know if they had ever seen such order and discipline in any other country and boasted that 'he was the greatest king in existence, that his people were as numerous as the stars, and that his cattle were innumerable'. To prove his point, he had the vast royal herds—the cattle sorted according to their colour—driven past for inspection. The white men were left in no doubt that the Zulu King was as rich as he was powerful.

Towards evening the dancers began to disperse. Instructions were given for the rest of the European party to be sent for—Peterssen and the others had been waiting on the other side of the valley—and the visitors were shown to a kraal where they could pitch their tents. Before retiring, the loutish Peterssen nearly ruined the happy proceedings with a tactless joke. He placed a musical box on the ground and, by surreptitiously striking the stop with a switch, caused it to start playing. At the sound of the music, Shaka gave a start, scowled, turned angrily on his heel, and strode off to join the last of the dancers. 'It seemed,' says Fynn, 'to produce in him a superstitious feeling.'

The King's anger did not last long. That evening he sent his visitors a sheep, a basket of corn, an ox and a three gallon pot of beer. Exhausted and hungry though they were, the white men felt honour bound to put up some sort of show before settling down to their meal. Not being able to equal Shaka's magnificent display, they contented themselves by sending up four naval skyrockets and firing an eight-gun salute. Shaka's reaction to this noisy demonstration has not, unfortunately, been recorded. While his people gaped in wonder, the King remained firmly in his hut.

In one account which Fynn gives of this first night at Bulawayo, he says that after dinner he was summoned to the royal seraglio. He found Shaka seated on a carved wooden chair, surrounded by some 400 girls. Two or three minor chiefs were also present. The conversation centred mainly on Fynn's reputed abilities as a doctor. Shaka had been far from pleased with the reports he had of Fynn bringing a woman back to life. He accused Fynn of wasting his medicine on menials.

'Are you then the doctor of dogs?' he growled. 'You were sent here to be my doctor.'

Shaka also enquired about the King of England. He wanted to know whether George IV was as great a king as himself. Bristling with patriotism, Fynn had assured him that the former Prince Regent was 'one of the greatest kings in the world'. (It was a statement which might have startled some of that monarch's subjects.) From then on Shaka, with instinctive majesty, was inclined to refer to George IV—whom he called umGeorge—as a royal brother. He now demanded that Fynn cure him of some unspecified complaint or, as he said, 'I will have you sent to umGeorge to have you killed.'

Faced with this bizarre prospect and with Shaka's refusal to specify what was troubling him, Fynn asked the King to stand up for examination. Shaka, a little affronted, eventually agreed to do so on condition that Fynn did not approach him closely. Some of the girls lit torches and the examination was conducted at a respectful distance. It did not take Fynn long to realise that the powerfully built King was, in all senses of the word, fighting fit. However, he was quick to notice some black scars on Shaka's body. Realising that these had been caused by the ministrations of the witch doctors, he hazarded a guess and said that Shaka 'had pains in his loins'. The correctness of this diagnosis caused a sensation. Shaka covered his mouth with astonishment; the girls gave Fynn a round of applause. The white man's magic was given a further boost.

Impressed by the young man's wisdom, Shaka asked Fynn to stay on for a month after his companions had left. Fynn agreed and

they parted the best of friends. Shaka was delighted with his new
doctor, Fynn was thrilled by his success, and George IV had been
spared a most embarrassing request.

[2]

The following day the Europeans presented Shaka with the gifts
they had brought. They found the King seated under a tree at the
upper end of the kraal surrounded by some 200 of his people. He
was being greased with a mixture of red ochre and sheep-tail fat in
preparation for his daily rounds. This public anointing took place
every morning. Shaka appears to have been obsessed by the need
to display himself naked before his subjects. His unhappy childhood
may have had something to do with this. If it is true that he had
been constantly taunted with genital inadequacy, he no doubt
welcomed the opportunity of proving that he was indeed every inch
a king. The morning ritual seems to have been his own innovation
and had nothing to do with Zulu custom.

For his attendants the ceremony was not without its dangers.
By assisting at the washing and anointing of the King they came as
close to him as anyone was permitted to come; Shaka was always
on the lookout for treachery. Those responsible for supplying the
water, grease and red ochre had to approach the King holding their
vessels and baskets at arm's length. Not until they were given the
signal to retire were they allowed to lower their arms. The slightest
false, or accidental, move could result in the offender being executed
on the spot. Nor did the presence of strangers help matters. All too
often Shaka used this ceremony to demonstrate his power and,
while talking to his guests, would casually order a few killings to
impress them. However, on this occasion the King was relatively
lenient: only one man was killed while Farewell's party watched.
It was the first of the many executions they were to witness during
their stay.

Once the King was dressed, the Europeans presented their gifts.
They had come well supplied. Besides a vast quantity of different
coloured beads—'far superior to those Shaka had previously
obtained from the Portuguese at Delagoa Bay'—Farewell had

collected a variety of woollen blankets, brass bars, copper sheets, some cats and dogs, a pig and a few pigeons. The prize item, however, was a full-dress military coat with gold lace epaulettes. Shaka received the gifts coolly but his satisfaction was obvious. He was extremely interested in the animals, particularly the pig. Unfortunately this quaint pet later disgraced itself by invading the royal milk stores and so frightening the women of the seraglio that it had to be killed.

That day there were further dancing displays and the Europeans did their bit by firing off a few more rockets. They had good reason to compliment themselves on the success of their visit. Shaka could not have been friendlier. Not until the fourth day did the white men experience a few qualms. They were taken to see the hillock outside Bulawayo where the bodies of those executed at Shaka's orders were left to rot. It was not a pretty sight. The corpses, some with stakes protruding from their rectums, were being devoured by hundreds of vultures which flapped obscenely amid the piles of decaying flesh. Having witnessed how capriciously Shaka ordered a killing, the sight of his countless victims was hardly reassuring. It proved too much for the jittery Peterssen. There and then he demanded that they dissolve the partnership and leave immediately for the Cape.

The party's confidence was somewhat restored the following day when Fynn gave another demonstration of the white men's magic. One of Shaka's trusted indunas was ill with fever and the Europeans were called upon to doctor him. Fynn's treatment was simple but effective. A little bleeding quickly reduced the man's temperature and within a matter of hours he reported that he was feeling better. Shaka was delighted. Fynn, with whom the King had long discussions every evening, was already an established favourite; now he was regarded as something of a miracle worker. For his companions, Fynn's elementary medical skills proved an undoubted boon.

Peterssen even tried to cash in on Fynn's popularity. Recognising that the surest way to Shaka's heart was through his imaginary ailments, the old man produced a little medicine of his own. He had brought with him what appear to have been some all-purpose purgative pills; these he offered to the King with an assurance that they were good for any disease. But Shaka was not so easily won over. Not only did he refuse to take the pills but he insisted that Peterssen give two to each of his indunas and then swallow two himself. When the indunas announced that the pills had no taste, the King agreed to swallow two but demanded that Peterssen do likewise. Unfortunately nobody noticed Peterssen slipping two more pills into his mouth and Shaka asked for the performance to be repeated. This time Peterssen refused and Shaka immediately became suspicious. He wanted to know why Peterssen was offering him medicine which he would not take himself. He was heartily supported by the now apprehensive indunas. Poor Peterssen, fresh from his visit to the gruesome hillock, apparently decided that he could better cope with the pills than the stakes and dutifully downed his final dose.

'The consequences of this to a person of 63,' says the sympathetic Fynn, 'does not require to be explained in detail.'

This purgative episode finished Peterssen completely. He made up his mind to return to the Cape as soon as possible and persuaded Farewell that the time had come to leave Bulawayo. Farewell could have had few objections. Having established friendly relations with Shaka, he had accomplished his main object. He was also no doubt anxious to complete the building of his trading post at Port Natal. Shaka was agreeable to the departure of the Europeans, stipulating only that Fynn must remain behind. Not knowing that Fynn had already agreed to this arrangement, Farewell had protested but the King remained adamant. When Fynn announced that he was not only willing but anxious to stay and explore the country, Farewell felt he was absolved from all responsibility. Arrangements were made for the African interpreter, Frederick, and the Hottentot servant, Michael, to remain with Fynn. The rest of the party started packing.

At a grand farewell ceremony next day, Shaka made the most of the occasion to impress his subjects. Some 25,000 people were gathered at Bulawayo; many of them arriving from outlying districts with their faces daubed with red, white and black clay. After the usual dancing and cattle displays, the King delivered a long harangue. He told the assembly to look at his guests and behold a wonder—white people! He was, he declared, the first of their kings to receive the subjects of umGeorge. Was not this a mark of his greatness? Did it not place him above their forefathers who had been too cowardly to receive a white man? The only white person previously to visit their country had been put to death as a monster who had sprung from the sea. Now that he had demonstrated his superiority, he expected his nation to treat the Europeans as kings and to respect them accordingly.

Calculated to inspire awe, there was nevertheless a great deal of truth in Shaka's words. His fearlessness and courtesy in receiving Farewell's party was a tribute to his statesmanship. He knew enough of the white people at the Cape Colony to make him suspicious of their motives. A lesser chief would not have hesitated to destroy what might well have been a threat to his supremacy. Despot that Shaka undoubtedly was, he was not without wisdom. From the very outset, he adopted a conciliatory attitude towards the whites.

Farewell and Fynn had been presented with five elephant tusks each: more were promised. When the Europeans eventually departed, Shaka supplied them with cattle for their journey. Fynn accompanied the party for a few miles and then returned to Bulawayo. He arrived back at the Zulu capital at sunset and was immediately summoned by Shaka. That evening their nightly conference lasted two or three hours.

[3]

Once Farewell's party had left, Shaka moved to a smaller kraal some fifteen miles away and sent for Fynn to join him there. The first couple of days at the new kraal passed pleasantly enough. Shaka delighted in teasing Fynn and spent hours debating the superiority of the black man over the white. The forefathers of the whites, he maintained, had been less than fair to their descendants. They had bestowed many gifts on the white men, but had deprived them of the greatest gift of all—a good black skin. He had no doubt that the whites were ashamed of their skin: why else did they hide it by wearing clothes? Nothing would persuade him that the whites would not give all they were worth for a handsome black skin.

The King was also scornful of the use the white men made of their manufacturing skills. He wanted to know, for instance, what they did with the hides of cattle. When Fynn explained that leather was used to make shoes and other articles, Shaka felt he had gained a point. Was not this further proof of lack of foresight on the part of the whites' ancestors? Had the white men been provided with tougher feet, they could have used their leather for more serviceable articles, such as shields. The Zulu shields were invaluable in battle. Dipped in water before an attack, they could protect his warriors against bullets and enable them to close with the white men before they had reloaded their guns. The whites would then have to drop their guns and run and, as they could not run as fast as a Zulu, they would be caught and beaten.

Trying to argue with the King, Fynn found himself at a disadvantage. Everything he said had to be translated by Jacob, who acted as interpreter, and Jacob wisely took care to soften Fynn's language. However, for the most part, there was no malice in Shaka's arguments. Only when others were present did he laughingly ridicule the ways of the white man; in private he was far more reasonable. He was anxious to learn as much as he could, without displaying his ignorance to his people. As in all else he did, there was a method in Shaka's quibbling.

But on one point he would not yield, either in public or private. He found the system of imprisoning criminals quite incomprehensible and sadistic. The only honourable way of punishing the guilty was by instant death. If a man was merely suspected of a crime he should be warned and set free. Nothing could be worse than keeping such men locked up indefinitely. Since Shaka had learned of the European penal system from Jacob, who resented his imprisonment on Robben Island, Fynn was unable to explain the need to safeguard the innocent and preserve life whenever possible. Jacob had no intention of admitting that criminals preferred imprisonment to death.

For all his disparaging remarks, Shaka never lost his respect for Fynn's medical abilities. He was continually asking his guest to treat him for minor ailments. But Fynn's skill as a doctor was to be put to a more severe test. Some days after the departure of Farewell, he was called upon to tend Shaka in dramatic circumstances.

It had been a day of festivity. A dance which had started in the morning had continued until early evening. Throughout the afternoon, Fynn had remained in his hut reading. As it began to get dark, however, he strolled out to watch the final stages of the celebrations. Seeing him, Shaka ordered some bundles of reeds to be lit to illuminate the dancers and then disappeared into the crowd. A few minutes later there was a sudden scream. The torches, which had been flickering erratically, were immediately extinguished, Fynn found himself standing in the darkness surrounded by a confused, shouting mob.

Having no interpreter with him, it took him some time to discover what was happening. Few wanted to stop and talk, those who did seemed as bewildered as himself. When he finally made sense of the muddled sign language, there was no mistaking the seriousness of the situation. Shaka had been stabbed.

Leaving the centre of the kraal, Fynn went in search of his servants. He found Michael sitting on a fence cheering loudly, under the impression that the general commotion was all part of the day's fun. Fynn quickly disillusioned him. He told him to find Jacob and bring some linen and camomile tea—the only medicine left—and prepare a lamp. As soon as Jacob arrived, they pushed their way through the crowd to Shaka's hut. It was impossible to get near the entrance. The way was blocked by a pack of women who started to claw at Fynn, pulling him backwards and forwards until his lamp went out. The crowd grew thicker, the screaming more hysterical.

As Fynn was about to make another attempt to enter the hut, he was grabbed by a man carrying a bunch of lighted reeds. Fynn's immediate reaction was to put up a struggle but when his arm was caught by another man he realised he was overpowered. Resigning himself to his fate, he allowed himself to be marched away. The men walked with him in silence for over half an hour until they reached a small kraal. Then they guided him into a hut where, to his intense relief, he discovered the wounded Shaka.

A determined attempt had been made on the King's life. He had been stabbed by an assegai which had passed through his left arm into his ribs. He was spitting blood. Fynn washed the wound with camomile and bandaged it with linen. There was nothing more he could do. Later a witch doctor arrived and, after administering a purgative, applied a mixture of cooling roots to the wound. Shaka, convinced that he was dying, cried throughout the entire night.

To the sobs of Shaka was added the wailing of his subjects. Having discovered where the King was hidden, a large crowd gathered outside the hut and their uncontrolled crying and shouting made sleep impossible. Each wanted to outdo the other in showing sympathy for the King. By the following morning the crowd was enormous. As more and more people pushed into the kraal, the behaviour of those surrounding Shaka's hut became more frenzied. Fynn was unable to find words to describe his horror while watching the mounting hysteria. In the full light of day, grief not only had to be felt but be seen to be felt. Men and women pummelled each other and threw themselves on the ground, not caring where or how they fell. Many of them injured themselves and fainted.

Orders had gone out that, while the King was ill, no one was allowed to wear ornaments, wash, shave their heads or eat. This had a terrifying effect on the women from Shaka's seraglio. Having kept the all-night vigil, they were parched and weak from hunger. Each of them wore four irremovable brass collars and, as the day grew hotter and their convulsions became more intense, they were almost suffocated by the tightness at their throats. Fynn threw water over some of them as they fainted, but his efforts brought little relief and several of the women died.

These deaths drove the crowd to further excesses. They began to attack and kill each other. 'Some were put to death because they did not cry,' says Fynn, 'others for putting spittle into their eyes, others for sitting down to cry, although strength and tears, after such continuous mourning and exertion, were quite exhausted. No such limits were taken into account.'

Luckily some medicine promised by Farewell arrived that day. Fynn was able to wash and dress Shaka's wounds and this brought the King some relief. All the same, it took four days before there was a noticeable improvement in his condition. Once it seemed that Shaka would recover, the killing of cattle was permitted and the starving crowd allowed to eat. On the fifth day the King began to regain his strength.

Rumour had it that the would-be assassins had been sent by Shaka's arch-enemy, the fugitive Zwide. Two regiments had been sent in pursuit of them and on the day of Shaka's recovery they returned with the dead bodies of three men. These bodies were laid on the ground outside the kraal, their right ears having been cut off, and the entire populace—some 30,000 of them—marched past, crying, yelling and striking the bodies with sticks which they left to form an enormous pile. That evening Shaka made his first public appearance. The national mourning song was chanted and the right ears of the suspected assassins were ceremoniously burnt in the centre of the cattle kraal.

News of Shaka's illness had been sent to Farewell. He immediately announced that he would return to Bulawayo and sent the King a present. A few days later he arrived with another member of his party. At a ceremony arranged for the handing over of Farewell's present—the King had been too ill to receive it earlier—Shaka expressed his gratitude to the Europeans. This gratitude took the tangible form of a grant of land to Farewell's trading company. In a lengthy document drawn up by Farewell, the white men were formally presented with a stretch of land, extending 100 miles inland and 25 miles along the coast, including Port Natal.

The contents of this document are said to have been explained to Shaka by Jacob—a fact to which Fynn and others testified—but whether the King fully understood what he was doing when he affixed his mark to the deed on 7 August 1824 is open to question. Certainly Farewell and his companions knew that by entering into such a transaction they were openly defying the specific instructions of the Governor of the Cape. This, however, did not seem to bother anyone.

The wording of the document was, to say the least, imprecise. The limits set on Farewell's territory were vague and it was not clear whether Shaka was giving or selling the land. Moreover, it stated that the King was offering land 'inherited' from his father— which shows that Farewell had no knowledge of Zulu history when he drew up the deed—and this statement alone might well have invalidated the grant. The fact that Shaka was made to refer to 'the year of our Lord eighteen hundred and twenty four' is some indication of how little he understood the words put into his mouth by Farewell.

Once the document was signed, Farewell assumed the status of an independent chief. In his new domain he had 'full power and authority over such natives that like to remain there'. Shaka guaranteed not to interfere with the traders and, without any return to himself, promised to supply Farewell with whatever cattle and corn he required. The agreement was entirely one sided. All in all, this shabby transaction reflects no credit on the man whom Shaka had treated so magnanimously.

Shortly after Farewell's arrival, a force of 7000 men was sent inland to revenge the attempt on Shaka's life. They had orders to destroy the kraals and kill all those who did not swear allegiance to the Zulu King. The Europeans witnessed the departure of this force and then took their own leave. This time Fynn accompanied the others back to Port Natal.

The visit to Bulawayo had undoubtedly proved profitable. Farewell had been in the country for little more than a month and already he was sole ruler, on paper at least, of a sizeable territory. He may not have found the gold he had hoped for, but he certainly had no cause to grumble.

[4]

Not everyone was so happy with the outcome of the trading venture. When Farewell and Fynn reached Port Natal, they found the disgruntled Peterssen still determined to return to the Cape. What is more, he seems to have unsettled the rest of the party: there was hardly a member of the expedition who did not share his feelings. And since the entire party had been engaged on short-term contracts, Farewell had no option but to let them go.

The main problem was one of transport. They had only the sloop *Julia* to convey them to the Cape and this somewhat rickety vessel was far too small to accommodate all those who wished to leave. It was therefore decided that the *Julia* should make two voyages. Half the would-be evacuees, including the much relieved Peterssen, were to leave immediately and the other half were to remain with Farewell until the *Julia* returned.

While the *Julia* was being prepared for her first voyage, Farewell staged another of his patriotic, highly irregular, demonstrations. Earlier he had solemnly raised the Union Jack and claimed Port Natal as a British possession; now, holding the dubious document he had obtained from Shaka, he repeated the performance. The cannon and musketry were fired and Farewell's domain was formally incorporated into the realms of His Britannic Majesty, King George IV. Impressive as this ceremony was, it is doubtful whether anybody—apart from the startled Africans living near

Port Natal—was particularly stirred by this waste of valuable ammunition.

Young Henry Francis Fynn attended the second flag raising and then left for another visit to Bulawayo. There was no question of his joining those who wanted to return to the Cape. He was enjoying himself hugely in Natal and his only desire was to see as much of the surrounding territory as he could.

On reaching Shaka's capital, he presented the King with yet another gift from Farewell and stayed long enough to witness the return of the regiments that had been sent to revenge the attempt on Shaka's life. The Zulu army had destroyed a number of kraals and returned with droves of cattle.

Restless as ever, Fynn made his way back to Port Natal and then embarked on another exploratory venture. This time he set off along the coast, in the opposite direction, hoping to reach the territory of Faku, the Mpondo chief. The going was hard. The entire coastal region had been devastated by the Zulu armies and the few, half-starved Africans that Fynn met were too poor or too terrified to help him. Having taken only enough food to last him four days, he quickly ran out of rations and was forced to return.

During his absence the *Julia*, with Peterssen and some others aboard, had sailed for the Cape. The rest of the party was busy building a fort. Fynn, however, had no interest in these operations. There was a message from Shaka waiting for him, asking him to visit Bulawayo. Immediately he again set off for the Zulu capital.

Shaka's spies had informed him of Fynn's attempt to reach Faku. Whatever promises the King had made to respect the independence of the Europeans, he was obviously keeping himself well informed about their movements. He now wanted to know more about Fynn's journey. His suspicions were quickly dispelled. When Fynn told him how badly he had fared, Shaka roared with laughter. He considered it ludicrous that anyone should want to explore such a barren territory. 'Moreover,' says Fynn, 'he wanted to know how I could expect to travel through those parts without his assistance, for obviously my troubles had all arisen out of his having killed off the inhabitants of the surrounding countries.' Fynn was unable to persuade Shaka that exploration was a goal in itself, that all he had wanted was to get to know the country better. Such things were beyond the King's comprehension. But the young man's eccentricity did not worry Shaka unduly. When Fynn left for Port Natal, two days later, they parted amicably.

Shaka's scepticism did not deter Fynn. He was still determined to visit Faku and, on his return to Natal, he induced another member of the party to accompany him. They took with them one of Farewell's European servants, two Hottentots and a plentiful supply of meat, biscuits, rice and salt fish. This venture was to prove more successful. Several months were to pass before Fynn and his companions returned to Port Natal.

The departure of Fynn's party coincided with the second voyage of the *Julia*. The sloop, having deposited Peterssen's party at Algoa Bay, had returned in November 1824 to pick up the remainder of those wishing to leave. There were eleven Europeans and an unspecified number of Africans on board the *Julia* when she sailed for Cape Town at the beginning of December. The ship was never seen again.

Some months later it was reported that 'a quantity of staves were picked up near Middle Point Natal by some of Mr Farewell's people, which leads them to conclude that she was lost near that place'.

The loss of the *Julia* was a bitter blow for Farewell. It meant that not only was his party sadly depleted but now he had lost his sole means of contacting the outside world. But he seems not to have despaired. He had a great deal of work on hand and this, at least, left him little time for brooding.

With Fynn and his companions away, Farewell had only three Europeans and three Hottentots to assist him. Of the three Europeans, John Cane, a burly, experienced carpenter, was undoubtedly the most useful and loyal; the twenty-two-year-old Henry Ogle was a competent foreman, but the third member of the party, Thomas Halstead, was a mere boy and somewhat dim-witted. The Hottentots were Farewell's personal servants: two men, Michael and John, and a woman named Rachel.

Small as the party was, they did not lack labourers. Shaka had seen to this. Having appointed Farewell a chief, he had supplied him with the nucleus of a tribe by sending 100 of his own people 'to reside near and protect the settlement'. Farewell was, in fact, well equipped to carry on until help was sent from the Cape Colony.

That help was not long in coming. The non-arrival of the *Julia* from her second voyage had caused consternation at the Cape and, at the end of April 1825, the authorities there despatched a small cutter, the *York*, to investigate the position of the traders at Port Natal. The *York*, commanded by Lieutenant Hawes, was away forty-three days and returned to Cape Town at the beginning of June. Lieutenant Hawes's report was by no means discouraging. He had found the Europeans living in three small huts and busy at work on a larger building.

'The party have been very healthy,' claimed Hawes, 'and represented the climate to be mild and good at all periods . . . They appear to have made but little progress in cultivation, probably from their limited numbers; they are much in want of supplies, and are entirely destitute of bread and flour, they have, however, an abundance of cattle, game, and fish, and may have as much Indian corn and vegetables as they choose to cultivate. They are upon the most friendly terms with the natives, and have the protection of Chaka, the King, who professes great respect for white people.'

There was no suggestion in the published report that any of the settlers wanted to leave and Hawes held out great hopes for their success. Farewell had just sent a man, under Shaka's protection, to Delagoa Bay and he was hoping that Fynn would make overland contact with the Cape Colony. 'The success of the party,' Hawes concluded, 'in their mercantile speculations is believed to be to the extent of their expectations, they appear only to want a vessel and supplies.'

The tone of Hawes's report was later to be distorted. This distortion gave rise to a legend that has persisted down to the present day. Farewell and his party were subsequently represented as being 'very much distressed' and anxious to leave Natal. The only reason they had refused to return with the *York*, it was claimed, was because some of the party were absent and this had decided them to wait for another vessel. Had this indeed been the case, the Cape authorities would undoubtedly have sent further assistance. But they did not: there was nothing in Lieutenant Hawes's report to cause concern.

No one appears to have checked the later embellishments (and they were to grow with the years) against Lieutenant Hawes's original report. Had they done so, they might have detected the origins of a very plausible hoax. This hoax was perpetrated some months after the *York*'s visit to Port Natal. It resulted from the reappearance of Farewell's erstwhile partner; the former midshipman and commander of the *Salisbury*—James Saunders King.

5

THE WRECK OF THE *MARY*

ON 10 JULY 1824, James Saunders King wrote a long letter to Earl Bathurst, Secretary of State for War and Colonies. King was then in lodgings off the Commercial Road in London; he had been in England since his arrival from the Cape some five months earlier. They had been a very busy five months. His letter to Earl Bathurst was written in an attempt to consolidate the promising venture upon which he was embarked.

Like Lieutenant Farewell, King had been quick to recognise the possibility of establishing a trading post at Port Natal. Unfortunately, he lacked capital and, unlike Farewell, he appears to have been doubtful about finding backers at the Cape. It was this that had sent him hurrying to London. Here he had successfully 'prevailed upon some respectable merchants to enter into the speculation' he had in mind. These tradesmen had agreed to fit out a small merchant brig, the *Mary*, and to entrust King with the management of a trading expedition, for which he was to receive 'a stated salary and other emoluments'. Pleased as King must have been to receive financial support, it did not meet all his requirements. He could take only a limited number of men with him and, knowing nothing of Farewell's activities in Natal, he was apprehensive about the chances of such a small band in the wilds of Shaka's country What was needed was a full-scale British settlement in Natal as soon as King had staked his claim to trading rights there.

To broach the possibility of such a settlement was the main purpose of King's letter to Earl Bathurst. He hoped to persuade the Secretary of State for Colonies to transfer the 1820 Settlers from their unsuccessful farms on the eastern border of the Cape Colony and establish them in Natal.

After outlining the way he had discovered Port Natal while in command of the *Salisbury*—taking care to make no mention of Farewell's part in the venture—King went on to describe the harbour and its surroundings in glowing terms. 'I should not my Lord have ventured to offer an opinion of the capability of the soil of this country,' he added, 'but having several very clever men who appeared perfectly acquainted with agricultural pursuits & who were unanimous in declaring that if the Government were acquainted with its advantages they would not hesitate to remove the unfortunate settlers thither [for] here they would in all probability succeed in their crops & have a Harbour which would enable them to export their produce to other countries in addition to this very spacious Bay which would afford shelter for such vessels as could not venture over the Bar with north-westerly winds—A chart of which & several sketches together with a few of their [the local Africans] weapons I am in possession of & will if your Lordship pleases forward for your Lordships Inspection.'

Earl Bathurst was sufficiently impressed by King's sketches and collection of weapons to grant him an interview and to recommend him to the Governor of the Cape. But this recommendation was confined to the commercial undertaking. King's suggestion of a British settlement in Natal was diplomatically ignored.

By the time King sailed from Plymouth in the *Mary*, on 29 February 1825, he had succeeded in ingratiating himself with officials at the Colonial Office and the Admiralty—although he had failed to have his renewed application for a lieutenant's commission recognised. Nor had he come any nearer to persuading the British authorities to send a garrison, let alone settlers, to Natal. But he was not dismayed by his failures. He continued to refer to himself as Lieutenant King and he was to persist in his efforts to have Natal colonised. These efforts were to contribute much to the distorted image of Shaka which was soon to be spread throughout Europe.

[2]

It took the *Mary* a full six months to reach the Cape. She was obliged to sail southwards by way of Rio de Janeiro and the island of St Helena. This long detour was not without its advantages. At St Helena, where the *Mary* arrived in June 1825, King made the acquaintance of a seventeen-year-old youth who was to be of great assistance to him in Natal.

The young man was Nathaniel Isaacs who, having been sent to St Helena from England some three years earlier, was then working in the store kept by his uncle, Saul Solomon, a reputable Jewish merchant on the island. King seems to have had a very persuasive way with impressionable young men; for, although the *Mary* was at St Helena for a matter of days only, by the time she sailed for the Cape at the end of June young Isaacs had agreed to join King's expedition. 'I readily embraced his proposition,' says Isaacs, 'particularly as he designed proceeding to the Cape of Good Hope, and from thence to the east coast of Africa to open an intercourse with the natives. My uncle immediately assented to my accompanying him, and I repaired on board his vessel.'

That Nathaniel Isaacs should so eagerly trust a passing sailor is, in some respects, curious. His knowledge of the sea was minimal and his earlier experiences on a long sea voyage would, one would have thought, have made him wary of the importunities of a strange sea captain. For, as a lad of fourteen, Isaacs had been entrusted by his family to the care of a Captain Johnson, master of the brig *Margaret*, who had undertaken to convey him to his uncle in St Helena. Not only had the voyage proved inordinately tedious but the attentions of Captain Johnson were hardly of the nature expected by Nathaniel's family. The drunk and lascivious captain had forgotten, as Nathaniel puts it, 'the civilities of a gentleman' and had promptly seduced his young charge. 'I was too young to attempt to expostulate with a man of his propensities,' explains Isaacs, 'and, as I was too weak to contend, I thought it discreet to succumb.' With this painful experience behind him, he should have had good reason for being suspicious of King's offer. However, he was undoubtedly bored with life at St Helena and the prospect of trading in an unexplored country overrode all other considerations. He set off, he says, determined to satisfy his curiosity and improve his fortune.

That Isaacs fell under the spell of James Saunders King there can be no doubt. Most of what is known about King comes from a eulogistic account written by Isaacs several years later. In this account he quotes from a journal which, he says, belonged to King. One of these quotes concerns the arrival of the *Mary* at Cape Town at the beginning of August.

According to King, the ship arrived too late in the season for him to continue his voyage along the coast. He decided instead to spend the next few months plying any trade he could pick up locally. Then it was that he heard that his 'old friend' Lieutenant Farewell was 'stranded' with a few companions in Natal. The last that had been heard of the party was when the *York* had visited Natal some three months earlier and there found Farewell 'very much distressed' and anxious to return to the Cape. King implies that it was the disturbing report of the *York*'s commander that inspired him to sail immediately to Natal to 'effect the recovery of my long absent friend'.

Touching as this might seem, King's tender concern is not very convincing. After their return from Natal, King and Farewell had become rivals. They had both had an eye on the trading concession in Shaka's country and each had been wary of the other. In his correspondence with Whitehall, King had made no mention of the part played by Farewell in their joint expedition; likewise Farewell had made no reference to King in the application he sent to Lord Charles Somerset before setting out for Natal. There was nothing in the *York*'s report to cause uneasiness about Farewell's position at Port Natal. Any concern subsequently expressed was undoubtedly whipped up by the opportunist King.

Later, when Farewell learned that King had posed as his would-be saviour, he was furious. 'I will not pretend,' he commented acidly, 'to account for Mr King's motives when he arrived at the Cape, for volunteering to go to Natal to my assistance, and setting on foot a subscription by advertisement to secure him the freight and expenses attending the voyage.'

Not only did King advertise for financial assistance from the merchants of Cape Town but he seized the opportunity of involving the Cape authorities in his venture. He applied to Lord Charles Somerset to 'grant him stores from the Ordnance to protect his vessel against the Natives'. The Cape Governor responded favourably by supplying King with two 12-lb cannon, twenty rounds of ammunition, twelve muskets and a hundred rounds of ball cartouche. But there was a stipulation: the loan of weapons had to be backed by a security of £100. This King raised by persuading a merchant, Francis Collison, to act as his guarantor.

By posing as a disinterested humanitarian, King had done very well for himself. He had succeeded in increasing his capital and obtained some much-needed armour. As he was, in any case, proceeding to Natal for his own gain, he had good reason to be thankful for Farewell's 'distress'.

The *Mary* set off on her widely acclaimed rescue bid on 26 August 1825. She immediately ran into adverse winds. A week later she was forced to return to Cape Town. Strangely enough, Nathaniel Isaacs, who recorded the voyage in detail, makes no mention of this initial setback but, as he was prostrated with sea-sickness during the first few days, he may not have realised what was happening. A second attempt was made on 2 September and the ship succeeded in reaching Port Elizabeth ten days later. After taking on more stores, King sailed from Algoa Bay on 17 September and, after battling against the wind, sighted Port Natal early in the morning of 1 October. The fact that it had taken well over a month to complete the voyage is, perhaps, some indication of the *Mary*'s performance at sea.

A strong wind was blowing when they anchored off the bay. King sent a party of sailors in a whaleboat to investigate the possibilities of crossing the sandbar. So heavy was the swell that they were forced to return without completing their mission. King then held a hurried conference of officers and crew. It was decided that they should lighten the vessel by dumping superfluous cargo overboard and risk the crossing, rather than remain exposed to the increasing gale. Once every spare article had been jettisoned, King ordered the ship about to face the sandbar. By this time the surf was crashing violently across the harbour mouth, flinging up towers of spray; it gave, says Isaacs, 'an appearance that would have unnerved any but an experienced seaman; the wind whistling through the rigging, seemed as the knell of our approaching destruction'.

How experienced a commander King was, one does not know. The admiring Isaacs pictures him as cool and intrepid, displaying a calm confidence. But it needed more than courage to take the flimsy *Mary* across such a hazard: the wonder is that the attempt was made at all. The closer they edged to the harbour mouth, the more terrifying the prospect seemed. 'We began rapidly to approach the rocks,' reports Isaacs, 'and every moment was one of immediate peril. I never contemplated witnessing such a scene. On one side, a beautiful and picturesque country presented itself, on the other, the agitated sea bubbling like a cauldron overspread with foam, from the dashing of its billows on the rugged rocks.' With a tremendous lurch, the ship bumped across the bar, sank into a hollow of sea and then rose buoyantly on a wave. The men gave a cheer. But their optimism was misplaced; the next swell struck the ship and drove her broadside to the waves. Pounded unmercifully, the rudder came adrift. King had no alternative but to order the men to take to the boats. For a few hours the *Mary* floundered, but her position was hopeless. The men salvaged what they could from the water-logged wreck, but most movable articles had been washed overboard.

Luckily no lives were lost. The men staggered ashore to be met by Thomas Halstead, Farewell's youngest assistant, Rachel, the Hottentot servant, five naked African men and a partly clad African woman. They were told that Farewell and John Cane, the carpenter, were on a visit to Shaka and that Fynn and his party had not yet returned from the Mpondo territory. Not only had King's party no means with which to effect their much-vaunted rescue, but there was almost no one for them to rescue.

[3]

King's position was far from enviable. Within a matter of hours he had lost all the assets it had taken him months, and a good deal of guile, to accumulate. His ship was wrecked, his cargo had been jettisoned, most of his tools and weapons were at the bottom of the sea. The outlook was grim indeed.

But not quite as grim as King and Isaacs were later to pretend. They were to represent themselves as castaways, cut off from civilisation and at the mercy of savages; and all through their selfless efforts to rescue Farewell. According to their version the only hope of survival lay in salvaging what they could from the wreck of the *Mary* and in building a new ship. That serious historians should have accepted this story without question is, perhaps, understandable. On the surface there is much to support it. But it is a rather cunning distortion of the truth.

Although King's motives in 'rescuing' Farewell are suspect, there is no doubt that his ship was wrecked. Nor was it untrue to say that he started to build a new ship. Indeed, work on the new vessel started almost immediately. King chose a sheltered spot on the southern shore of the bay, which he diplomatically named Townshend, in honour of one of his former naval commanders, Lord James Townshend, who was influential at the British Admiralty. John Hutton, the mate of the *Mary*, supervised this shipbuilding which continued for the next two and a half years, despite the fact that the self-styled 'castaways' were presented with several opportunities to return to the Cape: opportunities which they steadfastly ignored.

When Nathaniel Isaacs later published his highly coloured account of his experiences at Port Natal and bemoaned the fact that: 'Here I was destined to remain two years and nine months, an almost solitary European, wandering occasionally I knew not where, and in search of I knew not what,' he was purposely exaggerating his misfortunes. As nobody chose to contradict him, his story became accepted. It was to play an important part in assessments of the Zulu kings.

The fact of the matter is that, although the wreck of the *Mary* was a blow to King, it did not seriously interfere with his plans. He had never intended to rely entirely on the flimsy *Mary*. Lieutenant Farewell in a letter, hitherto overlooked, makes this quite clear. Before setting out for South Africa, King had, says Farewell, 'formed the design of building a small vessel at Natal, and had furnished himself with the necessary means for that purpose'. That Farewell was speaking the truth is borne out, not only by events, but by James Saunders King's earlier correspondence with Earl Bathurst.

When describing the advantages of Port Natal to Bathurst, King had been at pains to point out that 'near the anchorage is excellent timber for shipbuilding: it resembles cedar, also at the head of the Harbour are fine tall spars fit for masts etc.' In the circumstances, this observation can hardly be regarded as a coincidence. Nor was it coincidence that prompted King to employ as his chief mate John Hutton who was 'a practical shipwright, and had been brought up to the trade'. The wreck of the *Mary* merely made the building of a new ship doubly advisable, instead of, as was later represented, a dire necessity. Thus not only the lamentations, but the subsequent activities of Messrs King and Isaacs have to be viewed with the utmost caution.

Nathaniel Isaacs took no part in the urgent business of building a new ship. Instead, he wandered about interviewing the local Africans and inspecting Farewell's settlement, recording his impressions in his journal, which had been miraculously saved when so many essentials had been lost. He noted that Farewell and his party were living in temporary wattle and clay huts, close to the site of a large fort which Farewell was building as a permanent residence. The mud fort was designed in a triangle, intended to cover an area of two hundred square yards; provision had been made to mount cannon at each of its corners. A ditch was being dug around the perimeter and a house and store was to be built within its walls. Obviously Farewell had no intention of leaving Port Natal; there was not the slightest evidence to show that he was panting to be 'rescued'.

Two weeks after the shipwreck, the beefy John Cane arrived back from Shaka's kraal, bringing with him a number of cattle. He was welcomed by Rachel, with whom he had set up house, and he informed King and Isaacs that Farewell was on his way. Before Farewell reached the bay, however, the party welcomed another visitor. The day after Cane's arrival, a party of a hundred Africans, led by a tall, sun-burnt white man, staggered into the camp. The white man was so bizarrely dressed as to be scarcely recognisable. Heavily bearded and wearing a crownless straw hat and a tattered blanket, tied to his neck by strips of hide, he looked every bit as wild as his primitive followers.

He introduced himself as Henry Francis Fynn, just returned from a long tramp to the Mpondo territory.

Fynn had been away for over eight months. He had covered hundreds of miles, contacted Faku, the Mpondo chief, and collected a quantity of ivory. His journey had been packed with adventure and he kept the new arrivals open-mouthed with hair-raising stories of 'the many vicissitudes he had endured, and the obstacles with which he had contended, not only having been often without food, and ignorant where to seek it, but in daily terror of being destroyed by wild animals, or massacred by savage natives'. James Saunders King must have listened to Fynn's stories with interest: later he was to find a use for this adventurous young man's knowledge of Mpondoland.

Farewell turned up five days later. He reached Port Natal at night; the first indication that King and Isaacs had of his arrival was a gun-shot to announce himself. The only description of the meeting between Farewell and King is that given by Isaacs. He claims that Farewell had rushed back from Shaka's kraal to greet his 'old friend and companion Lieutenant King'. Isaacs was apparently quite overcome by the event. 'The meeting of two friends,' he says, 'under circumstances of so peculiar a nature, could not but be interesting to those who were witness of the scene; and the joy beaming in their countenances was too evident to admit of a moment's doubt, that the principals participated in the gratification which their dependants manifested. For my part, I could not conceal those impulses which so sudden and unexpected an event usually excites; and the tear of pleasure involuntarily flowed as I witnessed the outpourings of unaffected joy at this happy meeting.'

A manly tear might well have rolled down Nathaniel Isaacs's cheek. But it is doubtful whether Farewell and King were similarly affected, however delighted they may have appeared. King, having engineered the meeting, had every reason to put up a show of affection and Farewell—who then knew nothing of King's activities in England and Cape Town—might have responded. But underlying this apparent cordiality must have been an element of distrust. Far from bringing Farewell relief, the shipwrecked party had added to his problems. In fact, Farewell did not feel as cut off from civilisation as his would-be rescuers pretended. Shortly before he had set off for Shaka's kraal, he had been visited by Captain Owen's surveying team—who were still doggedly mapping the coast—and had received some welcome supplies. He had gone aboard the H.M.S. *Leven* to discuss his position with Owen and he could, had he so wished, have left Port Natal. Instead, he had been content to exchange ivory for supplies of flour, sugar, vinegar and three muskets and to remain at his settlement under Shaka's protection. The fact that he had at that time collected only three tons of ivory seems to have offset any feeling of isolation.

All King had provided was extra mouths to feed. 'I have every reason,' Farewell later complained, 'to consider myself a greater sufferer than Mr King, from the loss of the *Mary*, who, if he had any share in her, was exempted from any pecuniary loss, as she was well insured, whilst myself, induced by such friendly and disinterested appearances on Mr King's part, assisted in forming an establishment for him.'

According to Isaacs, Farewell gave the newcomers a most alarming account of Shaka, depicting him as a savage, blood-thirsty monster, and warned them not to let the Zulu King know that they had been shipwrecked. They were to pretend that they had been sent to Natal by the Cape Government to search for Farewell's party; Shaka, having heard of the extraordinary powers of the British nation, was said to be in awe of the Cape authorities.

If this were true, it is somewhat surprising that Farewell had been willing to remain so long at the uncertain mercy of a man whom he regarded as an ogre, without the backing of these same Cape authorities. King, despite his efforts, had brought no such backing yet, for all that, in the days to come, none of them were to appear unduly anxious to evacuate Port Natal. It is doubtful, in fact, whether the party did fear Shaka to the extent that Isaacs implies. Farewell's relationship with the Zulu monarch was, as it had always been, extremely friendly. Isaacs's description resulted from a determination to paint Shaka in lurid colours and to underline the need for official protection. He was, after all, the protégé of James Saunders King.

Significantly, Fynn tells another story. He claims that Shaka had already learned about the shipwreck and, as a result, had summoned the newcomers to visit him. This seems far more likely. Shaka's spies were everywhere. As Farewell must have known, it would have been impossible to keep secret a major event such as the wreck of the *Mary*. Both Farewell and Fynn were too well versed in Shaka's methods to contemplate such an obvious, extremely dangerous, deceit.

Whatever the truth, King lost no time in paying his respects to Shaka. Six days after Farewell's arrival, he and two sailors from the *Mary*, with a retinue of forty Africans, accompanied Farewell and Fynn to Bulawayo. Isaacs, much to his regret, was left behind.

[4]

Shaka appears to have taken an immediate liking to the smooth-talking King. He went out of his way to entertain the party, plying them with food and arranging for them to be amused. As always, his attitude towards the white men changed as soon as he was alone with them. In public he appeared formidable and aloof, but once in his private kraal, says King, he 'cast off his stern look, became good-humoured and conversed with us through our interpreters on various subjects'.

There were the usual displays of strength on both sides. On the second day of their stay, Shaka taunted the two sailors into demonstrating their fire-arms against wild animals. Unknown to King and Farewell, he persuaded the men to accompany him on an elephant hunt. When King and Farewell heard what had happened they rushed after the hunting party. But they were too late. They discovered Shaka sitting calmly beneath a large tree overlooking a valley: the sailors, accompanied by some warriors, had disappeared into the valley in search of the elephants. Having grave doubts about the effects of lead bullets on an elephant, Farewell and King took up a position some distance from Shaka. Apprehensively they waited for the sailors to reappear. Almost two hours passed before a messenger arrived and presented Shaka with an elephant's tail. It had been taken, he said, from an animal killed by the sailors.

'We could scarcely credit the fact,' reported King, 'but hastened towards the forest to join our people, and met them almost exhausted . . . It appeared that the natives drove the elephant from the forest to a plain, where the sailors placed themselves directly before the animal: the first shot entered under the ear, when it became furious: the other lodged near the fore shoulder, after which it fell, and soon expired. Had this affair turned out differently, we should, in all probability, have been held in a contemptible light by this nation, and awkward consequences might have resulted to the settlement.'

There was great rejoicing that night. Shaka's warriors lustily chanted their war songs, the elated white men responded with the opening chorus of 'God save the King'. When the words of the British national anthem were explained to Shaka he was delighted— this was the sort of patriotism he could appreciate. Everyone enjoyed themselves immensely and the celebrations lasted well into the night. For all that, the Europeans were up early next morning and paid Shaka their customary visit. They wanted, they said, to see the King in his war dress. Always willing to oblige, Shaka went to his hut and changed.

'His dress,' said King, 'consists of monkeys' skins, in three folds from his waist to the knee, from which two cows' tails are suspended, as well as from each arm; around his head is a neat band of fur stuffed, in front of which is placed a tall feather, and on each side a variegated plume. He advanced with his shield, an oval about four feet in length, and an umconto, or spear, when his warriors commenced a war song, and he began his manœuvres. Chaka is about thirty-eight years of age, upwards of six feet in height, and well proportioned: he is allowed to be the best pedestrian in the country, and, in fact, during his wonderful exercises this day he exhibited the most astonishing activity.'

It was on this occasion that James Saunders King drew the only known sketch of Shaka. Somewhat stylised—looking more like an illustration for a theatrical costume than a life portrait of the savage monarch—the drawing none the less met with Shaka's delighted approval. 'Indeed,' remarked Farewell, 'nothing pleases him more than for any person to admire his person of which he is very vain.' James Saunders King's stock must have risen tremendously.

Not only was King impressed by Shaka's physique, he was equally struck by the size of the Zulu monarch's seraglio. Shaka maintained a large household of women. The precise function of these women has, however, never been satisfactorily explained. Shaka always referred to them as his 'sisters', never as his 'wives'. As far as is known, none of them ever produced an heir. Shaka was to claim that his refusal to acknowledge children was prompted by a fear that an heir might one day oppose him. He gave James Saunders King to understand that he refrained from sexual intercourse to preserve his strength until he had achieved the goals he had set himself. This would also explain his insistence on celibacy among his younger warriors. There has been a good deal of speculation about Shaka's attitude towards sex.

One of his early biographers has depicted him as a great lover, secretly devoted to a girl he had known as a young man. No evidence is given for this somewhat novelettish theory and none of those who actually met Shaka mention such a liaison. Modern students of Zulu history, such as Professor Max Gluckman and Donald Morris, have ignored the suggestion. They claim that Shaka was impotent, probably a latent homosexual. Certainly his obsession with celibacy and his unnatural restraint in sexual matters—he was otherwise a full blooded man—seem to indicate deep-seated sexual complexes.

Given his rejection as a child by his father and the influence of his domineering mother, a recognisable pattern of homosexuality does present itself. Analysis of sexual traits on slight evidence, and at such a distance in time, must obviously be inconclusive, but Shaka's self-imposed celibacy was so at variance with other facets of his personality that it could well signify sexual aberration.

His emotional attachment to his female relatives was undoubtedly profound. He trusted them above his nominated counsellors; they occupied influential positions in the Zulu hierarchy. His mother's kraal, *emKindini*, ranked second only to Bulawayo in importance and his senior regiment was supervised by one of his aunts. The death of one of Shaka's kinswomen was treated as a national disaster. One such death occurred while James Saunders King's party was visiting Bulawayo; the Europeans were astonished at the way it affected Shaka.

One evening Fynn was summoned to the royal residence to attend Shaka's grandmother. The old woman was well over eighty and dangerously ill with dysentery; Fynn quickly recognised that there was nothing he could do. When he told Shaka this, the King burst into tears. 'Jacob, the interpreter,' says Fynn, 'told me of Shaka's great affection for his grandmother. When she happened to visit him he frequently washed her eyes and ears which were in a sad state because of her age; he also pared her nails and otherwise treated her as a father might his child. We could hardly believe that a man of an apparent unfeeling disposition could be so possessed of such affection and consideration for others.'

Fynn was with Shaka the following evening when a messenger arrived to announce that the old woman was dead. For several minutes Shaka sat staring in silence. Then his shoulders began to shake and he started to cry aloud. Soon the news spread and the entire kraal was in uproar. So frantic was the shouting and wailing that James Saunders King, who was in his hut, felt sure that Bulawayo was being attacked.

Farewell, on the other hand, was greatly amused by the proceedings. He noticed several new arrivals laughing and joking until they came within sight of Shaka, when they quickly changed their expressions and started to cry. 'I frequently saw some putting spittle in their eyes,' he says, 'and indeed their changing immediately by word of command from laughing to crying and wringing their hands, groaning, etc., for an old woman who not one of them cared a pin about, was a circumstance that made me keep to my tent as I could not avoid laughing.'

The noise continued for two or three hours. Then, after a short, deathly silence, it was followed by a doleful mourning chant which lasted throughout the night.

The old woman was buried next day, with all the honours of royalty. Instead of leaving her body in the veld to be eaten by wild animals, as was the custom for commoners, she was placed in a specially dug pit outside the kraal. Shaka did not attend the funeral. For several days he remained in his hut, refusing to see or speak to anyone.

When Shaka eventually agreed to see the white men again, they discussed the wreck of the *Mary* with him. King claims that they told him 'our vessel had sustained some damage, and we were in hopes, in about three months, to get her in order. We were apprehensive he might take advantage of our unfortunate situation, had he known she had been an entire wreck.' Why King considered that they would be safeguarded by a three-month limit, he does not say. Common sense should have told him that if the capricious Shaka wanted to harm them he would not need to wait three months: the mere flick of his hand was all that was required to have his orders carried out immediately. To give the despot a time limit was, one would have thought, to invite trouble.

Certainly Shaka had given the white men no reason for fear. Even King admits that the Zulu monarch made their stay at Bulawayo 'tolerably pleasant'. When the time came for them to leave, they were presented with 107 head of cattle. However barbarically Shaka ruled his own people, his attitude towards the whites was always hospitable.

After a journey lasting seven days, King and his companions arrived back at the bay. They found Nathaniel Isaacs in high spirits. Most of his time had been spent exploring the country and getting to know the local Africans. But not all the men from the *Mary* were as enthusiastic about Port Natal as young Isaacs. A month after King's return, he was faced with mutiny. John Norton, the second mate, and three sailors seized the *Mary*'s long boat and set sail for Port Elizabeth. Fynn claims that the mutineers went with King's blessing; Norton tells a different story. 'I requested permission,' he says, 'to fit up the Long Boat which I did with a deal of trouble and anxiety for the Master of the vessel used every means to prevent my sailing but I persevered.'

The loss of the long boat and half his crew was a serious blow to King. Hutton, the chief mate, now had only four men to help him in building the new ship. His work was slowed down considerably. The party looked like being marooned for a lot longer than three months.

By what was little short of a miracle, John Norton and his comrades reached the Cape Colony in their long boat. They sailed from Port Natal on 16 December 1825 and arrived at Port Elizabeth on 23 February 1826. As soon as he had recovered from the voyage, Norton informed the Governor of the Cape of his arrival. 'There now remains at Port Natal,' he wrote, 'the remainder of the Crew. Capt King as [sic] commenced building a vessel but in want of Tools for carrying on the building asks some assistance which I hope your Honour will be moved to send . . . I thought it was a duty to give as early information as possible.'

But somehow the news of the wreck had already reached the Cape. On 27 December 1825, Farewell's wife, Elizabeth, had written an impassioned letter to Lord Charles Somerset. She pointed out that it was almost two years since her husband had left the Cape Colony and that 'Capt King who went to his relief has been wrecked.' Unfortunately her wifely concern was somewhat marred by the strongly mercenary note that crept into her appeal.

'If there is a person,' she wrote, 'who is entitled to solicit the assistance of Government it is my husband, who has not only risked his life in order to form a settlement by which our savage neighbours may be civilised, and by which the peace of this Colony may be secured. Under this impression, I venture to intreat that your Lordship will be pleased to send a vessel to his assistance, and that the Commander of such a vessel be not only directed to bringing himself and party from thence if he wishes it, but also such produce, whether accompanied by himself or not, as he may be desirous of forwarding to the Colony. I am aware that in general cases it is contrary to the established wishes of Government to interfere with the transport of goods belonging to individuals, but in the present instance a deviation from that rule can be attended with no bad effect, and would by no means injure the shipping interest, as previous to Captain King's arrival no ship owner had the remotest intention of sailing a vessel to Mr Farewell's assistance.'

Lord Charles evidently had doubts about using a naval ship to transport goods from Natal. Elizabeth Farewell's letter was filed away marked 'not noticed'. However, the Cape authorities could not ignore the situation as described by John Norton. At the beginning of April 1826, H.M.S. *Helicon* was despatched to investigate the position at Port Natal.

6

'A DESPOTIC AND CRUEL MONSTER'

FOR ALL THE alarm and despondency of his later reports, James Saunders King could not have been unduly disturbed by his first impressions of Bulawayo. The report he made to Nathaniel Isaacs was sufficiently encouraging to make the young man determined to visit Shaka himself. During the next few months Isaacs was to busy himself travelling to and from the Zulu capital.

His first visit to Shaka came about almost by accident. Farewell had deposited a quantity of ivory near a river upcountry and he detailed Isaacs to collect it for him. Accompanied by young Thomas Halsted, whom he considered 'anything but intelligent', Isaacs set off a few weeks before John Norton staged his mutiny. That two teenage boys could be sent alone on such a mission is, perhaps, some indication of how little the traders feared their 'savage neighbours'.

Isaacs had the somewhat dubious advantage of riding a one-eyed, ancient horse, while Halstead and the African bearers walked beside him. Throughout their journey they were entertained at the kraals of minor chiefs. So much did they take this hospitality for granted that, when one of their hosts proved niggardly, Halstead had no hesitation in demanding that a cow be slaughtered. They were, he declared, 'on the king's business'. And slaughtered the cow was. For Isaacs the main attraction of these overnight stops was the undisguised admiration he commanded from groups of gaping young girls.

Once the ivory had been collected and sent back to the bay, Isaacs decided to continue on to Shaka's kraal. He took Halstead and six Africans with him and arrived at Bulawayo two days later. The two youths stopped at a stream outside the royal kraal to freshen up and then sent a messenger to announce their arrival. Word came back that Shaka would receive them immediately.

It was dark when they entered Bulawayo. They were led past fire-lit groups to the head of the kraal, where a huge semicircle of people were squatting round the King. Shaka sat alone on a rolled-up mat. Their African guide greeted the King with an upraised arm. Isaacs peeled off a smart military salute.

. Shaka was evidently amused at his cocky young visitor and was quick to have some fun at the boy's expense. First he asked Isaacs to step forward, enquired after Farewell, and then announced that there was another European at the kraal. The astonished Isaacs was introduced to a Portuguese soldier who had arrived from Delagoa Bay to buy some Zulu cattle. After this rather awkward introduction—neither of the white men spoke the other's language— Shaka dismissed Isaacs who, somewhat bewildered, was led round in circles until the King sent for him again. This time he was handed a piece of paper upon which Shaka had made an unintelligible scrawl. Isaacs was asked to decipher it. When he admitted that he could not read it, Shaka—always ready to show off in front of his subjects—gave a triumphant roar. The white man, he told the assembly, was baffled by his writing. The people applauded. The Portuguese soldier underwent a similar humiliation. Delighted with his joke, Shaka gave the white men permission to retire. They were shown to a hut where, after sharing some ribs of beef, they slept for the night.

The next day, after receiving Isaacs's present of brass bangles and sweet oil, Shaka again brought his visitors together. This time he asked the soldier whether the Portuguese were greater warriors than the English. According to Isaacs, the soldier freely admitted the superiority of the English and Shaka immediately announced that he and King George were brothers. 'He has conquered all the whites,' he crowed, 'and I have subdued all the blacks.' He then wanted to know from Isaacs whether umGeorge was as handsome as himself. Isaacs replied, with more truth than he owned to, that he thought not. This apparently delighted Shaka who then suggested that the two white men fight each other. Only by pleading that a treaty between their countries forbade such an exhibition were the visitors saved the embarrassment of coming to blows.

Despite Shaka's teasing, Isaacs seems to have enjoyed his visit until, on the third day, he was treated to one of the King's less humorous displays. He was summoned to attend Shaka's daily ablutions which, as usual, was accompanied by some summary executions. At a signal from the King, three men sitting near Isaacs were seized by executioners who 'took the criminals, laying one hand on the crown and the other on the chin, and by a sudden wrench appeared to dislocate the head. The victims were then dragged away and beaten as they proceeded to the bush, about a mile from the kraal, where a stick was inhumanly forced up the fundament of each, and they were left as food for the wild beasts.'

If this gruesome performance was staged to impress the young visitors, it certainly succeeded. Not surprisingly, Isaacs decided to leave the following day. Shaka was all charm. He gave Isaacs twelve head of cattle and then added two oxen in exchange for Farewell's dog which, despite Isaacs' protests, he summarily appropriated.

The journey back to the bay was far from easy. Three days from Bulawayo, the ancient horse collapsed and Isaacs, unused to walking at the best of times, suffered agonies marching barefoot through a thorn-bush jungle. His refusal to chew the thorns extracted from his feet completely bewildered his attendants, who assured him that this was a sure remedy against future inflictions. On reaching one of the kraals they had previously stayed at, Isaacs's flagging spirits were given an unexpected boost. His host, speaking mostly by sign language, gave him to understand that he owned an unusual animal. From the vague description of this one-horned creature, Isaacs decided that it could be nothing less than a unicorn. Unfortunately, his vision of achieving immortality as a naturalist was somewhat clouded when a search of the nearby kraals failed to reveal the fabulous beast. His host assured him that the animal had been taken to the interior and it would be kept for him when it returned. With this promise Isaacs had to remain content.

They reached Port Natal shortly before Christmas. On New Year's Eve a dance was held at Fort Farewell. The local Africans were invited, a bullock was killed, sea-shanties were sung and the Africans went reeling home after drinking two pails of grog. The year 1826 had got off to a good start.

By the beginning of February, cattle at the trading post were becoming scarce and Fynn was detailed to obtain some more from Shaka's kraal. Isaacs, now fully recovered from his earlier visit, volunteered to go with him. With goods for barter in short supply, they decided to impress Shaka by presenting him with the figure-head of the wrecked *Mary* together with twenty large neck bangles. They started out on 7 February, accompanied by some seamen and the usual African bearers.

They did not get far. The upcountry rivers were in flood and, after crossing two with difficulty, they were forced to turn back. By coincidence their last halt was at the kraal of the induna who had promised Isaacs his pet unicorn. He now undertook to send the animal after them. He was as good as his word. They had not marched far the following day when they were overtaken by a messenger leading the prize that was to bring Isaacs great renown. One look at the animal was sufficient to convince Isaacs that his fame would be short lived. Instead of the handsome beast with a flowing mane that he had been promised, he was presented with a decrepit, but unmistakable, he-goat that had lost one of its horns. He would, he decided, have to look elsewhere for immortality.

Heavy rains kept the rivers in flood for another month. Not until the middle of March, after a summons from Shaka, did the Europeans—Fynn, Isaacs and a seaman—again set out. The Zulu capital was in a state of chaos when they finally arrived there. It appeared that a revered old chief had died and Shaka, suspecting witchcraft, had embarked upon a series of smellings-out and mass killings. The rest of the population were, as usual, frantically displaying grief in the hopes of avoiding suspicion. Not all of them succeeded. 'Several of the people were knocked down in our presence and killed,' says Isaacs; 'all the huts were searched, and those found within forced out to share the fate of those who had been previously killed for not weeping.' The horrified Isaacs fervently hoped that something would be done to stamp out such barbarous customs 'for the sake of humanity and civilisation'.

Once the ritual mourning was over, Shaka sent for the white men and handed them a letter for Lieutenant Farewell. This letter had reached Bulawayo from Delagoa Bay; it had been sent by the captain of King's old ship, the *Salisbury*. The captain, having heard of the wreck of the *Mary*, promised to call at Port Natal on his return voyage. That this letter had been delivered in such a roundabout way shows that European distrust of Shaka was not, at that time, as widespread as was later supposed. Isaacs says he was delighted with the news. It came, he enthused, as a heaven-sent promise of deliverance from his hated exile.

For all that, the Europeans were in no hurry to return to Port Natal. They remained at Bulawayo for two weeks. Shaka was as hospitable as ever. Besides the usual singing and dancing, he organiscd a buffalo hunt, paraded his warriors and admitted the white men to his war councils. As always, he was full of questions about his brother umGeorge. He asked Isaacs how old the British King was and how many wives he had. When Isaacs told him that the ageing King set a national example by having only one wife, Shaka was delightcd. It was obvious that umGeorge had reached such an advanced age by practising a sexual abstinence similar to his own. Isaacs apparently received this tribute to the rakish British King's morals without blinking.

Shaka was also eager to know more about the Europeans' religion. He found the idea of a Supreme Being fascinating and was frankly astonished at the interpretation he was given of the origin of the world. He wanted missionaries to come to his country. They would, he said, be given cattlc in abundance if they could teach him to read and write.

Isaacs again suffered agonies with his feet on the homeward journey; the party made slow progress. On their second day from Bulawayo, they received a message to say that H.M.S. *Helicon* had called at Port Natal and had taken James Saunders King to the Cape. The news depressed Isaacs immensely. He did not blame King for seizing the opportunity to obtain help for the settlement, but bitterly regretted that he had not been rescued himself. That none of the other 'castaways' had bothered to accompany King, puzzled him not at all.

[2]

His Majesty's sloop *Helicon* arrived at Port Natal on 9 April 1826. Her commander, Lieutenant Wood, accompanied by a midshipman and four sailors, immediately rowed ashore. They found the traders in good spirits. 'The European Party,' they reported, 'are supplied by the Natives with cattle; they have abundance of Indian Corn, which they cultivate themselves, also plenty of milk and vegetables, the latter from seed saved from the *Mary* by Mr King. The harbour abounds with fish and there appears to be no danger from want of food.' Things, in fact, were very much the same as when the *York* had called a year earlier.

The account they were given of Shaka was not unduly alarming. He was said to be 'from 30 to 35 years of age, tall, very black, but well featured' and, although constantly at war with neighbouring tribes, was well disposed towards the Europeans. 'Mr Farewell and his Party,' the report went on, 'as well as the part of the crew of the *Mary*, that were left at Natal, are in good health. Mr King's vessel is more than half finished; her burthen will be from 40 to 45 tons. At first it was the intention to have built a small vessel of about 15 tons; but from the wood of the country being so large, it was found that it would require but a little extra labour to accomplish one three times as large. The Natives behave extremely well. Mr King had the assistance of as many as he required, to bring the timber for building his vessel from the woods near the shore.' This is very different from the gloomy picture painted by Isaacs.

The party from the *Helicon* was forced to remain on shore for a week. A heavy swell prevented them from reaching their ship earlier and, when they finally sailed for the Cape, James Saunders King was the only person who 'availed himself of the opportunity of returning' with them.

Quite obviously the settlers at Port Natal were in no desperate need of rescue. But the published report of the *Helicon* did not prevent King from glibly pretending otherwise. No sooner had he arrived in Cape Town than he set about advertising for financial support. He started by applying to the Cape authorities for help in purchasing a schooner. When his application was queried, he became petulant. 'The Crew of my wrecked vessel,' he asserted, 'are now wandering for sustenance amongst the Tribes inhabiting the Coast at Natal; the purport of my visit here is solely to assist them and to procure the means of conveying them with such part of my cargo as was saved from the wreck, to a Port of Safety. Under these circumstances and as the delegate of British Seamen in distress in a savage land I throw myself upon the Government of this Colony trusting that I shall not be considered as without some claim to their favourable consideration.'

As these same British Seamen in distress had so recently shown reluctance to be rescued by a Government ship, it is hardly surprising that the Cape officials remained unmoved by this impassioned plea.

His failure to melt the heart of the Governor must have decided

King to turn to the Governor's opponents. This meant appealing to John Fairbairn, the editor of the *South African Commercial Advertiser*. The feud between the Governor of the Cape and the Colony's only privately owned newspaper was as notorious as it was bitter. It had started shortly after the *South African Commercial Advertiser* was first published in January 1824 and had resulted in the closure of the newspaper four months later. Fairbairn's fight to establish his independence as an editor and to continue the publication of his newspaper—which reappeared in August 1824— became a *cause célèbre*, generally acknowledged as a triumph for the freedom of the press in South Africa. When James Saunders King approached Fairbairn, a year after the editor's victory, he must have been sure of a warm welcome. He had a story which would provide excellent copy for a controversial newspaper.

On 11 July 1826, the *South African Commercial Advertiser* published the first of two articles by James Saunders King. They were introduced by an editorial note which left no doubt as to the newspaper's sympathies. 'The following interesting Sketch of Lieut Farewell's Settlement at Port Natal,' it said, 'has been furnished by a gentleman on whose knowledge of the facts, and accuracy, full reliance may be placed. The intentions of the Colonial Government respecting this enterprise are not known. We trust the exertions of Capt King in his attempts to relieve his own men, and to assist this most intrepid and meritorious gentleman and his party, will be seconded—if not by the Government, at least by individuals here. The scheme promises to reward all parties.'

The first of King's articles was largely descriptive, relatively mild. He explained how Port Natal had been discovered by Farewell and himself and how the settlement had developed after Farewell's occupation. Stress was laid on the 'extremely great' sufferings of the party and upon his own efforts to build a new ship from the wreck of the *Mary*. In dealing with Shaka, he admitted that the Zulu monarch had not only granted the party a large strip of land but had assured the white men of his protection. He gave a detailed description of his own visit to Bulawayo and acknowledged Shaka's hospitality.

In the second article, published a week later, his attitude towards Shaka was more hostile. 'History, perhaps,' he declared, 'does not furnish an instance of a more despotic and cruel monster than Chaka.

His subjects fall at his word, he is aknowledged to be the most powerful ruler for hundreds of miles. . . . Chaka's strict discipline and method of attack is such that nothing in their warfare can possibly withstand the attack of the Zulus.' After describing Shaka's seraglio, he concluded: 'Of this establishment it would be impossible to say the extent; yet he will not allow that he cohabits with them, and to prove to his people this fact, when any of the women appear pregnant, they are instantly killed. He says, when he has defeated Esconyana [Sikhunyana], he will direct his force to the Frontier, and not leave a living soul or rest until he reaches the white people; he will then be satisfied and enjoy himself with his wives.'

The warning implied in this summary of Shaka's intentions is obvious. Already the colonists were plagued by frontier wars and marauding tribesmen who plundered the border area as a result of the pressure of Zulu attacks in their rear. If that pressure were intensified, the frontier farmers would be in even greater danger. Clearly something should be done to stop Shaka who, as King had shown, was well disposed to the whites and willing to grant them land. The logical course would be for the Europeans to reach Shaka before he attempted to reach them. This could be done by sending settlers, under military protection, to occupy Natal. Like many other statements made by James Saunders King, this thinly disguised hint was to prove suspiciously prophetic.

The appeal made by the *South African Commercial Advertiser* for private citizens to assist King bore fruit. A schooner, the *Ann*, was fitted out with supplies and King returned with her to Port Natal. The lurid picture he had painted of his men at the mercy of one of the cruellest despots in history, was somewhat belied by the presence of another passenger on board the *Ann*. This was Elizabeth Farewell. Whether at her insistence or at Farewell's request, King had agreed to take his partner's wife to a country which he had depicted as perilous for isolated whites. While one must admire Elizabeth Farewell's courage, one suspects the disparity between King's words and actions.

Farewell was not at the trading post to greet his wife. He and Fynn were away on a visit to Shaka. When the *Ann* sailed into the bay, on 6 October 1826, only Isaacs was there to welcome King back. As soon as the ship dropped anchor, young Isaacs clambered aboard; he was almost as embarrassed as he was surprised at meeting Mrs Farewell. He had lost most of his clothes when the *Mary* was wrecked and those he had saved were now practically worn out. Unkempt and in tatters, he made, he says, 'a sorry figure in the company of a lady'. However, after he had collected his mail from King, he was fitted out with new clothes by the crew of the *Ann* and emerged from below deck looking spruce enough to escort Elizabeth Farewell ashore.

Once Mrs Farewell had dutifully recovered from the shock of being surrounded by naked Africans, life at the settlement became almost civilised. Nathaniel Isaacs and John Hutton sipped tea with the new hostess at the fort and King joined them on tours of the nearby kraals. 'We had our little morning perigrinations and our evening conversaziones,' reports Isaacs, 'our visits on board the schooner *Ann*, and occasional trips to the dockyards, all designed to divert our female friend, and remove the gloom which the not finding her husband at home very naturally generated.' If it was not exactly gracious living, it served to smooth a few rough edges. John Cane was sent to Shaka's kraal to tell Farewell of his wife's arrival.

Isaacs wrote letters to his family and arranged for the captain of the *Ann* to take a cow to his uncle on St Helena. Needless to say, neither the distressed British seamen nor Isaacs—who so bitterly lamented missing the *Helicon*—showed any inclination to return to the Cape Colony on the schooner.

Farewell and Fynn arrived back two weeks later. Joyful as the reunion between husband and wife must have been, not everyone at Port Natal shared their happiness. Isaacs was away on a food-gathering expedition when Farewell arrived. He returned to find that Farewell and King had had a serious quarrel which they had subsequently patched up. Unfortunately, this reconciliation did not last long.

[3]

When James Saunders King had reported in the *South African Commercial Advertiser* that the Zulu monarch's first concern was to defeat 'Esconyana', he was telling the truth. The man he called Esconyana was, in fact, Sikhunyana, son of Shaka's old enemy, Zwide, of the Ndwandwe tribe. Although the exiled Zwide had been dead for some years, the Ndwandwe had by no means forgotten their defeat by Shaka. Sikhunyana had reorganised the Ndwandwe army and he now posed a serious threat to Shaka's supremacy. It was a threat that Shaka was determined to eliminate.

Shortly after King had left for the Cape, messengers from Bulawayo arrived at Port Natal. They brought a summons from Shaka for everyone at the settlement, black and white, to arm themselves and proceed to the Zulu capital. Sikhunyana was expected to launch an attack and Shaka was mustering his forces to resist.

According to Fynn, Shaka's summons created problems for the white men. 'Powder was scarce, and our arms out of repair,' he says. 'Moreover, we were aware that, by complying, we should be violating the laws of our country, and embarking on a course which could in no way prove beneficial to us. On the other hand, we dreaded the consequences that might ensue from refusing to obey the order.' While they were trying to decide what they should do, two more messages arrived from Shaka. The first informed them that their help would not be needed until the next full moon, the second was a request for a tent. Isaacs, accompanied by a Hottentot, John, and the interpreter, Frederick, was detailed to take the tent to Bulawayo.

After an arduous journey—he was not only developing boils, but a nasty kick in the groin from a pack-ox had almost crippled him—Isaacs arrived at the Zulu capital to find it highly active. Preparations for war were much in evidence. Shaka was busy drilling his uFasimba regiment. On seeing the tent, the King expressed great delight. He ordered it to be erected in his presence and declared that the very sight of it would strike terror in the hearts of his enemies. Isaacs was peppered with questions about the size of the British army. On learning that umGeorge's soldiers numbered more than all his men and cattle put together, the King became very suspicious. He told his indunas that he was afraid that the British would one day attack and defeat him. This immediately started an argument which ended in eight of the indunas being executed.

When the time came for Isaacs to leave, Shaka became surly. He wanted the young man to accompany him on his campaign. Only by promising to return with a force led by James Saunders King did

Isaacs finally obtain permission to return to Port Natal. If Isaacs is to be believed, Shaka was keen to have King join him but objected to Farewell whom he considered 'too much like an old woman'.

On his journey back to the bay, Isaacs met Farewell and Fynn travelling upcountry. They had decided to visit Shaka without their followers. Isaacs refused to go back to Bulawayo with them: he insisted that he had been told to collect King and the sailors before returning.

All was quiet at the Zulu capital when Farewell and Fynn arrived there. Of the frantic preparations witnessed by Isaacs, there was no evidence. Fynn was feeling far from well and Shaka received the white men sympathetically. He killed a fat bullock in their honour and seemed, says Farewell, 'very friendly and most happy to see us'. Among their equipment was a lancet which Shaka gleefully seized and amused himself by experimenting with it on the backsides of some of his indunas.

Two days later, however, the Zulu army had massed and was ready to set off. Nothing the Europeans could say succeeded in dissuading Shaka from including them in his force. Fynn claims that when they protested, the King became truculent. He threatened not only to punish them but to wipe out the settlement at Port Natal. In this he was supported by the interpreter, Jacob, who seized Farewell's musket and refused to return it. Rather surprisingly, Shaka then explained that he did not expect the white men to fight but wanted them with him as moral support. This, at any rate, is how Fynn explained his own participation in the campaign.

The entire Zulu force consisted of some 50,000 men, women and boys. Following in the wake of the army, the partly recovered Fynn was amazed at the organisation of Shaka's commissariat. The boys driving the cattle and carrying the warriors' sleeping mats were mostly under twelve years of age, some of them were not more than six. Besides them marched the regiments of girls, balancing pots of corn, milk and beer on their heads (once these supplies had been exhausted the girls were allowed to return home). The warriors were free of all burdens: except for their assegais and shields which, until they approached the enemy, they were permitted to roll up and carry on their backs.

For days the army marched in close formation across the hot, empty landscape. From a distance they were completely hidden by the huge cloud of dust raised by their stamping feet. There were few other signs of life. Most of the kraals they passed had been evacuated. The hard slog seems to have revived the ailing Fynn. Certainly he needed all the energy he could muster. During the day the heat was excruciating; at night the frost was so intense that several warriors froze to death in their sleep. Few halts were allowed. After one gruelling day's march, the thirst-crazed warriors of a forward regiment stampeded at a muddy stream, killing a number of men and boys in the confusion. Those who arrived after all the water had been drunk crammed wet mud into their mouths in an attempt to slake their thirst.

On the third day after leaving Bulawayo, Farewell was put out of action. Attacked by an enraged ox, he was so badly mauled that he had to be left behind. Fynn was ordered ahead to join one of the scouting regiments. Finally a halt was called in a dense forest and spies were sent to explore the enemy position. They returned to report that the Ndwandwe were massed close to a nearby mountain.

On the day of the battle, Fynn climbed to the top of the mountain to watch. The enemy army had collected near the summit of a rocky hill on the other side of the valley; above them were their women and children. When Fynn reached his vantage point, the Ndwandwe warriors were sitting, waiting for the Zulu attack. Shaka's men cautiously advanced until they were within twenty yards of the enemy. Still the Ndwandwe sat. Then Jacob fired three shots from his stolen musket. The first two shots produced only growls from the Ndwandwe. But, at the third shot, the two sides gave a tremendous yell, clashed together and continued stabbing at each other for about three minutes and then sprang apart. This hand-to-hand fighting went on at intervals until the Ndwandwe began to weaken. 'This,' says Fynn, 'urged the Zulus to a final charge. The shrieks now became terrific. The remnants of the enemy's army sought shelter in an adjoining wood, out of which they were soon driven. Then began the slaughter of the women and children. They were all put to death.'

The action had lasted little more than an hour and a half. It had been more of a *mêlée* than a staged battle. Shaka had remained in the rear and none of his customary strategy had been in evidence. Nevertheless it was an undoubted Zulu victory. Fynn estimated the Ndwandwe losses at not less than 40,000 men, women and children and 60,000 head of cattle. But the most important prize had evaded Shaka: Sikhunyana had not been captured.

The following morning, after a purification ritual, Shaka inspected his troops. Every chief was expected to pick out the cowards in his regiment—those who knew of no cowards invented them to please Shaka—and these unfortunates were immediately put to death. No fighting regiment was allowed to appear in front of the King before it had been cleansed by the witch doctors. Each warrior was given certain roots to eat—the number of roots depending on how many enemy he had killed—and part of the root was fixed to a piece of wood which the warriors then wore round their necks to proclaim their valour. After eating the roots, they went to a river to bathe and were then fed with meat from cattle killed on the day of the battle: this was the only nourishment allowed. When they appeared before Shaka they could not expect praise. The King merely pointed out the mistakes that had been made and then ordered the execution of his personally selected victims.

Fynn was horrified at the methods used to obtain information about Sikhunyana. A Ndwandwe woman and child were brought to Shaka for questioning. To induce the woman to speak, she was given some beer and beef. Once she had told all she knew, both she and the child were sentenced to death. Fynn pleaded to be allowed to take the child as his servant but he could do nothing to save the woman. A regiment was despatched to hunt Sikhunyana, but the Ndwandwe chief disappeared, never to be heard of again. Shaka had now achieved the first of the objects mentioned by James Saunders King.

Farewell, who had been cared for by women from Shaka's seraglio, had fully recovered when Fynn met him on the return march. Shortly before the army reached the Zulu capital, news was received of the *Ann*'s arrival and the two white men left immediately for Port Natal.

[4]

Although the quarrel between King and Farewell had quickly been patched up, their reconciliation was an uneasy one. Everyone at the settlement seems to have been aware of the unspoken hostility between the two men. It manifested itself in small things. When, for instance, King wanted to present Shaka with the gifts he had collected at the Cape, Farewell objected. As nominal head of the settlement, Farewell insisted that all dealings with Shaka should be done in his name. This, until King's visit to the Cape, had been the accepted custom; now King wanted to act on his own authority. In the end they compromised. The gifts—'a handsome brass crown, a quantity of beads, some blankets, and a plume of red feathers, with a quantity of peacock's feathers which he wanted for his warriors'— were taken to Shaka by Isaacs and one of King's African servants, Nasapongo.

Shaka received the gifts with feigned indifference. Only the brass crown seemed to rouse his curiosity. He made Nasapongo put it on and parade before his indunas. The peacock feathers he dismissed as quite unsuitable for his warriors.

As Nasapongo had accompanied James Saunders King to the Cape, Shaka questioned him about the number of soldiers and cattle he had seen there. The King also enquired about Elizabeth Farewell. Isaacs says that he wanted to know whether she was 'a pretty woman, and if she had any children; but did not express any desire to see her'. Many years later Mrs Farewell told another story. She informed a friend that she had been taken to see the Zulu King and that Shaka had 'determined to seize her and make her his wife'. Only by dressing her in men's clothes and smuggling her to a place of safety had her husband saved her from Shaka's clutches. How true this is one does not know. It seems highly unlikely. Not only would it have been out of character for Shaka to have behaved in such a way, but the fact that none of the other settlers mention the incident makes it extremely suspect. Both Fynn and Isaacs were at Port Natal throughout Elizabeth Farewell's stay; they would surely have heard of her narrow escape. It was the sort of story that would have fitted in well with the more lurid passages of Isaacs' account. Had it happened he would not have hesitated to use it.

As it was, Isaacs claims that Shaka showed more interest in the return of James Saunders King than in the arrival of Mrs Farewell. He regretted that King had not accompanied Isaacs and wondered what had prevented him from visiting Bulawayo. On the second day of Isaacs's visit, Shaka presented him with a bullock as a thanksgiving gift for King's safe return.

Shaka seemed in high spirits when he welcomed Isaacs. He was still celebrating his victory over the Ndwandwe; composing new songs and teaching them to his people. Isaacs was obliged to sit up late into the night listening to the incessant chanting. Then, quite suddenly, the King's mood changed. One morning he announced that he was troubled by a dream he had had. He had dreamt that 'a number of his boys had had criminal intercourse with his girls in the palace'. For the King to have had such a dream was as good as the debauch taking place. When Shaka went on to declare that he intended to punish the supposed offenders he was loudly applauded. 'Father kill them for they are not fit to live,' shouted the people.

Shaka needed no encouragement. The suspected boys and girls were ambushed in the cattle arena and preparations for the massacre began. Isaacs was summoned to witness the ghastly proceedings. Somewhat surprisingly, he says that it started with Shaka cruelly beating his mother, the ageing Nandi, whom he accused of not taking proper care of the girls. But there was worse to follow. The cowering youngsters were paraded before the King to be sentenced to death. 'He began,' says Isaacs, 'by taking out several fine lads, and ordering their own brothers to twist their necks, their bodies were afterwards dragged away and beaten with sticks until life was extinct. After this refined act of monstrous cruelty, the remainder of the victims in the kraal were indiscriminately butchered.'

The following morning there were more killings. Then, in another lightning change of mood, the King recovered his high spirits. That afternoon he again led his people in singing and dancing. Isaacs was among those who, in the evening, received a present of cattle taken from the kraals of Shaka's victims. He left Bulawayo the next day.

Compared with the Zulu capital, Port Natal was a haven of peace. But, for all that, it was not without its troubles. The tension between Farewell and King had heightened during Isaacs's absence: soon it was to come to a head and divide the traders into openly hostile factions.

7

DISSENSION AND A DEATH

THE MONTHS FROM November to February are the hottest of the southern summer. At this time of year the climate of the Natal coastal region can be extremely trying. The sweltering days are humid and enervating; the nights airless and oppressive. All energy is sapped, tempers are frayed, even the most placid of people become edgy.

For the settlers at Port Natal, living in a clearing hacked out of the pestilent bush, the hot November of 1826 proved particularly distressing. Farewell, who had moved into his large, newly built wooden house within the walls of the mud fort, was able to find some consolation in the company of his wife and a few amenities of civilised life. The rest of the party were not so fortunate. Scattered about the settlement in their windowless, mud and wattle huts, they found little to relieve the tedium of the long, uneventful days. John Cane was living with the Hottentot woman, Rachel, and there is reason to think that some of the others had already taken African mistresses; but it required more than women to make life at the settlement pleasant. The stifling heat had slowed down the ship building; the Africans were becoming fractious; and close confinement in their stuffy, rat-infested hovels had made the white men restless. With few distractions and no amusements it was, perhaps, inevitable that the traders should turn against each other. Some time during that November the uneasy alliance between Lieutenant Farewell and James Saunders King came to an end.

The precise nature of this final quarrel has always been something of a mystery. Fynn does not discuss it. Isaacs admits that a quarrel took place but is suspiciously guarded in referring to it. He says that a dispute arose 'on matters of a pecuniary nature' but refuses to give any further details. Both Farewell and King were dead by the time Isaacs published his account and this, he claims, obliged him to remain silent. 'To enter into the merits of the cause which ended in the division of friends, would be foreign to my purpose,' he wrote piously, 'I can only observe that I regretted it, and the death of Mr Farewell subsequently precludes my commenting on his conduct, as I conceive it my duty to abstain from remarks on those who cannot defend themselves.' Such praiseworthy sentiments are strangely out of character for the partisan Isaacs and must be taken with a very large pinch of salt. He was not always so reticent about presenting Farewell in an unfavourable light. On the other hand, he idolised King and one suspects his professed sensitivity was little more than an attempt to cover up for his friend.

For, if Farewell is to be believed, the 'pecuniary nature' of the quarrel reflected little credit on James Saunders King. A letter which Farewell wrote to the *South African Commercial Advertiser* shortly before his death sheds an interesting light on the mysterious quarrel. The fact that his letter was buried in the newspaper's correspondence columns, probably explains why it was subsequently overlooked.

According to Farewell, his relationship with King had never been easy: it is abundantly clear that, almost from the outset, the two men had recognised each other as rivals. Farewell says bluntly that the settlement which he helped King to establish at Port Natal, after the wreck of the *Mary*, was used 'to oppose me, and undermine my interests in a country which would have remained unknown, but for me, and on which I had expended very considerable sums, and exhausted all my means'. As far as the final quarrel is concerned, Farewell's explanation is brief but very much to the point. 'I shall merely state,' he wrote, 'that on my declining a proposal made me by Mr King, with a view of inducing me to resign all my interests in the country to him, that Gentleman thought proper to enter into a violent opposition, or rather hostilities against me.'

While it is possible that Farewell exaggerated King's demands, it is obvious that they quarrelled over the grant of land made to Farewell by Shaka. This, when one knows of King's activities in England and Cape Town, is a reasonable explanation of the breach between the traders. Unless he had a definite claim—or at least a share—in the land surrounding Port Natal, King could not hope to make a success of an independent trading venture. But this was something which neither he nor Isaacs wished to broadcast.

The quarrel split the camp into two hostile factions. Both Isaacs and Fynn sided with King. Farewell bitterly resented Fynn's defection. Not only had he brought Fynn to Natal but he had placed great trust in the young man's loyalty. Now, says Farewell, he 'deserted my employ, to join [King], without assigning any reason—leaving me alone opposed by the whole party, without the means of contending against them either as to trade or otherwise, or possessing a single witness whom I could call on to secure me from the false and malicious constructions then put upon whatever I did or expressed, as a justification for whatever they thought it their interest to do'.

Fynn's support of King is indeed puzzling. Of all the traders Fynn was undoubtedly the most courageous, the most honest. In later years he was to hold responsible positions in South Africa; he became regarded as an authority on affairs in Natal. He was revered by the white colonists and by the Zulu people. The only clue to his desertion of Farewell seems to lie in his comparative youth—he was still in his early twenties—and in King's persuasive personality. For there can be no denying that James Saunders King had a winning way with him. Not only had he completely captivated the susceptible young Isaacs, but he had greatly impressed officials at the British Colonial Office, enchanted the editor of the *South African Commercial Advertiser*, and induced the merchants of Cape Town to support him financially: even the suspicious Shaka was soon to fall victim to his magnetism. One had to stand at a distance from James Saunders King to detect his duplicity.

Fynn appears to have recognised this too late. During King's lifetime, Fynn remained implacably hostile towards Farewell. However, when he came to write his reminiscences, many years later, he seems to have had second thoughts. His account contains none of Isaacs's adulation of King and his attitude towards Farewell is discreetly impartial. He had need to think again. His loyalty to James Saunders King was to lead him into some very questionable situations.

The fault was not entirely one-sided. Farewell's obstinacy probably did much to alienate his former followers. Life in Natal had soured Farewell: he had become avaricious, touchy and, in many ways, a difficult man to get on with. Admittedly most reports of him come from hostile sources but, even allowing for this, he never strikes one as a man who could inspire fidelity. But he was wrong in claiming that Fynn's withdrawal left him entirely alone. At least one of his party remained true. John Cane, the down-to-earth carpenter, seems to have been immune to King's charm.

John Cane was not a man likely to be swayed by emotion. Then in his mid-twenties, Cane was the son of a London iron-worker. As a boy he had left home, hoping to become a sailor, but had quickly changed his mind after a few months at sea. In 1813 he had arrived at the Cape on board the *Hector*, signed off the ship, and found a job with a Cape Town wine merchant. But the wine trade had not suited him any more than had life at sea. He had somehow made his way to the eastern frontier where he worked at a Government farm and trained as a carpenter. Later, Fynn had also worked at the same Government farm and it might have been this connection which had attracted Cane to Lieutenant Farewell's expedition. But, whatever his initial relationship was with Fynn, it was to Farewell that Cane gave his loyalty when the settlement divided.

It is, in fact, Cane's testimony that inclines one to accept Farewell's version of the quarrel. Both Fynn and Isaacs must have known about Farewell's letter to the *South African Commercial Advertiser* but, significantly, neither of them replied to it. Cane, on the other hand, gave it his terse approval. 'I was most happy to see Mr Farewell's letter in your paper,' he wrote to the editor, some months after the letter was published, 'thereby giving that gentleman an opportunity of refuting the unfounded reports some idle persons have given to the transactions at Natal.'

The idle persons he referred to were probably members of Fynn's family. By that time many people had become interested in the transactions at Natal.

[2]

Both King and Isaacs were apprehensive as to how Shaka would react to the split in the traders' camp. There was good reason for them to think that by admitting to a division of interests they would rouse the Zulu King's suspicions. They had, after all, represented themselves as merchants whose only interest in the country was to trade with the Zulu nation. If they were now quarrelling among themselves—so soon after King's return from the Cape—Shaka might well question their motives in coming to Natal.

King decided to lose no time in reassuring the Zulu monarch. At the beginning of December 1826, he paid his second visit to Shaka. He was accompanied by John Hutton and one of the sailors; Isaacs joined them a few days later.

Shaka was then living at a new kraal. Towards the end of November, he had moved south of the Tugela and had established himself near the coast (at the site of the present-day village of Stanger) which he named kwaDukuza. Isaacs claims that Shaka intended Dukuza as a place to which he could retire when it was necessary for him to absent himself from Bulawayo. It is equally possible— and more likely—that, having eliminated the Ndwandwe, the King now felt free to give more attention to the Europeans and had thus moved his residence south. Port Natal was only a few days' march from Dukuza.

James Saunders King and his party were given a hearty welcome at Dukuza. Isaacs says that Shaka 'evinced great pleasure' at meeting King again. A cow was slaughtered in honour of the party's arrival and Shaka peppered King with questions about his visit to the Cape. Whether the quarrel with Farewell was discussed is not clear, but there seems little doubt that King succeeded in ingratiating himself with Shaka. There was no discord and, a few days later, King felt sufficiently reassured to return to Port Natal.

Isaacs is notably vague about the party's dealings with Shaka on this occasion and there is no way of knowing whether King was alone when he left Dukuza. Farewell implies that he was not. In fact, King's practice of installing his agents at the royal kraal became a sore point with Farewell. 'Mr King,' he says, 'had likewise the advantage over me, although he could not converse in the language himself, of generally having one or two of his party at Chaka's Kraal to attend to his interests there, and was no doubt indebted to these circumstances for any success he derived from Chaka, and prevented any false representations being made there against himself.'

Some weeks later King and Isaacs embarked on another expedition. They were searching for a navigable river on which to form a new settlement. With Farewell firmly in possession of Port Natal, it had become imperative that they find a port of some sort from which to operate. Fynn had already done some scouting. He had explored a district ninety miles north-east of Port Natal and had been allowed to return from there with seven hundred pounds of ivory. This encouraging haul and a favourable report on the nearby Umlalazi river had made King and Isaacs anxious to find out more about the region.

On their way north they stopped at Dukuza for a couple of days. Isaacs says that they informed Shaka of their intention to form a new settlement and the King not only gave them his blessing but promised them a large grant of land 'with exclusive right of trading to his dominions' if the Umlalazi proved navigable. The well-tried charms of James Saunders King were evidently taking effect.

Buoyed by the thought of putting one over on Farewell, King and Isaacs continued their journey. At the Umlalazi river they were entertained by the widow of Fynn's old friend Mbikwane. The aged Mbikwane (who had first conducted Fynn to Shaka's kraal) had recently died and the Europeans had greatly regretted his passing, but his widow proved every bit as friendly. King and Isaacs received a warm welcome. The day after their arrival, they waded along the flooded banks of the Umlalazi until they came to the mouth. Here their optimism soared. The inevitable sand-bar at the river entrance proved negotiable and there was good anchorage for small vessels. A quick survey of the surrounding country convinced King that he had found the ideal spot for a new settlement. The vegetation was lush, the rich soil was watered by innumerable springs, animals and fish were plentiful and the forests of the district were extensive. Equally important, from King's point of view, it was much closer to Zululand than was Port Natal.

Entranced by the scenery and backed by Shaka's promise of a land grant, King decided to stake his claim. Isaacs climbed to the top of a prominent sand hill, clutching a Union Jack which he solemnly planted as a token of possession. Whatever else they might have lacked, the traders were never short of a British flag when they wished to claim foreign territory.

The morning following their return to Mbikwane's kraal, King and Isaacs received disturbing news. They were awakened by an old woman who pushed her way into their hut and announced that two of Farewell's Hottentots, Michael and John, had raped the young

wife of a local chieftain. As these same two Hottentots had, on a
recent visit to Bulawayo, offended Shaka by starting a drunken
brawl, there was no mistaking the seriousness of the old woman's
message. Rape was a heinous crime in Shaka's calendar; it
could mean death for the troublesome Hottentots and ruin to the
traders' plans. King and Isaacs prepared to leave for Dukuza
immediately.

While they were getting ready, Michael and John showed up.
The Hottentots denied some of the accusations levelled at them but
admitted to the rape. King gave them a short lecture and packed
them off to Port Natal with instructions to keep well away from
Shaka's kraal. For some reason this warning was ignored. Shortly
after King and Isaacs arrived at Dukuza, Michael and John presented themselves at the kraal. 'Fortunately for all of us,' says
Isaacs, 'they did not enter the King's presence.'

Fortunate it was indeed. Shaka was in a cold fury. Reports of the
rape had already reached him and, as he made no distinction
between the traders and their servants—to him anyone who wore
clothes, as the Hottentots did, was a European—he was threatening
death to all the whites in Natal. While King and Isaacs were trying
to reason with him, John Cane arrived with an apology from Farewell. This seemed to placate Shaka. His mood changed. Instead of
demanding blood, he insisted that the traders join him in a military
campaign. 'Something must be done to appease the chiefs,' he
explained, 'or they will say I am not fit to command.'

Isaacs implies that this was just a ruse on Shaka's part to press the
white men into his service. How true this is it is not possible to say.
One only has Isaacs's word for it and, in view of later developments,
it is not beyond credibility that the offer came from the Europeans.
They stood to gain more from the arrangement than Shaka but, as
always, would have been unwilling to admit that they had volun-
tarily taken part in a tribal war. Isaacs's protestations on this
occasion are not very convincing. 'To go to war with such innocent
people, however, was painful,' he laments, 'it was, however, not a
measure of choice, but one of necessity, and we were led to hope
that, instead of any protracted contention, we might be able to
parley with them and bring them to terms.' Why, one wonders, did
he think a 'monster' like Shaka would be satisfied if the Europeans
simply persuaded his enemies to come to terms?

However it came about, four white men—Isaacs, Cane and two seamen—and seven armed Africans from the settlement were detailed to accompany the Zulu army on a military expedition.

[3]

The people against whom the Zulu army was moving were not so much a threat to Shaka as an annoyance. They were part of the Kumalo clan and inhabited the dense Ngome forest which covered a range of rocky hills beyond Bulawayo. Shaka had many scores to settle with the Kumalo: not the least being a long-standing grievance over the traitorous conduct of one of their young warriors to whom he had once been greatly attached.

This young warrior was a petty Kumalo chieftain named Mzilikazi. He had sought refuge with Shaka many years earlier when the Zulu King was campaigning against the formidable Zwide. Although Mzilikazi was related to Zwide he had had no reason to love his kinsman who had not only persecuted the Kumalo but had killed Mzilikazi's father. When Mzilikazi had offered to serve with the Zulu army, Shaka had welcomed him. The young Kumalo quickly distinguished himself and was soon established as one of Shaka's favourite commanders. But this happy relationship had not lasted long.

Shaka had entrusted Mzilikazi with an independent command and allowed him to return to his home on the fringe of the Ngome forest. Shortly before the white men arrived in Natal, the Kumalo chieftain had been sent, with two Zulu regiments, on a cattle raid into Ndwandwe territory. The raid was successful. Mzilikazi had returned to his home kraal with most of the cattle as well as the regiments under his command. Only a token number of the cattle were sent to Bulawayo and, as soon as Shaka became aware of this, he demanded the rest of the captured herds. Mzilikazi ignored the demand. Shaka was forced to take action.

Loath as he was to move against his protégé, Shaka first sent a small force to collect the stolen cattle and, when Mzilikazi fought and defeated this force, he had no alternative but to send a second, much larger force. This time Mzilikazi fled, taking with him some

three hundred Zulu warriors. In his flight northwards, he laid
waste to the country behind him and was joined by the remnants
of the clans he defeated. By the time he settled, in what was to
become the Transvaal, he had forged a new, formidable tribe
known as the Matabele. Originating from a nucleus of Zulu warriors,
disciplined by Shaka, this tribe eventually became a powerful
nation and its founder, Mzilikazi, was widely acknowledged as a
great African conqueror. For Shaka, however, the name Mzilikazi
meant treachery. He never forgot his favourite's defection.

The chief of those Kumalo who remained in the Ngome forest
was a man named umBeje. Although by no means as skilled a warrior
as Mzilikazi, he shared the Kumalo defiance. On a number of
occasions he had refused to co-operate with Shaka and had resisted
all attempts to coerce him. Such obstinacy could not go unpunished.
Shaka was determined to settle with the Kumalo once and for all.
He had already made two bids to come to grips with umBeje;
each time the jungle-like nature of the Ngome forest had defeated
him. There was to be no question of his army retreating a third
time.

If Isaacs really hoped to negotiate a peace with the Kumalo, he
must have been quickly disillusioned. When the small trader force
arrived at Dukuza, after collecting their arms, Shaka made his
intentions quite clear. The Kumalo clan was to be wiped out; not
a child was to be left alive. He would not listen to the argument that
women and children were innocent and could do no harm. 'Yes
they could,' he said; 'they can propagate and bring [forth] children,
who may become my enemies. It is the custom I pursue not to give
quarter to my enemies, therefore I command you to kill all.'

Despite these unmistakable instructions—which he duly recorded
—Isaacs continued to claim the role of a disinterested peace-
maker. Exactly how he intended to overcome Shaka's blood-thirsty
demands he does not explain. But, as it happened, neither Isaacs's
good intentions nor Shaka's threats were to be realised. The
campaign was almost farcical.

The main body of the Zulu army was already encamped on the
edge of the Ngome forest. They had, in fact, been there for three
months. When Isaacs's party, accompanied by twenty Africans
carrying shields and assegais, came trudging into the camp they
were met by some extremely apprehensive Zulu commanders. Torn

between the prospects of defeat in the dangerous forest and Shaka's wrath if they did not return victorious, they had been brought to a virtual standstill. The arrival of the white men did nothing to reassure them. They were afraid, says Isaacs, 'that we should strike terror by the application of our fire-arms in the attack, and thus at once subdue the tribe opposed to us, which would enrage their king at their want of skill, or, as he would call it, their want of courage, and subject them all to his implacable resentment'. Such a possibility represented the worst of all outcomes; it made the Zulu commanders unwilling to co-operate with the Europeans. Isaacs found all his attempts to contact the enemy undermined by false reports from the Zulu scouts.

Not until they had been at the camp for three days did an opportunity to attack present itself. A band of Kumalo were seen driving a herd along the edge of the forest; the seamen decided to lead a raiding party and seize the cattle. The result was unexpected. The herdsmen fled into the forest and summoned the entire Kumalo army; the Zulu warriors, seeing what had happened, massed behind the white men. Isaacs, who had rushed after the seamen and their raiding party, was pushed into the forefront. At the age of eighteen, with no military experience, he found himself at the head of a 5000 strong Zulu army preparing for battle.

'At this particular juncture,' he says, 'I felt no ordinary sensations of anxiety and apprehension.' One can understand what he means. While the witch doctors fussed about the Zulu ranks, flicking their ox-tails and doctoring the warriors for war, Isaacs murmured a short but heart-felt prayer: 'In Thee, O Lord, have I trusted, let me never be put to confusion.' Whatever his motives for joining the army, one must sympathise wholeheartedly with his plight. He had no alternative but to advance.

The Kumalo positioned themselves in small detachments along a series of rocky heights. Bravely Isaacs led his ten gun-carrying companions towards them, fully expecting the Zulu army to support him. How wrong he was. Before he had gone far he was amazed to discover that Shaka's legendary warriors were not following but had retreated speedily to the opposite side of a nearby river. Nothing daunted, the armed party pushed on up one of the enemy-held hills until they faced a party of fifty Kumalo. They stopped, sighted their muskets, and fired. The effect was electrifying. Not only did the enemy scatter but, looking back, the white men saw the entire Zulu army lying flat on the ground: every warrior covering his back with his shield.

The sight of 5000 prone Zulu warriors proved too much for the Kumalo. Connecting the sound of gun-fire with the falling of their apparently dead foes, they hastily retreated from the menacing white men. Taking up a position at the top of the hill, they screamed abuse and defied the traders to approach. Their hysterical panic gave Isaacs new confidence. He and his companions pressed on up the hill, firing at intervals and being answered with an occasional, bravely thrown, assegai. By the time they reached the summit, the hill seemed practically deserted. They pushed on until they came to a few empty huts. These they burnt in the hopes of inducing the enemy to surrender. There was still some scattered resistance from Kumalo hiding among the trees and one enemy commander tried desperately to rally his men. In the skirmish which followed this last stand, Isaacs, in the act of firing, felt something thud against his back. Thinking he had been hit by one of the stones that were being hurled—by women and children as well as warriors—he continued to reload his musket. As he did so, he noticed blood streaming down his leg; looking over his shoulder he was astonished to see the shaft of an assegai quivering in his back.

John Cane and some others tried unsuccessfully to remove the barbed spear from Isaacs's body; finally it was extracted by an African servant who skilfully loosened it by pressing his finger into the wound. Weak from loss of blood, Isaacs staggered to the bottom of the hill and pleaded with some Zulu warriors to help him. Their refusal so angered him that he at first hit out at them with a stick and then threatened them with his musket. The sight of the gun had a predictable effect: the warriors fled. Isaacs was left alone. Luckily he was soon joined by his companions who carried him back to the Zulu camp, where he spent an extremely painful night.

The following morning it was decided to leave Isaacs in his hut while the rest of the party resumed the attack. When the Zulu commanders heard that a second offensive was being planned, they hastily agreed to join the traders. Fearing that their earlier cowardice would be reported to Shaka, they assembled their warriors and, at ten that morning, the entire force started out.

Isaacs was left in the care of a witch doctor whose ministrations proved more alarming than helpful. He was awakened later that day by the return of the Zulu regiments. The army marched into camp shepherding a herd of half-starved cattle and goats which the Kumalo had surrendered without a fight. Still reeling from their experiences of the previous day, the Kumalo had been ready for peace at any price. The mere sight of the massed Zulu army, headed by John Cane, had been sufficient to frighten them into submission. Three of their envoys had approached the Zulu ranks and announced that they were prepared to accept any conditions as they were bewildered by the 'roots and medicines' that were being used and 'could not contend with people who spit fire'. Not only did they willingly hand over their cattle and promise allegiance to Shaka but, at the suggestion of one of the seamen, they had no hesitation in parting with ten young Kumalo girls to cement the new alliance 'by nuptial ties'. Everyone was happy.

This news cheered Isaacs but, when he tried to send a report of it to James Saunders King, he found his wound prevented him from writing. For three painful days he was forced to remain at the Zulu camp. By the time he eventually reached Dukuza, he had every reason to think that he had earned his new Zulu praisename—*Dambuza*, which he translated as 'the brave warrior who was wounded at Ngome'.

Shaka gave him no such praise. When he reported to the Zulu monarch—accompanied by James Saunders King, who had been anxiously awaiting his return—he was greeted by a cynical smile. Shaka examined his wound and informed him that he was lucky to be a subject of umGeorge; if any Zulu had returned with a wound in his back he would have been killed instantly. However, Isaacs's understandable anger turned to relief when he discovered that Shaka was merely teasing him. His obvious bravery was rewarded with a gift of four milch cows.

Isaacs is vague about Shaka's reaction to his warriors' failure to obey orders and obliterate the Kumalo. Having been at great pains to portray Shaka as an unrelenting, blood-thirsty monster at the beginning of the campaign, he did not bother to question his apparent *volte-face*. One is left with another unexplained contradiction in Isaacs's account.

One thing is certain, however. The Ngome expedition overcame

Shaka's scepticism about the white men's weapons: the effectiveness of gun-fire in a tribal battle had been proved beyond doubt.

[4]

Isaacs and King returned to Port Natal very much in favour with Shaka. Although King had taken no part in the campaign, he had been presented with seventy-eight head of cattle. He was not, however, so popular with his own people. For some inexplicable reason, John Hutton and the seamen chose this happy time to down tools. Nothing would make them resume their ship building. King promptly threatened to burn the vessel and march the rest of the party overland to Delagoa Bay. He despatched Isaacs to Dukuza to arrange for Shaka to provide an escort for the overland journey.

It proved unnecessary. Hardly had Isaacs arrived at the royal kraal than a message came from King to say that the quarrel with Hutton had been patched up. The ship building was going ahead. Unfortunately this did not solve all their problems. They were running short of supplies and were in desperate need of medicines. It was obvious that someone would have to make the journey to Delagoa Bay.

King's choice for this hazardous mission was extraordinary. Knowing full well the dangers involved, he sent a fifteen-year-old apprentice known as John Ross (his name was actually Charles Rawden Maclean; he changed it to Ross when he ran away to sea as a child) on a journey of 300 miles each way. No European had ever completed the trek to Delagoa Bay and back again. Some three years earlier one of Farewell's original party had attempted it but was never heard of again. None of this seems to have worried King—who professed to be devoted to young Ross—nor, for that matter, did it deter the boy himself. Shaka provided an escort and, to everyone's amazement, the plucky youngster returned in less than a month with the much needed medicines. The supplies had cost him next to nothing. A French slaver at the Portuguese settlement had been so impressed by his bravery that he freely provided all that was needed. Only later did Ross suspect the slaver of having designs on his Zulu escort. This, and the fact that the Portuguese imagined him to be a spy for Shaka—they could not believe he had been sent by a Christian—had hastened the boy's departure. On his way back he had carefully avoided Shaka's kraal for fear that his medicines would be commandeered. 'I cannot but conceive the journey of this lad,' Isaacs rightly remarks, 'as one that must be held as exceedingly bold, and wonderfully enterprising.'

By now James Saunders King appears to have had second thoughts about his proposed settlement on the Umlalazi. He and Isaacs were busy exploring other river mouths. On the way back from one of these expeditions, in July 1827, they met Shaka at his kraal for an important conference. Whether by design or accident, Fynn was also present.

According to Isaacs, Shaka expressed an urgent wish to meet his fellow sovereign King George. However, being apprehensive about his reception 'across the water' he thought it might be wiser if he first sent one of his chiefs as an envoy. He suggested that, as soon as the traders' vessel was ready, this chief should sail for the Cape under the charge of James Saunders King. There was another matter that was bothering him. Some time earlier Farewell had told him of a white man's preparation which could turn white hairs black. He said he wanted to obtain this for his ageing mother, Nandi. King was promised a huge reward in ivory and cattle if he returned with the magical mixture; he was, however, instructed to keep the proposed transaction a close secret. Knowing Shaka's fear of death and old age, the white men suspected that his concern was not only for his mother but for himself: he wished to ward off all signs of encroaching infirmity. Much was to be made of Shaka's vanity and his burning desire to obtain a bottle of macassar oil.

Although Fynn was at this meeting, he mentions it only in passing. However, after King and Isaacs had left Dukuza, Fynn was made to accompany Shaka to a place beyond Bulawayo, where the Zulu monarch was planning to establish a new residence. On their way, they skirted the former capital and passed close to Nandi's kraal.

Soon after work had started on Shaka's new residence, messengers arrived from Nandi's kraal to say that the queen-mother was ill. At first Shaka does not appear to have been unduly concerned. He despatched some of his witch doctors to attend his mother and sent her some European medicines he had obtained from the traders. But, as reports from Nandi's kraal grew worse, Shaka became more and more uneasy. Finally he decided to return to Bulawayo. He arrived there early one morning with his forces and immediately sent Fynn—whom he still regarded as his European doctor—to examine Nandi.

When Fynn arrived at the queen-mother's kraal, he found the sick woman's hut crowded with witch doctors and female servants. A fire had been lit and the heat and smoke inside the hut was such that Fynn had to drive out most of Nandi's attendants before he could breathe. The old woman was dying from dysentery and Fynn could do nothing for her. He returned to Bulawayo and told Shaka that the case was hopeless; he thought it unlikely that Nandi would live through the day.

Shaka received the news in shocked silence. He had been sitting surrounded by his regiments when Fynn arrived and, after dismissing the warriors, he continued to sit staring into space until word came that Nandi was dead. Then he rose, ordered his indunas to put on their war dress, and disappeared into his hut. A few minutes later he reappeared, dressed for battle; his face was smeared with coloured clay and for almost half an hour he stood among the assembled indunas with his head resting on his shield, occasionally wiping away his tears with his right hand. Not a word was said.

Fynn, who had been present at the death of Shaka's grandmother, watched apprehensively as the silent crowd waited for a signal from the King. He had some idea of what to expect. From the moment he had realised that Nandi was dying, he had been aware that her death would be accompanied by a display of frenzied mourning. But nothing in his experience had prepared him for the mass hysteria which now convulsed Bulawayo.

The long silence was broken by a terrifying yell from Shaka. After sighing deeply three or four times, he suddenly screamed: '*Maye ngo Mama!*' (Alas, my mother!). This cry was instantly taken up by the crowd. Frantically tearing off their ornaments they began weeping and howling uncontrollably. From the neighbouring kraals, people poured into the royal enclosure shrieking at the tops of their voices to announce their arrival. By early evening more than 15,000 delirious men and women were milling about Bulawayo; the number grew throughout the night as more and more regiments crowded into the capital. Next morning Fynn estimated that no less than 60,000 people were wildly lamenting Nandi's death.

The morning scene was horrific. Worn out from the excesses of the night, hundreds of mourners lay fainting from lack of sleep and food, while others trampled over them in renewed bouts of violence. Some forty oxen had been ritually slaughtered but no one was allowed to touch the meat which was being devoured by packs of dogs and vultures.

At noon the regiments formed a circle round Shaka, who led them in a war-chant, and then ordered several warriors to be executed on the spot. 'No further orders were needed,' says Fynn. 'But, as if bent on convincing their chief of their extreme grief, the multitude commenced a general massacre. Many of them received the blow of death while inflicting it on others, each taking the opportunity of revenging their injuries, real or imaginary. Those who could not force more tears from their eyes—those who were found near the river panting for water—were beaten to death by others who were mad with excitement. Towards the afternoon I calculated not fewer than 7000 people had fallen in this frightful indiscriminate massacre. The adjacent stream, to which many had fled exhausted, to wet their parched tongues, became impassable from the number of dead corpses which lay on each side of it; while the kraal in which the scene took place was flowing with blood.'

Fynn stood amid the carnage unharmed. At one stage a regiment of young warriors rushed at him with raised clubs and demanded to know why he was not crying but, when he stared at them without speaking, they backed away. He felt thankful, he says, not only that he was a British subject but that he had earned Shaka's respect. Even in this blood-crazed holocaust, Shaka's friendship proved all-powerful. Nevertheless, Fynn had every reason to feel thankful when, at sunset, a halt was called to the senseless killings.

Nandi was buried at her kraal the following day. A grave was dug inside her hut and, after she had been placed in it and covered with a mat, the hut was hacked down over the spot. Fynn was not at the funeral but he heard later that ten of the best-looking girls of the kraal had been buried alive in the grave. A regiment of 12,000 warriors was formed to guard the burial place for a year: they were supplied with 15,000 head of cattle taken from kraals throughout Zululand.

Even greater penalties had to be paid. Immediately after the funeral it was decreed that no crops could be planted for a year and that all milk drawn from cows during that period should be allowed to run waste on the earth. Any women found pregnant during the year were to be killed, together with their husbands. These appalling conditions—which entailed starvation for thousands—were enforced throughout the land. In the belief that Nandi had been killed by witchcraft, warriors were sent to scour the territory and punish those kraals that had not sent a mourning party to Bulawayo and could thus be suspected of conniving at the queen-mother's death. The most ghastly reign of terror ever known in Zululand had begun.

For three months Shaka's inhuman commands were obeyed. Then the King decided to make Dukuza his new capital and moved there with his regiments and cattle. Fynn was present at the installation ceremony which, in keeping with the mourning period, was accompanied by widespread lamentation. Shaka entered the kraal sighing and sobbing, pretending to stagger as he walked, and finally bursting into a loud fit of uncontrolled weeping. His cries were echoed by those of his people and joined by the bellowing of 100,000 oxen which had been assembled to appease the grief-stricken King. The climax of this emotion-fraught ceremony was reached the following day.

In the morning every cattle-owner brought a calf to the royal kraal. At a signal, the right side of each calf was ripped open and its gall-bladder extracted: the mutilated animals being left to die in agony. The warriors then circled Shaka and, as each regiment passed him, the cattle-owners carrying gall bladders left the ranks and emptied the bladders over the King. With this 'purification' of Shaka the taboos against growing corn and using milk were ritually lifted: the decrees against pregnancy, however, remained in force throughout the year.

The purification ceremony ended with a speech from one of Shaka's favourite indunas. He announced that Nandi had now become a spirit and would continue to watch over her son. 'But,' he added, 'there were nations of men, inhabiting distant countries, who, because they had not yet been conquered, supposed that they never should be. This was plain from the fact of their not having come forward to lament the death of the Great Mother of Earth and Corn. And, as tears could not be forced from these distant nations, war should be made against them, and the cattle taken should be the tears shed on her grave.'

According to Fynn this threat was directed at those tribes inhabiting 'Caffreland'—the territory separating Shaka from the white settlers on the frontier of the Cape Colony.

8

A CURIOUS UNDERTAKING

IN FEBRUARY 1828 the schooner *Buckbay Packet* called at Port Natal on its way to Delagoa Bay. The *Buckbay Packet* was one of the ships that James Saunders King had tried to persuade the Cape authorities to sell him when he visited Cape Town: now it was of little use to the traders. Farewell and King bartered some ivory for part of the schooner's cargo and entrusted the captain with some brass bangles to sell for them at Delagoa Bay, but this was as far as their interest went. It was just as well. Shortly after leaving Port Natal, the *Buckbay Packet* was wrecked and her captain died of fever on the coast.

But there was no longer any need for the traders to keep up the pretence that they were waiting to be rescued. By February 1828, the ship which they had started to build some two and a half years earlier was all but ready to put to sea.

For the astute King the first voyage of the almost completed ship was to be the culmination of a long cherished scheme. It must have been shortly after the departure of the *Buckbay Packet* that he paid an important visit to Shaka to put the finishing touches to his plans. Isaacs, who went with him, makes no mention of the visit. In fact, he implies that he was ill at this time and left it to King and Fynn to negotiate with Shaka. His signature on a document signed at the meeting between the Zulu King and the traders proves otherwise.

Fynn refers to the meeting but is vague about its proceedings. He says that Shaka presented James Saunders King with eighty-six elephant tusks and announced to his assembled people that the Europeans would 'bring back immense quantities of such things as they required. Afterwards, however, in his hut, he told Mr King to bring nothing but macassar oil. His people were dogs, he would give them nothing. All he wanted was macassar oil and medicine.' So intent is Fynn on emphasising Shaka's desire for macassar oil, that he makes no mention of the document the Zulu King was persuaded to sign.

This document, dated from 'Chaka's principal residence, Umbololi, February 1828' had been drawn up by James Saunders King. It empowered Shaka's 'friend James Saunders King' to take charge of a mission to King George IV. The British King was assured of Shaka's friendship and a treaty of alliance between the British and Zulu nations was to be negotiated. One of Shaka's principal chiefs, Sotobe, was to act as the Zulu representative. He was to be accompanied by the interpreter Jacob and an appropriate retinue. James Saunders King was instructed to take care of this delegation and to return with them to Shaka.

In return for these and other services—including 'his attention to my mother in her last illness'—King was to be granted full possession of a territory near the sea coast and Port Natal, together with a considerable stretch of inland country. The actual boundaries of this grant are vague but it is obvious that King had persuaded Shaka to cede him the territory already claimed by Farewell. King was also granted 'free and exclusive trade' in the Zulu domains.

This was the first stage of King's plan. He had been working towards it for months. Probably from the time that he had arrived in Natal, and certainly since his quarrel with Farewell, King had been determined to obtain this important trading concession. At the beginning of 1828—with the traders' ship very near to completion—he had stepped up his campaign. Shaka, during this periods, says Isaacs, 'evinced more friendship towards Lieutenant King, Mr Fynn and myself, than he had ever manifested before, though we had received ample proofs of his partiality on several previous occasions; whilst, on the other hand, he exhibited a cool indifference towards Mr Farewell'.

Precisely how King won over Shaka will never be known; but win him over he did. When the document was presented to the Zulu King, he duly 'signed' it with a lengthy scrawl which ran all over the paper. It was witnessed by Jacob, the interpreter, and Nathaniel Isaacs. James Saunders King was then appointed to nominal command of one of Shaka's regiments and presented with a head-dress of black feathers as a token of his status as a Zulu chief.

According to Isaacs, Shaka had originally wanted him to remain in Natal until King returned but, at the last minute, agreed to accept Fynn as a hostage in his place. He says that this change was caused by his illness; the fact that it was made (whatever the reason) might well explain why Isaacs claimed that sickness prevented him attending the meeting with Shaka. It suited the traders' book to pretend that Fynn was forced to remain in Natal by accident rather than by design. Fynn makes no mention of the change in plan, but agrees that he became a voluntary hostage. Why a hostage was needed is not clear.

The traders' ship was launched on 10 March. They called it the *Elizabeth and Susan*: *Elizabeth*, after Mrs Farewell—with whom King and Isaacs had remained friendly, despite their quarrel with her husband—and *Susan* after James Saunders King's mother. By the end of April the *Elizabeth and Susan* was loaded and ready to sail.

When the Zulu delegation boarded the ship, it consisted of those nominated by Shaka—Chief Sotobe and Jacob and their wives—as well as another chieftain, Mbozamboza (known to Isaacs as Unbosom Boozer) and Shaka's body servant, Pikwane. About the traders' party there is some doubt. It is generally admitted that the ship was commanded by John Hutton and that he was accompanied by King, Isaacs (now conveniently recovered), four of the seamen and Elizabeth Farewell. However, Isaacs says that Farewell also made the voyage. This seems very doubtful. Not only did the traders' quarrel make Farewell's inclusion unlikely, but Fynn states quite clearly that Farewell remained in Natal. Farewell's name is not mentioned in any of the ensuing official correspondence. The fact that Isaacs deliberately named Farewell as one of the passengers and continued to refer to him as such only deepens the mystery surrounding this peculiar mission. One can only suppose that Isaacs was trying to create a semblance of unity among the traders on this occasion; thus minimising James Saunders King's responsibility for the undertaking.

The voyage was far from smooth. A heavy swell made most of the passengers sea-sick: Chief Sotobe, King and young John Ross were the only ones not affected. They arrived at Algoa Bay on 4 May, four days after leaving Port Natal. The port officials who boarded the vessel expressed surprise at their safe arrival and were full of compliments for John Hutton's skill as a ship-builder. Next morning, King, Mrs Farewell and Chief Sotobe's delegation were taken ashore. The clothes-conscious Isaacs felt too scruffy to accompany them. In the remnants of a pair of duck trousers, a tattered home-made shirt and a civet-skin cap, he was reluctant to brave the stares of Port Elizabeth's inhabitants. Only when it became apparent that no clothes would be sent to the ship did he and John Hutton jump into a boat and, upon landing, dash straight for the nearest store, where they were fitted out and given their first civilised meal in months.

James Saunders King immediately sent word of his arrival to Cape Town and arranged to have his land grant attested. A few days later he received an official reply telling him to have the Zulu delegation entertained at Government expense until they could be conveyed to the Cape. On no account were the chiefs to be allowed near the frontier. Weeks were to pass without further official instructions from the Cape authorities.

Meanwhile the local military personnel were making their own enquiries. Exactly what was said to James Saunders King is not known, but it is obvious that his sudden arrival at the head of a mission from Shaka was regarded with the utmost suspicion.

One day, while King was away, Isaacs was visited by Major Josias Cloete, the commanding officer at Port Elizabeth. He announced that he had been instructed to find out the object of the mission. Having little faith in Jacob, he wanted Isaacs to interpret for him. The meeting he then had with Chief Sotobe was, according to Isaacs, more of an interrogation than an interview. The Zulu chieftains had been hospitably received in Port Elizabeth and, among other things, had been introduced to strong liquor. Already somewhat befuddled, Chief Sotobe became completely unnerved by Major Cloete's relentless questioning.

Isaacs gave what he described as a verbatim report of the meeting. Although this report was no doubt carefully edited, it is still possible to recognise the drift of Major Cloete's questions. First he wanted to ascertain the motives of Shaka's representatives, to find out how genuine were their powers to negotiate.

'What authority have you from your king to show that you are sent by him?' he asked.

'We have nothing,' replied Sotobe. 'We were sent with Lieutenant King.'

'Have you no sign, or token, or feather, or tiger's tail, or tooth, to show that you were sent by Shaka?'

'We generally send cattle,' said the chief, 'but as the vessel could not take them, Shaka has sent an ivory tusk.'

Having more or less satisfied himself on this point, Cloete endeavoured to persuade Sotobe to accompany him alone to Cape Town. The chief would not hear of it. Obviously acting on Shaka's instructions, he adamantly refused to be separated from James Saunders King. Sotobe's knowledge of the mission's aims appears, in fact, to have been extremely vague. It seems fairly obvious that the Zulu delegates had been included in the mission simply to give weight to King's representations; Shaka had entrusted King with whatever negotiations were intended and Sotobe was reluctant to speak without his white adviser. Nothing Major Cloete could say in this, or subsequent, interviews could change Sotobe's attitude.

'Lieutenant King is a chief in our country,' he explained, 'and sent by Shaka to communicate with the Governor, and we cannot go with any other but him; if we were to leave him what would our king think?'

'What is it that makes you adhere so much to Lieutenant King,' asked Cloete, 'do you always expect him to be with you?'

'Because,' replied Sotobe, 'our king has sent us with him, he is kind to us, and our king has given him every information respecting this mission, and we trust him, as we are unacquainted with your ways.'

This blind trust in James Saunders King frustrated all Cloete's attempts to arrive at a direct understanding with the Zulu delegates. No matter how he bullied Sotobe—in or out of Isaacs's presence— he could never overcome the chief's suspicions. It is obvious from Cloete's questioning of Sotobe that, from the very outset, the British authorities were suspicious of King. And from Sotobe's answers it is equally obvious that, before leaving Natal, King had ensured that he alone would control any negotiations.

When King learned that Major Cloete had been interrogating Sotobe behind his back, he was furious. Such behaviour was, he claimed, a lack of courtesy to him as a British subject. His indignation was echoed, as always, by the faithful Isaacs. But for all their fulminations, both King and Isaacs failed to answer certain essential questions. Neither of them gave a reasoned account of their mission, nor did they explain why they objected so strongly to the Zulu delegates being questioned privately.

Cloete's attitude might indeed have been lacking in courtesy but it was not unreasonable. He had, after all, a duty to confirm James Saunders King's credentials; the only way he could do this was by questioning Shaka's Zulu representatives. This, in itself, should not have unduly troubled men who had nothing to hide. If the mission was as innocuous as King and Isaacs liked to pretend, what harm could there be in Sotobe confiding in Major Cloete?

The churlishness of the British officials on this occasion has often been criticised. Isaacs's description of it as an 'insignificant display of paltry authority and petty power', has been widely accepted. The files of the Colonial Office, however, tell a different story. They show that Major Cloete had good reason for his suspicions: not the least being that Shaka chose this time to launch his long threatened attack on the frontier tribes.

[2]

If Henry Francis Fynn was forced to remain in Natal as a hostage, he was certainly not closely confined. This is evident from his own account of the events that followed the departure of the *Elizabeth and Susan*. He says that three days after King and Isaacs left, Shaka sent to Port Natal requesting that all the Africans at the settlement be sent to Dukuza to assist in recovering some stolen cattle. The command might have been thought suspect but, nevertheless, Fynn and Farewell obeyed it. Fynn then moved to a residence he had established at the Umzimkulu river, some eighty miles south of Port Natal. Two days after he arrived there, he was surprised to learn that Shaka was camped nearby. He was on his way to attack the Mpondo.

Since Fynn had long been aware of Shaka's intention to move against the frontier tribes, this news could hardly have been totally unexpected. All the same, he claims that he now realised why the

Africans from the settlement had been summoned to Dukuza. 'For the first time,' he says, '[I] saw into Shaka's scheme for obtaining our natives and Hottentots, for we had frequently told him we would not let our people assist him in attacking the amaMpondo.'

Fynn went to meet the Zulu army and next day Shaka moved into the Umzimkulu settlement. After a three days rest, the main body of the army was doctored for war and Shaka addressed them. He explained that the expedition had been planned to punish those who had not mourned Nandi and he ordered the warriors to exterminate all those tribes that stood between him and the Cape Colony. He then divided his force: sending one division to attack the Mpondos in the coastal region, while the other marched against the tribes further inland.

Eight days later word was received that the coastal force had passed the Mpondo territory and was about to cross the Umtata river further south. They had met with little opposition from the Mpondos who were reported to have fled as the Zulu force advanced. From then on news of the army's successes, both along the coast and inland, were received daily. In scenes of terrifying violence, Shaka's warriors swept through 'Caffreland'—plundering, looting, burning, killing.

Shaka remained at Fynn's settlement to await the outcome. According to Fynn, he spent most of his time decrying the abilities of his commanders and attempting to justify his attack. Fynn says they had a number of arguments about this. 'I told him,' claims Fynn, 'it was my opinion that if he wished to be on amicable terms with the Colonists a war on the Frontier tribes, as then going on on their borders, could not convince them of his being peacefully disposed.' To this Shaka replied that he could only treat the tribes as enemies; he was not prepared to play with them as the white men did. He pointed out that although the colonists had superior arms and forces, the frontier tribes continued to defy them by stealing their cattle and killing farmers. 'Black people who had committed an offence,' he is supposed to have said, 'should not be talked to but killed.'

Fynn asserts that it was he who persuaded Shaka to call off the attack on the Mpondos. He had met the Mpondo chief, Faku, on earlier trading missions and, knowing this, Shaka sought his advice.

Although the Mpondos had fled the Zulu attack, their crops had been destroyed and many of their women had been captured and sent back to Shaka. The King now asked Fynn whether he thought that Faku would be prepared to become his tributary if he promised to withdraw his army. Fynn thought this would be possible if Shaka returned the women captives and refrained from destroying any more crops. 'He accordingly sent messengers to Faku with proposals of peace,' says Fynn, 'at the same time returning the females as proof of his bona fides; he, moreover, directed his army to withdraw and to stop destroying the corn. Several chiefs of petty tribes in Faku's neighbourhood, with messengers from Faku, returned with the army to thank him for his liberality in thus sparing their lives. They were rewarded with presents of cattle, selected from those that had been taken from them.'

This is all Fynn has to say about Shaka's dealings with the Mpondo chief: significantly he makes no mention of visiting Faku himself.

Shortly after Faku's submission to Shaka, the main body of the Zulu army returned. The messengers who arrived to announce the approach of the triumphant regiments were dealt with severely. Shaka had them beaten with sticks and demanded to know why his commanders had not pressed on to the Cape Colony. The fact that his forces had captured some 30,000 head of cattle did nothing to lessen Shaka's show of anger. He kept the regiments four days before allowing them to appear before him and gave them to understand that only by their agreeing to another expedition—this time north-eastwards, towards Delagoa Bay—would he overlook their failure to reach the Cape. After the army had shown willingness to punish the north-eastern tribes (whom Shaka claimed had been cohabiting with Zulu women and had refused to mourn Nandi's death) the regiments were ritually purified by bathing in the sea. Orders were then given for the return march to Dukuza, where the army was to prepare for the new expedition. Fynn says that Shaka insisted on him accompanying the regiments on their homeward march.

This, according to Fynn's account, ended the campaign against the frontier tribes. It had been swift, deadly and, as far as plunder was concerned, largely successful. But there was more to it than Fynn admits.

News of the Zulu army's advance had quickly reached the Cape
Colony and created panic among the British settlers. All sorts of
exaggerated rumours had spread throughout the frontier districts.
There can be little doubt that James Saunders King's account of
Shaka, published in the *South African Commercial Advertiser* two
years earlier, had done much to make the colonists apprehensive
of a Zulu attack. In a book written at that time and published in
1827, George Thompson, a relatively liberal-minded Cape Town
merchant, had quoted King's account in full. It had confirmed
Thompson's own experiences among refugee tribes, displaced by the
rise of the Zulu empire, and led him to remark: 'The misery already
inflicted by the wars of this barbarian upon Caffer and Bechuana
tribes is incalculable, and is far from being confined to the massacre
and destruction directly occasioned by his arms. By plundering and
driving out the adjoining nations, he has forced them to become
plunderers in their turn, and to carry terror and devastation through
the remotest quarters of Southern Africa.'

Now, with King's warnings of Shaka's intentions still fresh,
the colonists received news of the approach—not of warring
refugee tribes, but of the Zulu King himself—with considerable
alarm.

There can be no doubting the fear and confusion into which the
Cape Colony was plunged. It is graphically illustrated by a report
which appeared in a Hamburg newspaper some months later.
Dated 13 June 1828, from Cape Town, it announced: 'The terrible
Chaka, chieftain of the African tribe of Wotodans [*sic*] advances,
at the head of thirty thousand men, against the Caffres bordering
on the Colony on the east, and there is no doubt that he will push
them upon the neighbouring towns. The proud conqueror has
already sent an Ambassador to us, to inquire whether we intend to
assist the Caffres, and to tell us, that if such were the case, he should
lay the Colony waste, and would try personally whether English
troops were so brave as he had been told. . . . 18th [June] Chaka
has beaten the Caffre King Vosani. 19th [June] Chaka advances
in forced marches towards Cape Town.'

The army authorities met the threat of invasion by mobilising all
available forces, military and civilian. Farmers were ordered to
report to Grahamstown—the inland settler town—and all frontier
posts were manned. On 25 June the Lieutenant-Governor of the

Cape, Major-General Richard Bourke (who had replaced Lord Charles Somerset in 1826) authorised a small force to enter the tribal lands beyond the frontier and investigate the position there. This force, which included a party of frontier Boers and a handful of British settlers, was under the command of Major Dundas, a former Civil Commissioner of the frontier district. It left Grahamstown on 1 July.

Dundas, a tall good-looking cavalry officer who had lost his left hand fighting in Spain, was both experienced and capable. Leading his party through the little-known territory, he was soon aware of the desolation created by the Zulu invasion. The entire countryside had been laid waste; the burnt and gutted kraals were littered with the corpses of women, children and animals. There were few signs of life and it was obvious that the invaders had already retreated. After two weeks hard riding, Dundas decided to leave the bulk of his force at a good grazing spot while he pressed on with a small escort to explore the country beyond the Umtata river. He intended to seek out Faku, whose kraal he had been told was near a large river some miles further on.

It was late in the evening of 18 July that he reached Faku's kraal. When he announced his arrival he was told that the Mpondo chief was away but had been sent for. The following day, after waiting several hours, Dundas began to suspect that Faku was deliberately evading him. He went to the kraal to find out and was not unduly surprised to find Faku hiding there with two or three attendants. He looked, says Dundas, 'most abject and dispirited . . . He was lying with his face upon the ground and only for a moment looked up when I came near him.'

At first, all Dundas's attempts to interest the chief in his mission failed. His overtures were invariably met with a blank stare. He explained that he had come a long way to offer friendship to the Mpondos; that he wished to contact Shaka and warn him that the white people objected to his invasion. On hearing this, he says, Faku 'looked most intently at me, with a view I presume of discovering whether there was any duplicity intended, but again his forehead was placed on the ground, as if dissatisfied with the result of his scrutiny'.

The reason for Faku's fear became apparent only later. Dundas eventually coaxed him into speaking with a small present of beads.

He then explained that the Zulu army had left his territory ten days earlier, after he had agreed to become Shaka's ally. He had lost all his cattle to the Zulu King, apart from a few beasts that had been returned after his submission. When Dundas repeated that the British wished to be his friends, Faku said that he was willing to believe this. 'He had thought otherwise,' he explained, 'as Chaka's people, who had been accompanied by a party of armed Englishmen in the attack upon him, had assured his people that resistance was unavailable & flight to the Westward useless as the Englishmen were the friends of Chaka and that the Englishmen with them were sent by their countrymen to the Westward to assist them in fighting and overcoming all the people between him & the country of the white men.'

When Dundas and his escort arrived, Faku had been convinced that more of Shaka's white friends had come to trouble him. This was why he had been reluctant to meet them. He apologised for his suspicions and told Dundas that 'we, with the exception of Henry Fynn and his small party with Chaka's army, were the only white persons his people had ever seen'.

Some time later, Fynn got to hear that a report had been 'circulated in the Colony of an intended invasion by the Zulus, with me at their head'. This he emphatically denied. He claimed that the British officers had been deliberately misled by their interpreters. There was good reason for this deception. After the Zulu regiments had retreated, an army of marauding tribesmen—displaced by earlier upheavals in Natal and led by Chief Matiwane—had tried to take advantage of the chaos in the frontier districts and plunder the defeated tribes. To counteract this threat, says Fynn, the interpreters had given false reports about him: they had wanted to give the British a strong reason for pursuing their would-be attackers. 'It was,' Fynn claims, 'a very shrewd political move on the part of the Frontier tribes to direct the British forces against Matiwane, as it prevented this chief from taking advantage of their distressed state.'

There is some truth in what he says. After leaving Faku, Dundas met Chief Vusani who informed him of a hostile force at the source of the Umtata river. Believing this force to be the Zulu army, Dundas went in pursuit. Aided by Vusani's warriors he then attacked the invaders and drove them from the area. Not being strong enough to destroy them completely, he did not follow up the attack but returned to the Cape Colony convinced that he had routed the Zulu aggressors. All he had done, in fact, was to repulse Matiwane's army, from whom Chief Vusani's warriors looted 25,000 head of cattle.

In the meantime, General Bourke had ordered a much larger force under Colonel Henry Somerset—son of Lord Charles Somerset —to mobilise on the frontier. Somerset had doubts about Dundas's report of defeating the Zulu army and, in August, hearing that hostilities had been renewed he marched into the tribal area. The frontier chiefs, including Faku, assembled an imposing force to assist Somerset but in the action which followed it was largely British arms which annihilated Matiwane's reorganised army. Even so, Somerset, like Dundas, had mistaken his enemy. 'The valour and enterprise of the troops I had the honour to command,' he reported, 'completely routed the Zoolah [sic] force on the 28th August after an action of several hours.'

The confusion which resulted from Matiwane's intervention has caused Fynn's statements to be accepted. Major Dundas's report has been ignored. Consequently the significance of Shaka's attack on the frontier tribes, coinciding with his mission to the British at Port Elizabeth, has been missed.

There is nothing in the interview that Dundas had with Faku to indicate that the Mpondo chief was trying to mislead the British. On the contrary Faku had first tried to avoid Dundas and when they did meet he was extremely reluctant to talk. What he said about his submission to Shaka and the loss of his cattle, fits in with Fynn's own version. This interview resulted, not in confusing directions from 'Frontier Chiefs', but in a direct statement from Faku. The Mpondo chief stated that Henry Fynn, whom he knew from earlier trading days, had arrived in his territory with a party of armed men. Dundas did not have to rely entirely upon his interpreter's word for this. Before he left Faku's kraal he was given tangible proof that Fynn had accompanied the Zulu army.

'That Fynn was present with the invading Army was verified to me beyond doubt,' he reported, 'as a man who had been wounded by a shot from a gun in both thighs was brought to me who said that the person who shot him afterwards saved his life and dressed his wounds and then told him that his name was Fynn and that his

Father lived in the great Town of the English where Chaka's people intended to go. Though Fakoo [sic] informed me that there were other white people with Fynn I have not been able to ascertain the point, perhaps he may have taken some Hottentots who are in that person's service for white people.'

Even had Faku wished to deceive Dundas, he could hardly have invented fresh gun-shot wounds. Nor would an experienced soldier like Dundas have mistaken such wounds. No other white men had then visited the area and the only guns known to be beyond the Umtata were those of the Europeans in Natal. The incidental information is also convincing. Only Fynn among the traders was likely to dress the wounds of a man he had shot and this characteristic touch seems beyond primitive invention. It is doubtful whether the wounded man would have known, had he not been told, that Fynn's father was then living in Grahamstown. There is, in fact, very good reason to believe that Fynn had assisted Shaka by using his panic-creating firearms.

General Bourke certainly thought so. Writing to the British Colonial Secretary, on 26 August 1828, he said: 'I have reason to believe the English at Port Natal have induced Chaka to suppose that his invasion of Caffreland would be favoured by the Colonial Government. On the late plundering expedition the Zoolah Leaders tried to impress the Tribes with this belief, and the presence in their ranks of an Englishman of the name of Fynn and some other persons either English or Bastard Hottentots, armed with muskets, seemed to prove this assertion.'

Nor did Bourke fail to connect this with James Saunders King's questionable mission at Algoa Bay. 'Mr Jas King whilst at Port Elizabeth,' he continued, 'expressed much disappointment at the front the Colonial Government had taken in opposition to the designs of Chaka, and I have little doubt that these designs were fomented & encouraged by King and the English of his party at Port Elizabeth for their own interested purposes. I have been informed that since the arrival of the English under Farewell & King at that place in 1825 Chaka's Forces have been accompanied on their marauding expeditions by one or more of these Englishmen who by their firearms contributed to the success of the plunderers and shared the plunder as their reward.'

[3]

It is impossible not to notice the discrepancy between the uncritical accounts of James Saunders King written by his devoted followers, Isaacs and Fynn, and the unbiased reports of those who had dealings with him outside Natal. Isaacs and Fynn—particularly the captivated young Isaacs—depict him as a disinterested trader battling against tremendous odds in a primitive country; King's recorded behaviour, both in London and Cape Town, shows him in a different light.

In London his correspondence with the Colonial Office reveals that he misrepresented the purpose of his trading mission in Natal— he made no mention of Farewell or his English backers—and that his main concern was to obtain official support for the venture. On reaching Cape Town he posed as Farewell's would-be saviour and thus gained financial and official backing for his 'rescue bid'. After the *Mary* was wrecked he did not acknowledge his prior intention to build a new vessel, but returned to the Cape in the guise of a ship-wrecked captain responsible for distressed British seamen. His failure to impress the authorities on this occasion led him to appeal to the Governor's opponents and thus gain further financial help. Details of his dealings with Farewell are suspiciously vague, but it is abundantly clear that he set out deliberately to undercut his rival and to win the support of young Fynn, Farewell's most valued helper. Even with Fynn and Isaacs he appears to have been less than honest: they continued to refer to him as a Lieutenant of the Royal Navy—a rank he aspired to but never attained. Precisely how he handled Shaka will never be known, but the events connected with his strange mission to Port Elizabeth seem to indicate a further, more serious, deception.

Having scotched Farewell and obtained a land grant of his own, King had achieved the first of his objectives: he now had an equal claim to the ivory trade in Natal. But he had never intended to set up an isolated trading post. However far he had succeeded in gaining Shaka's confidence, he obviously had doubts about the Zulu King. These doubts had been evident even before he arrived in Natal. From the very outset, King had endeavoured to obtain official protection for his trading venture. He had represented Natal as an

ideal place for British settlement, he had tried to involve the Cape
Government in the ill-fated voyage of the *Mary*, he had publicly
hinted that Shaka posed a threat to the Cape Colony which could be
overcome by taking advantage of the Zulu monarch's willingness to
receive white men. All these stratagems had failed. It had become
increasingly obvious that it would require a *fait accompli* to forge a
link between the Cape Colony and Natal. If the British refused to
approach Shaka, then Shaka must approach the British. In whatever
manner this juncture was arranged, James Saunders King would
have achieved his second objective.

It would surely be naive to imagine—against the background of
King's questionable dealings—that it was a mere coincidence that
Shaka should be attacking the frontier tribes at a time that King was
acting as his ambassador at Port Elizabeth. King clearly staged the
two events simultaneously; thereby hoping that he would be called
upon to bring about a *rapprochement* between the Colonial authorities and the Zulu King. By leaving Fynn to assist Shaka and act as
his adviser, King evidently hoped to control the situation.

But it had not worked out like that. From the moment King
arrived in Port Elizabeth he had been regarded with suspicion. He
had made matters worse by stalling for time—waiting for the attack
to be launched—and by not giving a reasoned explanation of why
he had brought the Zulu chiefs to the Cape Colony. 'The Officer
whom I sent to receive them,' General Bourke told the British
Colonial Secretary, 'has not been able to discover the exact object
of their mission.' No doubt King hoped that when he assumed the
role of mediator, his original intentions would be overlooked.
According to Bourke, he made no secret of his disappointment
when he learned that the Colonial forces intended opposing Shaka.

Everything had gone wrong. Shaka's regiments had failed to
reach the frontier, Major Cloete had become increasingly hostile
and the Zulu delegates had panicked. Bullied and insulted by
Cloete, and thinking the Zulu army was near the frontier, Chief
Sotobe and his companions had several times tried to run off and
make their way back to Natal by land. This only confirmed Major
Cloete's suspicions that they had been sent to the Cape as spies.
Finally, realising that there was nothing to be gained in Port
Elizabeth, the mission prepared to return to Natal. Here, at least,
they received prompt assistance from the Cape Government.

As soon as he received Major Dundas's report of Fynn's presence with the Zulu army, General Bourke detailed H.M.S. *Helicon* to take King's party back to Port Natal. 'The messengers from Chaka,' he reported to the Colonial Office on 28 August, 'of whose arrival at Port Elizabeth on the vessel of Mr Jas King one of the English party settled at Port Natal, I have had the honour to inform you in my previous despatches, left Algoa Bay on the 9 inst and were landed at Port Natal a few days after. To these persons and to Mr King, who returned with them, the views of the Colonial Government with respect to the invasion of Caffreland by the Zoolas have been explicitly declared . . . I am in hopes that as King is now fully convinced of the determination of the Colonial Government to oppose Chaka's progress in Caffreland, he may persuade that Chief to remain within his own ample territory, or if not, to turn his arms to some other quarter where less resistance may be expected.'

Nathaniel Isaacs, John Hutton and the rest of the seamen made their own way back to Port Natal in the *Elizabeth and Susan*. They were met at the settlement by Fynn who, according to Isaacs, informed them of what had happened during their absence. But evidently they had already been told that white men had been seen with the Zulu army, for Isaacs found it necessary to imply that Henry Ogle (one of Farewell's party) had been actively involved in the attack, not Fynn. Isaacs's version of Fynn's experiences is somewhat different from that given later by Fynn himself. Isaacs claims that when Shaka divided his forces—one to attack the coastal region, the other to march inland—he placed 'Mr Farewell's party with one division and our party with another, Ogle and the Hottentots accompanying them, whilst Messrs Farewell and Fynn sojourned with the king.' But, in his haste to shift the blame, Isaacs seems to have forgotten that he had earlier included Farewell in the mission to Port Elizabeth! There is reason to believe that Henry Ogle did indeed accompany Shaka's inland force, but whether he was actively engaged in the fighting is not clear. Certainly he was not the man referred to by Major Dundas.

The confused way in which Isaacs and Fynn report the entire episode merely emphasises their own participation in James Saunders King's devious plans.

But King's plans were soon to be forgotten. Trouble-fraught as had been their mission to the Cape Colony, their return to Natal was to prove disastrous. The events of the next few weeks were as unexpected as they were extraordinary.

James Saunders King had arrived back at Port Natal sick and depressed. Leaving H.M.S. *Helicon*, he had boarded the *Elizabeth and Susan* still anchored outside the bay; he was looking, noticed Isaacs, very ill. John Hutton's handling of the *Elizabeth and Susan* caused him further worry. Although the schooner successfully cleared the sand-bar, she had no sooner entered the bay than she ran ashore on a bank. Luckily there was no serious damage, but the ill-omened circumstances of their arrival were further emphasised when the Hottentot, Michael, was drowned while attempting to swim out to the ship. By the time King reached shore he was on the point of collapse. He had to be carried to his hut. His face was ashen and his bowels disordered. Fynn, after consulting Buchan's *Medical Work*, diagnosed a serious liver complaint.

It was left to Isaacs to report to Shaka on their visit to Port Elizabeth. Before doing so, he opened a sealed case which General Bourke had sent as a gift to the Zulu King. He was hoping that the novelty of the present would do something to offset the failure of the mission. He was quickly disillusioned. The case contained nothing more than some useless sheets of copper, a few cheap knives and trinkets and a piece of scarlet broadcloth. Knowing that such a paltry offering would only increase Shaka's disappointment, King and Isaacs added a valuable looking-glass and an assortment of medicines from their own scanty stock.

Even so, Isaacs was far from optimistic when, accompanied by Chief Sotobe and Jacob, he set off for Dukuza a few days later. On their way they met a messenger. He informed them that Shaka was furious with Sotobe for not reporting to him sooner and that, in his rage, he had thrown a bottle of medicine to the ground and 'broke it into a thousand pieces'. Isaacs was even further alarmed when one of his servants informed him that Sotobe and Jacob were concocting a story which would place the blame for the mission's failure entirely on the white men.

Isaacs's account of his meeting with Shaka is, of course, suspect. He claims that the King received him indifferently and looked at the presents with disdain. Sotobe then stood up and launched into a tirade against the Europeans; disparaging the size of Port Elizabeth and urging Shaka to have nothing to do with the British whose monarch was inferior to himself.

Another account of the meeting, reported in a Cape newspaper, says that Jacob joined in the attack by stating 'that Capt King was an outcast; that he was not an Englishman, and was not known by George's people; that the presents sent by the Government had been appropriated by Capt King to his own purposes; and that he was an Impostor'. This has a ring of truth about it, but Isaacs makes no mention of Jacob's intervention. He claims that Shaka merely asked why the presents had been taken out of the case and then accused Sotobe of not looking after his interests. He seemed satisfied with Isaacs's explanation that the gifts had been unpacked so that they could easily be transported and said that he was more pleased with the gifts from James Saunders King than those which General Bourke had sent. His interest was confined—if Isaacs is to be believed—to the presents; about the mission he appears to have asked nothing.

The report in the Cape newspaper was probably given by John Cane, who was at Dukuza when Isaacs arrived. Cane was also present that evening when Shaka examined Isaacs's gifts in private. According to Isaacs, it was then that Shaka's anger became apparent. He went through the medicines, enquiring the use of each, and when he discovered that the longed-for macassar oil had not been included he flew into a rage. He said he would send John Cane to the Governor of the Cape to find out if any of the presents had been stolen and to obtain the macassar oil. When Cane objected and explained that he had nothing decent to wear, Shaka seized an old Zulu cloak, threw it at Cane, and told him to prepare to leave.

This, at any rate, is Isaacs's story. 'The extraordinary violence of the king's rage with me,' he says, 'was mainly occasioned by that absurd nostrum, the hair oil.' He blamed Farewell for having told the King about macassar oil in the first place. For three days Shaka raged and stormed, threatening Isaacs with execution. Finally the young man decided that it would be safer if he left Dukuza.

On his return to Port Natal, he found that James Saunders King was much worse. Fynn, who had been treating him, now decided that he was suffering from pleurisy or dysentery. He dosed him with all the specifics mentioned in his medical book—calomel, jalap and Dover powder—and kept him on a diet of rhubarb, cinnamon and rice water. But there were no signs of recovery. King grew weaker by the day. Fynn and Isaacs sat by his side trying to cheer him. Not all their efforts were successful. When Isaacs told him that Shaka had sent John Cane overland to the Cape Colony, King became very agitated. 'Oh Nat,' he cried, 'what a pity it is that you have not an opportunity of writing to the Colony. Cane has gone away to injure me, that was the reason he did not call. Oh! What will my friends think of me?'

King died that evening, 7 September 1828, less than a month after his return from the Cape Colony. His last hours, from the accounts of Fynn and Isaacs, were reminiscent of a death scene in a Gothic novel. 'Mr Isaacs being in attendance,' wrote Fynn, 'called Mr Hutton and myself, he [King] requested us to take his hands, which we did; he spent several minutes in prayer, begging we would do the same for him. He said his only wish to live was for his dear mother and sister, praying for them, us, and himself alternately . . . he requested 60 drops of laudanum, and showed evident signs of a deranged mind and approaching dissolution . . . Mr King desired to be particularly remembered to his boy Jack (John Ross).'

They buried him on a height overlooking the bay. Hutton and the seamen carried the corpse, Fynn read the burial service and Isaacs cried. The funeral was attended by everyone at the settlement, including Farewell. The grave was marked by a large stone. When Shaka heard of King's death, he expressed sorrow and announced that he now regarded Isaacs as the traders' spokesman.

Fynn and Isaacs took seriously King's wish for them to communicate with the Cape Colony. They were equally anxious to counteract any harm that might be caused by John Cane, who they regarded as Farewell's agent. Fynn's younger brother, Frank, had returned on the *Elizabeth and Susan* and, shortly after King died, Fynn pencilled a despatch for his brother to take overland to the Colonial Government.

Young Frank Fynn, accompanied by two Africans and a Hottentot, marched along the coast and arrived safely at Grahamstown on 5 January 1829. He gave his despatches to his father, who was acting as correspondent for the *South African Commercial Advertiser*. A report of King's death appeared in the newspaper on 17 January. Not only did it describe the dying man's illness, but it viciously attacked Farewell for refusing to visit King shortly before he died.

This same story was later repeated by Isaacs and has been regarded as evidence of Farewell's callousness. However, Farewell emphatically denied it. He claimed that when he was first sent for he had no idea that King's illness was serious; when he did realise that King was dying he was unable to hurry because his leg had recently been dislocated. 'I set off for Mr King's habitation,' he said, 'where, I am sorry to say, I did not arrive till after his decease, and which no person could have regretted more than myself.' Even Isaacs admits that Farewell attended King's funeral.

The traders had need to stick together at this time. The failure of their mission, followed by the death of the most persuasive member of their party, made them apprehensive as to how Shaka would receive them in future. How much Farewell knew of his rival's intrigues is uncertain but, a week after King's funeral, he agreed to patch up his quarrel with Fynn and Isaacs and to accompany them to Dukuza. The truce was more diplomatic than real: they had to present a united front.

Shaka had summoned them to Dukuza so that the ritual attending King's death could be observed. When they arrived they discovered Shaka outside his kraal, presiding at the trial of six men accused of stealing corn. The traders had hardly sat down before two of the accused were ordered to be killed; two others tried to escape, were caught, and stoned to death. Isaacs was convinced, as always, that Shaka had staged these executions simply to frighten the white men.

When Shaka spoke to them, however, he was friendly enough. He seemed to regret King's death and assured them that he had recalled John Cane. His only complaint was that they had neglected the Zulu custom of bringing a calf for the cleansing ritual and he therefore had to supply an animal himself. The ritual took place next morning. One of the African servants cut the calf between the middle ribs and extracted the caul from its liver. The traders then approached Shaka and each of them took turns in sprinkling the caul around the King. This done, Shaka spoke in praise of the dead man and ordered the mourning period to end. Later, he presented the white men with two bullocks: one for their own use, the other to be sacrificed in memory of James Saunders King.

The rest of the day was taken up with discussions of a new mission which Shaka intended them to make to the Cape. Isaacs claims that he was created a Zulu chief and granted a tract of land similar to that formerly held by King. What Farewell had to say about all this is not recorded.

The traders set off for Port Natal with Shaka's good wishes ringing in their ears. It was the last time any of them saw him. On 24 September, five days after their return, a messenger from Dukuza staggered into the settlement, exhausted from running. He brought the most terrifying news. Shaka had been assassinated.

9

'WHAT IS THE MATTER, MY FATHER'S CHILDREN?'

EXACTLY WHAT HAPPENED at Dukuza on that September evening in 1828, has never been recorded. For once there was no European at the royal kraal with pencil and paper handy. Many versions of Shaka's assassination were to circulate, most of them contradict each other in detail, but they all more or less agree on the main points. It is also possible to trace with reasonable accuracy the outline of events leading up to Shaka's murder.

On his way back to Dukuza from the campaign against the frontier tribes, Shaka had been in a particularly sullen mood. He seemed to go out of his way to order killings. It was, of course, customary for him, immediately after a campaign, to execute those suspected of cowardice but, on this occasion, his wrath remained unappeased for days. Some idea of his smouldering anger—and the power he exercised—can be gained from an incident which occurred shortly before the army reached Dukuza. A number of herdboys were accused of sucking milk from cows in their charge. When it became obvious that the boys were guilty, Shaka flew into a rage and told them to report to the army (a mile or so distant) and say that he had ordered them to be put to death. Meekly the boys did as they were told and were instantly killed. There was no escaping the King's vengeance.

The army was welcomed home with noisy victory celebrations. Fynn, who had accompanied the regiments, left Dukuza for Port Natal the following day. Farewell was also at Dukuza at this time and remained there a while longer; it was from him that the Governor of the Cape later learned of the events which followed the army's return.

Shaka lost no time in organising his threatened campaign against the north-eastern tribes. Within days he had mustered his exhausted army and despatched them on a second gruelling expedition.

According to Farewell's report, he 'sent a force of about 3000
fighting men to the Eastwards and the Northwards of Mozambique
for the express purpose it is supposed of weakening his own Tribe &
exercising upon them more than usual brutality; this force marched
with provisions only for the advance & with orders not to fight until
that was expended.'

Fynn makes no mention of Shaka's intention to weaken his own
forces. If Farewell is correct, it could explain the haste with which
this second expedition was launched. Shaka is usually depicted as a
fanatic at this time: drunk with power, determined to crush all who
opposed him, acting in a maniacal fury. But it is also possible that
there was a method in his apparent madness. Those planning to kill
him were already active. Fynn was to claim that the assassination
plot 'had been long in contemplation' and was originally to have
been put into effect at his trading post during the frontier campaign
but 'an opportunity was wanting'. Shaka may well have got wind of
the plot and decided to send the army on an exhausting campaign
to prevent his enemies from exploiting dissatisfaction among the
warriors. This would explain Farewell's comment. It is, perhaps,
not without significance that four of Shaka's brothers (usually kept
well in the background) accompanied the army and that two of these
brothers—Dingane and Mhlangana—were among the leading
conspirators.

Shaka was undoubtedly afraid of *something*. Shortly after the
army had left, he realised he was defenceless and immediately
recalled the baggage-carriers. The warriors were instructed to
shoulder their own equipment, while Shaka formed the baggage
boys into a regiment which he called *Nyosi* (the Bees). As always, he
appears to have had more faith in the youngsters than in the
seasoned warriors.

News of the army's progress was prevented from reaching Shaka
by a hostile Swazi chief who evaded the Zulu regiments and then
intercepted and killed their messengers. The resulting silence seems
to have unnerved Shaka completely. Determined to assert his
authority, he turned upon the wives of his departed warriors. The
women were rounded up, accused of witchcraft, and then indiscriminately massacred. Horrifying stories were to be told about this
ghastly slaughter. It is said, for instance, that on one occasion
Shaka ordered the stomachs of one hundred pregnant women to be

sliced open so that he could examine their foetus. How true this is one does not know—it is typical of the stories told at the time; but it is emphatically stated that the killings took place. 'Dead bodies were to be seen in every direction,' says Fynn, 'not less than 400 or 500 being killed during the absence of their husbands at war.' Farewell also reported the massacre but the details he gives are so different from those given by Fynn that it is obvious that they were both relying on garbled accounts.

But there was nothing Shaka could do to ensure his safety. If he was hoping that his commanders would control his brothers, he was sadly mistaken. Dingane and Mhlangana, two deadly inseparables, had no intention of marching beyond reach of their quarry. Feigning illness—as they had done during the frontier campaign—they evaded the chieftain appointed to watch over them and made their way back to Dukuza. Here they contacted their fellow conspirator, Mbopha, Shaka's servant, and put the finishing touches to their fratricidal plan.

There was nothing particularly clever or subtle about Shaka's assassination. It was carried out boldly, openly, within sight of a crowd of witnesses. So simple was it that one wonders why the brothers had waited so long: there must have been many occasions as 'opportune' as that which they chose.

Late in the afternoon of 22 September, a party of frontier tribesmen arrived at Dukuza with a gift of crane feathers and animal skins. They had been expected earlier and Shaka, somewhat annoyed at having been kept waiting, went to receive them in a small dung-strewn kraal close to his main residence. He was accompanied by a few elderly indunas. Hardly had he sat down than he began slating the tribesmen for arriving late. It is not certain whether Shaka's servant, Mbopha, was present throughout the meeting or whether, as some say, he arrived later carrying a knob-headed stick in one hand and concealing a short stabbing spear beneath an animal-skin cloak. All agree that Mbopha had reason to fear Shaka's anger. Earlier, it seems, Shaka had dreamed that Mbopha had betrayed him and Mbopha had recognised the dream—like all Shaka's 'dreams'—as a threat to his own life. This may well have influenced the part he played in the assassination plot.

Dingane and Mhlangana had concealed themselves behind the kraal fence. While Shaka was berating the tribesmen, one of them signalled to Mbopha to clear the kraal. Springing to his feet, Mbopha joined in Shaka's denunciations. He then rushed at the tribesmen, beating them with his stick and driving them from the kraal. This unexpected move so astonished Shaka that he rose. He was about to recall the tribesmen when Dingane and Mhlangana leapt the fence and rushed at him with their spears. 'You shall never see the sun set again,' Dingane is said to have shouted as he sank his assegai into Shaka's back. Whether it was he or Mhlangana who struck first is not clear; in the frenzied stabbing all was confused. Somehow Shaka managed to push his attackers off. 'What is the matter, my father's children?' he gasped, as he reeled towards the kraal gate. Outside the kraal he stumbled and fell. The three conspirators closed in.

Some say that Shaka died pleading for mercy. One version has it, however, that before the final blow, he warned his brothers: 'As soon as I go, this country of ours will be overrun in every direction by the white man. Mark my words.' His prophecy was long remembered.

They left his body lying outside the kraal all night. Having steeled themselves to murder, the brothers were now terrified. They hoped the hyenas would finish their work and drag the gigantic corpse away. The thought of Shaka's ghost was as frightening as had been his living presence. Nor could the brothers find much reassurance among the people of Dukuza. An attempt was made to celebrate Shaka's death; to rejoice at the downfall of a tyrant. But it proved a half-hearted affair. A bullock was sacrificed and a war song chanted by the brave few who remained at the royal kraal: for the most part, the inhabitants of Dukuza, appalled by the crime, fled to spend the night hiding in the bush.

The next day Chief Sotobe and some of the elders asked for Shaka to be given a fitting burial. Dingane and Mhlangana, still extremely uncertain of themselves, agreed. They requested Sotobe to suggest some means by which 'they could repress Shaka's anger so that when he became a spirit he might assist them in their endeavours'. Sotobe recommended that they put a piece of cut loin cloth in Shaka's mouth to ensure the dead King's protection. When this had been done, a grave was dug and Shaka was placed in it and covered with a blanket. All his personal possessions, including several tons of beads and brass, were buried with him. After the grave had been filled in, a hut was built over it, and a guard set to watch the spot.

The mighty Shaka, founder of the Zulu nation. This
drawing by James Saunders King is the only authentic
portrait of the first Zulu King.

Two Zulu youths in dancing costume.
From the painting by G. F. Angas.

Zulu warrior in visiting dress.
From the drawing by G. F. Angas.

Lieutenant Francis George Farewell.
The only known portrait of the leader of the first
trading mission to Natal.

The Old House Museum, Durban

Henry Francis Fynn in middle age.
From the portrait by Frederick I'Ons painted shortly after
the disillusioned Fynn had left Natal.

The intense and dedicated Captain Allen Gardiner,
first missionary to arrive in Zululand.

Dingane in dancing costume.
When the Zulu King was shown
this and other drawings by Allen Gardiner,
he said they "hit him off exactly."

Dingane kills his brother. A modern African interpretation
of the assassination of Shaka, with the dying Zulu King
depicted as a Christ-like figure.
From the water colour by T. Livingstone Sango.

The approach to Dingane's kraal, emGungundlovu,
an impression by Captain Allen Gardiner, who
described it as looking like "a distant race-course."

The interior of Dingane's royal hut. The Zulu King
lies at the entrance surrounded by his women.
From the drawing by Captain Allen Gardiner.

(above) Kraal of Zulu refugees living in Natal.
South African Library

(top right) Christianity comes to Natal. One of the first
mission stations established near the border of Zululand.
South African Library

(opposite) The death of John Cane and Robert Biggar
at the battle on the Tugela, 17 April 1838. From a contemporary drawing.
Cape Archives

A romanticised portrait of Andries Pretorius, leader of
the victorious Boer commando against Dingane.

Mpande, Zulu King, brother of Shaka and
Dingane. From the portrait painted by G. F. Angas in the 1840s.

The captive Cetshwayo being deported from
Zululand at Port Durnford, 4 September 1879.

Cetshwayo photographed in exile.

Dinuzulu, Cetshwayo's luckless heir, as a young man.

Even in death, Shaka's fearsome power proved too strong for his murderers to ignore.

[2]

'What is the matter, my father's children?' Shaka had gasped. It is a question which has never been satisfactorily answered. Indeed few, if any, have considered that an answer was necessary. Shaka's death has been accepted in the simplest of terms. By and large, he has been depicted as a blood-thirsty tyrant whose assassination was inevitable. Blood-thirsty he might well have been, tyrant he undoubtedly was; but to accept his death as the unavoidable result of a ruthless despotism is an oversimplification. It is necessary to repeat his dying question: What indeed was the matter which drove his father's children to kill him?

The usual explanation given is based on Zulu tradition. It is said that the assassination plot originated in his own family. One of his father's maiden sisters—an embittered virago, Mkabayi (known as the Wild Cat)—is claimed to have harboured a vicious resentment against Shaka. Mkabayi was, by all accounts, a strange woman. From birth she had been overshadowed by a Zulu taboo. She was one of twin daughters born to Shaka's grandfather, Jama, and a long-held superstition decreed that the birth of twins was unlucky. Usually one of the twins was killed at birth but Jama had refused to dispose of either of his daughters and Mkabayi had suffered the stigma of her birth throughout her life. Whether she had befriended Shaka's mother, the outcast Nandi, or whether she resented her brother's unwanted wife, is a matter for contention: but she undoubtedly hated Shaka.

There is reason to believe that Shaka was unaware of Mkabayi's hatred for, when he usurped the Zulu chieftainship, he appointed his embittered spinster aunt as overseer of one of his regiments. The appointment did nothing to placate Mkabayi. For years she had schemed the overthrow of Shaka, so that her favourite nephew, Dingane, could take his place. Nandi's death, it is said, provided her with the opportunity she sought. By claiming that Shaka had deliberately poisoned Nandi and then used her death to persecute his people, Mkabayi was able to play on Dingane's ambition and involve him in the assassination plot.

There is undoubtedly a great deal of truth in this story and it has been readily believed. *Cherchez la femme* has, after all, tremendous popular appeal. Nevertheless, by itself, it does not explain the motivation and timing of Shaka's assassins. Whatever Mkabayi's feelings about Nandi were, they could hardly have influenced Dingane and Mhlangana. Like the rest of Shaka's family, they cared little about Nandi, and her death would not have roused them to vengeance. Nothing in Dingane's later career bears out the contention that he was so appalled by Shaka's cruelty after Nandi's death that he decided to rid Zululand of a tyrant. In fact, it is fairly obvious that Dingane and Mhlangana were spurred on purely by ambition; the question of why they acted when they did remains unanswered.

Shaka's filial massacres might well have turned many of his people against him, but there is nothing to suggest that his assassins were relying on popular dissatisfaction to achieve their ends. They returned to Dukuza alone; they acted in secret; and they did so a full year after Nandi's death. Shaka's dreadful fury during the mourning period had long since abated and those wishing to take advantage of the massacres for their own ends had, by that time, missed their opportunity. Indeed, unless something else had happened to embolden the conspirators, Nandi's death—for all Mkabayi's intrigues—seems too far removed to provide a satisfactory explanation of Shaka's murder.

But something else *had* happened. This, of course, was the ill-fated mission to Port Elizabeth and Shaka's abortive attempt to contact the Cape Colony. These events occurred too close in time to Shaka's assassination for them to be ignored.

Unfortunately the only full account of the happenings in Natal at that time is the one given by Henry Francis Fynn. For obvious reasons, Fynn did not tell the whole truth. However, what he does say is not without interest. Fynn's explanation of why the Zulu army failed to contact the Cape Colony is simple. He says that, at the last moment, Shaka recalled his commanders and secretly instructed them to turn back before they reached the frontier. Why Shaka—who had promised to 'open the road' to the white men—should have given such instructions is left conveniently vague. Moreover, Fynn (evidently sticking as close to the truth as possible) then appears to contradict himself. For he goes on to relate how, when messengers arrived to announce the return of the regiments, they were beaten with sticks. 'Shaka,' he says, 'wanted to know why they had not reached the Colony and defeated the tribes according to his orders.' This apparent *volte face* fits in well with the general description of Shaka as a capricious monster who deliberately contrived punishments for his warriors to indulge his power lust. But when one knows of the traders' involvement in the frontier campaign, a more logical explanation presents itself.

The only motive for James Saunders King's mission was that it should coincide with the Zulu army's arrival at the frontier. That the army did not reach the frontier means that something had gone wrong. Shaka's military tactics are well known; he rarely moved against an enemy without the help of advance spies. If these spies discovered that the colonists were arming themselves, not, as they had been told, to welcome them but to fight them, a quick retreat was inevitable. The Zulu commanders had sufficient experience of the traders' firearms not to risk advancing against a fully armed force. There is good reason to doubt that Shaka gave his regiments instructions to turn back before reaching the frontier. It seems far more likely that his anger at their return was genuine. The entire campaign had been something of a fiasco.

That the first attempt on Shaka's life was planned at this time is not without significance. Nor can Shaka's immediate decision to send the army on a second exhausting campaign be dismissed as a tyrant's whim. Whatever else Shaka might have been, he was no fool. Before James Saunders King had left Natal, Shaka had promised his people great results from contact with the white men. Just how extensive these promises were will never be known. When his army returned, he must have realised that, not only had his plans misfired, but that he had been misled by James Saunders King. For the first time (at least in recorded history) the all-powerful Shaka had been exposed as a dupe. No despot can afford to display an Achilles heel or admit to mistakes—particularly if he knows that his enemies are watching for signs of weakness.

The only detailed account of Shaka after his return from the frontier campaign is that given by Nathaniel Isaacs. From this one gets the impression of a hysterical fanatic behaving like a frustrated child. Certainly Isaacs had a basis of truth to work from. Shaka was undoubtedly furious with the traders for deceiving him and, as always, his anger was terrifying. When Isaacs went to report the failure of the mission, he felt the full weight of the King's wrath. 'Mr Isaacs,' Fynn reported to the Cape Colony, 'was very ill-treated, and his life threatened, and the situation of the Europeans rendered very unsafe.' Isaacs admits that his life was threatened but implies that this had nothing to do with the mission; it was merely the result of his neglecting to bring Shaka the promised macassar oil. The picture he draws of Shaka searching through the medicines and petulantly ordering John Cane to leave for the Cape to enquire about stolen gifts, is greatly distorted. It is one of the few episodes in Isaacs's account that is open to verification.

The truth is that John Cane was entrusted with a serious mission. He was sent to the Cape Colony with two Zulu chiefs, one of them being Mbozamboza (Umbosom Booser) who had accompanied James Saunders King on the *Elizabeth and Susan*. When the party arrived at Grahamstown, on 5 October 1828, Cane was hailed as the first white man to cross 'Caffreland'. (He had beaten young Frank Fynn to it by precisely three months.) The purpose of his mission was reported to the newly arrived Governor of the Cape, Sir Lowry Cole. Sir Lowry immediately gave instructions for Cane and the chiefs to be escorted to Cape Town by Captain Aitchison of the Cape Mounted Rifles. They arrived there at the beginning of November.

'The subject of the communication which Cane was directed by Chaka to make to me,' Cole reported to the Colonial Office, 'is as follows.

'Chaka expressed himself anxious to maintain friendly relations with the white people & willing to comply with their wishes when he clearly comprehended them but that from Mr King having told him one thing & Mr Farewell another he could not believe either, he therefore requested that an accredited agent from the Government might be sent to him in order that he might clearly and fully understand the desire of the Government to which he was perfectly willing to conform but which he might from ignorance oppose unless conveyed to him in the manner stated. Chaka added that he was not disposed to molest the frontier tribe of Caffers provided they did not provoke him by insulting messages (which he alleges

Hynza had done) and would permit him free intercourse with the colony an object which he had very much at heart & which he was determined to obtain at all risks, he particularly requested that a seal, some medicines, clothing and other articles might be sent to him.'

These are hardly the ravings of a petulant fanatic. Cole's report makes it abundantly clear that the frontier campaign had been launched primarily to enable Shaka to contact the whites in the Cape Colony. (Yet Fynn claimed that he had given his commanders secret orders to turn back.) It is also evident that Shaka blamed the intrigues of the traders for the failure of the campaign. Cane was given these instructions shortly after James Saunders King had returned from Port Elizabeth; it is obvious that, by that time, Shaka had lost faith in both Farewell and King. His anger with Isaacs is understandable. It had little, or nothing, to do with macassar oil. Medicines are included among his particular requests but these are secondary to the main object of Cane's mission: there is no specific mention of hair oil. All in all, Shaka had acted in a statesmanlike way. For Isaacs to pretend otherwise shows, once again, that he was trying to play down the failure of King's mission and to present Shaka as an irresponsible savage.

It is interesting, also, to note Sir Lowry Cole's reaction to this straightforward embassy. He displayed none of the distrust shown earlier towards James Saunders King and was quick to recognise John Cane's honesty. 'John Cane,' he reported, 'the man entrusted with this mission went in the service of Mr Farewell to Port Natal on his first settlement there & has since that period resided in Chaka's territory. He appears shrewd and intelligent & gave the enclosed statement of the state of Chaka's Country & that through which he passed.'

British officials have always been a favourite Aunt Sally for those writing about nineteenth-century Africa. It is therefore natural that the reports spread by King and Isaacs about the churlish treatment meted out to them at Port Elizabeth have been uncritically accepted. Cane's reception, however, shows that the Cape authorities were quite capable of recognising a reliable man when they saw one. Major Cloete's distrust of the first mission from Shaka undoubtedly resulted from the shifty behaviour of James Saunders King.

Big, bluff John Cane was a carpenter in the days when carpenters wrote little, if at all. He appears to have left no record of his experiences in Natal. This is a pity. Had he done so, a different picture of Shaka might have emerged. Certainly there was a distinct change in the tone of the newspapers at Cape Town after his arrival there. 'The frightful stories told of King Chaka,' reported the *South African Commercial Advertiser* on 15 November 1828, 'and which have for several years appeared in the English newspapers uncontradicted, are, we have reason to believe, mere fabrications. His enormous army, his shocking barbarities, and his projected conquests, partook too much of the marvellous not to gain easy credit among people fond of excitement. There are few monsters in the world. . . . If Chaka cut down the children of his subjects like hay, we suspect his army would have dwindled to something less than thirty thousand men.'

Three days earlier, an official statement from Government House had announced publicly that 'Chaka conceives he has great reason to complain of Mr King's conduct to himself and his Messengers.' It went on to say that Shaka had asked for a missionary to reside in his country and that Captain Aitchison had been despatched overland to Natal to establish 'a good understanding with Chaka'. News of the Zulu King's assassination had not then reached the Cape.

When one weighs the traders' deceit, exaggerations and evasions against the few available facts, it is obvious that they were doing their utmost to gloss over the importance of their ill-fated mission and the frontier campaign. Their failure to produce the results they had promised from these linked events must have influenced Shaka's actions prior to his death. If, as Cane's report stated, Shaka had lost faith in James Saunders King, there were others who drew confidence from the white man's betrayal. Shaka was no longer omnipotent. For once he seemed to be losing his grip. His behaviour after the return of his regiments from the frontier territory appears to have been inspired, not by a mad power lust, but by desperation. Events were to prove that his fears were well founded. A little over a month after the frontier campaign he was dead.

There is something reminiscent of a Shakespearean tragedy in the fact that Shaka's death followed so closely upon that of James Saunders King. Soon other actors were to be violently removed from the stage. The connection between these deaths is tenuous but significant. James Saunders King had much to answer for. He was one of the first Europeans the Zulu people had known. His intrigues might well have contributed to Shaka's downfall: they could also have sowed distrust of the white man among Shaka's successors.

[3]

As far as is known, Shaka was forty-one when he died. If he had come to power in 1817—the year Dingiswayo is said to have died—he had been the effective ruler of Zululand for eleven years. In that time he had forged one of the mightiest empires the African continent has ever known. Under his leadership, his small insignificant clan had risen from obscurity and given their name to an allpowerful nation. During his lifetime the Zulu army had been organised into a fearsome military machine which had transformed the age-old pattern of southern African society. The Nguni system of clanships and petty chieftainships had been replaced by a single, authoritarian state, feared by its neighbours and acknowledged far beyond its borders. Few leaders in history have accomplished so much, so quickly. Shaka not only established Zulu supremacy but ensured the lasting renown of his nation. For generations to come the word Zulu was to be synonymous with might. It was an awe-inspiring achievement.

But, like all such achievements, it was not come by gently. Shaka was a tyrant; he could have been nothing else. He rose amid appalling bloodshed. It has been estimated that no less than two million people died as a result of the upheavals created by Shaka. When the white men first arrived in Natal, they found the country desolate, the landscape littered with skeletons. Shaka reigned supreme because he had obliterated all semblance of opposition. He took no advice, he demanded blind obedience; he was intolerant, ruthless and inflexible. He knew nothing of the softer virtues, had he done so he would not have achieved what he did: his strength was derived from his callousness.

Living as he did, in the first quarter of the nineteenth century, it was inevitable that he should be compared with a contemporary despot: he has been called the Black Napoleon. But the comparison is more romantic than real. The system instigated by Shaka was unique. To compare it, even superficially, with that of a European power is misleading. The aims, methods and values of the white men were unknown to Shaka. The society he ruled and the opponents he fought were so far removed from the regimes of nineteenth-century Europe that to set his achievements against those of a sophisticated conqueror like Napoleon is meaningless. Shaka had no set objectives and was uninfluenced by political and moral considerations. He was guided by intuition; he learned from his own experience. It is necessary to realise this to appreciate his extraordinary genius.

Shocking as was his apparent cruelty, this also must be judged in isolation. The ethics of the white man meant nothing to him. He relied on his own interpretation of humanity. Treachery, disobedience and cowardice were, for him, the cardinal sins; he did not regard life as sacred—any more than did most of his subjects. When white men, fresh from Regency England, were plunged into a society that recognised none of their values, they were appalled. The fact that that society was rigidly organised only increased their horror: the frightful punishments inflicted by Shaka appeared to them all the more cold blooded. It was difficult to reconcile fine discipline with primitive values. But there was nothing so exceptional about the grim Zulu penal code. Shaka was by no means the only African ruler to order summary executions; he was, however, one of the few whose activities have been reported in vivid detail.

One must accept that European and African values were often irreconcilable. Nowhere was this divergence more apparent than in an early conversation between Fynn and Shaka. The Zulu King was flabbergasted to learn that the white men imprisoned offenders for months, even years. Such punishment seemed to him far more sadistic than the tortures he inflicted. To kill a man, however painfully, was preferable to the living death of confinement. As a warrior he could imagine nothing worse than a long, meaningless captivity.

'There are few monsters,' declared the *South African Commercial Advertiser* at the time of John Cane's visit to Cape Town. To make its point, the newspaper quoted the philosopher Hume. 'When I hear of a prodigy,' said Hume, 'I ask, whether it is more likely that this gentleman, the narrator, is deceived or wishes to deceive me, or that nature should change? I have known men lie but I have found nature very constant.'

The quotation is not without relevance. Reports of Shaka spread by the traders, make him appear an unnatural fiend whose activities went far beyond the dictates of even the most primitive code. He is shown as a mass murderer, a depraved ogre who revelled in the tortures he devised and drooled over his victims. 'History,' said James Saunders King, 'perhaps does not furnish an instance of a more despotic and cruel monster than Chaka.' Isaacs never lost an opportunity to describe Shaka's sadism in the most lurid detail. He more than supports King's theory. 'I am not aware that history,' he repeats, 'either ancient or modern, can produce so horrible and detestable a savage. He has deluged his country with innocent blood; he has forgotten the most sacred ties of affection, and, by a double murder as it were, compelled the agonising father to be the executioner of his own son, and the son to become an inhuman mutilator of his own mother.' But Isaacs was a sensitive soul. He claims that the only reason that he steeled himself to give such horrid details was to enable 'my readers to draw their own conclusions'.

He certainly knew his readers. Anyone wishing to present a lively picture of the monster Shaka can find plenty of material in *Travels and Adventures in Eastern Africa* by Nathaniel Isaacs. It does not do, however, to enquire too deeply into the authenticity of Isaacs's account. Many of his observations on Natal and Zulu customs are undoubtedly accurate and will be of lasting value. But when he comes to deal with the noble James Saunders King and the terrible Shaka his comments are, to say the least, suspect. The book is full of contradictions. Time and again Isaacs elaborates on his fear of Shaka whom, he claims, went out of his way to threaten and frighten the traders. Yet all that ever comes of these threats and fears are grants and favours from the Zulu King. Isaacs is quite capable of denouncing Shaka and grudgingly acknowledging a further kindness from the King in the same paragraph. The few episodes that can be checked by independent evidence, show that he deliberately distorted his account to blacken Shaka and cover up the activities of his idol James Saunders King. Even his claim to possess James Saunders King's journal is open to doubt. He quotes extensively from this so-called journal but—with one exception—his extracts

have been taken word for word from Cape Town newspapers. The
exception is a description of the wreck of the *Mary*, which could
have been taken from the ship's log. It is doubtful whether King
kept a journal; the letters he wrote to officials show him to have been
barely literate.

Isaacs's book was published in 1836. At that time he was still
hoping to persuade the British to occupy Port Natal. He needed to
gloss over King's intrigues: Shaka suffered as a result. Moreover, he
appears to have been studying books by other explorers and no
doubt he hoped that his would place him in their ranks. He had to
come up with something exciting: what better than an outsized
monster? There were sufficient facts for him to work from. Shaka
was undeniably a fearsome conqueror and a despotic ruler; but
Isaacs's portrait of him is, to use his own words, 'somewhat incredible, if not highly exaggerated'. It was meant to be. He admitted
as much in a private letter he wrote to Fynn, some years after Shaka's
death. Hearing that Fynn was contemplating writing a book on the
Zulu King and his successor, Isaacs was quick to offer his friend
some literary advice. 'Make them out as bloodthirsty as you can,' he
urged, 'and endeavour to give an estimation of the number of
people they have murdered during their reign, and describe the
frivolous crimes people lose their lives for. Introduce as many
anecdotes relative to Chaka as you can; it all tends to swell up the
work and makes it interesting.' When Isaacs wrote his letter,
he had to be careful lest it fell into wrong hands, but his
meaning is unmistakable. Nathaniel Isaacs could not be accused of
objectivity.

Fynn was more honest, less sensational. His account is far more
factual; it contains none of the purple patches Isaacs delighted in.
Even so, he was unable to ignore Isaacs's advice entirely: his own
activities in Natal had not been entirely blameless. He had some
covering up to do. What is more, his so-called 'diary' was written
many years after the events it describes. He is said to have lost the
original notes he was collecting for his book when they were
mistakenly buried with his brother Frank and he thus had 'to re-
write the whole of the contents from memory as well as he could'.
Unfortunately his memory was not all that reliable. The re-written
notes were fragmentary; often he gives more than one version of a
single incident; invariably the versions differ. It is possible that,

when recalling some events, he was influenced by Isaacs's *Travels and Adventures in Eastern Africa*.

Fynn does not dwell on Shaka's sadism to the same extent as does Isaacs. Nevertheless he gives many examples of torture and executions. The executions mostly result from some offence to Shaka, often a trivial offence. Fynn says, for instance: 'On one occasion I witnessed 60 boys under 12 years of age despatched before he had breakfasted.' Precisely why these boys were killed he does not say. The implication would seem to be that Shaka did not require a reason for butchery. But the most senseless slaying described by Fynn is that which occurred at Bulawayo after Nandi's death. Fynn's description of this massacre is often quoted as proof positive of Shaka's insane bloodlust. How valid this is remains open to question.

Fynn gives at least three versions of this episode. They all vary. In one he says Shaka ordered 'several men' to be executed; in another fragment he says the King commanded that one of his aunts, who had been on bad terms with Nandi, and all her girl attendants should be killed. The rest of the 7000 people who are said to have died on this occasion appear to have been victims of the mass hysteria that swept Bulawayo. Fynn had witnessed similar—though not such disastrous—hysteria after the first assassination attempt on Shaka. On that occasion Shaka had been taken away from the kraal, but the people continued to attack each other. In one of his versions, Fynn says that one word from Shaka would have stopped the slaughter which followed Nandi's death. But it is certainly arguable that, until the hysteria had spent itself, it would have been impossible for one man—even Shaka—to control the situation. Even Fynn admits that most of the deaths resulted from individuals 'revenging their injuries, real or imaginary'.

One could continue to analyse the occasions when Shaka is said to have instigated massacres but, in most cases, the reports are so conflicting or unsubstantiated that it is not possible to arrive at the truth. There is no doubt that Shaka was responsible for the desolation in Natal, but whether he was a lunatic mass murderer is another matter. The traders depicted him as such. Others have added touches of their own. By and large these reports, however suspect, have been accepted.

What is difficult to understand is the reaction of the traders. If they really believed that Shaka was a capricious, indiscriminate killer, then why did they remain in Natal? They were given repeated opportunities to leave but they refused them all. One would have thought that, with a monster like Shaka breathing down their necks, there would have been a mad scramble to board the first ship that called at Port Natal. Yet Farewell, Fynn, Cane and Ogle stayed for four years under Shaka; King, Isaacs, Hutton and the seamen were there three years. Young boys like Thomas Halstead and John Ross wandered about the country, apparently without fear. King even brought Farewell's wife to Natal.

Did they really think they would be protected by their white skins and magic medicines? Or were they so self-seeking that they were willing to risk their necks for a haul of ivory? Given their picture of Shaka, neither explanation is particularly convincing. A man who murdered his own family and wilfully massacred his own people could hardly be relied upon to respect a difference in skin colour indefinitely. Their medicines were limited and by no means infallible. Shaka is said to have commanded an army of 30,000; if, in one of his unpredictable moods, he had turned against the traders, their firearms would have counted for nothing. The chance of a fortune might have inspired them to take a reasonable risk, but it does not explain why they—down to the last seaman—willingly remained at the uncertain mercy of a savage extremist.

Summing up Shaka's character, Isaacs says: 'When he once had determined on a sanguinary display of his power, nothing could restrain his ferocity; his eyes evinced his pleasure, his iron heart exulted, his whole frame seemed as if it felt a joyous impulse at seeing the blood of innocent creatures flowing at his feet; his hands grasped, his herculean and muscular limbs exhibiting by their motion a desire to aid in the execution of the victims of his vengeance: in short, he seemed a being in human form with more than the physical capabilities of a man; a giant without reason, a monster created with more than ordinary power and disposition for doing mischief, and from whom we recoil as we would at the serpent's hiss or the lion's growl.'

Others have seized upon this portrait of a homicidal maniac and added colourful touches of their own. It never seems to have occurred to them to question Isaacs's lurid prose.

But the undeniable fact is that the traders did not recoil 'at the serpent's hiss or the lion's growl'. They stayed on for years with this terrifying fiend who, according to Isaacs, was continually threatening their lives. James Saunders King tried desperately to force the British to occupy Port Natal and thus provide the traders with protection, but his failure to achieve this did not prevent him, or the others, from returning to the Zulu territory. Just how afraid of Shaka were the traders?

There can be little doubt that the tortures and executions described by Isaacs and Fynn did take place. This was part of the Zulu system and was to be observed, independently, by others who later visited those Zulu rulers trained at Shaka's court. Painful death was the inevitable punishment for those who offended the King: and the King was easily offended. An ill-suppressed cough, sneeze or fart in the royal presence could result in a menacing finger being raised and the executioners moving in. The sixty boys whom Fynn says were put to death before breakfast might have done no more than titter at a serious gathering. Immediate death was the only punishment allowed for such offence. Was this, as Isaacs suggests, simply the means by which Shaka indulged a sadistic whim? If it was, then the traders had good reason for their professed fears.

But it seems more likely that Shaka's behaviour was not as erratic as they pretended. The Zulu system was based on a harsh, rigid, but recognisable discipline. By means of this discipline Shaka had made his army invincible; in the same way he had ensured his supremacy. From Fynn's description of the mass hysteria which was so easily generated among Shaka's subjects, it is obvious that the Zulu nation could never have reached the heights it did under a ruler less severe and determined than Shaka. To say this is not to excuse a cruel despotism, but to understand the motivations of an intelligent but barbarous ruler. Only by resorting to the abnormal could Shaka—like many another tyrant—retain his hold over his people.

The traders must have recognised this. They, as well as Shaka's subjects, must have been aware of the disciplinary code laid down by the King. They must have realised that, as long as they observed that code, they were safe. Safer in fact than a more ignorant and emotional Zulu. If one ignores Isaacs's false alarms, the only time the traders appear to have been in real danger was when one of their Hottentots raped a young Zulu woman. On that occasion the indunas were demanding reprisals; the traders were spared because of Shaka's intervention. They had more reason to thank the King than to denounce him as a sadistic pervert.

The only first-hand, detailed reports of Shaka are those given by his white visitors. Knowledge of the first Zulu King depends entirely on the biased observations of Isaacs and Fynn. Stripped of their subjective judgements, the few facts to emerge from these accounts are not entirely to Shaka's detriment. Confronted by a group of strange white men, with seemingly mysterious powers, the King offered them friendship when he might have destroyed them from fear. He not only welcomed them but gave every indication of wishing to meet their fellows. He granted them land, he supplied them with ivory, he fell in with their schemes. He stood between them and the wrath of his people. While Shaka lived no white man in Natal was harmed.

It is unfortunate that no contemporary Zulu account of Shaka exists. Did his people loath him as his enemies—both white and black—later maintained? There seems little evidence to support such a claim. Not even Fynn and Isaacs suggest the possibility of a popular rising against Shaka. The only recorded assassination attempt on the King, apart from that which killed him, was, as far as one can tell, that of an enemy agent. This might be explained, in part, by Shaka's iron-handed rule. Nevertheless, the Zulu were a warrior race, by no means servile, and when Shaka's brothers decided to strike they did so with relative ease. If discontent under Shaka was widespread, it was certainly not apparent.

But there is further evidence in Shaka's favour. Zulu sources are not entirely silent on the founder of their nation. Far from it. For generations oral tradition has hailed Shaka as the greatest of Zulu heroes. His name is frequently invoked in Zulu councils, his example is cited as a supreme authority. Any criticism of Shaka can, and often does, earn a sharp rebuke from Zulu elders and statesmen. He is the subject of eulogistic praise chants and poems; the hero of more than one African novel. The Zulu people have erected a monument in his honour at the site of his Dukuza kraal. When, in 1972, the Zulu Territorial Authority nominated a national day for the newly created kwaZulu, they chose the anniversary of their founder's assassination: Shaka's Day.

This, surely, is the supreme irony: the white men whom Shaka befriended reviled him, while his people—whom he is said to have tyrannised beyond endurance—revere his memory.

The first Zulu King must remain an enigma. Perhaps the most fitting epitaph to Shaka is contained in the concluding lines of *UShaka KaSenzangakhona* (Shaka, Son of Senzangakhona) by the Zulu poet, Dr B. W. Vilakazi:

> 'The nations, Shaka, have condemned you,
> Yet still today, they speak of you,
> Still today their books discuss you,
> But we defy them to explain you.'

PART TWO

DINGANE

THE UNSETTLED STATE

'IT IS BELIEVED that one of Chaka's half brothers named Dingaan will be elected his successor,' reported the *South African Commercial Advertiser* on 27 December 1828, 'and in the meantime, the affairs of the Zoolahs are administered by the Chief under whose hand Chaka fell; but until the election of his successor it is obvious that the country must continue in a very unsettled state.'

The newspaper was reporting Shaka's death. Although it gave a garbled account of the King's murder, it was correct in assuming that the elder assassin stood to gain most from his death. This was not as inevitable as it might appear. Age did not necessarily decide which heir would succeed to the Zulu chieftainship. It was customary for the chief to nominate his successor; his nominee then had to be formally accepted by the people. Shaka, unable to contemplate his own death, had acknowledged no heir. In fact, it is surprising that he allowed anyone with the remotest claim to the chieftainship to remain alive. That there should be any suggestion of an heir-apparent was, in itself, a tribute to the assassins' cunning. Only by years of studied self-effacement had they been able to survive. So little was known of them that it was automatically assumed that Shaka's eldest brother had the strongest claim.

The report in the *South African Commercial Advertiser* was the first that the Cape colonists had heard of a possible successor to Shaka. For this they cannot be blamed. The traders, from whom they got all their news, seem hardly to have been aware that the King had any brothers. Until Shaka's assassination, the names of Mhlangana and Dingane do not appear in their daily accounts. It is doubtful whether they so much as met Mhlangana; Dingane they were to come to know only too well.

The name Dingane means 'the needy one'. Why he should have been called this is not known. His name, like that of Shaka (Chaka, Tshaka) was spelt, for many years, in a variety of ways. The most popular early version was that given by the *South African Commercial Advertiser*—Dingaan. Isaacs spelt it, Dingān; others have preferred Dingana or Dingarn. Now it has been more or less standardised as Dingane.

However, unlike Shaka, Dingane has had no romantic stories told abcut his conception and youth. What few do exist are of doubtful origin. He was the son of Senzangakhona's sixth wife, Mpikase, and is said to have grown up under the influence of his maiden aunt, the scheming Mkabayi. It is thought that he was in his early thirties when he murdered Shaka; which would mean that he was born sometime during the 1790s. As a child he is supposed to have been aloof and morose; never mixing with the children of the kraal, always on his guard, often given to a petulant temper. The only youthful virtue claimed for him is an obsession with personal cleanliness. While still young he is said to have spent a great deal of his time bathing in streams and smearing his plump body with fat. He was also, it seems, inordinately modest. Shocked by his carefree companions, who thought nothing of relieving themselves in public, he would hide himself away and feel sick as he squatted amid the human excreta which littered the bush outside the kraal. If all this is true, he must have found the uninhibited tribal life of his childhood almost unbearable.

He was a big, lazy, sensuous boy (the one smell he enjoyed was that of cattle dung) and he grew into a big, lazy, sensuous man. Only in his features did he resemble Shaka; Fynn, in fact, detected a distinct family resemblance. He was tall, bronzed, muscular, with huge thighs—developed, it seems, by dancing, his only known voluntary activity—and, apart from three blackened front teeth, is reported to have been a handsome young man. As he approached middle-age he began to put on weight and lose his looks, but this did nothing to lessen his vanity. Conscious of his unsightly teeth, he developed a habit of speaking with his hand in front of his mouth; a habit which added to his sly, conspiratorial manner.

Information about his military abilities is equally scrappy. He had no natural love of fighting and, in his youth, tended to avoid the brawls which his companions enjoyed. The only two campaigns for which he is known to have been commandeered were the last two of Shaka's reign. On both these occasions he escaped the actual fighting by feigning illness. But he had ulterior motives for doing this and they must be regarded as exceptional. As a Zulu youth he would automatically have been conscripted into the army and to have proved himself in battle. Although he appears not to have distinguished himself, he must have fulfilled the requirements of a Zulu warrior. Brother or no brother, Shaka would undoubtedly have killed Dingane had he been suspected of cowardice.

Shadowy as was his early career, Dingane lost no time in asserting himself once Shaka was dead. He might have been indolent but he was not without nerve. Having steeled themselves to assassinate their brother, he and Mhlangana were propelled into further action. Neither of them trusted the other (there appears to have been no prior agreement between them) and each had his eye on the succession. But they could not yet afford to squabble openly. There were far greater dangers in the offing.

Not the least of these was Shaka's uterine brother, Ngwadi—the son born to Nandi after her expulsion from the Zulu kraal. Ngwadi had always been closer to Shaka than had been the sons of Senzangakhona. He it was who, by killing Senzangakhona's appointed heir, had paved the way for Shaka's usurpation of the Zulu leadership. As a reward, Shaka had allowed Ngwadi the same type of semi-independent command that he had once granted to his favourite Mzilikazi. Ngwadi's small force had not been commandeered for the campaign against the north-eastern tribes and, with the main body of the army still away, the assassins were afraid that Ngwadi might seize the opportunity to overthrow them. They determined to act before he did.

As the question of the succession could not be resolved until the army returned, Dingane and Mhlangana agreed to hand over the running of affairs to their fellow conspirator Mbopha. It was Mbopha who led the attack on Ngwadi. He mustered all the forces available at Dukuza—mostly the youthful *Nyosi* (Bees) regiment formed by Shaka before his death—but even so he was afraid to take on Ngwadi's experienced warriors in open battle. Moving stealthily through the night, Mbopha reached the enemy kraal at daybreak and launched a surprise attack. Unprepared as they were, Ngwadi's men put up a tremendous fight. They defended themselves, says Fynn, 'only as warriors of Shaka could do'. In the short, fierce action they accounted for all but twenty of Mbopha's three hundred men, before they were finally annihilated. They fought literally to the last man.

'Ngwadi alone,' it is said, 'made eight lick the dust before he fell, stabbed in the back by a boy during the battle.' The conspirators had nothing more to fear from Nandi's sons.

But they had much to fear from each other. Once Ngwadi had been removed, the contest between Shaka's assassins became more purposeful. Mbopha evidently backed Dingane to win but, at the same time, was careful to keep up a semblance of friendship with Mhlangana. No such pretence disguised the brothers' feelings. As the days passed they became more edgy, more openly suspicious of each other. The mere sight of Mhlangana sharpening his assegai was sufficient to throw Dingane into a panic. He immediately sent for Mbopha and accused his brother of planning to kill him. When Mbopha visited Mhlangana he found him equally apprehensive. Mhlangana ridiculed the idea that he was intent on murder but swore that he 'would not wait long and see such a fool as Dingane' ruling in Shaka's place. The least of his brothers would be more capable, he declared.

As so often happens with unrecorded Zulu history, there are several versions of how this deadly rivalry ended. From the mass of conflicting details, however, certain facts have emerged. One night in October an attempt was made on Dingane's life. An assegai was hurled in the darkness, but missed its target. Dingane escaped with a flesh wound. Shortly afterwards Mhlangana was stabbed to death. Some say that Dingane, aided by Mbopha and his sinister aunt Mkabayi, lured Mhlangana to the spot where he was killed. Fynn claims that Mhlangana was dragged from his hut and executed. Whatever the truth, the result is undeniable. By the time the army returned from its ill-fated eastern campaign, Dingane had disposed of his brother and consolidated his claim to the Zulu leadership.

The campaign had been a disaster. If, as Farewell suggested, Shaka had intended to weaken the army, he certainly succeeded. After leaving Dukuza in August, the *impis* (regiments) had skirted Swaziland and, after punishing a small eastern clan, had headed northwards. They intended to attack a more powerful tribe led by Soshangane, a refugee Ndwandwe commander. This tribe was established in Portuguese East Africa. To reach it entailed a gruelling march through pestilent country. Exhausted by the recent frontier campaign and forced to carry their own equipment, the half-starved army now had to contend with the twin plagues of primitive Africa—malaria and dysentery. By the time it reached Soshangane's territory, half the Zulu force was incapable of action. Disease, hunger and sheer fatigue had caused hundreds of warriors to collapse; others had been driven to desertion. Only the determination of their leader—the tenacious Mdlaka, one of Shaka's most capable commanders—had kept the impis on the move at all. To make matters worse, a Zulu deserter had given Soshangane ample warning of the army's approach. By the time Mdlaka was ready to attack, his enemy was waiting for him, concealed amid the rocks and bushes of a low lying hill.

Well versed in Zulu tactics, Soshangane knew better than to allow Mdlaka the benefit of a dawn offensive. On the night the Zulu impis camped before his rocky stronghold, he sprang a surprise attack on their left flank. In the resulting skirmish, the sleep-bemused Zulu panicked and fled; by the time their commanders rallied them, Soshangane's force had successfully retreated, having destroyed the best part of a Zulu regiment. Mdlaka was given no opportunity to retaliate. At daybreak Soshangane evacuated the hill and his warriors scattered into the bush country. The Zulu, after attempting a half-hearted pursuit, finally gave up and started for home.

The return march was a grim ordeal. Mdlaka had failed to capture any of Soshangane's cattle and his famished warriors were reduced to eating strips of their ox-hide shields. Any hope they might have had of plundering the wayside kraals was soon frustrated. 'The different tribes,' it is said, 'on hearing of their approach, sought safety in the thickets, taking with them their cattle, and setting fire to their cornfields.' In the region of Delagoa Bay they encountered a swarm of locusts and for days these insects were their only food. By the time they reached friendly country, some 15,000 warriors had died from hunger and sickness.

The remnants of the once powerful Zulu army were in no condition to dispute Dingane's *coup*; for the most part they were only too thankful to have escaped Shaka's wrath.

Dingane welcomed the warriors with 'liberality and kindness'. He promised an end to the tyranny they had known under Shaka and composed national songs denouncing the old regime. The future, he said, would be brighter. To those who had fully expected to be punished for the failure of the campaign, it all seemed too good to be true. They suspected a trick. Shaka, it was rumoured, was still alive. He had merely persuaded Dingane to pose as King so that he could test his subjects' loyalty. But these doubts were confined to whispered gossip; few had the will or the inclination openly to challenge Dingane's *fait accompli*.

One of the few not afraid of the new King was the redoubtable Mdlaka, commander-in-chief of the army. He regarded Dingane as an incompetent usurper, not fit to rule the Zulu nation, and said so openly. For a while Dingane allowed Mdlaka his head but, when an opportunity presented itself, his executioners moved in. The commander-in-chief was removed from the scene as summarily as had been Shaka and Mhlangana. It is said that, at the time of Mdlaka's killing, Dingane contemplated the murder of his younger brother Mpande. But Mpande—a good-natured, somewhat ineffectual young man—was popular with a group of indunas who successfully pleaded for him to be spared. Characteristically, young Mpande slipped quietly into the background where, fat and self-indulgent, he was to remain for several years.

Things had worked out well for Dingane. Not only had Shaka exposed himself to assassination but, by debilitating the army, he had ensured an easy passage for his successor. It had taken only a degree of cunning for the assassins to dispose of the seemingly all-powerful tyrant; with a little more cunning and a show of diplomacy, Dingane had been allowed to assume supremacy practically unopposed. For the time being, the new Zulu King could afford to display 'liberality and kindness'.

[2]

The traders at Port Natal knew little of the happenings in Zululand. What little they did know made them extremely uneasy. If proof were needed of their true attitude towards Shaka, it was certainly apparent after his assassination. Events were to show that they had regarded the 'monster' as their sole protector.

Their immediate reaction to Shaka's death was to build up the defences of the settlement. Expecting civil war to follow the King's downfall, they had good reason to anticipate an attack. Within hours of receiving the news, they had fortified the Townshend dockyard and made sure that the *Elizabeth and Susan* was in trim for a quick get-away. The following morning, says Isaacs: 'We got all the late Lieutenant King's effects on board in readiness for the worst.' For the first time in over four years they were actively preparing to cut their losses and sail for safety.

But they soon had second thoughts. That same evening a messenger arrived from Jacob, the interpreter, with an assurance that they had nothing to fear. Once the excitement caused by Shaka's death was over, said Jacob, the country would settle down peacefully. A few days later a similar message came from Dingane himself. He explained that Shaka had been killed because of his inhuman practises; that the white men should not mourn the tyrant but 'make themselves comfortable' under Dingane's protection. Somewhat relieved, the traders returned the compliment by assuring the new King that they were pleased with his news and considered that Shaka had received his just deserts. As a further token of their appreciation, they sent Jacob a bottle of brandy.

For all that, Isaacs was still none too happy. Now that James Saunders King was dead and the future uncertain, he felt the time had come for him to return to the Cape Colony. Whether he intended to leave Natal for good is not clear but, at the beginning of October, he began to prepare for his departure. He immediately came up against opposition from John Hutton, nominal commander of the *Elizabeth and Susan*. Hutton was a touchy man. He had, on several occasions, quarrelled with James Saunders King about the command of the ship he had built. Now he made it quite clear that he had no intention of taking orders from young Nathaniel Isaacs.

The feud, however, did not last long. A few days after the quarrel, Hutton fell sick and, despite Isaacs's noble-minded nursing, he died at the beginning of November. They buried him close to his former employer, James Saunders King.

Shortly after Hutton's death, the traders made personal contact with the new rulers of Zululand. The first of them to visit Dingane was Henry Francis Fynn. In a way, this was to be expected. Fynn had been the first to set off for Shaka's kraal and, in most matters, he had proved himself by far the most adventurous of the traders. Unfortunately, he has left no recollections of his first visit to

Dingane. He must have gone to Dukuza towards the middle of October; Isaacs reports him as returning from a trip to 'the princes' on the twenty-first of that month. Mhlangana was then still alive but, if Isaacs is to be believed, Dingane was very much in command. Fynn returned full of the reforms that had been instituted at the royal kraal. It had already been announced that some of the warriors, celibate under Shaka, would be allowed to marry. Dingane seemed to be doing all he could to win support among his people. 'This popularity,' noted Isaacs, 'increased daily.'

Other news trickled through to Port Natal. At the beginning of November, the traders learned that Mbopha had defeated the troublesome Ngwadi; they became more and more convinced that things would settle down under Dingane. Isaacs prophesied that the new regime would ensure a 'high state of prosperity' throughout the territory. This, however, did not deter him in his resolution to sail for the Cape. The truce with Farewell was still effective and Isaacs agreed to take him back to Algoa Bay. Fynn and Henry Ogle decided to stay at the settlement.

By 1 December the *Elizabeth and Susan* was ready to make her second voyage to the Cape Colony. As the ship glided out of Port Natal, young Isaacs looked back wistfully at the settlement. His thoughts, he says, were full of his 'valued companion and esteemed friend', James Saunders King.

[3]

It took the *Elizabeth and Susan* a full two weeks to reach Algoa Bay. The voyage, despite calm weather, was turbulent. A few days out from Port Natal, the crew became surly. Only with the support of Farewell and three of the men was Isaacs able to suppress a full-scale mutiny. This, however, was merely the beginning of his troubles.

At first the officials at Port Elizabeth seemed only too anxious to help him. He was given every assistance in arranging a settlement of James Saunders King's affairs. The Port Captain, Mr Francis—who had been intimate with King during the *Elizabeth and Susan*'s earlier stay—promised indemnification for the effects of King that were in Isaacs's charge. But this happy state of affairs did not last long.

Not knowing of Shaka's death, John Cane and the Zulu delegates had arrived at the Cape frontier, accompanied by Captain Aitchison, with the intention of continuing overland on the goodwill mission authorised by the Cape Governor. Soon after the *Elizabeth and Susan* docked, Captain Aitchison visited Port Elizabeth to interview Lieutenant Farewell. The news from Zululand made the Captain wary of proceeding to Natal. He sent to Cape Town for further instructions. The Governor replied promptly, putting a stop 'to the mission for the present & until I receive some information as to the consequences resulting from Chaka's destruction'.

Isaacs seems to have been startled to hear of Captain Aitchison's mission. He more or less admits this. He says that as soon as he had made the preliminary arrangements concerning James Saunders King's affairs, he set about writing his own versions of the happenings in Natal 'for the perusal and information of the colonial government of the Cape, hearing it was the intention of the governor to send a mission to the Zoolas'.

He did not get far with this attempt to justify himself. To his utter astonishment Mr Francis, the Port Captain, suddenly reversed his helpful attitude. He seized the *Elizabeth and Susan* on the grounds that the vessel was unregistered. Isaacs tried to oppose the seizure by ignoring James Saunders King's earlier arguments and claiming that the ship had been built mainly from the wreck of the *Mary* and was thus entitled to the *Mary*'s register. This made no impression on Francis. Nor did the fact that the *Elizabeth and Susan* had earlier been allowed to remain unmolested at Port Elizabeth and then been given a sea-letter to return to Natal. Acting on the provisions of the British Registry Act, he impounded the ship and announced his intention of selling her.

Once again Isaacs fulminated about the arrogance of petty officials. He later claimed that Francis had been inspired by avarice and had pocketed the money he obtained from the sale of the *Elizabeth and Susan*. But it seems far more likely that Francis was acting on instructions from the Colonial authorities. In either case, the Port Captain was within his rights. There was nothing that Isaacs could do about it. Extremely disconsolate, he made his way to Cape Town.

Not surprisingly, the Governor of the Cape refused his application for an interview. By this time Isaacs was feeling far from well; even his attempts to settle King's affairs proved more complicated than he had bargained for. Finally he gave up and booked a passage for St Helena. He arrived at the island on 5 March, after an absence of three and a half years.

Farewell's return to civilisation was equally discouraging. He also went to Cape Town in the hopes of impressing the Governor. Whether Sir Lowry Cole actually granted him an interview is not clear, but his report on affairs in Natal did at least reach the Governor's desk. Sir Lowry accepted his report of Shaka's death and Dingane's intentions. 'The character of the brother who is likely to succeed [Shaka] is described as mild and peaceable,' Cole reported to the Colonial Office, '& he seems desirous to live on friendly terms with his neighbours, I trust the bordering countries may now enjoy a state of tranquility which Chaka's restless and cruel ambition has so long denied them, a more bloodthirsty Tyrant never I believe having existed.'

Sir Lowry, however, was far from convinced by Farewell's explanation of his own activities in Natal. The new Governor had arrived at the Cape shortly after the abortive frontier campaign; he had been warned against the traders by his predecessor, General Bourke. Rightly or wrongly he was inclined to judge Farewell by the mischief which James Saunders King had created. 'I feel it impossible,' he said, 'to attach any credit to the contradictory statements of Lieutenant Farewell or King (the latter of whom died a few days previous to Chaka's being put to death) as these persons seem in their intercourse with Chaka to have had no other object in view but their personal advantage, and as far as I can judge from their proceedings they do not appear to be very respectable characters. Lt Farewell is now in Cape Town & inclined to return to Port Natal where he is desirous to induce this Government to form a settlement but even in his own interested statements he shows no ground whatever to make it appear desirable in any point of view. The harbour is insecure and fit only for small craft and scarcely any article of trade is to be procured except a scanty supply of Elephant teeth.'

Not only was Farewell unable to obtain assistance from the Cape authorities, but he lacked the persuasive personality that had won James Saunders King the support of the Cape Town press. His account of Shaka's assassination was fully reported but the newspapers were wary of advocating a British settlement in Natal. It is, however, interesting to note the puzzled change of tone in the *South African Commercial Advertiser* concerning Shaka. Having accepted John Cane's favourable report, the arrival of Farewell and Isaacs quickly put the newspaper on its guard again. 'Chaka, according to all accounts, was a cruel Ruler, and his miserable end was probably well merited,' it reported. 'To Europeans, however, he was uniformly kind, which is proof both of his discernment and their discretion; and it is rather at variance with the reports respecting his general character.' With so much contradictory evidence, it was difficult to know what to believe.

In January 1829, Farewell decided to cut his losses and return to Natal. He left Cape Town for the frontier town of Uitenhage, where he began to prepare for an overland expedition. He was at Uitenhage when the *South African Commercial Advertiser* published the report of James Saunders King's death which Fynn had sent to the Cape by his young brother Frank. To all the other slights he had suffered, Farewell now found added the public accusation of his having behaved callously to a dying man. He was understandably furious: not only at Fynn's accusations, but at the misrepresentation of his relationship with James Saunders King. On 24 January he wrote a spirited reply to Fynn's attack, outlining his dealings with King from the outset of their association. 'I imagine,' he said, '[Fynn's letter] was not intended for publication, or shame might have prevented the author erring so far from the real state of the case.' The short-lived truce between the traders was over.

But, as far as Farewell was concerned, there was worse to come. He now discovered just how profoundly his reputation had been harmed by the intrigues of James Saunders King. The official report, of white men accompanying the Zulu army, landed Farewell in serious trouble.

As soon as the report had reached Whitehall, the Colonial Office had notified the Admiralty of 'the presence of a lieutenant of the Royal Navy in Chaka's Territories' and asked for appropriate action to be taken. This had resulted in the Lords of the Admiralty sending Farewell a letter which threatened to cancel his leave of absence if it was found that he had 'given his countenance to Chaka, in this Chief's projects against the Caffres'. The letter was to have been delivered to Farewell by a specially appointed officer. By coming to the Cape Colony, Farewell had saved the officer a journey.

Just how much Farewell knew of, or was involved in, his rival's schemes it is not possible to say. An alliance between the traders, at the time of the frontier campaign, seems unlikely. On the other hand, Farewell was as anxious as the others for the British to occupy Natal. His first action on reaching Cape Town had been to renew King's plea for a British settlement. Mutual interest might well have triumphed over former enmities.

In a largely fictionalised biography, Farewell is depicted as the unsung saviour of the Cape Colony. It is claimed that he warned the Colonial authorities of Shaka's intended frontier attack, by sending a secret messenger ahead of the Zulu army. There is little evidence to support this. The claim appears to rest entirely upon an unsubstantiated statement made by Farewell after he had received the Admiralty's letter. The fact that he waited so long before revealing the important role he had played, makes his statement extremely suspect. Had he reported this to Sir Lowry Cole earlier there can be little doubt that—taken with the other information in the Governor's possession—his claim would have received serious consideration. As it was, Sir Lowry was unable to 'attach any credit' to what Farewell said. No record of Farewell's 'warning' has come to light.

Lieutenant Farewell had secrets of his own: secrets that were soon to die with him.

[4]

In the early months of 1829, Dingane first faced the possibility of rebellion. Shaka's assassination had so stunned his subjects that it had given Dingane the respite he needed to consolidate his position. He had been able to deal effectively with the handful of would-be rebels before they could organise a purposeful opposition, let alone a rebellion. But widespread acceptance of the new regime could not be expected to last long.

First to challenge Dingane was Nqetho, leader of the Qwabe clan, who sent a high-handed demand to Dukuza asking for the return of one of his kinswomen kept captive at the royal kraal. Dingane resolutely refused to comply. This seems to have unnerved Nqetho. When he heard that his demands had been dismissed, he panicked. Rallying his tribe with cries of liberty and a new life, he marched southwards, driving huge herds of cattle before him. The small Zulu force which Dingane eventually sent in pursuit of the rebels was repulsed after little more than a skirmish.

For all that, Nqetho failed to gain support from other clan leaders. The only chieftain to show interest in an alliance soon quarrelled with Nqetho, was promptly attacked, and lost all his cattle to the Qwabe.

A second, much stronger, Zulu force caught up with Nqetho some fifteen miles inland from Port Natal. But, strangely, the long expected battle with the rebels did not take place. 'The Qwabes', it is said, 'boldly stood their ground in anticipation of attack. As soon, however, as the Zulu force came up, although each army got ready for action, neither side felt disposed to attack the other.' What caused this unexpected paralysis nobody knows.

Certainly there was no battle. The Zulu contented themselves with capturing the Qwabe cattle and then retired. Nqetho, no doubt thankful to have been let off lightly, also beat a quick retreat. As most of the cattle he had lost had, in any case, been looted from his would-be ally, he had not suffered unduly. Taking the bulk of his herds—which he had earlier sent out of reach of the Zulu force— he continued his southward march; beyond the border of Natal, into Mpondoland. Here he established himself in the vicinity of the Umzimvubu river.

Faku, the neighbouring Mpondo chief, was far from happy at having these former Zulu warriors on his doorstep. Nevertheless, he took the precaution of 'entering into terms of friendship' with Nqetho. This was probably just as well. Within weeks of their arrival in Mpondoland the Qwabe impis were terrorizing the entire frontier district.

Dingane appears to have accepted Nqetho's escape philosophically. Whether he was told the full story of his army's refusal to fight is uncertain. The fact that the Zulu impis returned with a large haul of cattle and had executed a disloyal chieftain on the way, was enough to satisfy him. There were none of the killings which, in Shaka's day, would undoubtedly have followed the army's ignominious return.

But, for all his show of indifference, Dingane remained wary of Nqetho. Mpondoland was beyond his realm, but close enough to be dangerous. He sent a spy to Faku's kraal to keep an eye on the Qwabe. Faku, also watching Nqetho, was only too pleased to harbour Dingane's agent.

THE COMING OF STRANGERS

In April 1829, the bluff John Cane decided to return to Natal. Shaka's death had seriously undermined his mission and, for a while, both he and his Zulu companions seem to have been hesitant about facing the former King's assassins. However, the reports given by Farewell and Isaacs of Dingane's benevolent attitude towards the white men evidently gave Cane the encouragement he needed.

He was certainly not returning empty handed. His mission had aroused widespread sympathy in the Colony and enabled him to collect an impressive assortment of presents for the new Zulu ruler. So loaded were his oxen that his progress was painfully slow. It took him a full ten days to reach the Wesleyan Mission station at Butterworth, a little more than a hundred miles from Fort Beaufort. This, considering that he had earlier estimated that the entire journey could be accomplished in twenty days, was slow going indeed.

Shortly before reaching Butterworth, however, he was surprised to be overtaken by a party of white men, led by Andrew Geddes Bain, who were also making their way to Natal.

Andrew Geddes Bain, a Cape trader, had left the Colony about the same time as Cane but had travelled by a less direct route. Like many of the colonists, Bain had been stimulated by the reports from Natal and by the success of Cane and young Frank Fynn in travelling overland. Together with another trader, John Burnet Biddulph, he had decided to explore the territory between the Cape Colony and Natal in search of ivory. A few days out of Grahamstown, they had fallen in with yet another party making for the Zulu country. This party was made up of Henry Francis Fynn's father—also called Henry Francis—and his two younger sons, Frank and Alfred. Another of the Fynn brothers, William, had set off for Natal earlier. The Fynns were intending to join the settlement at Port Natal.

Bain and Biddulph had been delighted to meet the Fynn family. 'Frank,' noted Bain, 'had lately come overland from Natal & was consequently a valuable addition to our little party.' Now that they had met up with the other overland traveller, John Cane, the success of their expedition seemed assured.

They made their way slowly through the beautiful undulating country, crossing the Bashee and Umtata rivers with little difficulty. Their arrival at the African kraals invariably created excitement among the local tribesmen. The fact that they could communicate silently with each other by written notes was a source of never-ending wonder; one old chief evidently considered there was no limit to the fertility of their inventions. He arrived at their camp, says Bain, begging 'a little of some medicine to strengthen a certain member of his earthly tenement whose incapability he demonstrated to us, alleging at the same time that it waxed softer as the other parts of his body became stiff with years'. But they had to admit that they had no remedy for his flagging state. 'As we had no tincture of catharides [Spanish Fly] we could not administer to the old Chief's wants,' confessed Bain.

When the party arrived at Faku's kraal, they found the Mpondos enjoying a noisy harvest celebration. Naked men, befeathered, smeared with clay, and armed with clubs were lined up opposite a crowd of bare-breasted women who taunted them by slapping their hands in rhythm with their stamping feet and singing at the tops of their voices. Little notice was taken of the white men's wagons.

When Faku eventually came to greet the Europeans, he was full of complaints about the loss he had suffered to Shaka's impis, but he quickly brightened up when an array of presents was spread before him. So welcome did he make the party that they decided to spend a few days near his kraal. They were extremely impressed by Mpondo hospitality. On a hunting trip to the mouth of a nearby river, Cane and Bain failed to kill any hippos but were more than compensated by the friendliness of the local tribesmen. At one kraal they visited they were offered—but, says Bain, politely refused—the services of several Mpondo girls.

'I was afterwards given to understand,' Bain explained, 'that it was but a common rite of hospitality that was practised upon us & that all Amapondan virgins are *broken* in by strangers. I considered

those people the most friendly I had yet found among the Caffre
tribes & left them with regret at 3 o'clock in the afternoon.'

But, as they soon discovered, not all the local inhabitants were so
accommodating. After leaving Faku's kraal they struggled with their
wagons over a treacherous mountain range and then crossed the
Umzimvubu river. Here they decided to separate: John Cane and
old Henry Fynn taking a coastal route and Bain and Biddulph,
followed by the younger Fynns, travelling inland. The further they
got from the Umzimvubu the more disturbed the country seemed to
be. Everywhere there was evidence of faction fighting and Bain and
Biddulph were constantly approached by refugees seeking protection.

On 24 June, they learned the reason for the upheaval. Nqetho
and his marauding Qwabe were on the rampage, laying waste to the
entire district and sending the settled tribesmen flying. A week
later they found themselves surrounded by terrified tribesmen—all
hastily evacuating their kraals. The stream of refugees continued
and finally Bain and Biddulph decided to turn back. News that the
Qwabe had routed the young Fynns sped them on their way. The
entire country, says Bain, was in 'a state of consternation and
terror'.

John Cane and Henry Fynn Senior had also been forced back.
They managed to reach Faku's kraal in safety, but the experience so
unnerved old Fynn that he gave up hope of reaching Natal and
returned to the Cape Colony. His sons, like Bain and Biddulph, also
made their way back to the Colony and it was not until some weeks
later that young Frank Fynn again set out by himself and succeeded
in joining his brothers, Henry and William, at Port Natal.

Cane was still at Faku's kraal when a transport driver named
Whittle arrived there with the advance wagon of yet another
European party attempting to reach Natal. At the beginning of July,
Whittle had been sent on ahead by Lieutenant Farewell who was
waiting at the Cape for the birth of his first child before returning
to Natal himself. Farewell was nothing if not determined. Despite
opposition from the British authorities, he had busied himself
interesting various colonists in his trading venture and, by mortgag-
ing the land grant he had received from Shaka, had raised sufficient
capital to equip a sizeable overland expedition. Besides Whittle, he
now had four other European transport drivers and several
Hottentots in his employ. He had also persuaded an 1820 Settler,

William Thackwray, and a young naturalist named Walker to join him. They all arrived at Faku's kraal at the beginning of September.

Farewell took the news of the Qwabe marauders in his stride. He knew Nqetho from the days he had spent at Shaka's kraal and felt sure that he could deal with him. And at first it seemed as if he were right. The messengers he sent to Nqetho to announce his arrival, returned with assurances of friendship from the Qwabe chieftain. This lulled even John Cane into thinking they had nothing to fear.

After crossing the Umzimvubu, they were met by three Qwabe warriors who told them that Nqetho was waiting to receive Farewell at his kraal. He had collected some cattle for the Europeans and promised a further supply for the remainder of their journey. Still suspecting nothing, Farewell accepted the invitation. Some sixteen miles from Nqetho's kraal, he left Cane and the transport drivers in charge of the wagons and rode on with Thackwray and Walker and a party of Hottentots.

On arriving at the Qwabe kraal, Farewell was presented with an ox and shown to a place, outside the kraal, where he could pitch his tent. Nqetho was friendliness itself. That evening he paraded a number of captured horses before his guests and, by way of entertainment, instructed his warriors to torture the animals. Thackwray and Walker found this cruel demonstration extremely unsettling. Farewell remained unruffled. He remained confident despite several warnings from his servants that Nqetho was not to be trusted. Later that night, Thackwray's Hottentot interpreter, Lynx, crept into Farewell's tent and told him that the Qwabe were definitely planning to kill the party. Still Farewell refused to listen. He accused the Hottentot of cowardice and sent him away. Wisely, Lynx went back to his tent and loaded his gun.

The Qwabe, true to their Zulu training, closed in shortly before dawn. Silently they surrounded the white men's tent, cut the guy ropes and stabbed frantically at the collapsed canvas until they had killed the three Europeans. Then they turned on the Hottentots. Lynx, who had been waiting with his loaded musket, put up a determined fight and escaped, badly wounded, after killing three of his pursuers.

Two other servants managed to get away. They rushed back to the wagons to warn Cane and the others. Hastily Cane and his companions escaped into the night, crossed the Umzimvubu, and made their way back, some hundreds of miles, to the nearest mission station.

Farewell had died a year to the month after King and Shaka. Many reasons have been advanced to explain his murder. John Cane was convinced that Nqetho was revenging himself on the white men for a wound inflicted by a Boer outlaw. Fynn claims that in Farewell's party there was a son of the spy whom Dingane had sent to Faku's kraal and, although the boy was disguised, Nqetho recognized him and suspected the Europeans of acting as informers to the Zulu King. Isaacs puts the murder down to Farewell's foolhardiness.

Whatever the reason for the attack, the Qwabe did not enjoy their spoils for long. They were later routed by Faku who sent the remnants of the tribe fleeing to Natal where they were seized by Dingane and put to death. Nqetho was killed while trying to by-pass Zululand.

John Cane, on reaching the mission station, had intended to return to the Cape Colony. But once he had recovered his nerve, his old determination reasserted itself. Unimpeded by pack oxen and wagons, he and the Zulu delegates managed to slip through the hostile territory and reach Natal.

Although Dingane had scarcely known Farewell, he regarded the white man's death as an evil omen. Before allowing Cane to appear before him, he insisted on a full ritual purification. Cane, it is said, 'was forced to kill a calf at Dingaan's kraal gate and present him with an ox on the death of Farewell. The liver and gall bladder of the calf were required to be cut out at the gate and the gall sprinkled across the gate then round Cane: the other half required to be taken up to the king and sprinkled round him.'

[2]

At the beginning of his reign, Dingane undoubtedly intended to continue Shaka's policy of befriending the white men. One of his first acts had been to assure the traders that no harm would come to them. When Fynn returned from his first visit to Dukuza, he reported that the new ruler 'had been exceedingly kind to him'.

In the months following the departure of Farewell and Isaacs, Dingane seemed content to leave the traders to their own devices. At that time young Henry Francis Fynn and Henry Ogle were the only white men left at the settlement. Little is known about Ogle. He was a young man from Yorkshire who had come to South Africa with the 1820 Settlers and, at the age of twenty-four, had joined Farewell's first expedition to Port Natal. While Farewell was in command, Ogle had remained very much in the background. His decision to stay on with Fynn more or less established him as an independent trader. Like Fynn he had his own following among the local Africans and he is known to have had at least one child by an African woman. The two young men appear to have continued with their trading activities—bartering with the tribesmen and collecting ivory—without any interference from Dingane.

But it was more than a policy of friendship that diverted the Zulu King from the activities of Fynn and Ogle. He was very much occupied with his own concerns. During the early months of 1829, Dingane had his hands full dealing with the Qwabe rebels; and once Nqetho had fled Natal he turned his attention to more personal matters. He decided to build himself a new capital. Dukuza, where a mound of stones marked Shaka's grave, had too many unpleasant associations for Dingane to relish it as a permanent residence. His mind was full of new beginnings. In July 1829, he selected a site for his 'great place'. Some miles south-east of Shaka's first Bulawayo, was a fertile, well-watered valley said to be the birthplace of the founder of the Zulu clan. Here, on the slope of a low-lying hill, close to the stream which crossed the valley, the building of the new royal kraal was started. Dingane named it emGungundlovu, or The Place of the Great Elephant.

The new capital was similar to Shaka's great kraals. Some 2000 huts, in rows of six to eight deep, formed a tremendous oval which, seen from afar, looked 'like a distant race-course'. The vast central area was reserved for military and dancing displays and on the eastern side a thorn-bush hedge screened the thatched huts of the royal *isiGodlo* (seraglio). Although he had disposed of three-quarters of Shaka's 'sisters', Dingane retained over 300 girls for his own enjoyment. He produced no heirs but, unlike Shaka, made no claims to celibacy: his lusty appreciation of his plump, well-greased wives was apparent to all visitors to emGungundlovu.

The *isiGodlo*—closely guarded from all males—was dominated by the King's enormous hut. 'This house,' said a later visitor, 'is of considerable size, and was of sufficient height to stand erect even with a hat on in almost every part; but being only lighted from the low door, and the whole interior blackened by smoke, it had a most dismal and dungeon-like appearance on first entering ... The framework was supported by three parallel rows of posts [later decorated with elaborate beadwork] four being in the middle and three on each side ... the floor is remarkably even, and from being rubbed and greased has quite a polished appearance.' As many as fifty of the King's women could sit round the circumference of the hut with ease, while Dingane lounged on a reed mat at the doorway, his head resting on a hollowed wooden block. There was no furniture; only a few bead curtains decorated the windowless walls.

Dingane spent a great deal of his time in the *isiGodlo*. Visitors to emGungundlovu often had to wait days before he would agree to see them. On arrival they were made to sit outside the thorn-bush enclosure until the King had inspected them. This he did by mounting a specially built rise and peeping over the hedge; only for the very privileged would he emerge from his seraglio, rarely was anyone allowed inside.

Once established at emGungundlovu, Dingane reverted to type. His promises of reform were soon forgotten. As his position became more secure, so did the lessons he had learned from Shaka manifest themselves. Always on the lookout for treachery, he added his own refinements to Shaka's disciplinary code. 'It is death to cough before the king whilst he is eating,' noted a visitor; 'to break wind in his presence; to have an erection in his presence; to ease oneself or make water in his kraal; to sleep with a young Zoolo girl without the king's giving her; to eat green Indian corn before the king does, without his permission.' But, whereas Shaka's ruthlessness reflected an iron-will, Dingane's brutality mirrored little more than wilfulness fed on fear. He ruled by imitation rather than determination.

Nowhere was this more apparent than in his method of government. If Shaka was the embodiment of a warrior king, Dingane was very much the irresolute usurper. He took few decisions without consulting advisers. Two of these advisers—Ndlela, a slightly built, shrewd hereditary chief, and Dambusa, a haughty counsellor—

exercised tremendous influence on state affairs. Ndlela, commander-in-chief of the army, became Dingane's senior induna with powers equivalent to that of a prime minister; Dambusa was his inseparable assistant. Not only was Dingane guided by these indunas but, at times, he appeared fearful of acting without their consent. He insisted on them being present at important interviews and often hid behind their decisions to safeguard himself. Supplicants at emGungundlovu were informed that Ndlela and Dambusa were 'the King's eyes and ears, and that all matters of importance must first be notified to them before they could be expressed to him'. This was all that remained of Dingane's reforms. In place of Shaka's military dictatorship, there arose an ill-assorted triumvirate.

But, if Dingane was prepared to take advice, he did not allow this to diminish his status. He played his royal role to the full. Fat, lazy and self-indulgent, he lacked Shaka's commanding presence and relied on the trappings of kingship to impress his subjects. He adored dressing up. In public he invariably wore a cloak, wrapped round his shoulders and trailing the ground, designed to distinguish him from the most powerful of his indunas. He had a wide variety of these cloaks and nothing pleased him more than to be presented with material or ornaments for his royal wardrobe. Dressed in blue denim or green baize, seated on a high-backed chair—carved from a tree trunk—the King would spend hours drooling over his enormous herds. When absent from the *isiGodlo* he could invariably be found in the cattle kraals, gloating over his livestock like a miser counting out his money.

He was a man of large appetites. He ate well, drank huge quantities of home-brewed beer and grew fatter by the year. His only form of exercise was dancing, at which, despite his increasing weight, he was very nimble. During his reign the celebrations at the royal kraal lost much of their military significance and became little more than entertainments. Nobody enjoyed them more than the King. When he could combine his love of dressing up with his passion for dancing, his happiness was complete. He designed all his own dancing costumes. His arrival in the latest of these creations was the highlight of every ceremony. Preceded by a group of chanting women, he would thread his way through the dancers—bracelets flashing, amulets jingling and strips of leopard skin criss-crossed about his torso. Below his enormous paunch bobbed and dangled an assortment of animal tails; from the ring about his head a long crane feather sprouted heavenwards.

To the uninitiated, the gyrating Dingane was a bizarre sight. One spectator described him as the most grotesque figure he had ever seen. 'Tall, corpulent, and fleshy, with a short neck and heavy foot, he was decked out as a harlequin,' he declared, 'and, carried away by the excitement, seemed almost prepared to become one.' But the King's subjects delighted in his exhibitionism. As Dingane stamped and sweated through the dance, sending up clouds of dust, they leapt about him, joining in the songs he composed, clapping their hands and shouting his praises. 'To a bystander,' it was said, 'it has all the effect of the wildest battle scene of savage life, which it is doubtless intended to imitate.'

Not all gatherings at emGungundlovu were as merry, however. The killings ordered by Dingane were by no means confined to the offences of jittery individuals. Soon he was punishing whole clans for real or imagined slights. He thought nothing of enticing unsuspecting tribesmen and their families to appear before him and then, at the lift of his finger, turning them over to his executioners. The impalings, the crushing of skulls and the twisting of necks were daily spectacles at emGungundlovu. 'He massacred numbers with the same unsparing hand as his predecessors,' declared Fynn, 'though in a more treacherous and crafty manner.'

The devious ways in which Dingane ensnared his victims was no doubt responsible for hundreds of terrified Zulu men, women and children fleeing the country. This was a remarkable feature of Dingane's reign. However ruthless Shaka might have been, his own people remained loyal: hostile clans were attacked, disrupted and dispersed but very few individuals became voluntary exiles from Zululand. Once Dingane assumed power, the pattern changed. He waged few wars but desertion from his own ranks became widespread. Sometimes in families, sometimes in small parties, his subjects slipped across the border into Natal and sought refuge with those clans who would accept them. Many attached themselves to the traders at Port Natal. The white men were regarded as independent chiefs and, within a matter of years, their 'clans' had grown enormously. So many Zulu deserters flocked to Natal, in fact, that, in time, they created serious problems for their white protectors.

There was very little traffic in the opposite direction. Shaka's enemies hailed the death of the tyrant who had driven them from their homelands but, once Dingane was installed, few showed any desire to return. One of the rare clan leaders to take the new King on trust was Matiwane—the chieftain whose marauding army had lately terrorised the frontier district. He soon realised his mistake.

Matiwane and his clan, the amaNgwane, had fled Zululand during the early years of Shaka's reign. Since then they had lived a rootless existence; living off the land, attacking and butchering the weaker tribes they came across. Not until they were sent reeling back across the Umtata by Colonel Somerset's armed force had they met with any real opposition. This short but decisive encounter had weakened them considerably and when, shortly afterwards, Matiwane heard of Shaka's assassination, he decided to lead his shattered army back to their home territory. They were no longer a match for their enemies. On their way back to Zululand they clashed with a tribe from whom they had previously plundered cattle and who, as a result, were now notorious cannibals. The cannibals lost no time in revenging themselves. Not only did they decimate Matiwane's enfeebled army but literally ate up all the stragglers they could lay hands upon. There were very few of Matiwane's once fearsome marauders left by the time they reached Zululand.

All the same, they were given a warm welcome by Dingane. He listened sympathetically to Matiwane's promises of loyalty, presented him with 300 head of cattle, and allowed him to settle his people close to emGungundlovu. More presents followed; a happy relationship seemed assured. Unfortunately it lasted only a matter of months.

Bewitched by Dingane's kindness, Matiwane had no hesitation in answering the Zulu King's plea for assistance. Dingane claimed that some of the neighbouring tribesmen had been plundering the royal herds and that he was determined to punish them. Matiwane and his warriors were ordered to assemble at emGungundlovu. They arrived to find two Zulu regiments doctored and ready for battle. Dingane, as friendly as ever, pretended to consult Matiwane about the plan of campaign. Then, it is said, his attitude suddenly changed.

'Where are your people?' he demanded.

'Here they are, all that are left of them,' replied Matiwane.

'Then take them all away!' roared Dingane, as his warriors closed in.

Matiwane's little band was hopelessly outnumbered. They were seized and dragged away without a struggle to have their necks twisted. Their leader was not so fortunate: a particularly gruesome fate was reserved for Matiwane. He was taken to Dingane's execution hill—a rocky ridge beyond the stream outside emGungundlovu—where his captors first gouged out his eyes and then hammered pegs up his nostrils into his brain. His body was left for the vultures.

The murder of Matiwane was a significant landmark in Dingane's career. Not only did it demonstrate his treachery but it served as a warning to those who, at any time, had opposed Zulu supremacy. So that it would always be remembered, Dingane named his execution hill after his most distinguished victim. The hill became known as kwaMatiwane—the place of Matiwane—and as such was feared throughout Zululand.

[3]

At the end of March, 1830, Nathaniel Isaacs bounced back onto the Natal scene. He had spent several months on St Helena, regaling his relatives with stories of his adventures and complaining bitterly about the hostility of the Cape authorities. So incensed was he at being cold shouldered at the Cape that he had gone out of his way to interest visiting American seamen in the possibility of trading in Natal. Always adept at picking up passing sea captains, Isaacs eventually persuaded the master of an American brig, Captain Page of the *St Michael*, to take him back to Port Natal.

This, at least, is what appears to have happened. Isaacs claims that Captain Page was anxious to visit Natal and made him a 'liberal offer to accompany him in the capacity of supercargo, to which I cheerfully assented'. But one only has Isaacs's very doubtful word for this. There can be no doubt that Isaacs was planning to return to Port Natal. From his own admission, it is also clear that he was trying to enlist American aid to offset the hostility of the Cape authorities. Isaacs, in fact, had far more reason to propose the voyage than did Captain Page. But, however he engineered his return to Natal, one thing is certain: his reappearance on the scene resulted in another spate of misleading, contradictory and equivocal statements from the traders.

The *St Michael* sailed from St Helena on 18 February 1830, and anchored off Port Natal on the evening of 30 March. Entering the harbour proved as tricky as ever and Isaacs was kept on tenterhooks for almost two days before he was able to contact his friends on shore. He was met by John Cane, Henry Ogle and young Thomas Halstead. Later he was introduced to William Fynn, Henry Fynn's elder brother, who had reached the settlement some months earlier, after travelling overland from the Cape Colony. The traders were delighted to see Isaacs: they had a great deal to tell him.

Much had happened since Isaacs had left the settlement a year earlier. Farewell was dead, Nqetho had been defeated and Dingane was established in his new kraal at emGungundlovu. Despite the new reign of terror in Zululand, the traders had few fears about Dingane. As far as they were concerned, he could not have been more accommodating. He welcomed them to his kraal, left them to their own devices, and showed every sign of following Shaka's policy of befriending the white men.

Apart from the heartening news about Dingane, Isaacs found little else to cheer him at the settlement. The place had changed almost beyond recognition. The deaths of Lieutenant Farewell, James Saunders King and John Hutton had put an end to the enmities that had once divided the traders, but they had left Port Natal forlorn and dispirited. There was no recognisable centre of activity. The loss of the *Elizabeth and Susan* and the departure of the seamen had resulted in the abandonment of the Townsend dockyard; Fort Farewell was an empty shell. Wandering around Farewell's old residence, Isaacs found the deserted fort dilapidated beyond repair: the walls were falling apart, the three old cannon rusting.

But not all his old friends had disappeared. The day after his arrival Henry Fynn turned up. There was a joyful, backslapping reunion. Both Fynn and Isaacs had been youngsters when they first arrived at Port Natal, now Fynn was twenty-seven and Isaacs twenty-two. Fynn had been sent to Port Natal by Lieutenant Farewell, and Isaacs had been brought there by James Saunders

King; with their former employers dead, they considered it only natural to pool their resources and become partners. After sending word of his arrival to Dingane, Isaacs accompanied Fynn to his trading post on the Umzimkulu river.

Dingane was delighted to hear of Isaacs's return. Twelve days later a messenger arrived at Fynn's place with a present of cattle and an invitation from the King for the traders to visit emGungundlovu. They set off immediately. Calling at Port Natal, Isaacs collected some handsome presents from the cargo of the *St Michael*, begged a pack-bullock from Henry Ogle, and then, with Fynn and fifty Africans, headed for the royal kraal. He was expecting great things from the new Zulu monarch.

On their way upcountry they stopped for a night at the kraal of Jacob, Shaka's interpreter. In the upheavals of the past year, Jacob had fared better than most. He was now established as a semi-independent chief with an African following of his own. He gave Fynn and Isaacs an enthusiastic welcome and treated them, says Isaacs, 'with great liberality and kindness'.

Their reception at emGungundlovu was every bit as cordial. The gifts they had brought for Dingane produced squeals of delight. Beads, cloth, trinkets and blankets were spread before the King who, after a careful inspection, ordered the bulk of them to be sent to the royal enclosure and then made a great show of distributing the left-overs among his clamouring counsellors. No less generous himself, Dingane then ordered his warriors to scour the country for ivory. He regretted that he had so little on hand to offer his visitors but explained that the unsettled state of Zululand had prevented him from hunting. This he now intended to remedy. 'Whatever I can collect you shall have,' he declared.

Fynn and Isaacs stayed at emGungundlovu for four days. They were lavishly supplied with slaughter cattle, entertained with the inevitable singing and dancing displays. But the highspot of their visit came the night before they were due to leave. After supper that evening, Dingane summoned them to the *isiGodlo* and coyly asked whether they had ever seen him dance. When Isaacs admitted that he had never had this pleasure, the King was thrilled. Immediately he sprang into action. Summoning a group of girls, he waddled into his hut to set the stage for a performance his guests would never forget. It was very much a solo effort: the chanting, hand-clapping girls were kept well in the background. Puffing, grunting and sweating, Dingane went through a routine of elaborate hand and leg movements which astounded Fynn and Isaacs. 'He displayed extraordinary power of throwing himself into particular attitudes,' says Isaacs, 'which must have required great muscular strength to have accomplished, and this in fact his frame evinced.'

Merely watching this virtuoso display left the white men limp. By the time they sank onto their sleeping mats that night they were completely exhausted.

But there was more to the visit than singing and dancing. In between entertainments, the young men had several serious discussions with Dingane, one of which lasted over four hours. As always, Isaacs is rather cagey about these discussions. He confines himself to generalities, merely stressing points in his own favour. He says that Dingane urged him to remain in Natal and recognised the land grant which Shaka had ceded to him. At the same time he claims that the Zulu King wanted Fynn to become 'sovereign of Natal' and to act as his agent with the traders. Dingane was angry to hear that John Cane and Henry Ogle had taken over Lieutenant Farewell's cattle; he told Fynn to claim them. According to Isaacs, Fynn politely declined the offer of kingship as he doubted whether 'his countrymen would obey him' but, after a little persuasion, he agreed to act as Dingane's adviser.

For Dingane, Isaacs had nothing but praise. He considered him extremely shrewd—'his eye was keen, quick, and always engaged, nothing escaped him'—and dedicated to the peaceful progress of his people. In every way he differed from the ferocious Shaka.

If, between dances, the white men were shown over the bloody slopes of kwaMatiwane, Isaacs is careful not to mention this aspect of Dingane's benevolence.

Nor does he specify what return Dingane expected for his promises of friendship. This, in the circumstances, is hardly surprising. If John Cane is to be believed, the agreement between the traders and the King might not have been entirely one sided. A few months later, the Governor of the Cape was to learn from Cane that the *St Michael* had landed 'a quantity of Muskets, Cutlasses, gun-powder and salt which have been left under the charge of one of the crew named Nathaniel Isaacs a native of St Helena, who was formerly at Natal in the service of the late Mr King, & who probably brought the American Schooner into the Port. This person is stated to be instructing the Natives in the use of fire arms, & the Master of the vessel intimated his intention of proceeding to the United States, for the purpose of bringing out men & supplies with the design of forming a settlement at Natal.'

Isaacs, of course, denied the charge. The firearms, he explained, were merely a few old muskets that had been intended for Madagascar and which he had procured for his own use and protection. All the same, he made it quite clear that he had more faith in American enterprise than in the capabilities of the suspicious Cape authorities.

THE FLIGHT OF THE TRADERS

HAD HENRY FRANCIS FYNN accepted Dingane's offer to become King of Natal, he would not have had far to look for a crown prince. The Fynns were the most likely candidates for founding a white dynasty in Natal. In one way and another, the entire family was involved in the settlement at Port Natal. Although the elder Fynn had been forced to return to the Cape Colony, he was still regarded as the traders' ambassador in Grahamstown and, by the middle of 1830, his claim to represent the traders could be substantiated by the fact that he had no less than three sons living in the territory adjoining Zululand. The previous year his eldest son, William, had succeeded in joining Henry Francis; a few months later young Frank Fynn had again completed one of those lone, spectacular journeys to the settlement. All in all, the Fynns were no mean contenders for any 'crown' that Dingane might offer them.

Henry Fynn's only possible rival as leader of the traders was Nathaniel Isaacs but their visit to Dingane had cemented their partnership and they found that they could work happily together. By the end of June they had collected sufficient ivory, wood and Indian corn to despatch the *St Michael* to Delagoa Bay with a sizeable cargo. Expecting the ship to return within a matter of months, they then replenished their stock. The territory was more or less divided between them: Isaacs continued to trade with Dingane while Fynn contacted the isolated tribes of Natal. Soon the ivory began to pile up at Fynn's trading post.

The Fynn monopoly undoubtedly angered the other traders. Both John Cane and Henry Ogle appear to have resented being left out of the lucrative enterprise. Having no means of transporting their own goods by sea, they took a jaundiced view of Isaacs's dubious dealings with the Americans of the *St Michael*. This might well have coloured Cane's later report to the Cape authorities, but his accusations were not entirely without foundation.

Before long Cane and Ogle were to find allies in their opposition to the Fynn–Isaacs combination. At the end of July, three new-comers turned up at Port Natal. One was John Biddulph, who had earlier accompanied Andrew Geddes Bain and the elder Fynn on their unsuccessful attempt to reach the settlement. He brought with him an elderly Cape trader named Oughton and a Grahams-town merchant, James Collis. According to Isaacs, Collis had come, not only in the hopes of trade, but to spy out conditions in Zululand for the Cape authorities. They were welcomed by the traders and arrangements were soon made for them to visit Dingane.

The Zulu King was, as usual, delighted to meet the new white men, who lavished him with gifts and went out of their way to flatter him. So impressed was he that he was reluctant to allow them to leave until 'they gave a solemn promise to return and either settle permanently or engage in traffic with his people'. The promise was readily given. Collis was completely entranced by Natal, both as a country and as a trading proposition; by the time he arrived back at the settlement he had firmly made up his mind to return to Zululand and set up as an independent trader. But first he had to go back to the Cape to collect the necessary supplies. While he was preparing for his return, he and Biddulph spent much of their time hunting and were quickly brought into conflict with Fynn and Isaacs. The newcomers accused the traders of spying on them and interfering with their trade among the tribesmen. Angry messages were sent from their camp to Fynn's trading post. Isaacs professed himself at a loss to understand their unfriendly attitude. 'Far from manifesting any displeasure at their commerce with our people,' he complained, 'we had expressly consented to their engaging in it.'

Isaacs's concern might have been genuine. He, at least, did not want to discourage white men from settling in Natal; the more who could be persuaded to come, the better. This had always been James Saunders King's policy and Isaacs had fresh reasons for following it. He was beginning to have doubts about Dingane's benevolent intentions: the Zulu King was beginning to show a lively interest in the white men's firearms. The way this interest had manifested itself had given Isaacs a nasty jolt.

On a recent visit to the royal kraal Isaacs had been sent for by Dingane. He was told to present himself with a loaded musket. The order, he claims, struck him as rather odd but he nevertheless obeyed it. He found the plump King sitting in the cattle arena, surrounded by a crowd of people, and facing two dejected women. Isaacs soon discovered why he and his musket were needed. Pointing to the women, Dingane rapped out a command. 'They,' he thundered, 'are the wives of Nqetho, who killed Mr Farewell—go and shoot them.'

Isaacs was shocked, almost beyond words. He bluntly refused to carry out the order, saying that such a thing was unthinkable and would land him in trouble with the Cape authorities. His obstinacy surprised and angered the King. Scowling, he repeated the order. 'They killed one of your countrymen,' he snapped, 'and I insist on their lives being taken by the musket.' But Isaacs stood by his refusal. Eventually, when it became clear that Isaacs would not budge, a compromise was reached. Dingane's indunas—the ever-present Ndlela and Dambusa—demanded that the King be obeyed and, if the white man refused, the execution should be carried out by his African servant. Still protesting, Isaacs handed over his musket and pistols to his servant—who had evidently been taught to shoot—and insisted that the women be spared torture and killed by a single shot. The trembling servant then aimed the musket at one of the women and fired, hitting her in the breast and killing her outright. The explosion so terrified the guards that they immediately panicked and left the second woman cowering behind a reed mat which she held up for protection. Picking up one of Isaacs's pistols, the servant fired again, wounding the woman in the back. 'She started from her seat,' says Isaacs, 'running backwards, looking at her executioner with terror and anguish, while he loaded his musket. He fired at her again, and ended her miserable existence.'

This ghastly exhibition delighted Dingane. Sending for a pot of beer, he ordered a celebration. From then on he bombarded Isaacs with questions about the effectiveness of muskets. There were further, less gruesome, demonstrations. Isaacs was ordered to fire at a tree so that the King could examine the power of bullets. When Dingane discovered that gunshot could penetrate hard wood he was tremendously impressed. He asked to be given a musket to protect himself against witchdoctors and evil doers. Somehow Isaacs managed to talk him out of this, but he was extremely alarmed at the King's obsession with killing. It was inevitable that, when musing on Dingane's barbarous ways, Isaacs should reach the conclusion that only by contact with civilisation would the Zulu nation be redeemed. The necessity of Natal being occupied by a force which would protect the traders was, in his opinion, as urgent as ever.

Nor was Isaacs the only one anxious for the British to occupy Natal. This long held hope was very much in the minds of John Cane and Henry Ogle. They, it seems, were not so much afraid of Dingane as they were concerned at the disadvantages they suffered as traders. While Natal remained isolated there was little hope of their competing effectively with Fynn and Isaacs. They had no ship and the chances of transporting large quantities of ivory overland were extremely remote. Only if there was regular contact between the Cape Colony and a British garrison in Natal could independent trade be expected to flourish. With this in mind—and no doubt encouraged by the visit of Biddulph and Collis—they were preparing to approach the Governor of the Cape. Somehow or other they persuaded Dingane to send yet another mission of friendship to the Cape. The King, anticipating more novelties and gifts from the white men, readily agreed to allow them to act as his envoys.

John Cane, accompanied by young Thomas Halstead, left Port Natal on 15 September—shortly before the final departure of Biddulph and Collis. Two days later Henry Ogle and the interpreter Jacob, whom Dingane had detailed to escort the white men, followed and quickly caught up with him. Later, Isaacs was to claim that Jacob had resented joining the mission. But by that time the traders had good reason to attribute ulterior motives to Jacob. A scapegoat had to be found for the misfiring of yet another of their disastrous intrigues.

[2]

Cane and Ogle were given a hearty welcome at Grahamstown. Within days of their arrival the Cape papers were carrying enthusiastic reports about the potential of Natal and the friendliness of its new ruler. Dingane, it was said, was well disposed towards the white people and was anxious to have a missionary established in his country. It was all reminiscent of Cane's earlier visit as Shaka's envoy.

In a long letter to his superiors, the Civil Commissioner of the district went into raptures over the fertile soil of Natal, its lushly wooded hills, mild climate, plentiful rain and swollen rivers. He pointed out that if the British occupied this semi-paradise they would secure the entire southern coast of Africa, from the Cape to Delagoa Bay. But it would require prompt action. 'The information which I have received from these persons . . .' he declared, 'has strongly impressed me with the expediency or rather the necessity of the British Government taking immediate possession of that harbour & occupying the adjacent country *with the consent of the Zoola Chief* which there is no difficulty in procuring.' The fact that John Cane felt the need to emphasise that Dingane would give his consent seems to indicate that he was intending to act through the King rather than against him.

However, until word was received from Cape Town, the mission could not be officially recognised. For this reason Dingane's gift to the Governor of the Cape of four elephant tusks had to be declined. This put John Cane in a spot. The homeward march would be impossible if he remained there much longer: the rainy season would make the rivers impassable. In the end he decided to barter the tusks for some rolls of red, blue and green baize and a supply of beads, buttons and blankets. The exchange hardly provided him with an impressive royal gift but, in the circumstances, it was the best he could do.

He, Ogle and Halstead left Grahamstown in the first week of January 1831. By and large they could congratulate themselves; if they had not exactly achieved their object they had succeeded in arousing interest in influential quarters. Their mission, in fact, might have been an unqualified success had it not been for the surly Jacob who, not without reason, had become extremely suspicious of their motives.

Jacob, admittedly, had no reason to love the white men. And there was more to it than that. On his way to the Colony, Jacob had heard alarming stories about a recent commando that had been sent into the frontier districts to stamp out cattle raiding. It was rumoured that no less than four prominent chieftains had been killed and that the white men were planning to occupy the area and then march on to Zululand. In Grahamstown the widespread interest shown in James Collis's trading expedition to Natal seemed to confirm these rumours. The newspapers were recommending Natal as 'a most desirable settlement' and reporting that the 'Government have been made aware of this'. If any further proof of the white men's sinister designs were needed, it had come from Colonel Somerset who, as Cane's party were leaving, had said: 'I will not be long after you.' That Jacob should have assumed that Zululand was threatened is hardly surprising.

When Cane's party arrived back at Fynn's trading post on the Umzimkulu, Isaacs rode over to welcome them. He was surprised to learn that a military commando was shortly expected from the Cape and even more bewildered at Cane's reluctance to approach Dingane. The gifts that had been bought in Grahamstown were forwarded to emGungundlovu, but the King's envoys remained firmly in Natal. 'To my surprise, and the astonishment of everyone,' Isaacs reported a week or so later, 'John Cane, instead of proceeding to the king to announce his return, and the particulars of his mission, had gone hunting the elephant, whilst Jacob and Ogle remained at home, without evincing any intention of going to his majesty to communicate the result of their journey to the Cape authorities.'

This strange behaviour worried Fynn and Isaacs. Suspecting that the arrival of a military commando might mean trouble for them, they began to prepare for the worst. Dingane owed them fifty ivory tusks and, although the *St Michael* was not due back for some weeks, it was decided to collect these tusks immediately.

Isaacs and William Fynn left for emGungundlovu at the beginning of April. They had been on the road only two days when they learned from the induna of a wayside kraal that a messenger was hurrying ahead of them on the way to the royal kraal. This man had been sent by Jacob to warn Dingane that a white army was about to invade Zululand, that John Cane was waiting for the army and this was why he had not reported to the King.

That night the alarmed white men scribbled notes to John Cane and Henry Fynn, warning them what to expect. Disturbing as the news was, they decided that it would be better for them to face Dingane than to turn back as if they were guilty. The following morning they set off early and ran into a violent storm. For four days they battled through pouring rain, drenched to the skin, struggling to keep their horses on their legs.

When they eventually arrived at emGungundlovu, the King was waiting for them at the gateway of the *isiGodlo*, covered from head to foot in pink and white beads. The pink ones were wound round his body, criss-crossed over his huge paunch, while the white ones encircled his arms. 'These, with other decorations of bugles and brass,' says Isaacs, 'made him look singular indeed.' He immediately asked what gifts the white men had brought and was enchanted when, besides a supply of house-building tools, he was presented with a white mouse. Chortling with delight, he had the mouse sent to his hut.

The King then dismissed his guests without any further discussion. Knowing that Jacob's messenger had arrived, Isaacs found this extremely suspicious. He became more apprehensive when a group of young warriors followed him and Fynn to the entrance of their hut and then left them. That something was seriously wrong became only too apparent later that evening. Accustomed to being supplied with meat and beer, the white men were alarmed to find that the King had given no orders for them to be fed. Such a thing had never happened before. However angry Shaka had been, he had never starved his visitors. They had very little sleep that night.

Next morning Dingane sat waiting for them at the entrance of the *isiGodlo*. Tired, irritable and very hungry, they waited for his signal to approach. The King came straight to the point. And the point was that he felt he had been betrayed by John Cane. An impi was on the way to attack the disloyal envoy. He had sent John Cane on a goodwill mission to the Cape, he complained, and this was the result. Instead of coming to report to him, Cane had sent word that he was detained by the illness of Thomas Halstead. This Dingane did not believe. 'I am angry with John Cane,' he told Isaacs; 'I think he might deceive you as well as me.'

Isaacs bristled with indignation. He dismissed the idea that soldiers were on the way. Had an attack been contemplated, he said, he would have known of it. And if he had known of it, would he and Fynn have come on ahead? Dingane brushed his arguments aside. John Cane, he had heard, was hunting elephant. This had convinced him that the excuse of Halstead's illness was false. Cane was afraid to come to emGungundlovu because he had plotted with the white soldiers. Of that Dingane was certain.

Throughout the interview the King remained extraordinarily calm. There were no angry gestures, no shouting. He was just as calm when he told Isaacs of his intention to punish Cane. An impi had been sent to take Cane's cattle. The other white men need have no fear; no harm would come to them. He had sent a messenger to Henry Fynn telling him not to be alarmed and asking him to help in driving Cane from Natal. Only in this way could peace return.

[3]

Henry Fynn did not get Dingane's message of reassurance. He was not to be found when the messengers arrived. The warnings he had received earlier from his brother and Isaacs had put him on his guard. Perhaps he too was reminded of that earlier mission and its disastrous results. Certainly he trusted Dingane less than he had trusted Shaka. Shortly after he received the warnings, John Cane arrived back from his hunting trip in a state of panic. On the road he had heard that two Zulu regiments were on the way to attack the settlement. This was all that was needed to turn Fynn's apprehension into fear. Calling his people together, he rounded up some cattle and went into hiding in the bush. John Cane did the same.

They got away just in time. At dawn the following morning a band of screaming warriors surrounded Cane's huts and burnt them to the ground. They captured what cattle they could—mostly Halstead's, for Cane had driven his away—and returned triumphantly to emGungundlovu, leaving some of their men to guard the ruins. Significantly, they made no attempt to raid Fynn's place. Dingane had been true to his word; he meant to punish John Cane only.

From his hiding place in the bush, Fynn wrote a long letter to his brother and Isaacs who were still with Dingane. He explained what had happened, why he had fled and what he had managed to salvage. Their stock of elephant tusks had been concealed, he had rescued some of Isaacs's papers and had sent a special messenger to recover his brother's cache of Spanish dollars. He was also able to

report that the *St Michael* had arrived back at Port Natal ahead of
schedule. 'I am waiting a short distance above Mzoboshi's district,'
he said.

He had not long to wait. Isaacs and William Fynn came hurrying
back to Natal as fast as the King and the swollen rivers would allow
them. The rivers proved a greater obstacle than the King. Once
Dingane had stated his case against John Cane, his attitude towards
Isaacs and Fynn softened. He supplied them with food and treated
them as old friends. Isaacs and William Fynn left emGungundlovu
in a more optimistic mood than when they had arrived.

Their optimism did not last long. Once they had contacted
Henry Fynn and John Cane their doubts came flooding back. The
last of the Zulu army had retired but Cane's burnt-out huts were
glaring proof of Dingane's treachery. The King's promises of
friendship, they decided, were simply part of a deep laid scheme to
catch them off their guard when he launched a second attack. It
would be madness to stay any longer in Natal.

To evacuate the place, however, would not be easy. They needed
time. Their goods were scattered throughout the territory and they
could not leave without their precious ivory. Luckily they still held
a trump card. The *St Michael* had returned and the Africans were
suspicious of this floating fort and its terrifying cannon. As long as
the ship was in port they felt sure that Dingane would not attack
them. After weighing up their chances, they sent word to the King
that they were leaving but would wait for his reply as they felt
perfectly safe 'under the cover of the guns of the vessel'.

Dingane's reply came nine days later through Henry Ogle.
Apparently Ogle did not share the general alarm and had visited the
royal kraal. He said that Dingane was sorry to hear that they were
leaving and wanted Fynn to visit him.

More messengers arrived from emGungundlovu five days later.
They repeated Ogle's request. The King wanted Fynn to visit him.
Isaacs, Cane and the Fynns discussed the matter and decided that
they had better play for safety and answer the royal summons.
Henry and William Fynn started for emGungundlovu on 14 May.
With them they took eighty Africans loaded with gifts from the
cargo of the *St Michael*. Never before had such a collection of goods
been presented to the King. 'It consisted,' says Fynn, 'of beads of
various descriptions, brass bugles and other ornaments, snuff boxes,

iron pots and kettles, rugs, blankets, printed cottons, white and blue calico, Scotch plaid, and woollen clothes to the value of 2000 dollars.'

Dingane was pleased with the gifts but, even so, he was not as amiable as they had hoped: the ivory he gave them was far below what they had expected. And he was still uneasy about Jacob's report. He had every reason to be. Jacob had arrived at the royal kraal and what he had to say had convinced the King's indunas, if not the King himself. So that the matter could be thrashed out, it was arranged that Henry Fynn should confront Jacob in the presence of the indunas.

The traders always described Jacob as treacherous and vindictive, a liar and a rogue. He might have been all these things but the story he told was difficult to deny. On his way to the Cape, he told the indunas, he had met a refugee from the frontier district. This man had wanted to settle in Zululand as he found he could no longer live near the white men. The white men were not to be trusted. First they sent traders to take part of the land; then they took more land as well as cattle; next came the missionaries to build houses and subdue the tribes by witchcraft. There were now missionaries settled throughout the frontier district. Finally, warned Jacob, the soldiers would come and all would be lost. He had been told as much in Grahamstown by Colonel Somerset 'the terror of the Frontier tribes'. The soldiers were interested in Zululand. They had asked him what sort of country it was, whether it had good roads and plenty of cattle. John Cane had told him that settlers were preparing to leave for Natal. John Cane knew the soldiers were coming and had remained at home to guide them.

What could Fynn say? There was more than a grain of truth in all this. Whether he admitted it or not, he must have known that Jacob had reason to speak as he did. He could not argue, he could only fulminate. 'I declared the whole to be a tissue of falsehoods,' he says, 'invented by the interpreter himself, in order to be revenged on John Cane, and that time would prove the villain had long contemplated to induce His Majesty to injure us.' He listed Jacob's past treacheries and called upon friendly tribesmen to support him. The indunas heard him out in silence. They were not impressed.

Dingane remained aloof. When Fynn spoke to him later he refused to commit himself. He said he would wait and see. He might put Jacob to death but his mind was not yet made up.

The Fynns were left in suspense; they did not know where they stood. Not only Dingane but their own servants were acting strangely. One of these servants was a minor chief named Luki-limba whom Henry Fynn had once saved from Dingane's wrath. Lukilimba had spoken on Fynn's behalf against the accusations of Jacob, and Fynn had every reason to think he could trust him. But, one evening, Dingane sent for Lukilimba who later arrived back at Fynn's hut trembling. Unusual as this was, Fynn took it in his stride. 'I made no inquiry as to why he was so agitated,' he says.

He was soon to find out. The next morning he went to take leave of Dingane. Lukilimba went with him. Hardly had they entered the King's hut when, to Fynn's amazement, Lukilimba flung himself at Dingane's feet and begged to be allowed to leave Fynn's service. Dingane appeared every bit as startled as Fynn. He lectured Lukilimba on his ingratitude, pointing out that he owed his life to Fynn. But Lukilimba continued to whine and plead until the King finally, and reluctantly, gave way. 'Let us fall in with his request,' said Dingane to Fynn, 'then see when and where he will find a protector such as you have been.' It was arranged that Lukilimba should accompany Fynn back to Natal and then take his people to another kraal.

Fynn was puzzled and angry. He was at a loss to know why Lukilimba should so suddenly have turned against him. The man made no attempt to explain and Fynn was too disgusted to pursue the matter. They started back for Natal that day, leaving William Fynn to follow. On the second day out from emGungundlovu, Lukilimba broke his silence and explained his strange behaviour. It was all part of an elaborate plot hatched by Dingane and his indunas to separate Lukilimba from the white men. Why this should be necessary is not clear. According to Lukilimba, Dingane had sent for him and, in the presence of four indunas, had told him to plead for release from Fynn's service. Dingane, he claimed, was planning to murder the traders as soon as the *St Michael* had sailed. Luki-limba advised Fynn to lose no time in quitting Natal and promised that he would go with him. 'Rather than deceive you,' he vowed, 'I would eat the bones of my long deceased father.'

Fynn was forced to act swiftly and secretly. He had to avoid arousing the suspicions of the induna whom Dingane had appointed to accompany him back to Natal. That night he scribbled a hasty

note to Isaacs: 'Please come and meet me as soon as possible,' he
wrote. 'I am waiting for you at the Mdlothi River. I can't say any
more just now, only that there is nothing to fear, neither must you
let anyone know that there is news of consequence. Don't be the
least flurried, nor cause anyone else to be so. It's only news I've
heard.' He sent a similar note to his brother William.

Isaacs came hurrying and so did William Fynn, Frank Fynn and
John Cane. They consulted together and decided to flee, breaking
up into separate parties and taking different routes. William Fynn
went ahead to alert Faku, in case the Mpondo mistook the exodus
from Natal for another Zulu invasion. He was followed by his
brothers with their African dependants. John Cane rounded up his
people and headed for the bush. Isaacs took no chances: he rushed
back to Port Natal and boarded the *St Michael*.

William Fynn had no trouble in getting clear of Natal; his
brothers were not so lucky. At his first overnight stop, Henry Fynn
discovered that several of his herdsmen had absconded. Then he
hear rumours that Lukilimba was planning to desert him. He was
told that throughout the day Lukilimba and his brother had been
warning the Africans that if they continued on with the white men
they would be attacked and killed by Dingane's impis. It had been
Lukilimba who had persuaded the herdsmen to abscond.

Fynn was furious. Sending for Lukilimba he confronted him
with the rumours and asked him what his plans were. For once
Lukilimba stood up to him. He said he was afraid to go on; he was
afraid of being killed by the Mpondo or of being starved to death;
everyone was deserting and he intended turning back the next
morning. Fynn's patience snapped. 'I was on the point,' he says, 'of
taking hold of my pistol to shoot him.' He managed to control himself, but not for long. That night he was so angry he could not
sleep. He was still angry the next morning and his anger got the
better of him. After consulting some of his people, he took his pistol,
sought out Lukilimba and shot him.

Why Fynn, who was usually so level headed, should have acted
in such a passion is something of a mystery. Killing Lukilimba, of
course, solved nothing.

Dingane's warriors were scouring the country and seven days
later they caught up with the Fynns. They attacked, as Zulu impis
always did, at dawn. Henry Fynn was wakened by 'a violent noise

and commotion which proved to be the Zulus stabbing our people.
. . . The cries of those being murdered woke all the native chiefs, and
in a few minutes all had scattered and made off to various parts of
the bush.' In the darkness Frank Fynn was trampled on by the
warriors, but he managed to grab his musket and join his brother
and seven Hottentots. Blindly they fired in the half-light. The
gun-fire halted the attack and gave Fynn's party time to retreat to a
nearby rock. They held out here while the impi split into three
sections and tried to surround them. But, as the sun rose and the
bullets became more effective, the courage of the warriors ebbed.
They were Dingane's men, not Shaka's. The attack was called off;
the warriors contented themselves with looting Fynn's wagons and
driving off his cattle.

For the first time, white men in Natal had been attacked. Not by
the monster Shaka, but by Dingane on whom they had pinned such
hopes. It had been a short but costly encounter. Returning to his
plundered wagons, Fynn counted his losses. They were heavy.
Five men, twenty women and fifteen children had been killed; there
were seventeen wounded. Something like one hundred and fifty head
of cattle, as well as two horses, had been captured. The wagons had
been gutted—beads, cloth, medicines, food—everything had been
taken. 'All that we succeeded in recovering was two books,' says
Fynn.

Dispirited, living off what they could shoot, and half-expecting
another attack, they dragged themselves across the border into
Mpondoland. Word was sent to Faku to announce their arrival, but
the Mpondo chief was now wary of white men approaching his
kraal. He sent to the local mission station at Bunting to ask for
advice. The missionary, the Rev. W. B. Boyce, quickly came to the
refugees' aid. He told Faku that the Fynns were his countrymen and
must be helped.

And so, twenty-five days after leaving Natal, the sadly depleted
party arrived at Bunting where they were fed, clothed and nursed
back to health.

13

RECONCILIATION

DINGANE HAD ASSURED the traders that he desired only peace. He had given them to understand that he had no wish to emulate Shaka, that fighting was alien to his nature. 'I have given up going to war,' he had said, 'I mean to cultivate peace, and live on terms of good-will with all my neighbours, as being more congenial to my feelings, and more conducive to the welfare of my people.' These were strange words coming from a Zulu King. The traders had good reason for believing them to be false. But they were not entirely false. If Dingane was lying, he was doing so reluctantly; he may well have known that he would not be able to keep his word, but this does not mean that he had no wish to do so.

There is a temptation to think of Dingane as an archetypal ogre. A tyrant who snatches power by murdering his brothers, and retains power by treachery and cruelty, fits well into the mould of the stock villain. Such a man, it could be imagined, must of necessity be determined and ruthless, iron-willed and implacable. Such a man could be assumed to be eaten up with ambition, blind to his limitations, drunk with success and obsessed by a desire to further his conquests. Yet Dingane was none of these things. He was indolent, vacillating and self-indulgent. What energy he had, had been expended in assassinating Shaka, in killing Mhlangana, and in establishing himself as the undisputed Zulu King. Having keyed himself to accomplish all this, he would have liked nothing better than to have unwound; to have sat back to revel in his achievements. He would have been content with the flattery of his subjects and the caresses of his plump, fat-smeared wives; his happiness would have been complete if he could have been left alone to count his cattle, to design his costumes and to dance his dances. Much as he enjoyed exercising his authority, he had no particular desire to extend it. When he said that he did not wish to go to war, he was probably speaking the truth.

But, as he undoubtedly knew, a sybaritic life was not possible for a Zulu King. Shaka had decreed that the Zulu nation was an army; that the King must be a conqueror; that if enemies did not present themselves, they must be found. War not only ensured Zulu supremacy, it was essential to the nation's virility: a Zulu warrior was not a man until he had 'washed' his spear in enemy blood. To 'cultivate peace' would, for Dingane, be tantamount to engineering his own downfall.

Nevertheless he did not relish fighting. He lacked confidence in his own abilities as a warrior and was none too sure of his commanders. Mostly his martial efforts were confined to empty boasting. He liked to talk big, to make frightening noises, to strike menacing poses and to threaten, but when it came to fighting he was careful to pick his enemy and to choose the battle ground. His impis were kept busy chasing cattle stealers, disobedient tribesmen and rebellious clan leaders, but they rarely ventured beyond the borders of Zululand. When called upon to face a more serious challenge, Dingane's army had proved far from invincible. It had happened twice. Each time the outcome had been farcical.

First there had been the uprising of the Qwabe led by Nqetho. These rebels—by far the largest clan to defy Dingane—had been chased but not attacked. No attempt had been made to pursue them across the border into Mpondoland. Only when they had been defeated by Faku did Dingane's warriors mop up survivors who attempted to return to Zululand.

Equally undecisive had been Dingane's second encounter with a potentially dangerous enemy. This was Mzilikazi, the one-time favourite of Shaka who had fled to the north with a band of Zulu warriors and founded the nation known as the Matabele. It was luck, rather than valour, that aided Dingane in his first clash with the formidable Mzilikazi.

For, although Dingane would never admit it, Mzilikazi was a formidable foe. By the time Dingane came to power, his name was known and feared throughout southern Africa: that is southern Africa beyond the borders of Zululand. Mzilikazi was Shaka's protégé: he fought and thought in the manner of Shaka. His followers, the Matabele, had been welded together in the way the Zulu had been welded together—by conquest and absorption. They had attacked and 'eaten up' the tribes that stood in their way; killing the old and useless, recruiting the young and looting cattle, until Mzilikazi was as rich as he was powerful.

Like Shaka, Mzilikazi was a born leader. Early visitors to his kraal described him as dignified and reserved, cunning and suspicious, with a quick eye and a keen intelligence. He bore the stamp, it was said, of 'a man capable of ruling the wild and sanguinary spirits by which he was surrounded'. But he had something of Dingane about him as well. Success had made him fat and vain and this, in time, tended to detract from his inborn qualities. 'His appearance,' declared a later visitor, 'is rather effeminate and indicates that he leads a luxurious life, in his way . . . He idolizes himself, and causes himself to be idolized by his people.'

For all that, Mzilikazi remained a warrior. The Matabele had proved themselves in battle time and again. They dominated a huge territory north of Zululand and there were few—other than the Zulu King—whom Mzilikazi feared. His fear of Shaka, however, had been real and lasting and after Shaka's death it had extended to Dingane. He feared Dingane, not because of his military achievements—which were virtually non-existent—but because of his reputation as an assassin: any man who murdered Shaka must be mighty indeed. Mzilikazi kept well clear of the Zulu domains.

Dingane, in turn, was very conscious of the Matabele beyond his northern border. He knew that Mzilikazi was afraid of him. It was something he liked to crow about. Mzilikazi, he would say, was his 'dog' and some day he would deal with him. For there could be no doubt that, sooner or later, Mzilikazi would have to be dealt with. He was a Zulu renegade and his defection with Shaka's herds was a crime the Zulu nation had never forgiven: honour demanded revenge. But, although Dingane knew this, he did little more than threaten. He did not appear over-anxious to challenge the Matabele; indeed, he might never have done so had he not been pressed into it by his indunas and restless young warriors. The army was impatient for action and Mzilikazi with his stolen herds seemed an obvious target. At last Dingane could restrain his warriors no longer. In June 1830—a year before the white men fled—he ordered his impis, commanded by the astute Ndlela, to attack the Matabele and bring back the lost Zulu cattle.

The campaign took Mzilikazi by surprise. He was completely unprepared for the Zulu advance. The cream of his fighting force

was away in the far north, attacking tribes in the territory that was
later to be known as Rhodesia. All he could muster was an odd
assortment of veterans, herd boys and servants. None of the
neighbouring tribes would come to his aid. Yet he dare not evade
Dingane's challenge; he dare not yield his cattle without a fight. So
he collected his makeshift army together and sent it to meet the
Zulu impis.

As it happened, luck was not entirely on Dingane's side. From the
very outset this conflict between two mighty nations—the Zulu and
Matabele—seemed destined to end in a ludicrous skirmish. For
not only was Mzilikazi's army sadly depleted but the Zulu impis,
when the two forces met, were without a commander. Ndlela, with
the pick of his warriors, had dawdled on the way and his advance
troops faced the Matabele alone. Each side could only do their best;
neither had great hopes of success.

The battle, if such it can be called, started in 'the good old-
fashioned style'. Advancing to within a hundred yards of each other,
the two armies broke into a stream of abuse and sent their champions
out to fight single handed. Then the signal was given to attack. Each
side rushed forward, yelling, stabbing, locking shields and wrestling
foot to foot. It was a short, sharp struggle. The Matabele, finding
themselves hopelessly outnumbered, turned and fled. They were
pursued by the Zulu who hunted down stragglers until nightfall.
Then they retired to await Ndlela. By the time the commander-in-
chief arrived the following morning, the Matabele had vanished.
Contenting himself with setting fire to a few settlements and rounding up a few stray herds, Ndlela led his men back to Zululand. It
was hardly a victory; little more than a raid, it was typical of
Dingane's military exploits.

Dingane, of course, did not see it like that. Why should he
belittle a successful raid on the Matabele? If Zulu honour had not
been fully satisfied, it had at least been appeased. Mzilikazi had fled
with his warriors: Mzilikazi was still Dingane's dog. Now Dingane
could again settle down to the amusements that meant so much to
him.

But if the King fooled himself and his people, he did not fool
everyone. Nathaniel Isaacs had visited the royal kraal shortly after
the Matabele expedition and had found it necessary to revise his
earlier impressions of Dingane.

'There is nothing firm in the capacity of Dingān,' he declared, 'he is too vacillating, too capricious; and, to use an old phrase, there seems in him "nothing constant but his inconstancy".'

This inconstancy was very much in evidence during the King's crisis with the traders. At first—when he heard rumours of a white army approaching—he appeared resolute. He announced his intention of punishing John Cane and stood by it. He gave the impression of being unflustered, of knowing precisely what he was doing. But there was less to Dingane than met the eye. Once Cane had been punished, his resolution began to falter. He would no doubt have been content to leave the matter there and await events. By the time Henry Fynn visited him he had already begun to withdraw. He left it to his indunas to conduct the confrontation between Fynn and Jacob and he was far from firm when Fynn taxed him on the issue. The indunas were also behind the mysterious plot that had been hatched with Lukilimba. The attack on Fynn's party was the result of that plot and it is impossible to know how far Dingane went in condoning it.

What seems reasonably certain is that, as soon as the white men had escaped, Dingane took fright. His indunas could push him only so far. There was still the possibility of a white army advancing from the Cape; he could not risk the traders taking sides against him. It was essential for him to display friendship towards the whites. Within weeks of the Fynns fleeing Natal, Dingane was urging them to return.

[2]

Towards the end of August, 1831, the Rev. Mr Boyce—the missionary at Bunting, near Faku's kraal—received a pencilled note from John Cane. 'I seize this opportunity,' wrote Cane, 'to say we are all well in this quarter after living three months in the Bush, daily expecting the Zoolas to attack us. It all turns out however to be an alarm of our own fear: had Mr Fynn only staid there a few days more, he would not have been assegaied . . . His Majesty (Dingaan) has sent to me to send after him to inform him, should he be inclined to return he may.'

By the time this note arrived at Bunting, Fynn was no longer at the mission station. He had himself earlier received a message from Cane telling him all was well and had left immediately for Natal. He was not alone. At the beginning of August, James Collis had reached Bunting with his well-equipped expedition and the two men left Mpondoland together. The return journey proved almost as hazardous as Fynn's flight. They were plagued by freak storms which held them up for weeks. It rained incessantly, the rivers were flooded, their wagons got bogged in the mud, their food supplies ran low and several of their servants deserted. Collis, a seasoned African traveller, was to report that never before had he experienced such nightmarish conditions. Not until the end of September did they finally reach Fynn's old trading post on the Umzimkulu.

But Natal did wonders for their sagging spirits. Collis was soon writing ecstatically to the Cape, describing his joy at finding himself 'once more in this ever verdant country'. It mattered not that the relentless rains prevented them from at once reporting to Dingane. The King heard of their arrival and was quick to welcome them back. 'We received four oxen from him yesterday—four more today,' reported Collis.

The rains eventually stopped and Fynn and Collis went to emGungundlovu. Dingane received them as if nothing had happened. If any mention was made of Fynn's flight, neither of the traders recorded it. The King's immediate concern was that trading should begin again. He wanted more beads. Collis had brought with him a friendly letter from the Cape authorities and this he was made to read over several times until it was fully understood. Then Dingane dictated his reply. 'Tell the Governor,' he said, 'I am convinced of the goodness of the white people, who have always behaved well here; and I swear none shall ever receive any harm from me or my people. Now write on the paper the beads I want and I will give 100 cows and ivory, mind that!' Collis considered this an excellent beginning. 'I did better with him than the American vessel did either time,' he declared.

The only semblance of unpleasantness came when Dingane demanded that Fynn surrender some refugees whom he was harbouring at his trading post. These were survivors of a recent massacre. Using well-tried tactics, Dingane had enticed the entire Cele clan to one of his kraals and, suspecting them of treachery, had had them surrounded and killed *en masse*. A few had escaped and fled to Natal to seek the protection of the traders. Now Dingane insisted that they be returned to Zululand. The Cele, he argued, were his subjects and he wanted them back. There were far too many Zulu refugees in Natal as it was. The defections were undermining his authority. But Fynn, who had sent a full report of the massacre to the Cape, refused to be party to further executions. He said that if the King wanted to kill the refugees he would no doubt find a way of doing so whether they were returned to him or not. To this Dingane apparently had no answer and the argument fizzled out.

And so all was well again, or so it seemed. Dingane had welcomed the white men back, promised them friendship, and yielded to their pleas. There had been an argument about the Cele refugees, but nothing had been said about the Zulu attack on Fynn. The traders' flight and the events leading up to it had, it appears, been forgotten.

On one point, however, everyone agreed. The arch-villain, the double dealer, the hidden hand behind the whole unfortunate affair, was the unspeakable Jacob. The interpreter was the enemy of the white men. He had tried to turn Shaka against them; he was responsible for arousing Dingane's suspicions; his lies, his inventions and his alarming stories had misled the King and his indunas. Nothing could excuse his treachery. As long as Jacob lived there could be no peace in Natal.

John Cane felt particularly bitter towards the interpreter. He had suffered much from Jacob's intrigues and was determined on revenge. Once things were back to normal and the traders felt secure, Cane went to emGungundlovu and faced Dingane with Jacob's duplicity. The King agreed with all Cane said. 'I see now the untruth of Jacob's statement,' he replied, 'and I have allowed enough time for the [white] commando to arrive; therefore go down to the other white people and kill Jacob and you can take his cattle.'

But, for some reason, Cane was reluctant to kill Jacob. He had won his point but he had no wish to act as executioner. Instead he offered five head of cattle to anyone who would do the job for him. The offer was taken up by Henry Ogle. At the end of January, 1832, Ogle and some of his Africans went to the interpreter's kraal, surrounded it, shot Jacob, and appropriated seventy or eighty head of cattle. Few tears were shed for Jacob in Natal.

There was something inevitable about the interpreter's death. He had been fated to die by a white man's bullet. From the very outset, his association with the whites had been disastrous: the farmers had pursued him on the frontier, the military had imprisoned him, the traders had caused him to flee to Zululand and had followed him there to create further friction. Jacob was a marked man. He was also a rogue. It was an unhappy combination; it made his chances of survival slim indeed.

But whether he deserved to die as he did is another matter. The stories he had told Dingane were not as false as the traders made out. What he had seen and heard in Grahamstown had convinced him that soldiers were about to advance on Natal. And he was not entirely mistaken.

The reason why no white commando had arrive at emGungundlovu was not because Jacob had lied but because the necessary authority had been wanting. In Grahamstown the military had been willing enough to support the traders but they failed to obtain the backing of Sir Lowry Cole, the Governor of the Cape. Sir Lowry had considered the reports submitted to him to be serious but not urgent. He was not unduly bothered about the gun-running of the *St Michael*, although he did admit that the Americans might prove 'embarrassing' as neighbours. Nevertheless, he agreed that the Government should keep an eye on things in Natal. Writing to Whitehall, he had asked permission to send a responsible agent 'to ascertain the real wishes of Dingaan the Zoolah Chief'. But that was as far as he was prepared to go. There was to be no armed invasion of the country. The Governor's caution had killed Jacob as surely as Ogle's gun.

Dingane, persuaded that no invasion had been intended, had sanctioned Jacob's death. Others were not so easily convinced. The interpreter's warnings were not quickly forgotten. Some years later, when missionaries arrived in Zululand seeking to build a school, they found Dingane's indunas suspicious. They were confronted, says one of them, with Jacob's prediction 'that one white man after another would come into the country and want to build a house, and live in the country, till at last an army would come and take the country from them'.

Who can say that Jacob was lying? The time would come when Dingane would have reason to regard him as a prophet.

[3]

The traders quickly settled down again. Most of them were now back in Natal—Henry and Frank Fynn, John Cane, Henry Ogle and Thomas Halstead, as well as James Collis—only William Fynn and Nathaniel Isaacs were missing. William Fynn was with his family in Grahamstown and Isaacs was back on St Helena: both of them intended returning to Natal, but Isaacs never did.

There can be no doubt that Nathaniel Isaacs was an enterprising and extremely brave young man. It had required courage to survive the uncertainties of Natal. But his most recent experience— his narrow escape on board the *St Michael*—had decided him to put first things first. Now, more than ever, he was convinced that there could be no future in Natal until the traders were given military protection. This had been drummed into him by his friend and hero, James Saunders King, and events had shown how right King had been. All the intrigues of the traders to promote a British settlement had ended in disaster. Things had gone from bad to worse. King, Farewell and Hutton were dead; Shaka had been replaced by Dingane. Nothing would ever be achieved by half-baked conspiracies in Natal. For pressure to be brought on the authorities, a much broader campaign was needed: a campaign which would arouse sympathy for the traders and promote commercial interest in Natal. It was Isaacs's intention to launch such a campaign.

He started by arranging for extracts from his diary to be published in the *South African Commercial Advertiser*. Then he sailed for Cape Town where he was given an enthusiastic welcome by the colonists. Interest in Natal was, he found, very keen indeed. Unfortunately this interest was not shared by the Governor. When, in September 1832, Isaacs tried to obtain an interview with Sir Lowry Cole, he was cold-shouldered. This was probably no more than he expected—he was accustomed to being snubbed by Colonial officials—but it more or less put an end to his making headway at the Cape. He decided instead to continue his campaign in England. He knew a member of parliament who might help him by raising the matter in the House and he intended to tackle an influential emigration committee. This, and the publication of his diary, would, he felt sure, focus attention on Zululand. Always the optimist, he seems to have had little doubt that he would succeed in 'getting Natal settled'.

In the meantime he busied himself in Cape Town, seeing this one and that and picking up what news he could of Fynn's activities in Natal. He found plenty to interest him. The newspapers were full of reports from the traders and their various contacts in the Cape. Isaacs was particularly pleased to read an account, written by Fynn, of the massacre of the Cele clan. This was just the sort of thing that was needed to draw attention to Dingane's ghastly methods of government. He was also delighted to learn that Fynn was thinking of writing a history of the Zulu people. Handled in the right way, such a work would add substance to the points he hoped to make when his diary was published in full. Before leaving for England, he wrote a long letter to Fynn. This was the letter in which he gave his friend some valuable literary advice.

He could not be too explicit. Communication with Natal was still uncertain and there was always a chance that a letter could fall into wrong hands. But, for all that, his advice was clear enough. He was extremely anxious, he said, to read Fynn's work. He hoped it would set out the policy of the Zulu Kings. In his own book he intended to illustrate the treachery of both Shaka and Dingane and he hoped Fynn would do the same. 'Make them out as blood-thirsty as you can,' he recommended.

In England Isaacs set to work trying to interest the appropriate authorities and businessmen in his scheme for settling Natal. He issued a long, somewhat confused, prospectus for a joint-stock company which he hoped would finance a properly organised trading venture. But it came to nothing. His book, *Travels and Adventure in Eastern Africa*, published in two volumes in 1836, was as colourful as he promised it would be, but it was regarded more as an adventure story than as a scientific study. Written in lurid, flowery prose, it makes entertaining reading but it is full of contradictions and hopelessly biased.

Yet it had a profound influence on the early history of Natal. Shaka is depicted as an unmitigated monster and little attempt is made to assess his complex role as a warrior king. Dingane fares slightly better. Isaacs did not want to frighten potential settlers in Natal and, after giving various contradictory assessments of the

King, he came down in Dingane's favour. Europeans, he says, had nothing to fear from Dingane: 'So long as they abstain from intrigue, or from those petty jealousies among themselves, by which one attempts to impugn the other before the king, for the purpose of exciting his wrath.' Unfortunately, Isaacs had learned this all-important lesson too late.

He was never able to put his good advice into effect. His days in Natal were over. As late as September 1840 he was writing to Fynn, promising to return to South Africa and three years later he renewed an official claim he had made for land in Natal, but his claim was unsuccessful and, as far as is known, he never travelled south again. The last thirty or forty years of Isaacs's life were spent in west Africa, exporting arrowroot and groundnuts to England and dabbling in the illegal slave trade. He died, aged sixty-four, at Egremont in Cheshire, England, in 1872.

Isaacs's career in Natal was coloured by his unquestioning devotion to James Saunders King. King had brought him to Africa at the age of seventeen and, impressionable youngster that he was, Isaacs had followed his smooth-talking friend blindly. To cover up for King's double dealing, he discounted the friendship shown to the traders by Shaka; he was reluctant to admit that the Zulu kings had any redeeming qualities. There is a great deal of truth in what he says, but all too often his writings have been accepted uncritically. His diary is regarded as a primary source for the pioneering days in Natal but it is too biased—particularly where Shaka is concerned—to be reliable. When he told Fynn to make the Zulu kings 'as bloodthirsty as you can', he summed up his own approach. His portrait of Shaka is an obvious distortion but, for want of other evidence, it has resulted in a legend of a Zulu monster. Shaka, for all his ruthlessness, deserves more credit than Isaacs allows him.

But it is impossible to dislike Isaacs entirely. He was the most flamboyant of the traders: he had all the push, all the audacity and all the breeziness of a true adventurer. He was a born optimist, always ready to take a risk and quick to recover from any misfortune. Irresponsible he might have been, an opportunist he undoubtedly was, but he was a loyal friend and a lively, intelligent and plucky companion. Such things matter in an isolated trading post.

Isaacs wrote of his contribution to early Natal as a trader. What he did not mention was his more personal involvement with the Zulu. If one were to believe all he says, his years in Natal were as chaste as they were noble. Time and again he described how he was forced to turn down the offer of beautiful Zulu girls because he could not conform to the Zulu marriage customs. But, of course, marriage, Zulu or otherwise, did not enter into it. He had his African followers and, like the other traders, he had his African mistresses. There is no knowing how many children he fathered in Natal. Only two are on record.

He mentioned one in the letter he wrote to Fynn from Cape Town. He asked Fynn to take charge of a son he had been forced to leave behind. The boy was to be taken to the Bunting mission station, baptised Henry Porter Isaacs, and educated by the missionaries. 'I know him to be a child of gifted talents,' wrote Isaacs, 'he will doubtless make great progress under the tuition of Mr Boyce.' And years later a traveller was to mention an African who 'had married the mother of Mr Isaacs's daughter'.

This is all that is known of Isaacs's Natal descendants. But, as with *Travels and Adventure in Eastern Africa*, it is probably not the full story.

14

'SUCH A FINE PLACE!'

BY THE BEGINNING of 1832 Dingane was about thirty-seven years old and had been King for over three years. To all outward appearances he was every bit the despot, the worthy successor of Shaka. He was a big, bronze man, six foot or more in height, large-boned, fleshy, with huge thighs and an enormous paunch. Yet, despite his apparent grossness, he gave the impression of tremendous dignity. He held himself erect, had a stately walk and spoke with authority. There was nothing slothful about him. He was fat but not flabby, his muscles were firm and well developed, his eye was keen, he was agile and alert. Both in his manner and in his bearing he lived up to his praise name—'the great elephant'.

The elephant was the symbol of Zulu majesty, a symbol which Dingane guarded jealously. If one of his subjects dared so much as stand on a dead elephant he was suspected of trying to sap the King's strength and was immediately executed. There were other taboos, all strictly enforced, all carrying the death penalty and all designed to glorify Dingane.

No Zulu was allowed to sit on a chair. The only chair in Zululand was Dingane's 'throne' carved from a single block of wood and sacrosanct to the royal buttocks. Should a commoner merely squat on a box he was thought to be emulating the King and his days were numbered. Zulu men and women were permitted to wear black, blue or brick-coloured beads but it was more than their lives were worth to be seen in the King's scarlet or striped beads. No one could eat green Indian corn until it had been tasted by Dingane; only those with masterly control over their emotions and natural reactions could survive watching the King feast. Those approaching Dingane, even the indunas, did so with their heads lowered; his attendants had to walk three yards behind him and anyone passing him on the road was obliged to make a circuit of at least fifteen yards. . . . The list was as endless as ignorance of its requirements was fatal.

The royal mystique created by Dingane fascinated visitors to emGungundlovu. One of the first to record the prohibitions and punishments in detail was Dr Andrew Smith, who visited the King in April 1832. Smith was an army surgeon who had arrived at the Cape in 1820 and had subsequently made a name for himself as a naturalist and explorer. It had long been his ambition to visit Zululand. In 1829 it had been announced that he intended to make a scientific investigation of the country. He had been prevented from doing so by Shaka's assassination. When he eventually set out, at the beginning of 1832, his expedition received little publicity. He had good reason not to draw undue attention to himself. There was more to his trip than a desire for scientific information: he was, in fact, the responsible and disinterested agent chosen by Sir Lowry Cole to investigate conditions in Dingane's territory. Until his report was in the Governor's hands, it was necessary for Smith to act with caution.

It had taken Smith almost three months to reach Port Natal. He was accompanied by an army friend, Lieutenant Edie, and a young Boer named Hermanus Barry; while travelling through the frontier districts, the party was joined by two German naturalists. Somewhat mixed, both in composition and motives, this semi-official expedition was to have considerable impact on affairs in Zululand.

Precisely what Sir Lowry Cole instructed Smith to investigate is not known. By the time Smith left the Cape Colony the Governor had not received authorisation from Whitehall for the expedition and his instructions were probably given verbally. Only the disjointed notes made by Smith and the German naturalists have survived. They are concerned mainly with Zulu customs and manners and provide some interesting sidelights on the sexual activities of the local inhabitants, both black and white.

John Cane was reported as living, not only with Rachel, the Hottentot woman, who was childless, but with an African woman, by whom he had had a number of children. Fynn, Ogle and Collis were less discriminating. They appear to have followed Zulu custom and, as minor chiefs, had their own harems. Each of them, it was recorded, lived 'with several Kaffer women'. This freedom from restraint was equally obvious in the Zulu kraals. Among the advantages of Dingane's regime was the lifting of the marriage restrictions imposed by Shaka and, by the time Smith arrived, permission to marry had been extended to practically all the regiments. It had resulted in a wild scramble for wives. Within months men, forced into celibacy by Shaka, had married eight or ten women. Smith considered this sudden demand for wives somewhat excessive: to meet it Dingane would need to conquer a great many enemies. Polygamy was not, however, without its advantages. 'It is no uncommon thing,' noted the doctor blandly, 'for a woman to hold a light whilst the husband has connection with another wife'.

Other marriage customs were not so cosy. When a woman had a difficult labour, Smith discovered, it was usual for string to be tied round both her ankles and pulled by people outside her hut until the child was delivered. Some women had borne so many children that they required a permanent bandage round their stomachs for support. No woman was allowed to beat her male children; if she did, the boys were allowed to kill her and this, according to Smith, happened frequently. Many of the men suffered from a disease known as *juvela* which resulted in painful elongation and swelling of the penis. 'The men die from it,' says Smith, 'and all men who have connection with women so affected catch it.'

But, by and large, Smith was delighted with Natal and Zululand. The people, he found, were handsome, intelligent looking and seemed far superior to the frontier tribesmen. The country itself was all the traders had reported it to be: lush, fertile, well watered and eminently suitable for colonisation. Abundant crops were obtained twice a year and the hills were covered with dense forests. Everything the traveller hunted for in other parts of South Africa was close at hand in Natal. He was astounded at the number of rivers, rivulets and rills throughout the country.

Nor was he alone in his opinion. Hermanus Barry, the Boer of the party, was in raptures about Natal from the moment they arrived. 'Almighty,' he declared, 'I have never in my life seen such a fine place.' Barry was a farmer and knew what he was talking about. Others, besides Smith, were to be fired by his enthusiasm.

There was no doubt about it—Dingane's country was a veritable paradise. There was only one drawback: that was Dingane himself. Dr Smith did not warm to the King. He had very little good to say about him. He admitted that Dingane seemed well disposed towards the British, would probably enter into an alliance with the

Cape, and wanted nothing more than to continue trading with the colony, but he was doubtful whether his word could be trusted. In Smith's opinion, Dingane was completely unreliable, an ogre, unable to command the loyalty of his people and unworthy to rule. He had good reason for thinking this. On his visit to emGungundlovu Smith caught a glimpse of the horror that lay behind Dingane's royal pretensions. He was shown portions of the bodies of Dingane's wives whom, it was said, the King had executed a few days earlier for annoying him with their foolish chatter. He was told of the refugees who had fled to Natal. He heard of the Cele refugees whose deaths the King was still demanding. He saw that Dingane was suspicious of the white men; that he would discuss the requests of the Cape authorities only when his two indunas, Dambusa and Ndlela, were present. Such a man did not inspire confidence. He was treacherous and unpredictable and white settlers would not be safe while he reigned. It would be better for everybody if he were disposed of. His removal, claimed Smith, would not be difficult.

'If a military party were to be posted near the bay,' wrote the doctor, 'I would engage in twelve months after its arrival to be able to dethrone Dingaan by means of the very people who are at present his support. It is impossible for men to feel attachment to such a monster; and it appears to me an act of great inhumanity to permit his murdering, torturing and destroying even hundreds of his subjects in the course of a day, when only the most trifling exertion would be required to effectually restrain him.'

This is a bold statement for a man who was in Natal for less than a month. Granted that Smith saw all he claims to have seen at emGungundlovu, his assertion that hundreds were murdered in the course of a day is an obvious exaggeration. But then Dr Smith was given to making bold statements on questionable evidence. Some twenty years later he was to distinguish himself, as Director of the Army Medical Service, by blandly assuring Florence Nightingale that no additional medical supplies were needed in the Crimea. But there is something familiar about his confident prediction of Dingane's overthrow. He was evidently relying more on what he had been told than on what he had observed.

Sir Lowry Cole had selected Smith as an impartial observer. He had wanted a report uninfluenced by the interests of the traders.

But the Governor was asking the impossible. Smith, for all his scientific training, was no more impartial than other white men visiting Natal. He could speak no Zulu, he relied on the traders for information, his notebooks are riddled with second-hand opinions. The stories he tells of Shaka, for instance, are the stories told by Fynn, Farewell and Isaacs. The conclusions he reached are the conclusions reached long before by James Saunders King. This is not to say that he was mistaken in describing Dingane as a monster, but it does throw doubt on his role as a disinterested man of science. The whisperings of the traders can be traced in all the early accounts of the Zulu Kings.

That Dr Smith was biased in favour of commercial enterprise became only too apparent on his return to the Cape Colony. His written report to the Governor, if it existed, has been lost, but there is plenty of evidence of his activities on behalf of the traders. He busied himself contacting leading Cape citizens and collecting details of the early expeditions to Port Natal. The account he gave of Natal's economic potential—coupled with the reports of Nathaniel Isaacs—aroused considerable interest among the merchants of Cape Town. At the end of 1833, Smith was invited to address a group of merchants at the Cape Town Commercial Exchange; as a result of this meeting, a memorial was drafted for public discussion.

The public meeting, held on 20 January 1834, attracted widespread attention. Men from all over the colony flocked to hear the views of prominent citizens 'on the subject of a military occupation and settlement of Port Natal'. Tributes were paid to the selfless endeavours of James Saunders King and Lieutenant Farewell. Natal was described in glowing detail. Dr Smith and Nathaniel Isaacs were quoted as authorities. The first speaker was quick to anticipate opposition and dismissed the suggestion that military occupation would imply aggression before it was made. No such thing was intended, he assured his audience. The country had been depopulated by Shaka and would provide an excellent starting point for the spread of 'Christianity and civilisation'. Others were only too eager to support this noble aim. They also revived several old fears. Attention was drawn to Shaka's alarming invasion of the frontier districts in 1828, as well as to the gun-running of the St Michael. Occupation of Port Natal was represented as a worthy crusade; essential to British prestige and the safety of the Cape;

that it might also provide an extremely lucrative trade was made to appear incidental.

As a result of this meeting, a petition was drawn up. Signed by one hundred and ninety residents of Cape Town and addressed to 'His Majesty the King in Council', it requested that steps be taken for setting up a Government establishment at Port Natal. It was supported by a memorandum on the history of Natal written by Dr Andrew Smith. The Governor of the Cape forwarded it to London. Nine months later the petitioners received a reply from the King in Council. Their request was turned down. The finances of the Cape, it was explained, would not stretch to the founding of a new settlement.

It was going to take more than a petition and statements from Dr Smith and Nathaniel Isaacs to move the British Government.

[2]

A Zulu King had to act as a Zulu King. New warriors had to be initiated in battle; enemies had to be punished or frightened off; wars had to be found and fought. Dingane was given little time in which to relax.

Soon after the departure of Dr Smith from emGungundlovu, the indunas were again clamouring for action. They wanted another attack launched on Mzilikazi. Dingane appears to have been reluctant. He refused to allow certain of his commanders to take part in the campaign. But the indunas had their way and the commanders went. The impis left Zululand at the end of June, or the beginning of July, and returned at the end of August.

Little is known of this campaign, but it seems that Mzilikazi's army again managed to escape the full force of the Zulu attack. Later it was reported that the Zulu impis met a contingent of Matabele warriors who asked 'why they did not come on and meet the fighting men who were coming up'. No explanation is given for what was obviously a hasty retreat on the part of the Zulu commanders. The army straggled back to Zululand, having lost three regiments and captured only 140 oxen. The campaign was an abysmal failure: of that there is no doubt.

Dingane was furious. For once he stopped playing the king and acted like Shaka. From those regiments which had not seen action he demanded compensation: each man had to surrender a cow or one of his sisters in lieu of a cow. Those suspected of cowardice were put to death. Blood flowed freely on kwaMatiwane. The commanders whom Dingane had earlier forbidden to fight were now executed for running away from the fighting. Dingane turned on his defeated impis as determinedly as Shaka had punished his successful army. This military massacre was something new: Dingane had never dared so much before.

When the news of the executions reached Natal, the traders were shocked. Fynn, in particular, was alarmed by Dingane's severity. He was still far from easy about his prospects in Natal. The brush he had had with the Zulu impi had chastened Fynn; he was uncertain of Dingane's intentions towards the Cele refugees who still claimed his protection. There was no knowing where or when the King might strike again. If a new attack was made on the traders, it could prove even more devastating than before.

For not only was the white settlement larger, but there were now white women living in Natal.

The women were the wives of three traders named Cawood. They had arrived in Natal at the beginning of 1832. The news of Fynn's reconciliation with Dingane had inspired more traders to leave the Cape Colony. In February 1832, a Mr C. J. Pickman had reached Natal, after a rough four months journey, and shortly afterwards the Cawood party had turned up in five wagons, loaded down with goods for barter. Besides the biblically named Cawood brothers—Joshua, James and Samuel—and their families, there were two other traders in the party.

Fynn had not welcomed this influx. He wished Port Natal to be occupied, but not by unprotected women and children. And certainly not by families like the Cawoods. The Cawoods were religious, given to praying loudly, at length, and in public. Their like had not been seen in Natal before.

When the Cawoods held a prayer meeting, they invited the local Africans to attend. One of the dour-faced brothers would stand beside his wagon and praise the Lord while the others sat in silence; a silence followed by doleful hymn-singing. Fynn found it all quite alarming. 'How must this appear to the Zoola eyes?' he demanded.

'When they invoke their spirits in going to war, a Chief stands in the midst of the people, invoking their spirits for their assistance in the intended attack, the people all in mute silence till he is done, when the war-hoop is sung in a most solemn manner.'

With the King in a suspicious, bloodthirsty mood, the prayers of the Cawoods might well turn him against the traders again. Rumours of a white army approaching had prompted his earlier attack. Knowing little or nothing of the white man's religion, how was Dingane to know that the Cawoods were not the forerunners of a war party?

And the Cawoods, indirectly, were to be the cause of the next brush between the white men and the Zulu impis. It happened the following year. It was a mistake—a genuine mistake this time—but it was frightening and caused the traders to flee Natal a second time.

Dingane's anger at the failure of the campaign against Mzilikazi was undoubtedly profound. He was determined to assert himself. He sought a new enemy; an enemy his warriors could handle. He fixed on a tribe living close to the Mpondos.

This time Dingane tried to be too clever by half. Wanting to surprise his enemy, he ordered his impis to take a roundabout route. First they were to march into the wastelands north of Zululand and then turn westwards and descend on the unsuspecting enemy tribe. But it did not work out like that. The wastelands could not support an army: there were no crops, no cattle, no kraals to plunder and soon the Zulu impis were starving. Warriors, reduced to eating their ox-hide shields, died in their hundreds. They lost their sense of direction. Those who did not starve to death started killing each other.

Of the enemy tribe there was no sign. The only humans encountered by the survivors of the starving army were a few Hottentots camped near the Umzimkulu river. The Hottentots were elephant hunters, armed and dressed like Europeans and the warriors mistook them for white men. Approaching the camp, a Zulu patrol first begged meat and then attacked the Hottentots, smashing their muskets, looting the wagons and killing the entire party with the exception of a youth whom they took captive. The army then moved on into Mpondoland where it was reported that they had attacked and killed a party of white men.

Henry Ogle, who was hunting in Mpondoland, was the first trader to hear of the attack. He was shown a spade which the Zulu marauders had taken from the Hottentots. He thought he recognised it as belonging to the Cawood brothers who were also hunting in the area. Ogle immediately scribbled a note to John Cane saying that the Cawoods had been murdered and a Zulu attack could be expected.

Cane, who had been the first victim of the previous attack, was taking no chances this time. He organised his African followers into a fighting force and pounced on the dispirited Zulu impis as they approached Port Natal. A terrible slaughter followed. The Zulu were too exhausted to fight back and Cane's men, armed with muskets, killed over two hundred warriors before the attack was called off.

Not until the following day did the traders come to their senses. Then they met to discuss the affair and quickly realised their mistake; they were also aware of what it could, and most likely would, lead to. The facts spoke for themselves: no Zulu force had been sent to attack them but they had attacked a Zulu force. Dingane would surely retaliate. How could they expect anything else? The conference did not last long. Once again they hastily packed their wagons and headed for Mpondoland. This time they felt sure they would never return.

But, of course, they did.

Henry Ogle had been the last to leave and he was overtaken by Zulu messengers who had been sent in search of the Europeans. He returned with them to Natal and was assured by Dingane that there was nothing to fear. The King, however, was in two minds about whether or not the white men should return. There appeared, he informed Ogle, to be something obstructing the friendship between them. True as this was, it did not prevent the white men from slowly making their way back. The rift was patched up by Ogle in August 1833 and by the beginning of the following year all the original traders—with the exception of the hymn-singing Cawoods—had more or less settled down again.

And the settlement continued to grow. In May 1834 it was reported that some thirty persons, backed by Cape merchants, had left Grahamstown with the intention of forming 'a permanent establishment in the vicinity of the port'. These newcomers had been given every encouragement. Some four months earlier the widely publicised meeting, inspired by the report of Dr Andrew Smith, had been held in Cape Town and the reports from Natal were more optimistic than ever. Not only had Dingane allowed the traders to return but he had ordered his people to abandon Natal and settle beyond the Tugela. Shaka had earlier granted Natal to Farewell and King; now it looked as if Dingane was prepared to honour the agreement.

But not everyone was happy. The old-timers, who had once roundly denounced Shaka as untrustworthy, were now having second thoughts about their old protector. Things would have been very different had Shaka lived. Dingane was far too unpredictable to inspire confidence. 'What a contrast there is between Shaka's government and his,' lamented Fynn. 'If he, Dingane, had the same power as Shaka had, it is evident the people would respect Europeans more than has of late been evinced, if his conduct towards them did not give scope for such outrageous conduct, taking away their lives and property.'

If Fynn's facts and syntax were a little shaky, his meaning was abundantly clear.

[3]

'Almighty,' Hermanus Barry had exclaimed in Natal, 'I have never in my life seen such a fine place!' He had gone on to say that if the British made Port Natal a magisterial district he would gladly leave the Cape Colony and settle there.

Barry was half Briton, half Boer: he had an English father and an Afrikaans mother. His national loyalties were therefore inclined to be divided. The fact that he had accompanied Dr Andrew Smith's semi-official expedition seems to indicate that his sympathies were with his father's people, the English, and he would, as he said, have been happy to see the British occupy Natal. But there were many among his mother's people who felt differently. Reports from Natal had aroused widespread interest in the Cape Colony and nowhere was that interest so intense, or so purposeful, as among the Boer population. Many an Afrikaans farmer would have welcomed the opportunity to leave the Cape and settle in Natal, but, unlike Barry, they wished to escape, rather than court, British protection.

The Boers were descendants of the original white settlers at the Cape. These settlers had come to South Africa in the seventeenth century as employees of the Dutch East India Company. They had come mostly from Holland but over the years they had absorbed other emigrants from Europe, mostly French and German, until they were regarded as a distinct nation: they were not Dutchmen, Frenchmen or Germans but white Africans or, as they became known, Afrikaners.

In Afrikaans, the language of the Afrikaners, Boer means farmer. But the Boers were more than farmers: they were tough, rugged individualists who formed the solid core of their people. The Boers had pioneered southern Africa. They had broken away from the original settlement in the western Cape to search for the two things which, next to God, they prized above all else: land and freedom. They were born conservatives and born rebels. Their deep attachment to their land was equalled only by their fierce resentment of any interference in their way of life. To escape the restrictions of the Dutch East India Company, they had moved further and further away from Cape Town. They had declared themselves independent and set up their own republics. But they could never escape completely: authority—first the tentative authority of the Dutch East India Company, then the more resolute authority of the British—had a way of catching up with them.

The British had first occupied the Cape temporarily at the end of the eighteenth century and then permanently in 1806. Their coming had naturally been resented by the Boers. Not only were they foreigners with a minimal understanding of conditions at the Cape, but they brought with them concepts, both civil and religious, which were anathema to the Cape farmers.

The Boers were, for instance, unable to accept black men as their legal equals; they were vehemently opposed to laws under which a master could be charged for ill-treating his servants. It was not that the Boers were the sadistic task-masters they were often made out to be: their relationship with their servants was no worse, and often much better, than existed in contemporary Europe. But it was a feudal relationship in which the authority of the Boer patriarch was supreme and unquestioned. A farmer would no more recognise the right of outsiders to come between master and servant than he would allow interference between parent and child. For the Boers, British law did not represent justice; it was an unwarranted encroachment which undermined the God-ordained structure of their society.

Nor were matters helped by the missionaries who followed the British to the Cape. The Boers were a religious people but their interpretation of Christianity differed vastly from that of the clergymen who invaded the Cape. Essentially Calvinists, steeped in the teachings of the Old Testament, the Boers had little in common with the philanthropic evangelism of the missionaries. The differences which separated them from the newcomers, both in law and religion, boiled down to much the same thing: the ideals of a patriarchal society were inevitably opposed to concepts of equality and brotherhood. So profound were these differences that they were bound to clash.

And clash they did. Circuit judges touring the Cape Colony all too often found against the Boers on charges levelled by the missionaries. The fact that many of these charges were trumped-up, or ill-founded, only increased the bitterness of the farmers. In 1815 tensions came to a head when a recalcitrant Boer repeatedly refused to answer summonses issued by a Graaff Reinet court and was eventually shot by a party—mostly Hottentots—which was sent to arrest him. The incident sparked off a rebellion among the neighbouring farmers, who called upon a local African chieftain to assist them. Although the rising received little support, the gruesome public hanging of five of the ringleaders added considerably to the growing Boer resentment of British rule.

But the dissatisfaction of the Boers was caused by more than resentment. There was, among other things, the question of land. The Boers loved their land. They loved the vast farms with horizons unclouded by smoke from their neighbours' chimneys; they felt hemmed in on holdings of less than 6000 acres. They wanted such farms, not only for themselves but for each of the sons of their large families. It had been the search for land, as much as the search for freedom, that had caused them to spread across the Cape. But they were unable to expand indefinitely. As they moved eastwards with their cattle, they collided with other herdsmen seeking new grazing. The Bantu tribes they encountered presented a more formidable barrier than had the indigenous Hottentots and Bushmen of the western Cape. It had been necessary to observe a frontier between black and white; a frontier that had constantly to be defended and redefined in the vain hope of preventing cattle thieving and friction.

And with the rise of Shaka and the expulsion of the settled tribes in Natal, the pressure on the frontier had become greater, the friction had increased.

Attempts by the British to strengthen the frontier had merely complicated matters. The arrival of the 1820 Settlers had caused a further drain on the available land. More and more the frontier Boers felt themselves deprived of their rightful inheritance; more and more they felt themselves exploited by the British who afforded them little protection from the marauding tribesmen and who paid scant regard to their needs.

Not the least among their needs was the need for a cheap and stable labour force. This was something the British authorities had once recognised. They had introduced laws which prevented the roving Cape Hottentots from moving from one district to another without a pass from a magistrate; thus tying the Hottentots to the farms and turning them into serfs. In 1828, however, these controversial pass laws were repealed. There was an immediate outcry from the farmers, English and Afrikaans, who claimed that the Hottentots would become vagrants or, even worse, would be able to demand higher wages

Hardly had this furore died down when more alarming news reached the Cape. In May 1833, the British parliament passed an Emancipation Act by which all slaves in the British Empire were to be set free by the end of the following year. This came as a severe blow. Unpopular as was the Act, the Boers were later given more justifiable grounds for complaint when it was announced that compensation for the loss of their slaves—about a third of what had been promised—was payable only in London, 6000 miles away. Slave-owning was indefensible and its abolition long overdue, but until it was abolished it had been perfectly legal and, by having to pay agents to act for them, many of the farmers suffered serious loss.

The frontier Boers did not own as many slaves as farmers in the more settled western Cape, but the news of the Emancipation Act added to their many grievances. It looked as if the philosophy of the hated missionaries was gaining ground and there was nothing they could do about it. There was only one answer. They would have to clear out of the Cape Colony—trek, take their families and cattle and find a new country; a country where they would be free of political interference, where they could live their lives according to their beliefs.

But where were they to go? The Boers were singularly incurious and knew little of the country outside the Cape Colony. The tales told by hunters and travellers in the north-western regions were hardly encouraging. There were vast expanses of semi-desert, poor grazing and little water. The territories to the immediate north were more promising but were said to be bounded by formidable mountain ranges; the tribesmen there were more organised and might prove aggressive. Nor were they better informed about the land beyond the eastern frontier. Until the return of Andrew Smith and Hermanus Barry they, like the other colonists, knew no more about Natal than what the traders had reported. Could such reports be trusted? Could they risk large-scale emigration in any direction? How far would they have to trek before finding the country they sought? Where, indeed, was the Promised Land?

They decided to find out. They decided, as they were wont to say, 'to make a plan'.

In the middle months of 1834, three exploring parties secretly left the Cape. They were known as the *kommissie trekke*: they were instructed, or commissioned, to report on the possibilities of settlement beyond the borders of the Cape Colony. They rode out in three directions: to the north, the north-west and to the east.

How much the eastern *kommissie trek* was inspired by Hermanus Barry is not certain. Barry had made no secret of his enthusiasm for Natal and his word would probably have counted for more than that of the traders. Certainly the Boers knew of Andrew Smith's expedition. In travelling through the frontier districts and Mpondoland, they kept close to Smith's route (which had earlier been detailed in the *Grahamstown Journal*). They went by wagon—twenty-one men and one woman—and called on the local chieftains who made a great show of entertaining them. Faku is said to have been overjoyed at hearing they were looking for land. He urged them to settle close to him. He said he would welcome a buffer state between himself and Dingane, particularly a well-armed white state. The Boers made no promises. Their leader, the short, stocky, dynamic Piet Uys, said he would look at the country first; if he decided to return, he would bring with him enough white men to prevent Dingane from ever making trouble again. One wonders whether Dingane, whose spies were everywhere, got to hear of this threat?

The traders at Port Natal were delighted to see the Boers. Over the last few months the settlement had grown considerably and one of the newcomers, Richard King, son of an 1820 Settler, offered to act as their guide. They were told that Dingane's spies had already informed the Zulu King of their arrival and, as soon as they had established themselves at the Umvoti river, young Dick King was sent hurrying to emGungundlovu to explain why they had come. Dingane did not exactly welcome the news. He appears to have been cagey, refusing to commit himself one way or the other until he had spoken to Piet Uys. Dick King was sent back to the Umvoti with an escort and told to bring the Boers to the royal kraal.

Uys was willing enough to visit Dingane but, just as he was about to start out, he went down with fever and had to be confined to his wagon. His companions were reluctant to move without him. For days they hung about waiting for Uys to recover, until the Zulu escort sent by Dingane became restless. Eventually it was decided that a small party, led by Uys's younger brother, Johannes, should undertake the mission.

Arriving at the Tugela, the Boers found the river in flood and impassable. All they could do was shout messages to the tribesmen on the opposite bank. Word was sent to Dingane but, despite the King's instructions that a raft be built, no closer contact was made. Neither the Boers nor the Zulu escort seemed anxious to brave the angry current. In the end Johannes Uys gave up. He had not seen the King but he was satisfied with what he had heard—or what he thought he had heard—from the tribesmen across the river. He returned to the Umvoti camp highly optimistic.

The King, he was to report, wanted the Boers to return to Natal. He wanted them to come in their hundreds. Natal was vacant and Dingane would grant vast tracts of land to white settlers. This, said young Uys, is what the tribesmen had told him.

So the Promised Land had been found. There was no time to confirm the good news. Rumours that a war had broken out in the frontier districts made it imperative that the Boers return to the

Colony immediately. As soon as Piet Uys had recovered, the Zulu escort was presented with gifts and a stallion for Dingane, and the party inspanned their wagons and left. They reached the Cape Colony safely. There was no doubt in their minds that Natal, in all its beauty and promise, was the land their people sought. They had no doubt that they would return and live in peace.

But they should have had doubts. Had they troubled to find out a little more about the Zulu King, they might have suspected those garbled promises. For it is highly unlikely that Dingane said all he was supposed to have said. It is extremely doubtful whether the King would, at that time, have encouraged white settlers to come to Natal. He was already unhappy about those who were there. There had been too many 'misunderstandings'; there were too many Zulu refugees sheltering with the traders. Only a few months previously Dingane had ordered his people to withdraw to the other side of the Tugela. Only a few months previously he had told Henry Ogle that he was doubtful whether the white men should return. Why should he now wish more of them to come?

Obviously there had been a misunderstanding. It was the first of the many misunderstandings that were to plague Dingane's dealings with the Boers.

[4]

If the Uys brothers were full of hope, the more experienced Fynn brothers were by no means as optimistic. In September 1834, Henry and William Fynn packed their bags and left Natal. This time they were not pursued by Zulu impis, real or imaginary; this time they went of their own accord.

Henry Fynn never explained his departure. He gave no reason why, after ten years of struggle and uncertainty, he decided to abandon life as a trader and to enter government service. He was undoubtedly disillusioned. He had lost most of his friends and saw little hope for the future. The long-looked for military protection had never materialised; there seemed little chance of it coming now. He had admitted as much shortly after his most recent return to Natal. 'Dingaan,' he wrote, 'has been told these five years, that an authority was coming to him from government, it however does not seem likely that the government will bother with this place till they find that ultimately must be so.' But that would not be yet: it would not be for a long time.

Fynn must have realised this and decided that he could not wait indefinitely. He had arrived in Natal as a hopeful young man of twenty-one; he was now thirty-one and no longer hopeful. The time had come to think of a more settled, a more secure, career. He had not far to look. During the frontier war that had sent the Boers hurrying back to the Cape Colony, Fynn was employed as head-quarters interpreter to the Cape Governor. He continued to act as a government agent and eventually settled as British Resident in Mpondoland.

In 1852 Fynn returned to Natal after an absence of eighteen years. The place had changed considerably by then. The British had at last moved in, a town was developing at Port Natal and the future seemed assured. But it had all come too late to be of any real benefit to Fynn; he received little or no compensation for his pioneering efforts. He came to be respected as an expert on early Natal and on the traditions and customs of the Zulu people, but the fortune that he and Farewell had hoped to realise eluded him as surely as it had eluded his companions. He died, aged fifty-eight, in 1861, in a house almost within sight of his original camping place. To the very end the government refused to acknowledge his claim to a modest land grant.

The members of the original trading parties were fading from the scene like—one hesitates to say it—the ten little nigger boys. One by one, Farewell, King, Hutton, Isaacs, Fynn and young John Ross died or disappeared

And now, by 1834, there were three: John Cane, Henry Ogle and Thomas Halstead. The three junior members of Farewell's party stayed on; but only one of them was to survive the vagaries of Natal.

15

A MAN OF GOD

LATE IN THE afternoon of 10 February 1835, Dingane peeped over the fence of his *isiGodlo* to inspect a new visitor to emGungundlovu. He found himself gazing at a tall, gaunt man, whose intense expression, pursed lips and level stare made him unlike any white man the King had ever met. Dingane was fascinated. For several minutes he continued looking at the man without saying a word. Then, evidently satisfied, he pointed to an ox standing nearby and said: 'There is the beast I give you for slaughter.' With that he disappeared from view. Dingane had come face to face with his first missionary.

The missionary was Allen Francis Gardiner, son of an English country gentleman, and a former officer of the Royal Navy. Then forty years old, Gardiner had come to Africa to spread the word of God and to recover from a personal tragedy. He was a deeply, almost fanatically, religious man. Only his love of travel and adventure equalled his unquestioning piety. He had inherited his religious beliefs from his devout parents who, when he was a boy, had opposed his wish to join the British navy on the well-founded grounds that such a career would lead him from the paths of righteousness. But young Allen had had his way. Shortly after his fourteenth birthday he had enrolled as a cadet at the Royal Naval College, Portsmouth, and two years later embarked on his first sea voyage in the warship *Fortune*.

Gardiner's parents need not have worried unduly. There was little chance of their son going seriously astray. He was far too earnest, far too dedicated. As a young man he did, it is true, abandon his Christian beliefs but his conscience appears to have nagged at him. In 1820, during a severe illness, his doubts surfaced; he took stock of his life and decided to devote himself to missionary work. His conversion, however, conflicted with his career. He was then a naval lieutenant and, on recovering his health, returned to sea and was eventually promoted to the rank of captain. A more profound shock was required to wean him from the navy.

At twenty-nine he had married Julia Reade, a young woman from Oxfordshire. They had five children. The marriage lasted over ten years, until May 1834, when his wife died. So shaken by her death was Gardiner that he swore to give the rest of his life over to the conversion of primitive peoples. This time he was true to his word. By August of that year he was on his way to Natal as a missionary.

Africa was Gardiner's chosen field. He had asked to be sent to the mysterious continent where slavery, savagery and superstition were rife. Why Natal in particular was selected is not clear. There were few white men there, little was known of the Zulu people and a lone, inexperienced missionary would be faced with tremendous obstacles. It may have been the missionary society, primed by their Cape representatives, who decided on Natal; they may have wished to test the zeal of their new recruit. Certainly no more zealous, more single-minded Christian could have been chosen. Allen Gardiner hurried to Natal with all the confidence of a fervent novice. If Dingane did not see the light it would not be Gardiner's fault.

But he was helped by more than high hopes. Allen Gardiner could, when he wished, be extremely persuasive. This had been demonstrated on the voyage to South Africa. One of the passengers on board ship—a well-born Pole named Berken—had been so impressed by him that, by the time they docked at Cape Town, Gardiner had gained his first follower. Berken decided to break his journey to Australia to explore the Cape Colony. At first Berken had intended to travel only as far as Grahamstown, but he was still tagging along behind the missionary when Gardiner started for Natal.

The journey through the frontier districts proved tough going. They narrowly escaped the fighting that had recently broken out and, as it was summer, were held up by swollen rivers. Eventually Gardiner was forced to leave Berken with the bulk of their luggage and travel ahead with two servants. Even so, he lost two horses and, on one occasion, was reduced to eating cheese rind and a packet of damp sugar, before he finally limped into Port Natal. None of this doused Gardiner's fiery spirit. After a brief two-day rest at the bay, he borrowed a wagon from James Collis and set off, as determined as ever, for emGungundlovu.

[2]

He arrived at the royal kraal exhausted. Nevertheless, when
Dingane sent for him, he lost no time in presenting himself. Having
been inspected by the King over the fence, he waited to see what
would happen next. He quickly found out. Within minutes Dingane,
wearing a blue dungaree cloak, edged with white tape, waddled out
of the *isiGodlo* gate. Gardiner was most impressed. The cloak was
well-worn, tarnished, and trailed in the dust, but this did not
detract from Dingane's regal bearing. Once in the arena, he
straightened up, walked with a measured step and looked every bit
the king. He did not, however, walk towards Gardiner. He had
other duties to perform.

Earlier the missionary had noticed several piles of newly slaughtered oxen close to the *isiGodlo* fence. With a word here and a nod
there, Dingane now proceeded to distribute this meat among a
crowd of crouching warriors. At the King's signal the warriors
darted forward, one by one, collected their rations and rushed off,
holding the meat aloft and singing Dingane's praises. Gardiner
watched this ritual—undoubtedly arranged for his benefit—
spellbound. Like Shaka, Dingane knew how to stage manage an
introduction.

Not until all the meat had been distributed did Dingane appear
to notice his guest. He crossed slowly to where the missionary was
squatting and stood motionless until his throne had been placed
behind him. Then, seating himself, he began to pepper Gardiner
with questions. How had his guides behaved? Why had he come?
Was he a trader? Who was this God he spoke about? What presents
had he brought? Who was his king? How did his king govern?

Gardiner answered as best he could. He tried to explain
Christianity. He assured Dingane that religion had brought great
advantages to heathen people. He apologised for not having a present for the King and explained that in his haste to reach
emGungundlovu he had been forced to leave his gifts behind: they
would be arriving shortly. His king, he said, was King William,
who governed with the help of his great men.

Dingane smiled indulgently. He doubted whether his people
could learn from Christianity and refused to commit himself on the

question of allowing Gardiner to teach. He was obviously sceptical about King William's power. The only thing that seemed to impress him was the fact that the missionary had arrived empty-handed. Gardiner had got off to a bad start. When he was dismissed he was told to bring 'the Book' he had spoken about on his next visit.

That was not until three days later. Gardiner was informed that the King was unwell and could not see him, but it seems more likely that Dingane was deliberately holding himself aloof. White men visiting emGungundlovu were expected to bring presents. The King was not prepared to put himself out for those who did not.

The second interview was held in the *isiGodlo*. Gardiner, clutching his Bible, was ushered into the royal hut where Dingane, attended by two women, was stretched out on a mat, his head resting on a hollowed wooden block. He asked to be shown the Bible. After riffling through the pages, he handed it back and told Gardiner to read to him. Selecting what he considered appropriate passages—those dealing with death, damnation and judgement—the missionary read until he was interrupted. The King had a few pertinent questions to ask: 'Where was God? How did he give his Word? Who would be judged on the last day? What nations would appear? Would his be included? Would he live forever if he learned the Word?'

At last Gardiner thought he was getting somewhere. But he did not advance very far. Dingane was interested, was friendly, but he remained evasive. Gardiner's hints about establishing a mission were brushed aside. That, said the King, was something for his indunas to decide. He suggested that Gardiner consult Ndlela and Dambusa.

Introduced to the indunas, Gardiner discovered where the real power at emGungundlovu lay. 'Hitherto,' he says, 'I had been treated with great civility by all, but an unaccountable change was now apparent.' Ndlela and Dambusa were openly hostile. They treated the missionary with contempt, they had him followed, they encouraged people to insult him, they prevented him from seeing the King. He could rarely leave the kraal without being ordered to return and, on one occasion, a huge warrior seized him by the shoulder and turned him about as he was heading for the gate. His Christian patience was sorely tried. When he complained, the indunas laughed. Yes, they admitted, they had sent messengers to fetch him; no harm was intended; they merely wanted him to sit down and talk with them. Gardiner knew better.

He could not understand this hostility. Not until later did he learn the cause of it. Then he was told about Jacob's prophecy: the warnings about missionaries heralding the coming of the white men.

Things improved slightly when Gardiner sent to Port Natal to find out what had happened to his luggage, but there was no real improvement until the long-awaited presents for Dingane arrived at emGungundlovu. Then things brightened up considerably. Gardiner was gratified. He had taken a great deal of care in selecting gifts for the King. The prize article was a red baize cloak, with a long silky nap, which Gardiner—advised by one of the Fynn brothers—had bought in Grahamstown. He was told that both the colour and texture of the cloak would please Dingane. They certainly did. The moment the cloak was unpacked, Dingane seized upon it. He had it displayed in every possible manner: first on his own shoulders, then on one of his servants—who was made to turn and twist so that the drape could be admired from every angle—then two men were ordered to run to and fro, with the cloak rippling in the air between them, and finally it was hung on a fence for public viewing. After that Gardiner did not see the cloak again. Dingane had it put away for highdays and holidays.

There were plenty of holidays while Gardiner was at the royal kraal, but none grand enough to warrant the red cloak. Once Dingane had got over his sulks, he went out of his way to entertain the missionary. He ordered his wives, veiled with brightly coloured beads, to dance for Gardiner and had great fun in making some of the women hide until the missionary found them by following the written instructions of his interpreter. The bewilderment of the women at being discovered without a word said, amused Dingane immensely. 'Dingarn,' remarked Gardiner, 'with all his barbarity, is dearly fond of a joke.'

But he was making precious little progress.

Dingane had become more accessible, more amenable and seemed well-disposed towards the missionary. Gardiner had proved a source of never-ending novelties. His monocle made an excellent burning glass (the King had experimented with it; first on the grass, then on a warrior's arm). The ticking of his watch had proved so amusing that the King had tried to steal it and gave it up only on being promised another in return. Dingane felt he had much to learn from Gardiner. But this did not include the white man's religion. He showed little real interest in Christianity and avoided all questions to do with a possible mission station.

In the end Gardiner tried to force the issue. He hinted that he was about to return to Port Natal and needed to know where he stood. As always, Dingane referred him to the indunas. As always, Ndlela and Dambusa were evasive, if not downright rude. They told Gardiner that the entire male population was about to depart for emBelebeleni, a military kraal, and advised him to follow the King there for an answer. He had no option but to do what they told him.

Arrival at emBelebeleni did nothing to cheer the missionary. The kraal was grossly overcrowded and Gardiner had trouble finding accommodation. He and his interpreter were forced to spend a miserable night sleeping on the rock-like floor of a small hut already occupied by two Africans. Next morning he had great difficulty in rounding up Ndlela and Dambusa for the long promised discussion.

The conference was held under a large, shady tree. Dingane sat on his chair, flanked by the indunas, while Gardiner and his interpreter squatted in front of him. Once again the missionary tried to explain the blessings of Christianity. He made a point of emphasising that he had no wish to interfere with Zulu laws and customs. A prominent feature of his religion, he claimed, was honour and respect for kings and all those in authority. This is what 'the Book' taught. Dingane listened but said nothing. It was left to Dambusa to reply: he quickly demolished Gardiner's arguments.

They had no wish for such teaching, he said. The missionary spoke words they could not understand, they would never understand them. If Gardiner wanted to instruct them he could stay and teach them how to use a musket; this was the sort of thing they were interested in. Gardiner protested that he was a man of God, not a man of war. It made no impression. Ndlela joined in and supported Dambusa: it was muskets or nothing.

Finally Dingane spoke. He would not, he said, overrule the decisions of his indunas.

And so Gardiner gave up. Declining Dingane's invitation to stay for the twenty days dancing that was about to start, he made preparations to leave. Two days later he said a formal goodbye to the King. The entire kraal was summoned for the leavetaking. Dingane asked the missionary to return and suggested that he build a school at Port Natal and teach the people there. Gardiner grasped at this slight straw. 'I told him,' he says, 'that I hoped he would soon alter the word he had spoken, and that whenever he wished a teacher for his people, he must send me a message to Port Natal.'

It was more of a gesture than a hope. Gardiner had spent over a month with Dingane and had gained nothing more than an offer to teach the Zulu warriors musket shooting. But he did not despair. He took comfort in the thought that his ways were not God's ways and, so long as he kept faith, a way would be opened to him. He had very little else to hold on to.

[3]

If Dingane did not want a missionary there were others who did. On his return to Port Natal Gardiner was handed a letter signed by eight of the principal traders—including John Cane, Henry Ogle and James Collis—asking him to establish a mission station at the bay. Gardiner was quick to respond. Never one to sit idle, he recognised that there was plenty to keep him busy while waiting for God to move Dingane. There were some thirty Europeans now living in Natal as well as thousands of Africans, all of them deprived of religious teaching. He started immediately.

The day after he received the traders' letter, he held two open-air meetings: preaching to thirteen of the settlers in the morning and to one hundred and fifty Africans in the afternoon. He explained that he would continue to minister to the Natal community until the necessary buildings had been completed and arrangements made for a Church of England clergyman to take over. Four days later he selected a site for his mission on a hill overlooking the bay, which he named Berea, and was given title to the land by an agreement signed by the traders. Within a week he had started a school and, in true missionary spirit, had distributed lengths of calico to his pupils 'that they might appear decently dressed'. Christianity had indeed come to Natal.

Whether the traders' request to Gardiner was inspired by the need for spiritual uplift is another matter. The presence of a missionary at Port Natal undoubtedly added to the status of the settlement. Pleas to the Cape authorities for protection had previously been tainted by commercialism; now their claim to be agents of Christianity and civilisation was given more substance. It might well result in the Flag following the Cross. Certainly the need for a military contingent was as strong, if not stronger, than ever.

For the newcomers had inherited all the problems of their predecessors. They remained, despite the increase in numbers, a small white community, isolated and vulnerable, with an unpredictable savage king breathing down their necks. And Dingane's breath was far from comfortable. As more and more Zulu deserters flocked to Natal, so the King's demand for their return became more insistent. The dilemma Fynn had faced with the Cele refugees had grown a hundred-fold. There was no telling how long Dingane's patience would last; how long it would be before he decided to claim his renegade subjects by force. Not without reason, the traders lived in daily fear of a Zulu attack. Precautions obviously had to be taken.

It is not without significance that, shortly after Gardiner started his mission, a general meeting of the traders was called to discuss the position. On the missionary's advice, plans were made to protect the settlement and a system of mutual help agreed upon. A month later another meeting was held in John Cane's shack. This time it was decided to negotiate a treaty with Dingane. Gardiner was to visit the King again and promise that, so long as the traders were left in peace, they would refuse to accept any more deserters from Zululand. Those refugees then living in Natal were, however, to be exempt.

Once more Gardiner left for Zululand. He found the King still on his royal progress, living at another of his military kraals. This time the missionary had come well prepared. He had brought with him a sack full of unusual, if somewhat improbable, presents. Included among the rolls of calico, ribbon and looking-glasses were a pair of naval epaulettes, a silk sword belt, a telescope, three small gilt bracelets, several coloured engravings of English scenes and field sports and full-length portraits of George IV, in his robes, and William IV in naval uniform.

Dingane was ecstatic. He arranged to have the epaulettes sewn onto his new red cloak, hung the sword belt round his neck, amused himself gazing at the moon through the telescope and exclaimed over the coloured prints. He was suitably impressed by the portraits of the British kings and, on looking closely at the figures in a view of Brighton Pavilion, was astonished at the white man's custom of walking arm-in-arm with women. Equally astonished was he when, as he sweated to thrust his podgy fingers through the gilt bracelets, Gardiner informed him that such ornaments were usually worn only by ladies. 'Ah!' grunted the King, temporarily abandoning the struggle, 'they shall not wear them here.'

During the first interview no mention was made of the purpose of Gardiner's visit. The King had been informed why the missionary had come but deliberately avoided the subject. Dambusa and Ndlela were away and, until they returned, no important discussion could take place.

When the indunas arrived, two days later, Gardiner was ready for them. Knowing how obsessed Dingane was with dress, he turned up for the conference in full naval uniform. The effect was more than he bargained for. For several minutes the King stared at him speechless. Then, heaving himself from his chair, he waddled over to Gardiner for a closer inspection. The missionary explained that this was his war dress and that he always wore it when he approached his own king. Dingane's hands were everywhere; he examined every piece of braid, every tassel. So fascinated was he by the sword that, in the end, Gardiner presented it to him.

Once the discussion got under way, Gardiner's hopes rose. Dingane listened while he explained the traders' proposals and seemed immediately interested. He heard Gardiner out and then, idly picking at the *isiGodlo* fence, he agreed to the plan. He said he was prepared to ignore the past offences of his subjects in Natal and to promise that no harm would come to the traders, but he doubted whether the white men would keep their word.

'I observed here,' said Gardiner stoutly, 'that "true Englishmen" never broke a treaty; that it had always been our boast to adhere to them; and that, if he had met with white people who had deceived him, he had been unfortunate—they were not the right sort of Englishmen".'

Immediately recognising Gardiner as the right sort of Englishman, Dingane pointed a finger at the missionary and said he was satisfied. Now he was dealing with a great chief. Now all would be well. The naval uniform had not been worn in vain.

Gardiner left Dingane sheathing and unsheathing his new sword and was not a little surprised to notice that, deeply embedded on the King's fat wrist, were three lady's gilt bracelets.

For the next few days things went smoothly. Even Dambusa and Ndlela, after being presented with lengths of cloth and a few naval buttons, seemed well disposed towards Gardiner. They claimed that they had previously misunderstood his motives but now that the treaty had been concluded they recognised that he was the King's friend. The words of the treaty, they said, had gladdened their hearts.

On his last Sunday he was summoned to a meeting with Dingane and the two indunas. He found them seated close to the *isiGodlo* fence. Once again he was asked to explain his religion and once again he launched into a long sermon on the benefits enjoyed by nations who believed in God. While he spoke, he says, Dingane 'appeared deep in thought, looking earnestly at me, and occasionally, as though abstracted, picking blades of grass from under his chair'. But the King was far from abstracted; he was listening intently. When the missionary had finished, he turned to the indunas and said: 'Now you must decide.'

And decide they did. To Gardiner's amazement they decided in his favour. God's news, declared Dambusa, was good news. They had been mistaken before, the treaty had changed their minds. The missionary could stay and teach: not at the capital, as he had hoped, but at a site close to the Natal border. Were there any further requests?

The jubilant Gardiner assured them that they had granted all his heart desired.

But there was a snag. Dingane now had a request. There was a certain refugee at Port Natal he wanted returned; a man who had not been mentioned in the treaty. Gardiner hesitated and then agreed. He was prepared, he said, to make this one concession: if the man could be found he would be sent back.

It was a mistake. A few days later, as the missionary was about to leave, Dingane made further demands. This time he wanted a large party of refugees exempted from the treaty. But Gardiner would not hear of it. The treaty would become meaningless if he continued to make exemptions. Dingane had given his word and he must keep it. In any case, he explained, the terms agreed upon had already been sent to Port Natal and could not be altered. Much to his relief, Dingane let the matter drop. No more was said about the refugees.

[4]

Gardiner was soon given the opportunity to prove that he was the right sort of Englishmen to observe a treaty. On his way back to the bay he stopped at a kraal, close to the proposed site of his new mission station, and learned that a woman of high rank, accused of adultery, had fled to Natal with two servants and three young children. He had no alternative but to hurry after them.

On reaching Berea he immediately gave orders for the woman and her servants to be taken captive. Once the prisoners had been rounded up and shackled in pairs, Gardiner again left for Zululand. He did not relish his role as gaoler. There was little hope of Dingane sparing the prisoners' lives and Gardiner dreaded the thought of their dying heathens. 'Poor creatures,' he lamented, 'on the verge of eternity, and yet ignorant of the immortality of the soul, and unconscious of a future state of existence. Their apprehensions of sin were nearly as dark, imagining that there were but three kinds—adultery, witchcraft, and speaking evil of the King.'

They reached the royal kraal late one afternoon. A huge crowd had gathered and, as Gardiner led the wretched captives into the cattle arena, they burst into song. For Dingane, peeping over the *isiGodlo* fence, it was a moment of triumph.

'He appeared in high glee,' says Gardiner. 'His women were all singing around him; and on my seating myself, he pointed to me and said, that it was on my account this rejoicing was made. I could have burst into tears.'

The singing, led by the King, was followed by dancing and beer drinking. Gardiner sat through it in agony. The noise was deafening and the thought of the prisoners trembling at his side made it impossible for him to move his head: he could not bring himself to meet their eyes. Finally the celebrations ended. Dingane disappeared from the fence and, a few minutes later, strode into the arena wearing a multi-coloured cloak and a pink ribbon round his head. A semi-circle of warriors formed round him; the trial of the prisoners commenced.

It was, of course, a mere formality. Dingane acted as accuser and judge. Witnesses were called and questions asked, but it was all meaningless. The verdict was never in doubt. One by one the four were pronounced guilty and sentenced to death.

Next morning Gardiner decided he must do his Christian duty. When Dingane sent for him, he again put on full dress uniform and went to the interview determined to plead for the prisoners' freedom. But Dingane would have none of it. The missionary, he said, was expecting too much; what he asked was against the customs of the country—evil doers must be punished. After a little more argument, however, he informed Gardiner that it had been decided the previous night to modify the sentences. 'They are all,' sighed Gardiner, 'to be kept in confinement and I fear this will be for life.'

Precisely what confinement for life meant, he discovered the following day. One of his servants told him that the prisoners were starving, that they had been given no food since their arrival. Fearing the worst, Gardiner immediately tackled Dingane. The King told him not to interfere. He had done his duty by delivering the prisoners tied and bound, now he must keep away from them.

'*Their bonds must kill them!*' thundered Dingane.

This was worse than anything Gardiner could have imagined. He was thrown into black despair. 'Inhuman wretch!' he moaned. 'The death they had so much dreaded would have been a mercy compared with the torture of lingering out a few more days of painful existence, and at last falling the famished victims of hunger and want.'

Gardiner's journey back was far from pleasant. Awaiting him, as he was only too aware, was another grim task. He had delivered the adultress and her servants but her three young daughters had escaped; Dingane demanded that the children be surrendered. Having insisted that the King keep to the word of the treaty,

Gardiner had been forced to send word ahead that the girls be caught and imprisoned until he arrived to arrange their return.

The children were duly sent to Dingane and nothing more was heard of them. Three weeks later Gardiner learned that the adult prisoners had been put to death shortly after his departure. The executions were said to have been ordered by Ndlela, against the wishes of Dingane and Dambusa. Gardiner found this difficult to believe. 'The fact is,' he wrote, 'these three great personages have a most convenient method of placing upon each other the responsibility they would evade.'

But if the treaty brought distress, it also gave the traders a measure of security. As long as they played their part and refused to harbour deserters, there was a reasonable chance that they would be left in peace. Dingane's word might not be his bond, but it at least offered some assurance. For the first time they were able to think in terms of a permanent settlement.

On Tuesday, 23 June 1835, a meeting was held in a smoke-filled hut at Port Natal to discuss the laying out of a township. Boundaries were drawn, plots allocated, housing regulations decided and a Town Committee—which included Allen Gardiner, John Cane, Henry Ogle and James Collis—elected.

It was agreed that the town be named in honour of the new Governor of the Cape, Sir Benjamin D'Urban; but soon the apostrophe was dropped and it became and has remained—Durban.

'THE MISSIONARIES WILL BUILD HOUSES...'

CAPTAIN ALLEN GARDINER, self-chosen missionary to the Zulu King, was finding the ways of the Lord in southern Africa mysterious indeed. His sole purpose in coming to Natal had been to convert the heathen but, far from achieving this, he was becoming more and more involved in secular matters. It worried him. 'Full well do I know and feel,' he declared, 'that whenever a minister of the gospel turns aside to mingle in politics, insomuch has he departed from his evident path of duty.'

Like other missionaries in Africa, both before and after him, Gardiner could find no sure guide outside his own conscience. The circumstances were such that it was impossible to divide religious and secular responsibility. To interpret his duty too narrowly might well result in his defeating his own ends. Both Dingane and the traders regarded him as the leading representative of the Natal community and, until such times as he was relieved of this position by civil authority, he must continue to act as he saw fit. But it was not easy. 'Most gladly,' he sighed, 'would I divest myself of all responsibility in these matters, which are quite foreign to the objects I have in view.'

The trouble was, of course, the more deeply involved he became in secular affairs, the more entrenched became his position as spokes-man for the traders. That Dingane regarded him as such was made only too obvious in the next dispute between the King and the white settlers. It was an issue which only Gardiner could resolve.

On 26 June—three days after the founding of Durban—Thomas Halstead returned from a hunting trip in Zululand with alarming news. Dingane, he said, had expelled him from the Zulu territory and had given orders that no kraal was to supply him with milk or provisions. He had been instructed to inform the Europeans that all trade with Port Natal was now prohibited and that in future no

white man, other than Gardiner, would be allowed across the
Tugela. Why this should be, he could not say: he had hurried back
to Natal without waiting for explanations.

Gardiner was completely bewildered. Rumours had trickled
through to the traders that all was not well in Zululand but they had
not expected such a sudden and drastic move on Dingane's part.
It was a negation of the treaty. It put Gardiner in an invidious
position. Like it or not, he would have to visit Dingane and he was
far from happy about making the journey alone. There was talk
among the local Africans that the King intended to lure him to
emGungundlovu and then hold him hostage. But it was a challenge
he was forced to accept. He left Durban a few days later, doubtful
whether he would return, and fully expecting a stormy reception.

But he was wrong. Arriving at the royal kraal he discovered
Dingane contentedly counting his cattle and full of concern for his
well-being. A bullock was slaughtered in his honour and, after a
few words of welcome, the King advised him to rest. They would
have time, he said, to talk later.

The promised discussion, however, was postponed for several
days. Whenever he tried to arrange an interview he was told that
the King was busy supervising building operations in the kraal. It
was suggested that if he had anything to discuss he should consult
Ndlela and Dambusa. The indunas, when he eventually tracked
them down, were not particularly helpful. They pretended they
had no idea why Dingane had forbidden trade with the white people.
All they were prepared to admit was that the King was angry with the
traders for breaking the treaty. Word had reached emGungundlovu
that certain white men were encouraging deserters and even smuggling young Zulu women into Natal in their wagons. Acknowledging
that Gardiner probably knew nothing of these incidents, the indunas
promised to do what they could to arrange an interview with the King.

For once they were as good as their word. Two days later Gardiner,
accompanied by Ndlela and Dambusa, was again summoned to the
isiGodlo. Dingane was in a surly mood. After listening to the missionary's complaints, he repeated the accusation made earlier by the
indunas and claimed that Thomas Halstead had falsely used his
name by making a local headman surrender cattle on 'the King's
order'. How could he be expected to observe the treaty when the
white men acted like this?

Gardiner had to admit that Dingane's anger was justified. He promised to investigate the incidents and swore to return any more deserters found at Port Natal. The word that had passed between them, he told the King, would not fall to the ground.

Dingane was quickly won over. He said he recognised Gardiner as 'Chief of the white people' and looked to him to keep the traders in check in future. He went further. A chief, he said, must have power and to ensure the missionary's power he was prepared to grant him land. Gardiner would then properly rule the people in his territory.

But Gardiner was not so sure. He protested that he had no wish for power; he had come to Natal to teach, not rule. In any case he doubted whether the traders would acknowledge his authority. After some hesitation, however, he agreed to accept the chieftainship on condition that it met with the approval of the Governor of the Cape. He would consult, he said, with the 'Great Chief at Grahamstown'; only with his permission could a mere missionary assume such responsibility. With this Dingane appeared satisfied. He then instructed Ndlela and Dambusa to explain the precise limits of the proposed land grant.

There must have been a flurry of ghosts in the veld. For the territory that Dingane was prepared to make over to Gardiner was the same, more or less, as that ceded by Shaka: first to Farewell, then to King, then to Isaacs.

[2]

And so, tormented by doubts, Gardiner was lured further from his chosen path. He consoled himself, however, with the thought that there were certain circumstances in which a man of God had a duty to support 'such civil authorities as may be requisite for the suppression of vice, and the well-being of the community in which he resides'. The situation he faced was clearly such a case. A well ordered society was essential to the spread of the gospel; the lawlessness of the traders was undermining his mission. It was a duty he could not escape.

But on one point he was determined. He would not assume

authority over the traders without official sanction. To obtain this, he decided to travel to the Cape Colony immediately. This proved easier said than done. The frontier districts were again in turmoil and travelling was precarious. However, after two abortive attempts, he eventually reached Algoa Bay by an overland route at the beginning of December 1835.

As luck would have it, the Governor of the Cape, Sir Benjamin D'Urban, was visiting Port Elizabeth when Gardiner arrived there. The missionary immediately arranged for an interview. Sir Benjamin was delighted to hear of the plan proposed by Dingane. Since his appointment as Governor, a year or so earlier, he had become increasingly concerned at the irregular situation in Natal; a treaty between the traders and the Zulu King would, he thought, be a worthwhile step. D'Urban had no hesitation in giving it his blessing. In a letter to Dingane, dated 5 December 1835, he wrote:

'I rejoice to hear the good word which has passed between the Chief and Captain Gardiner, and of the treaty concluded between them for the town and people of Port Natal.

'An officer on the part of the King of England, my master, shall speedily be sent to Port Natal, to be in authority there in place of Captain Gardiner, until his return, and to communicate with the Chief, Dingarn, upon all matters concerning the people of Natal. By him I will send to the Chief presents, in token of friendship and good understanding, of which I hereby assure the Chief, in the name of the King my master.'

It was the closest the traders had yet come to receiving official recognition.

Gardiner's return to Natal was to be delayed. He had made up his mind first to travel to England to report his progress to the missionary society and, if possible, to arrange for a Church of England clergyman to assist him. Having consulted with the Governor, he galloped on to Cape Town and sailed from there two weeks later. D'Urban had to find another emissary to deliver his letter to Dingane.

The man he chose was Benjamin Norden, a Jewish merchant from Grahamstown. Norden had long been interested in Natal. His firm, in fact, had backed James Collis's original expedition and until recently Collis had acted as his agent at Port Natal. A few weeks earlier, however, news had reached the Cape Colony that Collis had been killed in an accident. On 24 September, while working in his powder magazine, Collis had misfired a gun and caused some fifteen hundred pounds of gunpowder to explode, blowing himself, his infant son, and two servants to smithereens. On hearing of the tragedy, Norden had chartered a brig, the *Dove*, to fetch Collis's family and merchandise from Port Natal. He was only too ready to act as the Governor's agent.

Dingane went out of his way to welcome Norden. When he heard that a messenger from the Great Chief at Grahamstown was on his way, he sent two hundred warriors to escort the merchant to emGungundlovu. He could hardly wait to see what presents had been sent. He was in for a disappointment. Norden had assembled a handsome collection of gifts—including 'an elephant chair ... constructed at Grahamstown especially to suit his Majesty's tastes'—but when they were unpacked the King was clearly unimpressed. There was nothing among the rolls of cloth, beads and brassware that he did not already possess; he was amazed at the Great Chief's stinginess.

However he cheered up when D'Urban's letter was read. He said he was pleased to hear that his good friend Captain Gardiner was well and that he looked forward to the arrival of the Governor's representative: it was wrong that so many people should be allowed to live in Natal without a commander. To prove his good faith, he loaded Norden with ivory and provided an army of bearers to carry it to Port Natal. Unfortunately his efforts were wasted: the officer promised by D'Urban was never sent.

But Gardiner's post was not left entirely vacant. If the Cape Government was negligent, God had not been idle. Dingane did not remain long without a missionary. Hardly had Norden left emGungundlovu when a messenger arrived there to report that no less than three clerics were camped outside the kraal and wished to see Dingane. They had come, the King was told, from a 'country three moons over the great sea'.

They had come, in fact, from Boston, Massachusetts. They had been sent to Africa by the American Board of Commissioners for Foreign Missions. They were part of a mission that had arrived at the Cape several months earlier with instructions to contact the 'Maritime Zoolahs [Dingane's people] and the Inland Zoolahs [Mzilikazi's people]'. There were six missionaries in the party, three of whom had been assigned to Mzilikazi, and three to Dingane. The first three, accompanied by their wives, had set off for Mzilikazi's country almost immediately, but those assigned to Dingane— Aldin Grout, George Champion and Dr Newton Adams—had found travelling to Natal extremely difficult. With a war raging in the frontier districts, they had been forced to wait until they could beg a passage with Benjamin Norden on the *Dove* to Port Natal. Before sailing from Port Elizabeth they had been given some friendly advice by Captain Gardiner: he told them to approach Dingane with caution. Wisely they had left their wives in the Cape Colony while they scouted out the land.

On arriving at Durban, they had been distinctly shocked by the promiscuity of the traders. 'We found at Natal about thirty white people, two white females, one a married woman, the other living with one of the settlers, but not married,' reported the scandalised Aldin Grout. But that was the least of it. 'Most of the white men,' he added indignantly, 'have under them Zoolahs and control them as Chiefs, *and most of them have one and some five or six black wives.*' Wifely status was, of course, purely nominal; darkest Africa must have seemed murky indeed. Hoping for better things, the missionaries started for emGungundlovu. When they arrived there, on 16 January 1836, they found that Norden had already left.

Dingane, after keeping them waiting for a day, received them with great pomp in the cattle arena. Seated on the 'elephant chair' presented to him by Norden, the King was dressed in his ceremonial red plush cloak and wore a band of red baize round his forehead. George Champion was greatly impressed by the formality of their introduction. Some fifty or eighty men were seated in a semi-circle round the King and a solemn silence fell over the kraal as the missionaries were led up to the throne. Not until the presents were ritually laid out was there any animation. Then Dingane became excited. 'He examined minutely the articles brought,' says Champion; 'the razor, the umbrella, the pictures, and the lock of a tin trunk given him. A few beads also, a knife, a tea canister, and some handkerchiefs were among them. He appeared much pleased and said he would like to see our wagon. This he inspected narrowly. He found a piece of green baize which he fancied, and we gave it him.' God had undoubtedly scored a point over Sir Benjamin D'Urban.

But on the question of establishing a mission station, Dingane was as evasive as ever. He entertained the missionaries daily during their week's stay, but was reluctant to discuss the purpose of their visit. That, he said, was something for his indunas to decide.

Ndlela and Dambusa were away but a conference with three other indunas was arranged on the last day of the missionaries' stay. It followed much the same pattern as earlier discussions with Gardiner. The indunas were openly hostile. They reminded Dingane of Jacob's prophecy that the missionaries would be followed by an army of white men who would take over the country. It would be unwise to let these teachers settle in Zululand, they said. Dingane agreed. He said the Americans must first build a house in Natal, make that their home, and then come and see him again. 'If you succeed in teaching my people to read and write,' he added, 'you must come immediately to me and teach me and my chiefs to read and write, and then I should want schools in all my country.'

With this the missionaries had to be content. On their return to Port Natal it was arranged that Grout and Adams should go back to the Cape Colony on the *Dove*, collect their wives, and then travel overland to Natal. Champion remained behind to select a suitable spot for their first mission station.

By the time Grout and Adams returned with the women, Champion had already converted some shacks on the Umlazi river into a school and started teaching. He had twelve pupils, one of them the son of a white settler. News of this school soon reached Dingane. So impressed was he with what he heard that, when the missionaries next visited him, in July 1836, he reversed his decision and promised them a site in Zululand. He was still determined, he assured them, to learn to read.

He kept his promise. Towards the end of the year, George Champion started the first mission in Zululand. He built his station some ten miles north of the Tugela, close to the site chosen earlier by Allen Gardiner, and called it *Nginani*—I am with you. God had come to Zululand by way of America.

How far the indunas went along with all this one does not know. They had little option but to agree with the King, but may well have had misgivings. Ominously, Jacob's prophecy was being realised. The missionaries had come, as he had warned they would; they had built houses, as he had said. How long would it be before

the white army arrived? And how long would Dingane last after
that?

[3]

If Dingane had reached a *détente* with the missionaries, his
relationship with the traders was still far from happy. Port Natal
was now crowded with newcomers, not all of whom were prepared
to observe Gardiner's treaty. Many resented the missionary's
interference, doubted his authority, and objected to the restrictions
which the treaty placed on their freedom to hunt and trade.
Inevitably, their defiant attitude led to trouble.

A crisis was reached in June 1836. Two African hunters, employed by one of the traders, abducted some of Dingane's people
and, as was to be expected, the King retaliated. All entry into
Zululand was stopped immediately. Luckily not all the traders were
hot-headed and irresponsible. Some of the older hands realised the
foolishness of defying the King. One such was John Cane who,
aided by two of the American missionaries, called a meeting of the
whites at Durban and persuaded them to renew allegiance to
Gardiner's treaty. Dingane was appeased, but not blind to his
advantage. Cashing in on the traders' conciliatory mood, he
demanded their assistance in a campaign against the Swazi chieftain,
Sobhuza.

The attack on the Swazi was long overdue. For some time this
tribe had infuriated Dingane with their cattle raiding activities.
Now, with the help of John Cane and a party of armed whites, the
King intended to recover his stolen herds and redeem his honour.
The white men's firearms were essential to the campaign. By
retreating into the rocky hills beyond the Pongola river, the Swazi
had safeguarded themselves against the traditional Zulu method of
attack; it would require gunfire to dislodge them.

And so it proved. When John Cane and his men, accompanied
by Ndlela and a Zulu impi, arrived at the Swazi stronghold, they
found it impossible to get to grips with the enemy. Sobhuza's
people had taken refuge in a gigantic cave at the top of a steep hill
overlooking a gorge and had assembled mounds of boulders to roll

down on their attackers. Acting on Ndlela's advice, Cane abandoned all thought of scaling the hill. Instead he led his men up a height on the opposite side of the narrow gorge and called across demanding the Swazi surrender. He warned them that refusal would result in their destruction by his weapons of thunder. When the Swazi ignored this threat, a volley was fired and some were killed. With that the enemy panicked.

Suddenly a Swazi woman, carrying an infant, appeared at the edge of the cliff with a young boy at her side. Screaming, 'I will not be killed by thunder, but will kill myself,' she pushed the boy into the gorge and leapt after him. A few more shots were all that was necessary to ensure complete surrender. Cane collected some fifteen thousand cattle and drove them back to emGungundlovu.

There are varying accounts of how Dingane acknowledged this victory. Some say he was preparing to kill Cane and his men but fear of the white men's firearms prevented him from doing so. Others claim he was highly gratified and rewarded Cane lavishly. In either case, it was the traders' weapons that triumphed.

That Dingane appreciated this there can be no doubt. Shortly after the Swazi campaign the King again demanded the traders' assistance: this time in an attack he was contemplating on his old enemy Mzilikazi. For some reason this attack did not materialise, but Dingane continued his demands. He insisted that the white men sell him guns. Some did. A number of elephant guns are recorded to have been sold at steep prices and, on one occasion, Dingane confiscated six muskets from a party he accused of hunting in a prohibited area.

How effective these weapons were is open to question. Dingane still knew little about firearms and, according to one report, the traders made a point of removing the mainspring or an essential screw from the guns before handing them over. But this might well have been the usual face-saving excuse made by traders suspected of supplying arms to the Zulu King. At least one of them is said to have arranged for a 'boy to cast balls at the King's residence'. Presumably this boy knew enough about weapons to teach Dingane a thing or two.

At all events, neither Cane's armed support nor the sale of guns did much to ease the tensions. Hunters, fearing further confiscations, tended to avoid Zululand; the settlers at Port Natal remained jittery. Little was needed to bring about another confrontation; when it came, it was more serious.

The trouble originated with one of Dingane's periodic clan massacres. Suspecting a tribal chieftain named Dube of treachery, Dingane planned the wholesale destruction of his followers. The King's tactics were painfully familiar. Dube's people were ordered to collect poles from a nearby forest and assist in the building of a new palisade at emGungundlovu. Unsuspectingly, some five or six hundred members of the clan reported to the royal kraal, were trapped in the cattle areas, and clubbed to death. Dube himself was not present and, on hearing of the massacre, attempted to flee. He was eventually tracked down and killed. Others took fright. Two small clans bolted across the Tugela and sought refuge at Port Natal. They were followed by Dingane's messengers who threatened that unless the fugitives were returned, the white settlement would be attacked.

This time the traders stood firm. They rejected the objectionable treaty as 'most cruel and utterly impractical'. If Dingane attacked them, they told the messengers, he would meet with resistance. To prove their determination, they immediately set about fortifying the settlement.

The crisis brought to the fore an ex-army officer, Alexander Biggar, who, together with his son Robert, was beginning to play an important role in the affairs of the traders. A former captain and paymaster of the 85th regiment, Biggar had been cashiered from the army in 1819 following a scandal involving the misappropriation of regimental funds. The following year he had arrived at the Cape with the 1820 Settlers where, before long, he was again in trouble with the authorities. After a disastrous career as a farmer he had finally decided to try his luck in Natal. He had arrived at Durban shortly before the departure of Allen Gardiner and, having no love for missionaries, had quickly emerged as a determined opponent of the treaty with Dingane. The threat of attack now provided him with the opportunity he had been seeking. A leader was needed; Biggar was quick to assume authority.

As the elected commandant of the 'Port Natal Volunteers', he organised the local Africans into a body of troops, appointed captains—including his son, Robert, John Cane and Henry Ogle—amassed supplies and commenced building an imposing stockade.

In a proclamation, dated 4 May 1837, he called on the inhabitants of Durban to hold themselves ready in cheerful obedience to his orders. There was no shortage of these orders. During the next few days a stream of instructions flowed from his 'headquarters'. By the 13 May he was able to announce his satisfaction with 'the unanimity that prevails amongst all ranks and classes, and the activity displayed in carrying on the Public Works'. In Alexander Biggar the traders had at last found their long-awaited military protector.

Unfortunately he was given no chance to demonstrate his abilities. Dingane, hearing of the preparations at the Port, quickly climbed down. In a message to Biggar, on 26 May, he swore by 'the bones of his fathers' that he had no intention of attacking the settlement. It had all been another of those regrettable mistakes; he would never dream of killing a white man. Biggar, after thanking everyone concerned, had no alternative but to disband the short-lived Port Natal Volunteers.

But the settlers had had a nasty scare. They had been forced to threaten Dingane with warfare. That the King had climbed down was no guarantee that the danger had passed. How long would it be before another incident occurred? So long as Dingane's tyrannical rule continued, his victims would seek refuge at Port Natal. Under the terms of Gardiner's treaty the King would insist that the fugitives be surrendered; there would be a never-ending series of dangerous confrontations. The traders were convinced that the only way to deal with the situation was to adopt a 'firm attitude'. The treaty was unworkable; it would have to be scrapped.

Their decision was no doubt influenced by the return of the instigator of their troubles. On 24 May 1837—two days before Dingane's apparent capitulation—Captain Allen Gardiner, with a new wife and three children of his first marriage, arrived back in Durban. He landed at the settlement weighed down with grief. Some two weeks earlier his eldest child, a girl of twelve, had died at sea and his first act on reaching the Berea mission had been to prepare a grave for his first born. He played no part in the settlement of the crisis.

This did not mean that he intended to remain aloof from the traders' affairs. Far from it. He had come back commissioned to act as a magistrate, had decided to make Natal his home, and was resolved to organise the traders into a law-abiding, Christian community. That he had set himself a formidable task, he was fully aware. News that firearms were being sold to Dingane had already reached him and caused him considerable alarm. He had warned the Cape authorities of the dangers involved. 'In the course of a very few years—perhaps not many months,' he had predicted, 'the Zulu army, led by a second Chaka, may, with muskets in their hands, not only sweep all before them in Natal, but, encouraged by such partial success, even dispute the very boundaries of our colonial territory.' The gun-running would have to stop. As Gardiner saw it, his first duty was to organise a police force, build a gaol, and apprehend offenders. But it was not to be that simple.

The trouble was, Gardiner had no real authority. Britain still refused to become actively involved in Natal and the missionary's appointment as magistrate was purely nominal. Any criminals sent to the Cape Colony would be dealt with, but there could be no question of financing a police force in Natal. If Gardiner was to make any progress, he would require the voluntary co-operation of the traders and this, as he soon discovered, was not forthcoming. Few men in Natal—with the possible exception of Dingane—were, at that time, more unpopular with the white community than Allen Gardiner. He was given a very chilly reception.

[4]

It was largely his own fault. In his fervour to win souls for Christ, Gardiner had blinded himself to all other considerations. For all his professed reluctance to become involved in politics, he had not hesitated, while in England, to whip up secular support for his mission. This had led him even further from the paths of righteousness.

Shortly after arriving in London, at the beginning of 1836, Gardiner had discovered that a Select Committee of the House of Commons was investigating the treatment of aborigines in British Colonies. He had immediately offered to give evidence. His testimony was, to say the least, extremely one-sided. The traders at Port Natal were represented as a crowd of immoral trouble makers who defied Dingane's orders, harboured deserters, lived in a degraded state, fought among themselves, and showed little sense of responsibility. Dingane, he admitted, was a ferocious tyrant given to child murder and other atrocities, but this simply strengthened his case against the traders. How could a disorganised rabble be expected to deal with such a despot?

Some of this, as the American missionaries had discovered, was true enough. The traders were a rough lot, not overscrupulous, living for the most part in hovels, and not enamoured of authority. But they had much to complain of and their motives in protecting Dingane's victims were not entirely selfish. Gardiner gave little recognition to their side of the story and, as there was no one to speak on their behalf, his distorted account was readily believed. The result was that when the Cape of Good Hope Punishment Act—designed to discipline the frontier Boers—became law in August 1836, its provisions were extended to include the settlers at Durban. News of this had infuriated Alexander Biggar and his cronies but, at the time, it looked as if Gardiner had scored an important point: British authority, if not British protection, had been tentatively cast over Natal.

Gardiner had spent the rest of the year writing a book on his African experiences (which he concluded with a plea for military occupation of Natal), finding a new wife, and addressing meetings of the Church Missionary Society. His efforts were well rewarded. His 'fervour and eloquence' at the anniversary meeting of the Church Missionary Society inspired the Rev. Francis Owen to offer his services as a missionary in Zululand; and Lord Glenelg, the Secretary of State for Colonies, agreed to Gardiner's appointment as a Justice of the Peace at Durban. By the time he was ready to return to Natal, Captain Gardiner had every reason to congratulate himself. Unfortunately his achievements proved more theoretical than real.

The traders might not have appreciated the ways of God, but they were fully alive to the ways of the world. They knew that Gardiner's magisterial powers were inoperable. They told him as much when, on 1 June, he called a meeting to announce that as a commissioned Justice of the Peace he held authority over the white settlers at Durban. Only a few Europeans attended the meeting but there were enough to give the missionary a rough ride. They questioned him vigorously on his so-called powers and flatly rejected the proclamation he read forbidding the sale of firearms to

Dingane. In a protest which they later sent to the Cape they pointed out that Natal was not an acknowledged part of the British dominions, but a free settlement. How, they wanted to know, could Captain Gardiner settle criminal cases when his supposed powers were limited to British subjects and gave him no right to 'punish any act of aggression committed by the native population, or by other Europeans, upon the British residents of Natal'? Offenders, in any case, would have to be tried in the Cape Colony and they were not prepared to allow Gardiner the right of arrest and detention until decisions on his reports were received from the British authorities. The proposed system was wide open to abuse. The traders wanted none of it.

An attempt by Gardiner to change his tactics and base his authority on the land grant awarded to him by Dingane was also treated with contempt. Dingane, claimed the traders, had no right to the land which had already been ceded to the white men by Shaka. 'If desolating a wide extent of country by fire and sword,' they declared, 'if murder of the inhabitants in cold blood as well as in battle, if cruelties the most unheard of to the aged and defenceless, the women and children, could give such a right—such a right had Chaka, and none other.' The intrigues of James Saunders King were indeed bearing fruit. To bring any semblance of order to Natal or establish a workable agreement with the Zulu King had become practically impossible. Such was the conflict of authority, and the vagueness of the claims on either side, that any solution to the problem would inevitably involve force.

Gardiner gave up. A few days after his stormy meeting with the traders, he packed his bags and moved some twenty miles north to the Thongathi river where he established a mission station, known as *Hambanathi*—Go With Us. From here he continued to bombard the Cape authorities with complaints about the traders' refusal to co-operate with him and the hopelessness of his position. It did no good.

Help of a sort came, however, from another direction. At the end of July, the Rev. Francis Owen arrived at Port Natal with his wife, sister, and a Welsh maid called Jane Williams. The Owen family, having sailed to the Cape with Gardiner, had taken some months to reach Natal. In order to acclimatise himself to the country, Francis Owen, a thirty-five-year-old, somewhat naive and earnest, London-born parson, had decided to travel from Port Elizabeth by the overland route. The journey had proved instructive, if not particularly encouraging.

Owen had been shocked at the frontier tribesmen's incessant demands for presents, astonished at their indifference to the word of God, and dismayed by their reluctance to acknowledge themselves as sinners. No amount of effort on his part—and he struggled valiantly—could overcome their suspicions. His entreaties to them to abandon their wicked ways and attend the mission stations, invariably met with the same response: they would be willing to serve God when told to by their chiefs, not before. By the time he reached Durban, where he was met by Captain Gardiner, Owen's views on the conversion of the heathen were far from rosy.

But he remained hopeful. He had picked up a smattering of the Nguni language and was convinced that once he could preach to the tribesmen in their own tongue he would win them over. That they would be susceptible to religious teaching he had no doubt; even their superstitions he regarded as an uncomprehending acknowledgement of the supernatural. It was all a matter of communication. 'I trust,' he noted in his diary, 'I shall better know, after every succeeding conversation, the proper way of bringing forward the truth.' In this spirit he travelled on to visit Gardiner at *Hambanathi*, leaving his family at Durban.

Gardiner was delighted to have him at the mission. Owen had arrived at an opportune moment. Some weeks earlier the missionary had visited Dingane and had been partly compensated for the slights he had suffered at Durban. The King, unlike the traders, had proved extraordinarily co-operative. Not only had he rejoiced at Gardiner's return but, by the end of the visit, had given permission for a mission station to be established at emGungundlovu. Anticipating Owen's arrival, Gardiner had dashed back to *Hambanathi* to report the good news to his superiors in London. 'Dingarn,' he wrote, 'has promised to have a hut erected ... for the Mission Station near [emGungundlovu] with a door high enough to admit of its being entered without crawling.'

There had been a slight disagreement about the location of this unusual hut. At first Gardiner had wanted it built on a hill close to the royal kraal but Dingane had objected that it would overlook the place where his wives bathed. Eventually another hill, about a mile and a half from emGungundlovu, had been agreed upon. The mission would still be within sight of the King's residence. Dingane, in fact, had chosen the site with care; he wanted, he said, to be able to keep an eye on the missionaries through his telescope. Gardiner had accepted this. He was in no mood to protest. The erection of the hut represented a great step forward: it more than made up for the traders' refusal to build him a gaol.

Hardly had Owen arrived at *Hambanathi* than he and Gardiner set off for emGungundlovu to keep the King to his word. The meeting was an undoubted success. Dingane was on top of his form. Apart from a few awkward questions after Owen had preached a sermon on the resurrection of the body (Would his wives rise from the grave? Why didn't the dead get up now?) the King went out of his way to accommodate the white men. Work had already begun on the mission hut and it promised to be all that Dingane had claimed for it. Some twenty feet in diameter, it not only had a high door but was lofty enough for a tall man to move about inside without discomfort. There was one slight drawback, however: Owen found the outlook rather bleak. 'It is on top of a hill commanding a view of the whole town . . .' he reported. 'A stream of water washes the foot of the hill; but the trees, shrubs and everything conducive to comfort or beauty seem far away.'

Another unpleasant feature, which he did not comment on at the time, was the view it gave of the infamous execution hill—*kwa-Matiwane*. The significance of that blot on the landscape was to become apparent later.

Returning to Durban, Owen spent two weeks there and then engaged Dick King, the young man who had acted as guide to the Boer trekkers, to take him and his family by wagon to emGungundlovu. With him went Richard Hulley, an interpreter, and his family. On the journey upcountry they stopped to visit Gardiner and the American missionaries and arrived at the royal kraal on 10 October. Dingane was as affable as ever. When Owen's wagon drew up outside the *isiGodlo*, the King, wearing his green baize cloak and a 'gay red' headband, peeped over the fence and then came hurrying out to shake the missionary's hand. It was a momentous occasion. Mrs Owen, her sister-in-law and maid were the first white women to visit emGungundlovu. Dingane, whose only knowledge of European beauty had been gained from faded prints, was unashamedly intrigued. Peering into the wagon, he begged the women to climb out so that he could inspect them closely. The ladies, in their sombre bombasine and bonnets, evidently met with his approval. He 'surveyed them all,' says Owen, 'with minute attention and silent pleasure'. The mission had got off to a good start.

The solitary mission hut, for all its spaciousness, proved hopelessly inadequate for Owen's mixed, straight-laced party. There could be no question of communal sleeping and, until more huts were built, his sister and maid were obliged to sleep in a tent, while the interpreter and his family occupied one of the covered wagons. None of this seems to have bothered Owen. His main concern was to start a school. Within a few days he had arranged to teach fifteen young boys sent to him by Dingane. He left the more mundane affairs to the women.

But, for all his dedication, Owen found it difficult to make progress. His lessons were continually interrupted by Dingane who sent for him on the slightest pretext. The King, highly amused at having a tame white man on hand, would spend hours teasing the missionary about religion, discussing the British royal family, or exploring the possibility of obtaining gun-powder from Port Natal. Owen found it all very irritating.

He was slightly appeased when the King suddenly asked to be taught to read. Never one to waste time, Owen set to work immediately and was astonished at the speed with which Dingane mastered his first lesson. He proved, says the missionary, 'an apter scholar than for his age I could have imagined him to be'.

But not everyone shared the King's enthusiasm. In an interview Owen had with Ndlela, the induna made it quite clear that he considered reading a pastime for children. Ndlela was extremely suspicious of Owen. A few days earlier he had told one of the American missionaries who visited emGungundlovu, that he was 'opposed to the missionaries coming into the country' and was 'angry with the King for allowing Mr Owen to settle at the capital'. Now he was anxious to impress Owen with his own standing at the kraal. He went to great pains to point out that, although the King was head of the nation, he could do nothing without the consent of the indunas and that he and Dambusa were two of the most important indunas. It was more than a hint; it was a warning.

Significantly, after this interview, attendance at Owen's school fell off and, when he complained to Dingane that the indunas did not want him to teach, the King more or less admitted that there was nothing he could do about it. He had given his permission for pupils to attend but he could not defy the indunas. Like Gardiner, Owen was made to realise that politics could not be kept out of religion in Zululand.

Politics of another sort were soon to cause him even greater distress.

On 26 October Dingane sent for Owen and handed him a letter that had just arrived. He asked the missionary to read it. Dated from Durban, the letter announced the arrival in Natal of a large party of white emigrants from the Cape Colony. They had come, it said, in peace and wanted permission to visit emGungundlovu to arrange for a grant of uninhabited land in which they could settle. It went on to describe how and why the emigrants had recently fought and defeated Dingane's greatest enemy, Mzilikazi, and was signed by the leader of the party—Pieter Retief.

The Boer trekkers had returned to Natal. This time they had come to stay.

'OTHER WHITE PEOPLE WILL COME...'

THE GREAT TREK, as it became known, has been described by Professor Eric Walker as the 'central event in South African history'. The gradual exodus of thousands of Boers from the Cape Colony, starting in 1835, was to transform the face of southern Africa. These courageous and dauntless emigrant families, seeking new lands and a new life, free from interference and the hated restrictions of British authority, were, after years of privation and struggle, to found new republics in the wilderness and to establish a way of life which, in one way or another, profoundly influenced the political and social thinking of succeeding generations of white South Africans. The effects of the Great Trek are still very much in evidence today.

It started slowly. The return of the *kommissie trekkers*, at the end of 1834, did not result in an immediate stampede from the Cape Colony. Despite encouraging reports from the northern and eastern territories—particularly Natal—there was no rush to leave. Roots are not easily torn up. It was easier to dream of a new life than to face it. Decisions had to be reached, affairs settled, and plans made, before vague yearning could be turned into resolute action. Indeed there were many who clung to the hope that it would not be necessary to trek: that conditions in the Cape Colony would alter, that the British would have a change of heart, that all would come right in the end. They were to be disappointed.

The first two parties of trekkers set off separately in 1835, joined forces, and then travelled together northwards hoping eventually to branch off to Portuguese East Africa and find an outlet to the sea: an outlet essential to their survival and independence. They were followed by two larger parties who, in 1836, crossed the Orange river, journeyed on into the territory later known as the Orange Free State, and then came to a temporary, but lengthy, halt. After

making a treaty with a local African chief, who ceded them a large
tract of land, they formed settlements which, in time, became a
focal point for trekkers leaving the Cape Colony.

It was never intended that these settlements should be permanent.
This was not the Promised Land; that still had to be found. The
question was, where to seek it? Some were in favour of turning
eastwards, crossing the formidable Drakensberg, and entering Natal
from the north. The account given by Piet Uys of the glorious, ever-
green country adjoining Dingane's territory, had met with an
enthusiastic response. Not only did Natal seem to offer all the
trekkers required—grazing land, water, timber and an equable
climate—but it had the added advantage of possessing a navigable
harbour.

There was, in fact, only one drawback. English settlers were
already established at Port Natal and were known to be eager for the
British to occupy the country. How long would it be before their
incessant requests for military protection were met? Was it not
likely that, by settling in Natal, the trekkers would merely be
preparing the way for the very forces they were attempting to
escape? If the British occupied Natal, they would be back where
they had started. The risk, thought many, was too great to take.
They considered it wiser to join the earlier trekkers in the north and
take a chance of finding a port in Portuguese East Africa.

The problem of which direction to take was greatly aggravated by
personal quarrels and jealousies among the leaders. These tended
to divide the scattered followers into factions. Parties were sent out
to explore the alternative routes and attempts were made to establish
a central authority, but it seemed impossible to arrive at a common
agreement. The debate was still raging when, at the beginning of
1837, Pieter Retief arrived on the scene. By that time the endurance
of the trekkers had, in many ways, been sorely tried.

Piet Retief was then in his mid-fifties. Tall and sturdily built, with
a face framed by dark hair and a grey-flecked beard, he was an
impressive looking man. His glance was penetrating: his manner
friendly, though somewhat solemn. He exuded a restless energy.
Restlessness had, in fact, characterised much of his early career.
As a young man he had spent much of his time journeying about the
Cape Colony and it was not until he was thirty-four that he had
married and established himself as a building contractor in Grahams-

town. By the time the English settlers arrived in the eastern Cape, in 1820, Retief was recognised as one of the wealthiest and most respected men in the district: he also became Field-Commandant of the local burger levy. But he seems to have been temperamentally unsuited to business life. Often his duties as Field-Commandant took him away from Grahamstown and his contracting business suffered. A series of unfortunate building transactions finally resulted in his being declared insolvent; he was forced to retire to his farm in the Winterberg. For all that, his integrity was never in doubt and he continued to command respect from all sections of the community, white and black.

Retief was a born leader. He and another trekker personality, Gert Maritz, are said to have been instrumental in organising the *kommissie trekke* of 1834. Both men were particularly impressed by the report brought back by Piet Uys from Natal. Yet, despite his enthusiasm, Retief—who had recovered some of his fortune as a farmer—was late in leaving the Colony. Not until the beginning of 1837 did he finally despair of his prospects in the British-ruled Cape and decide to join the trekkers.

Before leaving he issued a manifesto which was published in the *Grahamstown Journal*. In this finely worded proclamation he set out his reasons for leaving the land of his birth and announced the course he intended to follow in the wilderness. 'We will not molest any people, nor deprive them of the smallest property,' he stated; 'but, if attacked, we shall consider ourselves fully justified in defending our persons and effects to the utmost of our ability. . . . We propose . . . to make known to the native tribes our intentions, and our desire to live in peace and friendly intercourse with them.'

This reassurance was then doubly necessary. A few months earlier the trekkers had experienced the first opposition to their movements from an African tribe. They had clashed violently with Mzilikazi's Matabele.

News of the Boer exodus from the Cape Colony had aroused Mzilikazi's suspicion and greed. He regarded the convoys of wagons, manned by armed white men, as a threat to his supremacy and looked enviously at the trekkers' herds. In August 1836 he had struck. A Matabele impi, some 600 strong, had first attacked a party of white elephant hunters and then turned on the nearest trekker encampments. At the first camp the Boers, despite the

warnings of survivors from the hunting party, were caught unprepared. The screaming Matabele warriors descended on the settlement, killing most of the inhabitants, taking three children captive,
and sweeping off all the livestock. Returning with their loot to
Mzilikazi's kraals, Mosega, they gathered reinforcements and set
out to destroy another encampment on the Vaal river.

This time they met determined opposition: the Boers were
waiting for them. The little trekker party—seasoned veld fighters,
accustomed to tribal warfare—had hastily resorted to their traditional
method of defence by forming their wagons into a *laager*. The
wagons were drawn up in a semi-circle with the river behind them,
lashed together, and the spaces between the wagons filled with
thornbush. Inside this tented fortress, the men took up their
positions at the narrow openings while the women and children
stood behind them ready to reload their guns. The Matabele were
completely outwitted. For almost six hours a thousand maddened
warriors charged the wagons, shouting their war cries and hurling
their assegais, only to be repeatedly driven back by the fire of some
thirty guns. Over 150 Matabele were killed before the attack was
called off at three that afternoon; the whites had lost one boy and a
handful of coloured servants who had been unable to reach the
laager when the fighting started. Such was the outcome of the first
battle in which warriors, trained by Shaka's discipline, were pitted
against a Boer laager.

When the next attack was launched, on 15 October, both sides
had had ample time in which to prepare. This time the Boers
formed a laager on a small hill, later to be known as Vegkop (battle
hill.) Fifty heavy wagons were drawn into two concentric squares;
the smaller, inside enclosure, was roofed with planks and raw hide
and acted as a shelter for the women and children. Nothing was
left to chance. Chains kept the wagons firmly in position, the spokes
of the wheels were threaded with thornbush branches, each of the
forty men was armed with two or three guns to allow time for
reloading. The Matabele army was said to number some 9,000. The
battle lasted little more than an hour—to the Boers it seemed an
eternity.

The fury of the attack was terrifying. Hissing and chanting, the
warriors surged round the wagons, hurling their assegais high to
fall into the laager, dashing forward to tear at the thornbush

barricades or, in desperation, trying to rock the wagons apart. Some climbed on the wagon canopies and attempted to leap into the enclosure—one getting close enough to have his hand severed by a furious trekker woman. But they were no match for the Boer sharp-shooters. With deadly aim the defenders kept the mass of Matabele at bay, while the bodies of the more reckless warriors piled up round the laager. Again the attack had to be called off. This time the casualty list was even more devastating. It is claimed that 430 dead Matabele littered the veld in the vicinity of the laager and more are thought to have been shot by Boers who pursued the retreating impis. Two trekkers were killed and fourteen wounded. A greater loss was that of their livestock: one hundred horses and practically all their cattle and sheep were driven off by the Matabele. The trekkers were left victorious but destitute.

There was no chance of the attacks going unavenged. The Boers, no less than the Matabele, prized their cattle: their animals were their life's blood. At the beginning of 1837, a combined party of 107 Boers set off on a punitive expedition. With them went a mixed contingent of local tribesmen; some mounted, some on foot. They reached Mosega after a thirteen day march and fell upon the sleeping village at dawn. The Matabele were caught off guard. Living at Mosega were three American missionaries assigned to Mzilikazi's 'Inland Zoolahs' and one of them described the sudden-ness of the attack. 'Early in the morning,' he reported, 'I was awakened by the firing of guns; I arose and looked and saw the farmers on horseback, pursuing and shooting the natives, who were flying in every direction.'

The Matabele, despite their numbers, did not stand a chance. Mzilikazi and his chief indunas were away at a military kraal fifty miles to the north and, although the warriors at Mosega put up a brave fight, they could not withstand the gunfire. By mid-day the fighting was over. After 400 warriors had been killed the Matabele fled, leaving the Boers to burn the kraals and depart at leisure with 700 head of cattle. The Americans, fearing Mzilikazi's vengeance, decided to abandon their mission and join the trekkers. They had little option. The attack, declared one of them, 'made our field of labour an awful desolation.' A few months later they joined their companions in Zululand.

Dissension was still rife among the trek leaders when Piet Retief joined them two months later. Adversity had not made for unity. Old quarrels still festered, future policy was still vague. Many hailed Retief's arrival as a possible solution to their problems.

And for a while it looked as if it was. Almost immediately Retief, backed by his old friend, Gert Maritz, was elected Governor and Commandant-General of the 'United Laager.' In June a formal constitution was drawn up. But even Retief, with his talent for diplomacy, could not reconcile all the dissidents. The bickering continued until Retief, impatient with the uncertainty, decided to go ahead with his plan to move to Natal. Patrols were sent to explore the passes over the Drakensberg and, at the beginning of October, Retief with thirteen companions and four wagons made the steep descent into Natal. He intended to contact Dingane and arrange for a place of settlement.

The majority of trekkers were prepared to follow Retief as soon as he sent word for them to join him. Some, however, were still uncertain. Not only did they doubt the wisdom of moving to Natal but they were wary of leaving before finally disposing of the Matabele threat. Mzilikazi was still at large and, until he was vanquished, they felt their future was in jeopardy. Preparations were even then being made for a second, decisive, attack on the Matabele.

Piet Retief and his advance party reached Port Natal on 19 October. They were heartily received by the traders. Alexander Biggar, still the leading light, quickly drew up an address of welcome and canvassed local residents for signatures. Retief was touched. In his reply to the welcome he assured the traders that he shared their friendly sentiments and had no doubt that, with God's help, events would work out to their mutual interest. Biggar was also convinced of this. The arrival of the trekkers was, in his opinion, opportunely timed: at last the traders would be given substantial support in their stand against Dingane. He said as much in a letter he sent to the Cape Colony a few days later.

'The conviction,' he wrote, 'that we shall, for the future, be permitted to live in peace, and be freed from the constant, though idle, threats of Dingane, had infused a lively spirit amongst us. We can now proceed with confidence, and an assurance that our future exertions will no longer be cramped by doubts of our stability; but rewarded with the fruits of our industry.'

He was being dangerously optimistic. That same day Piet Retief, having announced his arrival to the Zulu King by letter, left Port Natal for emGungundlovu.

[2]

The day after he received Retief's letter, Dingane instructed Francis Owen to read it to Ndlela. While the missionary read, the King and the induna listened in silence. Not by a blink of the eye did they give any indication of what they thought of the message. Dingane, in fact, immediately changed the subject. Taking the letter from Owen, he made movements with his fingers to show that he wished to hold a pen and be able to write, and went on to ask questions about the history of writing. Ndlela said nothing.

There can be no doubt that this show of indifference was a pretence. The information given by Retief was not entirely new to Dingane. He had, for some months, been aware that the white men were on the move. He was fully aware of the clashes with Mzilikazi and knew all about the burning of Mosega. Indeed he had been quick to take advantage of the Matabele disaster. Two or three months earlier he had mobilised his warriors, had them 'fortified against all ill and charmed to every success', and sent them on a secret raid against the weakened Mzilikazi. Once again the Matabele had been taken by surprise. In their first encounter with the Zulu impis they had been forced to abandon their livestock—including cattle and sheep looted from the trekkers. But they had quickly recovered, pursued Dingane's army and recaptured some, but by no means all, of the plundered herds. As always when Zulu met Matabele the campaign had been only partly successful; but Dingane had been well pleased. He had made a point of bragging to Owen about the raid, claiming that only ten of his warriors had been killed and displaying some of the captured oxen which, he said, 'were only a few and that the whole fold was full of them when the army first returned.'

But, as he must have known, Dingane's exaggerated success owed much to Mzilikazi's preoccupation with the white men. Now those same white men were coming to emGungundlovu. The King could not have been happy at the thought. And Ndlela, always conscious of Jacob's prediction that a white army would follow the missionaries, must have been equally disturbed. They had much to discuss.

Five days passed before Dingane was ready to reply to Retief's letter. Then he sent for Owen and dictated a message which the missionary considered eminently fair. The Zulu impis, said the King, had returned from Mzilikazi's territory with 110 sheep belonging to the Boers and he was now anxious to return those sheep to their proper owners. Unfortunately some of these animals had died on the journey to Zululand, so he could only send their skins. He regretted that his warriors had captured only nine of the Boers' stolen oxen and that these had since died. Such honesty was, for Dingane, remarkable. He seemed intent on quietening any fears the Boers might have. The following day he instructed Owen to write another letter, this time to Port Natal. 'It was,' says the missionary, 'to purchase more gunpowder with 3 elephants teeth.'

Piet Retief arrived at the royal kraal on 5 November. He was accompanied by two trekkers and Thomas Halstead, who was to act as interpreter. Dingane, wearing a splendid cloak of broad black, red and white stripes and seated on the chair given to him by Benjamin Norden, received them immediately. 'You do not know me, nor I you,' he said to Retief, 'and therefore we must first become better acquainted. You have come a long distance to see me, so you must first have rest and amusement.' This more or less set the tone for the first few days. Amusements there were aplenty. Cattle displays, dances and mock battles were staged to entertain and impress the visitors.

Francis Owen, who was forced to attend, seems to have found the celebrations a little frightening. There was something sinister about Dingane's continual bragging. After one sham fight, in which companies of young men charged about, brandishing sticks, whistling, leaping at each other and sweating profusely, the King was at great pains to stress that this was one of his *smallest* regiments. His boast was echoed by the warriors, who kicked their shields and shouted: 'We are as hard as stones: nothing shall harm us.' Then, in a dense mass, they formed a semi-circle and stamped out a war dance, with Dingane leading the singing. It was all too much for

Owen. Seeing another huge party assembling, he asked permission to leave.

Piet Retief and his companions sat through it all, every day, for hours. With a farmer's eye for cattle, Retief was more impressed by Dingane's herds than with the 'terrific exhibition' of the warriors. The discipline of a herd during one of the ox dances, he considered remarkable. All three Boers were amazed at the never-ending processions of cattle. Their reactions were no doubt noted by the sharp-eyed King.

But it was not all fun. On the fourth day a meeting was called and they got down to business. Dingane was at last ready to discuss Retief's request for land. He announced that he had been in touch with Allen Gardiner, who had agreed that the land ceded to him should now be handed over to the Boers. This, said the King, he was prepared to do.

'With the request you have made for land,' he announced, 'I am quite willing to grant it.' But there was a condition. Retief first had to demonstrate his good faith. Cattle had recently been stolen from a Zulu outpost by mounted raiders, dressed in European clothes, and claiming to be Boers; Dingane now insisted that Retief prove that his people were not responsible for the raid. He was to do this by recapturing the cattle and bringing them, and the thieves, back to Zululand.

The trekkers had no hesitation in agreeing. They already knew of the cattle raid and assured Dingane that the culprits were not Boers but followers of a tribal chieftain named Sikonyela. Some of Sikonyela's people were known to dress as white men. Then, said the King, 'you must prove this.'

Owen, who was called to translate the agreement into English, was extremely nervous about the entire business. He let Retief know this. The transfer of the land grant was, in his opinion, illegal. While in England, Gardiner had formally handed over this territory to the British Government and had no right now to give it to the trekkers. Dingane was aware of this. What if the traders at Port Natal refused to accept the new agreement? What if they insisted that the land be occupied by the British? Would the trekkers be prepared to become British subjects again? No, said Retief, they certainly would not. If this happened, the Boers would move further north and seek an equivalent land grant. But he was not unduly worried by such a possibility. His main concern was to clear his character with Dingane. It was first necessary to recover the stolen cattle from Sikonyela.

Owen became even more alarmed. He considered such talk dangerous. White men should not become involved in tribal disputes. What if there were bloodshed? Surely a more peaceful solution could be found. Why did the Boers not confront those who claimed that white men were responsible for the cattle raid and prove that this was not true? But Retief had already tried, and failed, to convince Dingane of this. He assured the missionary that his venture would be bloodless. Sikonyela, he claimed, knew enough about the Boers to hand over the cattle without fighting.

But Owen was still unhappy. When he read over the agreement to Dingane, he again pointed out that the land had been handed over to the British Government. The King paused for a moment and then said: 'I will speak to Mr Retief on that subject when he returns with the cattle.' There was nothing more Owen could do.

Others also tried to warn Retief. On his way back to Natal he called on George Champion at the American mission and was given some timely advice. Champion told him to be careful of Dingane and not to return to emGungundlovu without a sizeable escort. Two years' practical experience in Zululand had taught Champion that the Zulu King was not to be trusted; he felt sure that Dingane was plotting to kill Retief and his party. But Retief would have none of it. It took a Boer, not an Englishman, he said, 'to understand a Kaffir.' When Champion pointed out that he was not English but American, Retief was amused: the difference, he replied, was so small it was not worth talking about.

English or American, what did it matter? A missionary was a missionary: a Boer was a Boer.

Retief was being very foolish. He was in no position to scoff. What did he know of Dingane after a few jolly days at emGungundlovu? His common sense should have made him suspicious. Why should Dingane promise so much, for so little? Indeed, why should he welcome the Boers as neighbours? They were not traders: they would not lavish him with gifts. (It is not clear whether Retief had even taken any presents to the King.) They were not missionaries: they had not come to teach his people. He was not looking for protection: he was quite capable, if necessary, of punishing cattle thieves himself. His relationship with the whites had never been easy; Retief must have known about his quarrels with the traders. Why should he now invite a veritable army of white men to settle on his doorstep? How could he be expected to trust men who announced that their firearms had recently put the entire Matabele army to flight? Would any ruler—white or black—so readily enter into an agreement from which he had nothing to gain and everything to lose?

But none of this was apparent to Retief. In fact he seems to have gone out of his way to make matters worse. Of all Retief's rash actions, the letter he sent to Dingane shortly after leaving em-Gungundlovu was the rashest. It simply invited trouble. For not only did he again refer to Mzilikazi's defeat, but went on to lecture Dingane on the fate which awaited evil rulers.

'From God's great Book we learn,' he wrote, 'that kings who do such things as Matselikatse [sic] has done are severely punished, and not suffered long to live and reign; and if you wish to hear more fully how God treats such wicked kings, you can enquire of all the missionaries in your country.'

The implications of this letter were all too clear. Nor could the fact that he went on to assure Dingane of his friendly intentions have disguised the thinly veiled threat.

What is also clear from the letter is Retief's idea of 'understanding the Kaffir.' His tone throughout is pious, cajoling, and unmistakably patronising. Like many another man of his time, he obviously considered that Africans, regardless of their standing, should be treated as children: one must be kind but firm. Unfortunately he was dealing with the wrong man. Dingane, whatever else he might have been, was no child. He could recognise a threat when he saw one. And by linking the threat with the teaching of the missionaries, Retief added fuel to a longstanding suspicion. Jacob's prophecy must indeed have appeared to be coming true. Had Dingane and the indunas needed further proof of the danger posed by this 'white army', Retief's letter undoubtedly provided it.

According to George Champion's interpreter, Joseph Kirkman, the Zulu King had already taken steps to safeguard himself. No sooner had Retief and his party left emGungundlovu than Dingane sent orders for them to be attacked. A clan chieftain was told to invite the Boers to his kraal, entertain them with food and dances, and then put them to death. Had this happened Dingane would no doubt have disclaimed all knowledge of the murder. But it was not to be so easy. For some reason, the chieftain disobeyed the King's order and was himself attacked. Over 600 people are said to have been slaughtered by the Zulu impi which Dingane sent to punish the disobedient clan.

Doubts were later expressed as to whether or not Dingane *had* given orders for the Boers to be killed. It was said that he attacked the clan for some other reason. Be that as it may, the story was widely believed at the time and quickly spread, causing considerable alarm.

Meanwhile, unaware of the tumult in his wake, Piet Retief rode confidently through Natal.

[3]

While Retief had been busy in Zululand, the trekkers had not been idle. Those who opted to follow the Natal party had crossed the Drakensberg by selected passes and established camps between the upper Tugela and Blaauwkrantz rivers. The waiting period had not been easy. They had been plagued by thunderstorms and wild animals and plunged into despair by rumours that Retief and his companions had been murdered. There was great rejoicing when, on 27 November, their leader rejoined them.

From both sides there was much to report. Retief gave an account of his dealings with Dingane and the trekkers had news of a second, devastating, attack on Mzilikazi. At the beginning of the month a well-equipped commando had again invaded Matabele territory and, after a series of short, sharp encounters, had sent Mzilikazi's army reeling into the unknown north. One of the threats in Retief's letter had, in part, been realised. Now he had only to deal with Sikonyela's cattle raiders.

He lost no time. Meetings were immediately called, a plan made, and at the end of December a party of Boers—accompanied by two of Dingane's indunas and Thomas Halstead as interpreter—left for Sikonyela's territory.

Before leaving, Retief wrote another tactless letter to Dingane, informing him of Mzilikazi's defeat and explaining that the Boers had killed 500 Matabele and captured 3000 head of cattle without losing a man themselves. According to Owen, who read the letter to the King, this news did not appear to disturb Dingane. He already knew of the Matabele campaign from his spies. The missionary himself, however, was less complacent. 'It is not without apprehension and a lively interest,' he noted in his diary, 'that we trace the course of the Dutch and wonder how it will terminate, especially in what way the Zooloos themselves, if they are not extremely cautious of offending or giving just provocation to this powerful body, may be affected by them.'

For all his show of outward calm, the same thought must have occurred to Dingane. The King must also have been disturbed to hear that parties of trekkers had come streaming into Natal without waiting for his permission.

Retief had promised Francis Owen that there would be no bloodshed in his dealings with Sikonyela. Nor was there. When the confrontation with Sikonyela took place, not a bullet was fired. The bewildered chief was at a loss to know why the Boers had come for him (he was expecting the Zulu army) and when one of them offered him a pair of handcuffs as bracelets he obligingly walked into the trap. Once the handcuffs had been snapped onto his wrists, Retief announced that he was under arrest and would remain a captive until the stolen cattle had been handed over. Sikonyela was in no position to argue. Not only did he give orders for the cattle—some 700 head—to be rounded up, but agreed to surrender a number of his horses and rifles to Retief as punishment for his people posing as Boers.

Once the Zulu cattle had been handed over to Dingane's indunas, the Boers released the hapless Sikonyela and rode back to their camps to auction off the rest of the plunder. All in all, it had been a highly successful expedition. Or so it seemed to Retief. But he appears to have misinterpreted Dingane's instructions. The King had specifically asked for Sikonyela to be sent to emGungundlovu together with *all* the cattle taken by the Boers, whether they belonged to the Zulu herds or not. What, in fact, Dingane had meant by this was that everything captured on the expedition should be handed over to him. As was to become apparent later, he considered that by holding on to the horses and rifles Retief had broken his word. It gave Dingane yet another reason for thinking that the white men were incapable of honouring an agreement with the Zulu King.

By the middle of January, Retief was ready to return the captured cattle to Zululand. Not all the trekkers thought this a wise move. The story—that Dingane had ordered Retief's death—spread by survivors of the clan massacred by the Zulu impi, had reached the trekker camps. Many believed it. They told Retief that he was taking a grave risk in returning to emGungundlovu, personally. They maintained that it would be better if he sent someone else and remained behind in command of the camps. Gert Maritz was among those who had doubts. He offered to take a small party and deliver the cattle himself: if anything went wrong, he argued, he would be less of a loss to the community than Retief.

But Retief would not hear of it. Dingane was expecting him, he said, and he had no intention of offending the King by showing a lack of trust. This, at least, is the reason usually given for Retief's ignoring the warning; but there is probably a stronger explanation of his seemingly reckless behaviour.

From the very outset, doubts had been expressed about possible British claims in Natal. No one knew this better than Retief. The question had repeatedly arisen during his negotiations with Dingane. Owen had been at pains to point out that Gardiner's land grant had been given to the British Government. How valid this argument was is open to question, but Retief knew full well that if his own claim to land was to be recognised, he would have to rely on more than vague promises. Why else had he insisted that his expedition against Sikonyela be explained in writing? But reference to a land grant in that agreement had been far from specific. Had not Dingane said that he would discuss the matter more fully when Retief returned? Moreover, the King had assured Owen that he had no intention of giving the Boers the land about Port Natal. 'He had merely said,' reported Owen, '"Go and get my cattle and then I will give you land *somewhere*," he *means* Umselekaz [Mzilikazi] late country, but he has been leading them to imagine it is Port Natal.' Owen had told Retief about this.

Retief could not afford to leave matters so vague. He needed a harbour for his people and he was determined to have Port Natal. He had already told the traders as much. On his way back from emGungundlovu he had called at the Port to announce that, once matters had been settled with Dingane, the traders would be welcome to stay but that they would have to submit to Boer authority.

His attitude is understandable. The trekkers had endured much. They had struggled against tremendous odds, suffered severe losses, been brought close to despair. Was all this to result, as some had predicted, in uncertainty and possible compromise with the very forces they sought to escape? Not if Retief could help it. He was determined, as far as was within his power, to secure the independence of his people. This meant reaching an unequivocal agreement with the Zulu King. Such an agreement might not be foolproof but without it how could the trekkers claim any authority? In the manifesto he had published before leaving the Cape Colony, Retief had declared that the trekkers would not molest any people or deprive them of the smallest property. As a man of honour, he had to hammer out this land question with Dingane. It was not something he could leave to others.

And so, at the end of January 1838, Retief, accompanied by sixty-six Boer volunteers, set off again for emGungundlovu. They arrived there on Saturday 3 February.

Dingane was expecting them. He had, in fact, been awaiting their arrival somewhat impatiently for days. A week earlier, he had received a letter from Retief telling him that the Sikonyela affair had been settled and that the Zulu cattle were to be returned. Retief also admitted that he had released Sikonyela and was keeping the horses and guns he had appropriated. This did not please the King. He was furious that Sikonyela had been allowed to go free and considered that the horses and guns were rightfully his property. The following day he sent for Owen and dictated a strongly worded letter to the Boer leader. He accused Retief of lying and of breaking his promise to deliver Sikonyela to emGungundlovu in shackles. His anger alarmed Owen who eventually persuaded him to tone the letter down. But although Dingane agreed to modify his language concerning Sikonyela, he stood firm by his demand for the horses and guns. Only when these were handed over would he be prepared to give land to the Boers. 'The whole communication,' lamented Owen, 'was indicative of the cruelty, artfulness, trickery and ambition of the Zooloo chief'.

By this time Owen was thoroughly disillusioned about Dingane.

His last few weeks at emGungundlovu had been hellish. Not only had the King continued to interrupt his work, sending for him at all hours of the day, demanding to be taught how to shoot and scoffing at his religion, but, on one occasion, he had sent men to ransack the mission on a flimsy pretext and had then shown reluctance to apologise. Nor had things been made easier by the alarming rumours that followed the mysterious Zulu attack on the recalcitrant clan. So disturbing were these rumours that Allen Gardiner had sent word to Owen offering him refuge should it be necessary for him to flee the Zulu capital. More than once the despairing Owen had been driven to commit the safety of his family to God's care and pray for deliverance. 'I am not without fears for our safety,' he confessed to his diary, 'but desire to have my soul in readiness for death!'

Added to his many miseries was the fact that he had difficulty in communicating with Dingane. His interpreter, Richard Hulley, had gone to Port Natal, leaving his family in Owen's care. Had it not been for the chance visit of fourteen-year-old William Wood—son of a Port Natal trader, who spoke fluent but limited Zulu—he would have had no mouthpiece in his uneasy dealings with the King. That Owen desperately sought consolation in prayer is hardly surprising.

But then things seemed to brighten. On the day before the Boers arrived, Dingane sent for Owen to write another letter to Retief. The King's attitude had changed radically. He was now his old self: a bundle of fun. The thought of getting his cattle back, he said, had made his heart content. Owen was to tell Retief that he was welcome and could bring *all* his people with him, but they were to come without their horses. When the missionary asked how they would reach the capital without their horses, the King quickly relented. Let them come with their horses, he declared. Let them bring their horses and dance on their horses and he would arrange for his warriors to perform so that it could be seen who could dance best. No mention was made of Sikonyela's guns and horses. All that seemed to be forgotten. Owen went away convinced that Dingane intended no treachery.

This conviction did not last long. That evening, watching from the mission station, he saw several Zulu impis entering the capital in war dress.

[4]

The noisy arrival of Retief's party the following morning did little to comfort Owen. Driving the Zulu cattle before them, the Boers careered up to the royal kraal in a cloud of dust, firing their guns and creating a tremendous commotion. Once in the great arena, they were surrounded by the huge crowd that had been assembled to meet them. Then, on Dingane's request, they demonstrated how they danced on horseback by staging a mock fight. Watched by the gaping crowd, they thundered about the arena, charging at each other and, says Owen, 'making the air resound with their guns'. Nothing like it had ever been seen in Zululand before: so many white men, so many horses, and so much dust and noise.

All things considered, it is difficult to imagine a more inappropriate spectacle. Here indeed was a white army. The war dance performed by the warriors afterwards must have appeared tame in comparison.

At noon Owen strolled over to the kraal to greet the Boers. He found them resting under some euphorbia trees outside the gates. They were friendliness itself: full of stories about the Sikonyela campaign and amused at the missionary's concern about the disputed loot. That, they assured him, had been easily settled. When Dingane had sent to demand the guns and horses, Retief had simply pointed to his grey hairs and told the messenger to inform 'his master that he was not dealing with a child'.[1] No more had been heard of the matter. It showed what firmness could do.

[1] It has often been suggested that by demanding guns and horses from the Boers, Dingane was trying to disarm them. According to this familiar interpretation, the Zulu King is said to have demanded that the Boers hand over *their own* guns and horses but was foiled by Retief's astuteness. This seems most improbable. A close study of the sole source for the incident—Francis Owen's diary—shows that Retief's appropriation of Sikonyela's guns and horses was a burning issue between Dingane and the Boers. So incensed was the King about this that, only a few days earlier, Owen had vainly attempted to persuade him to modify his language on the subject in a letter written to Retief. It was only to be expected that both Dingane and Owen would raise the matter with the Boers as soon as they arrived. The relevant passage in Owen's diary states: 'The answer he [Retief] gave to Dingaan when he demanded the guns and horses was to show the messenger his grey hairs and bid him to tell his master that he was not dealing with a child.' He then goes on to discuss the raid on Sikonyela. There

The following day was a Sunday and the Boers promised Owen that they would attend his service at the mission. He was disappointed when they did not show up. Had they insisted on observing the Sabbath, he thought, it might have had an 'amazing influence' on Dingane's mind, but the sound of singing and dancing coming from the great kraal quickly convinced him that once again God had taken second place to the Zulu King.

The festivities started at sunrise and went on for the best part of the day. Dingane was in his element. There was nothing he enjoyed more than a good day's dancing. Whether the Boers shared his enthusiasm is another matter. Retief was anxious to get down to business. He had prepared a treaty which, if he could persuade Dingane to agree, would give him his Promised Land. The terms were crystal clear.

'Know all Men by this,' it read, 'That whereas Pieter Retief, Gouvernor of the Dutch emigrant South Afrikans, had retaken my Cattle, which Sinkonyella had stolen; which Cattle he, the said Retief, now deliver unto me: I, DINGAAN, King of the Zoolas, do hereby certify and declare that I thought fit to resign unto him, Retief, and his countrymen (on reward of the case hereabove mentioned) the Place called "Port Natal," together with all the land annexed, that is to say, from Dogela [Tugela] to the Omsoboebo [Umzimvubu] River westward; and from the sea to the north, as far as the land may be usefull and in my possession. Which I did by this, and give unto them for their everlasting property.'

It is incredible to think that Retief expected so powerful a ruler as Dingane to hand over this vast territory—without the promise of trade, or other assistance—for such a slight service: particularly when Retief had already benefited by the loot he had taken from Sikonyela and which he refused to surrender. But apparently he did. And sometime during that day, during a pause between the

---

can be little doubt that by speaking of *the* guns and horses (rather than *their* guns and horses) Owen was referring to the contentious loot taken from Sikonyela. The fact that he links the King's demand directly with the discussion of the Sikonyela raid underlines this. It would have been both foolish and unnecessary for Dingane to arouse the Boers' suspicions by attempting to disarm them at this stage. Zulu custom dictated that arms were not allowed to be carried in the King's presence and, as events showed, this custom ensured that Dingane could render the Boers defenceless when and how it suited him.

dances, Dingane appeared to agree to the terms which were read to him by the Boers' interpreter, Thomas Halstead. Whether, as is usually assumed, the King then fixed his seal to the treaty is open to question. The treaty is dated for that day—Sunday, 4 February 1838—but Dingane had reasons to delay finalising the agreement.

The following day was again taken up with singing and dancing. Zulu impis were still streaming into emGungundlovu and by this time they could be numbered in their thousands. But still they came. That evening a regiment known as the 'Wild Beasts' passed close to Owen's mission, loudly chanting a war-song. Listening to them, young William Wood—the only one who understood Zulu—turned to Owen's maid, Jane Williams, and said: 'You will see that they will kill the Boers tomorrow.'

Jane was shocked. Already nervous—she had witnessed a great many executions on kwaMatiwane—she seemed to think that the boy was deliberately trying to frighten her. She rounded on him. 'Don't say so,' she snapped, '—you told me the King said a long time ago that he would kill you, because you talked so much.' But young William was serious. He repeated the warning.

Early next morning two or three Boers called at the mission to beg some coffee or tea for the road. They were leaving that day, they said, to return to their wives and children. Owen invited them to stay for breakfast and asked them what they thought of Dingane. They were most enthusiastic. 'They said he was good . . .' recalled the missionary. 'He had promised to assign over to them the whole country between the Tugala and the Umzimvubu rivers, and *this day the paper of the transfer was to be signed.*' (Emphasis added.) Owen's statement is borne out by George Champion who, writing a few weeks later, claimed: 'The papers were to be signed on Tuesday and Mr Retief was to leave on his return.' If this, as it seems, was the case, then it fully explains the supposed mystery of Retief's subsequent behaviour. How could he leave emGungundlovu before the treaty was signed?

But not everyone at the mission was as optimistic as the Boers. Jane Williams, who supplied the men with tea and coffee, says that William Wood now repeated to the Boers what he had told her the previous evening. Nor, apparently, was this the first time he had warned the Boers. On an earlier occasion, he had considered Dingane's manner so suspicious that he had made a point of telling

Retief's men to be on their guard. They had not taken him seriously. 'We are sure the king's heart is right with us,' they had smiled, 'and there is no cause to fear.'

Certainly Retief could have had little fear when, an hour or two later, Dingane sent for him to bring his party unarmed for a final meeting. Why should he have been suspicious? Had he not been plagued by alarmists' talk from the very outset? Nothing had come of it: Dingane had gone out of his way to be friendly. Why, having set his heart on getting the land grant clarified, should Retief turn away now? Even had the treaty been signed, to have shown a lack of trust at this stage would not have promised well for the future. Retief had to go and he went.

That the Boers were asked to attend the meeting unarmed was not unusual: weapons were not allowed in the King's presence. According to William Wood, Retief and his men had been wandering about unarmed throughout their stay. It would have looked strange indeed if they had taken their guns to this last meeting.

Dingane received the trekkers sitting in his arm-chair, surrounded by two of his choice regiments—the 'White Shields' and the 'Black Shields'. Ndlela and Dambusa squatted on either side of the King. After discussing—and probably signing—the treaty, Dingane wished the Boers a pleasant journey back to Natal and offered them some sorghum beer. At that, the warriors began to stamp out a dance: rattling sticks against their shields and chanting Dingane's praises. Retief was invited to sit next to the King; the rest of the party sat on the ground a short distance from the throne.

The dancing continued for about a quarter of an hour. Everything was much as usual. The Boers, chatting idly among themselves, had no reason to be suspicious; they had sat through similar displays for days on end; soon they would be on their way; soon they would be back with their families. They were completely unprepared for what happened next.

Without moving from his chair, Dingane suddenly shouted: '*Seize them!*'

Before the Boers could scramble to their feet, the warriors were upon them. They had no chance to escape; they could not even defend themselves. The only weapons they possessed were knives but, in the suddenness of the attack, few managed to unsheath them. Those who did were quickly overwhelmed. For every Boer there were several warriors. Sustained resistance was impossible. Fighting, kicking, trying desperately to hold on to their knives, the Boers were hauled through the dust past Dingane, who sat motionless on his throne, roaring: *Babulaleni abathakathi!*—Kill the Wizards!

As the last white men were jostled from the kraal, the King rapped out another order. 'Take the heart and liver of the king of the Boers,' he shouted, 'and place them in the road of the Boers!'

Dragged to the summit of kwaMatiwane, the Boers were clubbed to death. Some were impaled. Others were said to have had their eyes gouged out. Retief was pinioned and forced to watch his men—including his son—tortured and killed before his own skull was cracked by the heavy knobbed sticks and the King's last orders obeyed.

Among the bodies littering the bloody slopes of kwaMatiwane was that of the only trader in the party—Thomas Halstead. His death held a special significance.

Some fourteen years earlier, as a simple-minded youngster, Halstead had landed at Port Natal with Lieutenant Farewell's original party. He had endured all the hardships of those early days, braved the uncertainties, faced the fears, and had seen men come and go. Why he refused to give up remains a mystery. Of all the early pioneers, Halstead was the least known—even his age is uncertain. Isaacs claimed that he was dim-witted, but he had learned Zulu and, to a certain extent, won the trust of the Zulu Kings. Dingane was to say that he had not intended Halstead to die but his orders had been misunderstood in the confusion.

But if Halstead died by mistake, his death was not undistinguished. He had been the first to recognise the meaning of Dingane's sudden order. 'We are done for!' he had shouted and had then pleaded in Zulu to be allowed to speak to the King. Dingane appeared to wave his protests aside. As the warriors closed in, Halstead put up a brave fight—ripping the body of one Zulu with his knife and cutting the throat of another—before he was overpowered.

His mutilated corpse was left with the others to feed the vultures which descended on kwaMatiwane.

'A WHITE ARMY WILL FOLLOW...'

WHILE THE BOERS were being dragged from the great kraal, Francis Owen sat reading his Bible in the shade of one of his wagons. Family prayers had just ended and the women were busying themselves in the huts: it was February, one of the hottest months of the year, and it was important to get the work done before the sun rose too high. They had heard nothing unusual and, apart from having the Boers to breakfast, the day seemed much like any other.

The first indication they had that all was not well was when a Zulu messenger 'covered with perspiration' came panting up to the mission and demanded to see Owen. He had been sent by Dingane to prevent the missionary from panicking. The King, he announced, had discovered that the Boers were planning to murder him and had decided to kill them, but no harm would come to anyone at the mission: the missionaries were King George's children and not deserters like the Boers who deserved to be punished. What had Owen to say to this?

What could Owen say? His first thought was naturally for his family and dependants—now huddled round him, speechless with fear. With white people being killed, what would happen to them? He dare not risk offending Dingane by protesting; even less could he risk sending a warning to the Boers. He stared at the messenger, not knowing what to say. But the silence was quickly broken.

One of the Zulu maid servants suddenly shouted: 'They are taking the dogs away to kill them!' Turning towards the great kraal, the petrified whites became aware of the commotion there. They watched in horror as the warriors streamed through the gate and dragged their victims up the slopes of kwaMatiwane. Owen fell to the ground; his wife and sister clung to each other. Poor Mrs Hulley, the interpreter's wife, broke into hysterical sobs and had to be comforted by Dingane's messenger who told her to 'be still' and not weep as no harm would come to her. Jane Williams was dazed by the noise and frightfulness of it all. 'If I had understood the Zulu or the Dutch language,' she claimed, 'I would have understood many of the exclamations which were being made at the scene ... I do not think half an hour elapsed between the seizing of the Boers and the end of their slaughter.'

Eventually Owen pulled himself together and sent a guarded reply to Dingane's message. He would have gone himself but he could not bring himself to ask young William Wood to accompany him and interpret. The boy was terrified. So, for that matter, was Owen. When a group of warriors later approached the mission carrying their shields, the missionary called his family together and began to read a psalm. But he could not continue. 'I began to tremble,' he lamented, 'lest we were to fall the next victims.'

The danger passed. Owen and William Wood stood at the door of their hut watching the executioners return to the kraal, where Dingane still sat in solitary state, barking out orders and receiving homage. They heard the warriors shout in triumph as they presented the King with Retief's heart and liver wrapped in cloth.

At this time two unsuspecting white men—young James Brownlee, an interpreter, and Henry Venable, one of the American missionaries—arrived at the gates of the kraal. Brownlee had come in answer to a summons from Dingane who, claiming that Thomas Halstead had been lying to him, had earlier wanted another interpreter: Venable had taken the opportunity to accompany Brownlee. On arriving at the kraal the two men immediately became uneasy. The only sign they could see of the Boers was a pile of firearms and baggage, guarded by a group of warriors. When they asked where Retief and his party were, they were told that the white men had gone hunting. Despite repeated requests to see the King they were not allowed inside the kraal. An hour or so later, Ndlela sent for them and abruptly informed them of the massacre. The King, he said, had killed the Boers because they intended to make war on him. When Venable, rather ineptly, raised the question of religious teaching, the induna 'made an indiscribable face' and asked why he did not teach the warriors to shoot and ride. Ndlela had other things on his mind.

Leaving the two men, the induna returned to Dingane's side in the great arena. William Wood, still watching intently from the mission, saw him and Dambusa take up their positions close to the throne. Then the warriors fell into line and staged a mock attack; rushing up to Dingane, brandishing their shields, and yelling: 'We will go and kill the white dogs!' At an order from the King, the warriors wheeled and rushed in a body from the kraal.

Neither Francis Owen, who had his telescope fixed on the kraal, nor William Wood, needed to be told what was about to happen. 'They are (I cannot allow myself to doubt),' declared Owen, 'sent to fall or join others who have been ordered to fall unawares on the main body of Boers who are encamped at the head of the Tugala.'

The orders had been given by Dingane, but he was not solely responsible for what happened that day. As had been repeatedly made clear to visitors to emGungundlovu, the King made no important decisions—particularly military decisions—without consulting the indunas. There can be no doubt that Ndlela and Dambusa played a decisive part in the plot against the Boers. Both these powerful men had been active at every stage of the proceedings. Dambusa later openly admitted that he had goaded Dingane into action; Ndlela's distrust of the white men was well known. Yet, all too often, their influence on the King had been ignored.

This is not altogether surprising. Dingane was the key figure and both Ndlela and Dambusa preferred, when they could, to act behind the scenes. Often this had made their behaviour appear sinister to the white men; they were regarded as Dingane's evil geniuses. But were they? It is more probable that they acted as they did for good reason. To have openly challenged the King's authority would have destroyed the unity which, as Shaka had demonstrated, was essential to Zulu supremacy. The King was the focal point of the Zulu nation; he had to appear all-powerful. Ndlela and Dambusa no doubt realised this; they had tried to guide the King without usurping his role as law-giver. The trouble was they had poor material to work with. They were no match for the King's vanity.

Time and again they had warned Dingane of the danger of white intruders. They made no secret of their hostility towards the missionaries and were obviously behind the various attempts to expel the traders from Natal. But all their efforts had been undermined. Dingane, flattered by the white men's attentions and dazzled by their novelties, had not wanted to listen to his indunas. He had compromised and vacillated until he had found himself faced with a threat which even he could not ignore. That things had reached this critical stage was no fault of the indunas; now they could only repeat the advice they had given earlier. Unless Dingane destroyed the white men, the white men would destroy him. Had not Shaka, with his dying breath, said as much? Had not Jacob repeated the warning more forcibly? The indunas might have been responsible for the attack on the Boers, but they were not entirely to blame. Both Ndlela and Dambusa were to pay dearly for the loyalty they had shown, and continued to show, to their King.

It is not certain whether Ndlela led the attack on the trekker camps; as commander-in-chief he probably did. To him the annihilation of the Boers was all important. Ten days after leaving emGungundlovu, the impis were ready to strike. The Boers were caught completely off guard. For, although Retief had left strict instructions that they were to stay together, the trekkers had become careless. Their wagons were, for the most part, now spread out in small groups over a wide area. They were neither prepared for an attack nor were they seriously expecting one. There had been rumours that Retief had been murdered—someone is said to have heard a Zulu shouting this from a hilltop—but few, if any, believed it. Why should they? Similar stories had proved false before.

Only Gert Maritz, the temporary leader in Retief's absence, seems to have been in any way concerned. After waiting anxiously for Retief's return, he eventually sent out a small scouting party. He then rode about the encampments, warning the trekkers to go into laager: not many obeyed. A matter of hours later the Zulu warriors emerged from their hiding places.

The impis fell on the outlying clusters of wagons in the middle of a moonless night. The trekkers—some alerted by their barking dogs, others warned by the noise of a neighbouring attack—put up a brave and desperate fight. But they were hopelessly outnumbered and pitifully confused. As they battled in the dark to grab their guns, they were enmeshed in a tangle of black shapes—hissing, stabbing, tearing their wagons apart. It was a night of unmitigated horror.

Men, separated from their families, saw their wives and children hacked to death before they could reach them; babies were snatched from their mothers' arms and battered against the wagon wheels; pregnant women were horribly mutilated—their breasts cut off, their stomachs ripped open. The shouts of the warriors mingled with the screams of their victims. Only a few escaped.

There were instances of great heroism, of astonishing bravery and miraculous escapes, but nothing could disguise the magnitude of the disaster. Not until the next morning was there any organised resistance by the camps further back. By the time Gert Maritz led his men out, the main Zulu force had retreated, leaving behind them the corpses of forty-one white men, fifty-six white women, one hundred and eighty-five children and some two hundred coloured servants. It was far and away the greatest catastrophe suffered by the trekkers. When, in time, they came to found a town at the site of the holocaust, they called it simply Weenen—the place of weeping.

The Zulu impis drove some 25,000 head of trekker cattle before them as they marched homeward. They approached the capital in triumph. But there were no white men on hand to witness Dingane's rejoicing.

The missionaries were no longer at emGungundlovu.

[2]

Three days after the massacre of Piet Retief's party, Francis Owen's interpreter, Richard Hulley, returned to Zululand from Natal. He had earlier been sent with a Zulu escort to invite Allen Gardiner and John Cane to attend the meeting between Dingane and the Boers. His mission had been unsuccessful. Neither of the men had been willing to accept the invitation—Gardiner had said he considered it unsafe—and Hulley was faced with the unpleasant task of reporting his failure to Dingane.

Knowing nothing of what had happened in his absence, he was none the less made apprehensive by the murmurings among his Zulu companions. His apprehension turned to alarm when, on approaching the capital, he noticed a huge flock of vultures blackening the sky above kwaMatiwane. 'At once,' he says, 'I suspected that there had been evil work going on.' His fears were quickly confirmed. Riding on a little further, he saw the bloodstained sleeve of a white shirt lying at the side of a path leading to the execution hill. This, and a pile of saddles stacked against the main entrance of the royal kraal, told him all he needed to know.

Waiting only to send a message to Dingane announcing his return, he galloped furiously to the mission station. To his horror he found the place silent and deserted. Leaping from his horse, he rushed to the hut recently built for his family. Throwing open the door, he reeled back in dismay. 'On the table,' he says, 'I saw plates and cups, with the remains of a meal but not a person was to be seen.'

But, as he turned away, he suddenly heard a child shout. His little son was running towards him from Owen's hut.

'Father's come!' screamed the boy, rushing into his arms. Immediately the rest of the family appeared at the door of the missionary's hut. They had been at prayers and had not heard him arrive. Soon he was surrounded. His wife clung to him sobbing, his children pulled at his jacket, and the Owens stood dazed with relief.

'I cannot tell,' declared Hulley, 'how thankful I was to find them all safe.'

But there was little time for thanksgiving. Hulley hardly had time to swallow a cup of coffee before Dingane sent for him. The King had been waiting impatiently for the interpreter's return; he greeted him like a long lost friend. They had, claimed Dingane, a lot to tell each other. He was full of explanations. He wanted Hulley to know that he was not responsible for the ugly turn of events. 'I must tell you,' he said, 'that during your absence the Boers arrived. I kept them waiting as long as I could expecting you to return with Captn. Gardiner and John Cane, when I could keep them no longer, I had them put out of harm's way.' The fault, apparently, was not Dingane's, but Hulley's, Gardiner's and Cane's.

Hulley was not convinced and, when he hesitated to agree, the King turned unpleasant. Why, he wanted to know, had Gardiner and Cane not come when they were sent for? What had they heard to make them keep away? They were like all the other white men. The whites did not love the blacks and never would. Well, he had sent his army to deal with the rest of the Boers. It was a pity Gardiner and Cane had not shown up; they fully deserved the same treatment. They had disobeyed his orders in the same way as the Boers, by allowing Sikonyela to go free, had disobeyed him. He thought it a good idea to get rid of all his enemies in one stroke.

As Dingane ranted on, Hulley became more and more nervous. On returning to the mission, he told Owen that he intended to take his wife and children away immediately. With the King in his present mood, it would be madness to stay. After a little hesitation, Owen agreed. It was not an easy decision to take. Owen had set his heart on converting the Zulu. So far he had failed to win a single soul for Christ. On the other hand, he had no wish to be caught in the war which he felt would be bound to follow once the Boers discovered what had happened to Retief. The fact that he would not be leaving any converts behind made it easier for him to abandon the mission. Selecting a roll of red cloth as a parting present, he went the following afternoon to tell Dingane that he was leaving.

Much to Owen's surprise, the King proved extremely understanding. He was astonished that the missionary expected a war to break out but agreed to let him go. So conciliatory was he that Owen, who had expected opposition, felt it was all too good to be true.

And he was right. The following day Dingane, unpredictable as ever, sent for Owen and Hulley. He threw a terrifying tantrum. He demanded to know why they had come to Zululand in the first place. Nobody had sent for them. He had not asked them to come, nor did he want them there. When Captain Gardiner had left for England he had promised to return with a ship-load of presents: instead he had come back with Owen. Why? As King, he had been *forced* to build a hut for the missionary; he had not wanted to; he had never intended white men to build houses in his country. What was behind it all? He had a good idea. Servants at the mission station had told him that Owen spied on emGungundlovu through a telescope; that he had sympathised with the Boers and had fainted when he saw the Boers slaughtered; that he was always talking against the King; that his wife and sister had called the King a murderer and a rogue. To prove his point he sent for Owen's servants and made them testify against the missionary.

Owen was shocked. He had trusted the servants and had never expected them to turn against him. As best he could, he tried to defend himself. How, he asked, could the servants know what he had said when they could not speak English? He was quickly cut short. The servants, thundered Dingane, did not have to speak English—they could read faces.

Once again Owen mentally committed his soul to God. This time there could be no doubt about it: his family's hours were numbered.

'I composed my mind while the chief was speaking,' he says, 'to think of another world to which my spirit would fly.'

And at the mission station, his trembling wife and sister, frantic at having their servants sent for, watched nervously through the telescope, expecting any minute to see Owen and Hulley dragged through the kraal gates to join the decaying corpses on kwaMatiwane.

But they were all wrong. Dark one minute, light the next, Dingane's moods came and went like summer storms. Seeing Owen's fright, he quickly changed his tone. He was not angry, he said; he merely wished to show the missionary his faults. Perhaps it was as well that Owen was leaving, because otherwise he would have been forced to send him away. But before he left there was something he could do: he could write a letter from the King to the Governor of the Cape. Sending for pen and ink, he dictated a letter explaining that he had killed the Boers in self-protection. He did not want white men to settle in his country, he said; they could come and visit him but they could not build houses.

How different things would have been if he had listened to the indunas and made these conditions earlier.

There were cheers at the mission station when Owen and Hulley finally emerged, quivering and tense, from the royal kraal. Immediately the women started packing boxes and loading the wagons; they were determined to leave at once, they could endure no more.

For Owen, the leave-taking was a sad admittance of failure. The betrayal of his servants had robbed him of his last glimpse of success: not only had he failed to reap a harvest but even the seeds of friendliness had fallen on barren ground. Yet he was not without a bitter hope. Behind it all there had to be a divine purpose. Retribution must surely follow, the Boers would act and God would triumph.

'God is now humbling the pride of the nation,' he wrote, 'and the chiefs in particular, he has permitted them to fall by their own pride, self conceit and wickedness into such an atrocity as will in all probability bring ruin upon themselves and the nation, from which it will never recover and thus the way will be prepared for the missionaries of the word.'

He had done with charity. But if his words smacked more of

anger than of forgiveness they were, in the circumstances, understandable. As it proved, they were also prophetic.

Owen and his party made their way slowly to Natal, stopping for several days at the American missions. The entire countryside was bristling with rumours; garbled reports of the Zulu attack on the Boer encampments had begun to trickle through; everyone was jittery. The Americans were hastily preparing to follow Owen's example and evacuate Zululand.

When they eventually managed to cross the swollen Tugela and reach Gardiner's mission, their fears for the Boers were finally realised. Not only had Dingane sent a message to say that the trekkers had been massacred, but had invited Gardiner to visit the encampments and see the havoc created by the impis. This, claimed the King, was what would happen to all those whites who disobeyed him. He was angry with the traders for not having visited him and threatened to descend on Port Natal one night, drive all the people away, and build a settlement there for himself. Equally alarming was the news that the traders, under Alexander Biggar and John Cane, were organising an expedition to invade Zululand and avenge the death of Thomas Halstead. Far from escaping a war, Owen was headed for an explosive area.

Tension was high at Durban when Owen's party reached there on 10 March. The traders had assembled a huge army of their African followers and were on the point of setting out for Zululand. Owen considered this the height of folly. There seemed little reason and no justification for the proposed invasion. To his mind the traders were merely taking advantage of the unsettled situation to indulge in 'plunder and revenge'. He told them as much, heatedly. On being invited to visit their camp, he harangued them on the sinfulness of their doings and threatened them with the anger of God. But they were no more prepared to listen to the missionary than had been Dingane. The time for sermonising had passed.

The traders' expedition, led by John Cane wearing an ostrich plume in his old straw hat, set off three days later. As a makeshift army it was not unimpressive. Some two thousand Africans, carrying banners inscribed '*Izinkumbi*' (locusts) and 'For justice we fight', had rallied to the traders' cause. Mostly refugees who, at one time or another, had sought sanctuary at Port Natal, they were out for Dingane's blood. Bellowing a war-song as they marched—'The wild beast [Dingane] has driven us from our homes, but we will catch him'—they seemed to one petrified newcomer to Port Natal like nothing less than a herd of angry bulls.

A few days later it was learned that Cane had been contacted by the Boers, who were also planning to invade Zululand. It was expected that the two expeditions would join forces.

By this time Allen Gardiner, his family, and the American missionaries had arrived at Port Natal. With the exception of one of the Americans, Daniel Lindley, they had all decided to quit Natal. A few days after Cane's departure, they boarded a ship waiting in the harbour and sailed for the Cape Colony. Owen, still undecided about his own future, watched them go with a heavy heart. The Americans hoped to return, and did, but Gardiner was leaving for good: his brief, ill-fated, attempt to bring light to Africa had ended. For three years he had struggled, only to find every hand turned against him, every hope shattered—in the end even Dingane had turned on him and sent warriors to plunder his mission. For the next thirteen years he ranged the earth, Bible in hand, in a series of futile missions to primitive peoples. He finally died of starvation in Patagonia on 6 September 1851. In a last, characteristic, message—written a few hours before he died—he wrote: 'I neither hunger nor thirst, though five days without food—marvellous loving kindness to me a sinner.'

The day after Gardiner and the Americans left, Owen moved his tents and wagons onto an island in the bay. Like some of the other settlers, he felt that only the sea could protect him from a possible Zulu attack. Nevertheless, he continued indefatigably with his missionary work: starting a school, visiting the sick and lecturing dissolute traders on the evils of drunkenness. He was as busy as he had ever been when, at the beginning of April, John Cane's expeditionary force returned.

They had not met Dingane's army, nor had they joined up with the Boers: they had not even crossed the Tugela. In northern Natal they had launched a somewhat cowardly attack on one of Dingane's vassal tribes and, with most of the grown men being away, had had little difficulty in seizing some 4000 head of cattle and 500 women and children before marching back to Durban. Cane had lost only two men: one he shot himself for pilfering, the other died of snake bite. It had been a small price to pay for such splendid loot.

Owen was appalled at this evidence of lawlessness. 'There is no king in Israel,' he moaned, 'every man does whatsoever is right in his own eyes.'

Such had been the state of Natal for many years.

[3]

The Boers in the meantime had mounted their own expedition, or commando.

For several days after the Zulu attack, the trekkers had been on the point of despair. Their position seemed hopeless; some talked of abandoning Natal, others began to pack. But Maritz, stoutly supported by the women who demanded that their dead be avenged, succeeded in rallying them. New laagers were formed and fortified and an appeal was sent for reinforcements. By 6 April a commando of 347 men was ready to leave for Zululand.

The Zulu army was waiting for them. Dingane's spies had been active and Ndlela had been given ample time to muster a huge force and deploy it strategically in preparation for the attack. The Boers were lured into a cunningly arranged ambush.

On 11 April the commando, heading for emGungundlovu, sighted a party of Zulu and gave chase. As the Zulu fled into a pass in the surrounding hills, one of the Boer columns—led by Piet Uys—galloped after them. They were quickly cut off from the rest of the Boer force by Ndlela's warriors. Separated and taken by surprise, the two Boer columns were thrown into confusion. While those outside the valley attempted a half-hearted charge, Uys, trapped in the hills, bunched his men together and rode headlong at the encircling Zulu horns. His bid to blast a passage through Ndlela's ranks was only partly successful; for, although most of his men reached the open, he and nine others—including his gallant young son, Dirk—were overtaken and killed.

The Zulu army pursued the remainder of the Boer force for several miles and then gave up. With the advantage of superior numbers and fighting in their own terrain, Dingane's warriors could claim an undoubted victory in their first encounter with armed Boers. A week later they were equally successful in a more bitterly contested clash with the traders.

The loot taken by John Cane by no means satisfied the inhabitants of Durban: they had their plunder but, to Owen's dismay, still thirsted for vengeance. Shortly after Cane's return, a second expedition, commanded by Alexander Biggar's son, Robert, set off for Zululand. Cane, who before leaving sent his half-caste family to join Francis Owen on the island in the bay, had good reason to be apprehensive of a Zulu attack: it was already known that Dingane had offered a reward for his life. Altogether there were seventeen white men in the traders' force.

They met the Injandune regiment of the Zulu army just beyond the Tugela on 17 April. This regiment, said to be in disgrace for having recently lost its commander in a raid on Mzilikazi, was now nominally led by Dingane's sybaritic brother, Mpande, who, for the past few years, had been living in virtual obscurity at a kraal in southern Zululand. But Mpande, like Dingane, was no soldier and the defeat his warriors inflicted on the traders was undoubtedly due—though he was reluctant to admit it—to the skill of his indunas, Nongalaza, Umahlebe and Zulu. Once again the Zulu commanders lured their enemy into a carefully prepared trap.

The traders first sighted a small Zulu contingent near the summit of a hill beyond the Tugela. Expecting a quick and easy victory, they immediately stormed the hill. But, before they could reach the top, some 10,000 warriors rose from the long grass and fell upon them. In the ferocious battle which followed, the traders were doomed from the outset. By the sheer weight of numbers—numbers which increased with the sudden arrival of Ndlela's impis—the Zulu army proved more than a match for their opponent's firearms. Nor were matters helped when some of the Natal Africans panicked and tore off the white calico strips which they wore to distinguish them from the enemy: in the confusion of naked black bodies, many were killed by their own comrades. The death toll was enormous. Before they were finally overcome, the traders are said to have accounted for some 3000 Zulu, while they lost more than 1000 men. Of the seventeen white men, only four survived: among the dead were the two leaders, Robert Biggar and the mighty John Cane.

After fourteen precarious years, Cane, the hefty, well-meaning carpenter whom the Zulu kings had at one time regarded as their trusted ally, had paid the price of pioneering in Natal: he died, like most of his early companions, without reward or recognition. But it is doubtful whether he sought either: a born adventurer, he died as he had lived—facing danger for its own sake. Now, of Farewell's original party, only Henry Ogle remained.

For some reason, Ogle, who seems to have preferred acting on his own, had refused to march with Cane and Biggar. But he had allowed several of his 'clan' to join the expedition and it was one of his Africans, fleeing from the Tugela battle, who first brought news of the disaster to Port Natal. Francis Owen was visiting Ogle when the exhausted warrior staggered into the settlement. He says the scene which followed was heart-rending: 'The tumultuous cries of the distressed women whose husbands were supposed to have been slaughtered made the air resound. One woman was seen walking with her hands at the back of her head crying mournfully "Booya Baba," return my father. An English woman among the rest was almost frantic with grief.'

After vainly, and typically, pleading with the sufferers to turn to God, Owen hurried back to his family. He, like everyone else, was convinced that the Zulu impis would follow up their victory by attacking Durban. Luckily, a brig, the *Comet*, had just arrived in the harbour. That night the Owens, joined by other settlers, went on board.

The next few days were tense. On 23 April, Alexander Biggar called a meeting on shore and it was unanimously agreed that they should make common cause with the trekkers and accept Boer authority once the country was settled. The only one with doubts was Francis Owen. When he asked whether they would accept the establishment of an English mission in Natal, he was heatedly shouted down. The traders had had more than enough of missionaries in Natal. They told Owen so in no uncertain terms. But the argument proved academic. That night the Zulu impis were sighted: the whites scrambled back on board the *Comet*, their Africans fled to the bush.

Ten days later the *Comet* put to sea with Owen and his family still on board. They had watched from the ship as the Zulu army had plundered Durban and, when the impis had left, they had gone ashore to inspect the damage.

The place was a desert. The traders' huts had been ransacked, their cattle driven away, their stores of cloth, calico and beads carried off. At Gardiner's Berea mission house, Owen found there was 'scarcely anything whatever left but provisions of various kinds, salt, sugar, flour etc., which were scattered on the floor and in the midst of which lay half covered soiled immense quantities of books'. Dingane had never mastered the printed word.

'It is with deep regret and great disappointment,' the forlorn Owen reported to his superiors from the *Comet*, 'I inform you of the painful necessity which puts an end (at least for the present) to our mission at Port Natal.'

Francis Owen remained three more years in South Africa. He worked mainly at mission stations in the Cape Colony and then returned to England where he found more suitable employment as a parish priest. High-minded and unworldly, he was never really cut out for the hardships of missionary life. He died in November 1854, at the age of fifty-two. He was thus spared the unsubstantiated calumnies that were spread after his death—accusing him, Gardiner, Cane, Ogle and others, simply because they were English, of inspiring the murder of Piet Retief. Not only is there no credible evidence to support such accusations but they show a complete lack of understanding of the Zulu King. Why should Dingane have required outside help or encouragement to rid himself of a potential threat?

The sacking of Durban did more than put an end to Owen's career in Natal. It brought a fresh personality into prominence. Dingane's brother, nominal commander of the marauding impis, took full credit for driving the white men into the sea. Zululand now had a new name to reckon with: Mpande—The Root.

[4]

Dingane certainly had reason to congratulate himself. His warriors had marched against both Boer and Briton and had returned triumphant. The white men's firearms had not proved as formidable as he and his indunas had feared. But he did not underrate the effectiveness of guns in battle and appears to have used the weapons taken from Retief's party to give his warriors some practice in shooting. When, in August, he again sent his impis to attack a Boer laager, many of the Zulu were armed with muskets. Not that it did them much good. The warriors handled their weapons clumsily, their bullets fell short, and the Boers valiantly withstood a two-day siege which ended with the impis retiring. For all that, it was another terrifying experience for the trekkers, who, as one of the women put it, felt the 'whole of heathendom' had descended upon them and only by God's help had they survived.

The outlook for the trekkers was grim indeed. Retief's murder and the two crippling Zulu attacks had robbed them of some of their best men and most of their cattle. Provisions were low and, to add to their misery, heavy rains had set in, turning the crowded laagers into seas of mud. During the weeks following the sacking of Durban, they had contacted the remaining handful of traders, under Alexander Biggar, and had obtained some supplies of vegetables—salvaged from the gardens of the Natal Africans—and a few other provisions which the traders had wisely hoarded on the islands in the bay. Help had also come in answer to the appeals they sent to their countrymen in the Cape Colony.

Slight as it was, such aid had strengthened their determination to hold out. 'Tears of gratitude were seen on every cheek,' reported a Boer delivering supplies from a frontier town, 'while others weeping and sighing said, "*Let our faith be on the Lord, for he will deliver us.*"' Despite everything, they were inclined to trust God in Natal, rather than the British in the Cape.

They needed all the faith they could muster. There seemed no end to their tribulations. Both within and without the laagers, the forces of evil seemed bent on their destruction. Hardly had they recovered from the Zulu attack in August when, on 23 September, Gert Maritz, who had been ill for weeks, suddenly died. Although not universally popular, Maritz had helped inspire the trek movement and, for some, his loss was as great as that of Retief. His death was mourned by all. The gloom in the camps deepened.

Then, when things were at their blackest, the long looked-for light appeared. First a vessel called at Port Natal, bringing substantial supplies from well-wishers in the Cape Colony and then, on 22 November, Andries Pretorius arrived at the laagers.

Pretorius, a tall, impressive-looking and prosperous farmer from Graaff-Reinet, had earlier informed the trekkers that he was on his way. Even before Maritz's death they had eagerly looked forward to his coming. With Pretorius's appearance on the scene, the trekkers undoubtedly felt that the moment had produced the man. He was immediately elected Commandant-General. 'This man,' declared Piet Retief's widow, 'has been sent by God to help us. He will fight our cause. He will help us take vengeance.'

Few, least of all Pretorius himself, could have doubted that she was right. Then approaching his fortieth birthday, Andries Pretorius was a man with a mission. Earlier, while Retief was still alive, he had briefly visited Natal and had then made up his mind to join the trekkers. News of the Zulu attacks had done nothing to deter him. Seasoned as a fighter in the frontier wars, he regarded these setbacks as a call to him to assume the leadership of his people; to avenge the death of Retief and bring peace to the blood-soaked land. Dedicated and resolute, he approached his appointed task with unflinching confidence.

Within days of his arrival at the laagers, a council of war was called and a punitive commando mounted. It set out in search of Dingane on 27 November.

By far the largest and best organised expedition the trekkers had mounted, Pretorius's force consisted at the outset of 464 men, including coloureds, and a train of sixty-four wagons. As they advanced slowly into Zululand, Pretorius proved himself every bit as efficient as he was determined. He established a proper chain of command, took his officers into his confidence, handled his men firmly but tactfully, sent out scouting parties and nightly posted sentries to watch over the strongly formed laagers. There was to be no repetition of previous mistakes.

Nor was morale neglected. Not the least of Pretorius's qualities as a leader was his appreciation of the religious sentiments which inspired his men. Nothing consoled the trekkers more than the conviction that they were walking in the way of the righteous and, to ensure God's blessing, the commando was assembled after a few days out to observe a pious vow. Solemnly it was pledged that, should God deliver the enemy into their hands, they would honour the day and date of their victory each year as a Sabbath and enjoin their children to follow their example. Having rejected the Church evangelical, in the shape of the missionaries, Dingane was now to be brought face to face with the Church militant: Christianity was invading Zululand sword in hand.

Other forces were also mustering. Two weeks after Pretorius's departure for Zululand, news was received at the trekker encampments that British troops had landed at Port Natal. Alarmed at reports of the upheavals in Natal, the Governor of the Cape had at last sent eighty men of the 72nd Highlanders, under Major Samuel Charters, to Durban. But a Government proclamation made it quite clear that this occupation was merely a temporary measure to keep the peace. It was not intended as the first step towards 'colonization or annexure to the Crown of Great Britain'.

All the same, there must have been a round of celestial applause from Port Natal's dear departed as the red-coated soldiers scrambled ashore. How these British boys would have been welcomed ten years earlier! Now there was only Henry Ogle to appreciate the significance of the moment. He may or may not have rejoiced to see the dreams and schemes of Farewell and King realised at last—albeit half-heartedly—but he would have found few to share his reflections: the trading community had so diminished that not even the bellicose Alexander Biggar was there to greet Major Charters and his men.

Biggar was again on the war-path. Word of Pretorius's expedition had quickly reached Durban and Biggar, with a few other traders, had immediately rounded up a troop of Natal Africans and hastened to join the Boers. His little army, together with a contingent of Boers under Karel Landman, had joined up with the commando shortly after Pretorius crossed the Tugela. The combined force continued northwards into Zululand.

They were watched every step of the way. Dingane's spies were known to be active and there was an occasional skirmish with Zulu patrols. Pretorius was left in no doubt that an enormous force was on its way to head him off. He was given ample time to select a battle site.

On Saturday 15 December, reports were received that the Zulu army was in the vicinity. The Boers went into laager on the banks of the Ncome river. It was an excellent defensive position: one side of the laager was protected by a steep-sided hollow, another by the river which, at that point, was very deep. 'The Lord,' declared one of the trekkers, 'in His holy providence, had appointed a place for us, in which He had determined that the fight should occur.'

The wagons were lashed together, rawhide was stretched from

wheel to wheel, ladders were placed in strategic positions, and two small cannon, brought by Pretorius, were mounted in readiness. Behind each wagon were piles of reserve guns and ammunition. That night lanterns were lit inside the laager, to guard against surprise, and the Boers slept fitfully, waiting for the attack. It was half expected that the Zulu army, which had been sighted that afternoon and was massing on the opposite side of the river, would strike under cover of darkness.

But the night passed quietly. At daybreak, the Boers began to take up their positions behind the wagons. As the sky slowly lightened, they saw a frightening sight: 'all of Zululand' faced them, sitting ring upon ring, in deathly silence. Hardly had Pretorius given the order to open fire than the warriors rose. Hissing, chanting and rattling their stabbing spears against their shields, they charged the wagons. There were, it is said, some 12,000 of them.

As the Zulu closed in, the Boers kept up their steady fire. The air was split by the thunder of guns; smoke billowed above the wagons; piles of black bodies littered the veld and the river banks; the waters of the Ncome ran red as bleeding warriors reeled and tumbled headlong into the stream. The sun rose on a crystal clear day and the aim of the Boers became more accurate, more deadly. Finally Ndlela and Dambusa, commanding the impis, were forced to order the warriors back. The laager remained impregnable; not a Zulu had reached it; not a defender had been killed.

The warriors retired, sat, recovered their breath, and charged again. Inside the laager, the Boers grabbed gun after gun, thrust powder and shot into hot barrels—often without stopping to ram it home—and continued their unremitting fire. The cannon pounded away through the openings in the wagons, adding their deafening roar to the crack of the muskets and the screams of the attackers. As wave after wave of warriors broke against the wagons, there was no time to think, no time to doubt. 'Of that fight,' claimed one trekker, 'nothing remains in my memory except shouting and tumult and lamentation, and a sea of black faces; and a dense smoke that rose straight as a plumb-line upwards from the ground.'

For two hours the Zulu battled fearlessly to get to grips with their enemy, only to be mown down before they could reach the wagons. Against the Boer defences and the Boer gunfire they were helpless. Nothing in their training, nothing in their experience, had prepared them for such warfare. At last, exhausted, and impeded by their mounting dead, they began to waver; the attacks began to slacken off. Sensing victory, Pretorius was quick to take advantage of the lull. Through gaps in the wagons, parties of mounted Boers thundered out, scattering the warriors in all directions. The Zulu offered little resistance. After a short, brave stand the dispirited impis turned and fled.

The Boers hunted down stragglers for several hours and then returned to the laager. They had lost not a single man and only three—including Andries Pretorius—had been wounded. In the immediate vicinity of the wagons, the bodies of dead Zulu dotted the veld 'like pumpkins on a rich soil'. How many warriors had fallen it was impossible to say: certainly more than the original estimate of 3000.

So many lost their lives in the Ncome that the name of this little known stream was changed. The epic clash was henceforth to be known as the Battle of Blood River.

'AND THEN ALL WILL BE OVER'

IT IS OFTEN claimed that the battle of Blood River broke the power of the Zulu nation. But how true is this? Zulu power, crippled by the death of Shaka, had been on the decline for years. Dingane had merely survived on his predecessor's reputation.

In his ten-year rule, Dingane had never fought a major campaign, let alone won a major victory. His army, when tested, had all too often proved irresolute, if not downright defeatist. More than once his warriors had returned without completing their mission: the attacks on Mzilikazi, probably the most important of Dingane's reign, had ended as little more than glorified cattle raids. In fact, had the white men not appeared, one wonders how long it would have been before Mzilikazi got Dingane's measure. The shadow of Shaka was already growing dim. What small successes Dingane could claim were the result of cunning and treachery. It had required no military valour to lure defenceless clans to his kraal and massacre them

Dingane was full of show but, unfortunately, he rarely showed to advantage. He never accompanied his army and was incapable of inspiring heroism. Had he not repeatedly displayed a reluctance to fight? How could his warriors have faith in the campaigns forced upon the King by his indunas? This was not how Shaka had forged the Zulu nation.

And not only did Dingane lack Shaka's genius but he lacked Shaka's gifted commanders. He had murdered them as he had murdered Shaka. Ndlela and Dambusa, loyal and brave as they were, showed little talent for warfare. Their strategy, such as it was, depended more on brute force than on judgement. To have allowed a powerful enemy like the Boers to fight on chosen ground was foolish. Not to have recognised the futility of charging an impregnable laager, bristling with guns, was madness. Would Shaka, a master tactician, have been so rash? It is open to doubt.

Dingane was not Shaka and the power he wielded was merely a distorted reflection of Shaka's. The battle of Blood River did not break Zulu power: it exposed Dingane's weakness. That this had not happened sooner was Dingane's good luck; that it happened when it did was the misfortune of the Zulu people.

There could be no question of the Boers resting after their victory. They had by no means finished with Dingane; they had too many scores to settle, too many debts to collect—not least being the valuable herds taken during the disastrous Zulu raids. The day after the battle, Pretorius broke up his laager and rode on to emGungundlovu.

The commando arrived at the Zulu capital three days later to find the great kraal deserted and the *isiGodlo* a smouldering ruin. Dingane had set fire to his royal quarters and fled: taking his wives, his cattle and his servants with him. There was not a soul to be seen; it was obvious that the evacuation had been a panic measure.

Searching the abandoned huts, the Boers discovered an amazing collection of treasure horded by the Zulu kings over the years: iron, copper, ivory and a wide assortment of European utensils and novelties. Evidence of the contact between the traders and the rulers of Zululand was there in abundance. The Boers unearthed many forsaken gifts—including two useless brass cannon—which appear to have passed unrecorded. Who had presented Dingane with cannon? Or were they relics of the days when Farewell and King were courting Shaka? It must have broken Dingane's heart to sacrifice so much valuable loot.

Pretorius and his men went into laager a short distance from the kraal before investigating further. They climbed kwaMatiwane and stumbled on the remains of Piet Retief's party. Exposed for months to sun and rain, the bodies were decaying and scarcely recognisable. But details of the ghastly executions were only too apparent: the hands and feet of some of the skeletons were bound with leather thongs, from others the lethal impaling stakes protruded. 'The sight of them,' sighed Pretorius, 'must have moved the most unfeeling heart.'

They identified Piet Retief from scraps of clothing adhering to his bones. Close to his body was a water bottle and a pouch containing the fatal treaty bearing Dingane's seal. So much had rotted away but, as if by a miracle, this incriminating document had remained intact as testimony to Retief's last, grimly mistaken, hope. It was visible proof, if such were needed, of Dingane's infamy; as such it was reverently preserved by the Boers.

The skeletons were gathered together and buried, on Christmas day, in a communal grave. On the same day a year earlier, Francis Owen had sat listening to celebrations in the great kraal marking the beginning of the harvest. He had regretted that no voice was raised to honour the Christian God. Now the voices could be heard acknowledging the Christian God but a more gruesome harvest. Zululand could never be the same again.

The Boers, however, were set on reaping more than sorrow. Sending out patrols, they began to search for the fugitive King. There were few indications of his passing. Not until three Zulu were ferreted out in the bush near emGungundlovu did they receive news of Dingane's whereabouts. Two of these warriors were immediately sent to contact the King and demand his surrender; the third was kept for questioning.

His name was Bongoza and he claimed to be one of Dingane's indunas. He also claimed to hate the King. He was willing to tell the white men all they wanted to know, and more. Dingane, he said, was defenceless, his defeated army had scattered and he was hiding with his cattle in the bushveld to the north-east. He offered to lead the Boers to the King's new grazing grounds.

That the man was lying was obvious. Pretorius knew well enough that, though victorious at Blood River, he had by no means put the entire Zulu army out of action. From the very outset he had suspected that Bongoza had been sent to lure the Boers into a trap. But Dingane had to be found somehow and Pretorious pretended to fall in with the plan. The following day, at Bongoza's suggestion, he moved eastwards, to a ridge overlooking the valley of the White Mfolozi river. Here the Boers went into laager and Pretorius rode out to survey the scene below. In the valley there were, as Bongoza had promised, great herds of Zulu cattle tended by what looked like a few herdsmen. The sky was overcast and it was not possible to see distinctly.

To reach the valley it was necessary to descend a perilously steep ravine. Pretorius, still suffering from the wound he had received at Blood River, did not feel up to it; he handed over command to Karel Landman. The following morning Landman and a commando of 300 men set off. They were accompanied by Alexander Biggar and his Natal Africans and guided by Bongoza. Before they left, Pretorius warned them to take care, to send out scouts, to be on guard against a trap, and to keep a watchful eye on Bongoza. He was none too happy as he watched them canter towards the edge of the ridge.

The climb down was hard going. The men had to dismount and lead their horses, stumbling over loose stones and scrambling across rocky rivulets. They were urged on by whispered instructions from Bongoza. The further they descended, the clearer became their view of the valley. About half-way down they were brought up short. A Zulu impi suddenly emerged from a wood in the valley and dashed away towards the river; so obvious was their flight that the Boers immediately became suspicious. Bongoza was quick to reassure them. The fleeing warriors, he explained, were all that was left of Dingane's army. Cautiously they continued the descent.

That they were being led into an ambush soon became apparent. As they neared the bottom of the ravine a shout was heard, Bongoza disappeared, and warriors sprang out of hiding on all sides. What had looked from a distance to be a herd of cattle was now seen to be Zulu crouching beneath their shields. Finding themselves cut off, the Boers held a hurried consultation; then, instead of retreating into the hills as the Zulu obviously expected, they mounted and raced for the river, firing in every direction.

Once across the Mfolozi, the commando swerved in an arc and, while a rear-guard opened fire at the pursuing Zulu horde, they headed upstream hoping to recross the river. In the running fight there were several skirmishes and the warriors—some mounted and some with guns—were still hot on their heels when the Boers plunged back across a tributary of the Mfolozi. Fording the swiftly flowing stream proved more difficult than they had anticipated. As horses and men splashed and struggled in the water, six Europeans, including old Alexander Biggar, were stabbed to death. Most of the Natal Africans were shot by Boers who mistook them for Zulu.

The fighting continued sporadically until late that evening, when the main body of the commando met an armed patrol which Pretorius, alerted by the shooting, had sent to reinforce them. Together the two forces made their way back to the laager. By midnight all the Boer stragglers had returned. No more white men had been killed; the Boers' greatest loss had been the seventy or more Natal Africans who had died as a result of their own wild shooting. It was impossible to estimate correctly the Zulu dead; Pretorius considered that at least 1000 warriors had been killed.

Once again the Boers could claim a victory. This time, fighting in the open, they had outwitted the enemy and escaped from a carefully laid trap. It would require great ingenuity to get the better of the Boers: greater ingenuity than Dingane's commanders possessed.

Experience, however, had taught them the futility of attempting to storm fortified wagons. For three days Pretorius remained in laager, hoping for a further attack, but nothing more happened. Finally he withdrew and led the commando back to Natal. On the way he destroyed a number of kraals and rounded up all the livestock he could lay his hands upon. By the time he arrived back at the Boer encampments he had recovered some 5000 head of cattle and 1500 sheep.

The trekkers gave him a tumultuous welcome. All the hopes they had placed in him had been fulfilled. In little over a month he had defeated the Zulu army, avenged Piet Retief, put Dingane to flight and replenished the depleted Boer herds. Not for nothing was Pretorius hailed as the leader of the *Wen* (Victory) *Kommando*.

[2]

But what of Dingane? Where was he? What was he up to? Unfortunately there is no way of knowing. His activities were no longer being recorded by his white scribes; his movements and his intentions at this time are largely a matter of conjecture. All that can be said with any certainty is that, at the beginning of 1839, he moved further north to the region in which Shaka's old enemy, Zwide, had once lived. Here he established a new capital; another emGungundluvo, smaller than his former residence and planned, it seems, with an eye to possible further retreat into the mountains and forests beyond. Lacking Shaka's resolution, he undoubtedly viewed the future with great uncertainty. His dancing days were over; the Boers, he knew, would come after him again: now he could only wait on events.

Meanwhile the trekkers were busy establishing themselves in Natal. With their worst fears behind them they could at last think of a permanent settlement. While Dingane was occupied in building the huts of his new capital, they began to prepare a capital of their own.

They moved their encampments to a spot some fifty miles from Durban where, amid the hills of the lush hinterland, they divided a tract of land, unloaded their wagons, and started to till the fertile soil. At first little more than a glorified laager, the settlement quickly began to take shape. By the middle of March, Pretorius could report that: 'A large, pleasant, and well-watered town ... begins daily to raise its head above the surrounding hillocks; 300 beautiful erven [plots] have already been given out, surveyed and partly planted.' Administered by an elected Volksraad (the Boer legislature and executive authority) the fledgling town was named Pietermaritzburg after the two dead trekker leaders—Pieter Retief and Gert Maritz.

But Pietermaritzburg and the new emGungundlovu were not the only centres of power. There was also Durban, where the British troops were now firmly encamped. On the very day that Boer fought Zulu at Blood River, Major Charters had hoisted the Union Jack at Port Natal and taken temporary possession of the harbour and surrounding country in the name of his sovereign. He had, by then, already informed the trekkers of his arrival, making it clear that they were still regarded as British subjects and that they were expected to accept his authority. Pretorius, who had been told of this on his return from Zululand, had made it equally clear that he did not intend to budge. 'To ask us to return to the colony,' he growled, 'will be useless.'

There was, in fact, very little that Charters could do. His force was small and his authority, to say the least, very tenuous. Apart from impounding a consignment of arms destined for the Boers, he confined his activities to wordy proclamations. Then he gave up altogether. On 20 January 1839, he handed over command to Captain Henry Jervis of the 72nd Highlanders and rode back overland to the Cape Colony.

So there they sat: the Zulu at emGungundlovu, the Boers at

Pietermaritzburg and the British at Durban. Three irreconcilable forces had formed an all-too-familiar pattern. Boer, Briton and Bantu faced each other, each waiting for someone to make the first move. After weeks of turmoil, events had ground to an uneasy standstill.

It was Captain Jervis, a conscientious but limited officer, who first attempted to break the deadlock. Finding his authority challenged by the Volksraad—he tried unsuccessfully to arrest a young Boer charged with wounding an African—he turned his attention to Dingane. Through the medium of Port Natal's oldest resident, Henry Ogle, he contacted the Zulu King in the hopes of arranging a peace conference with the Boers.

Dingane seized upon the suggestion. In Jervis's approach he saw a possible solution to his dilemma. If he was to escape the persecution of the Boers, he needed allies; what better allies could he have than the British? Were not the Boers deserters from the Cape Colony? Had he not, in the past, exchanged friendly messages with the Governor of the Cape and welcomed loyal subjects of the British sovereign? And had it not been agreed between himself and one of those subjects, Captain Gardiner, that deserters should be surrendered and punished? Here, surely, was a way of ridding himself of these frightening newcomers.

Ever the great showman, Dingane fully appreciated the drama of his predicament. The reply he sent to Ogle, through one of his servants, was as highly coloured as it was cautious. 'I am,' he declared, 'on the brink of ruin.' If Jervis could suggest a way in which he could come to terms with the Boers, he would be willing to co-operate. But he left no doubt as to how he would like things settled. 'I have never acknowledged the Boers,' he stressed, 'and never will. The English I always have, since Farewell's arrival at Natal . . . I am in great trouble. Tell the English Government to assist me, and send the Boers out of the country.' Of Retief's murder he refused to speak.

Jervis made no promises. The messenger was sent back and Dingane was requested to send a deputation to speak on his behalf. A few days later three indunas arrived at Port Natal. It was agreed that, as a preliminary to a lasting peace, the Zulu would restore the cattle and arms they had taken from the Boers. This, apparently, was as far as Jervis was prepared to commit himself.

The Boers, on the other hand, were far from happy with the way things were going. Much as they wanted peace, they objected to negotiations being conducted behind their backs and placed no reliance on the Zulu King's promises. 'When Dingaan makes propositions of peace,' declared Pretorius, who arrived at Port Natal on 20 March, 'his murderous intentions are at their height.' If Dingane preferred to forget the Retief massacre, others did not. Nor were matters helped by Jervis's refusal to hand over the Boer arms impounded by Major Charters. All in all, Pretorius felt he had scant reason to trust either the Zulu or the British.

But, things being what they were, Pretorius was in no position to argue. Stifling his doubts, he eventually agreed to meet the Zulu delegates in the company of Captain Jervis. The conference was held in a field close to the bay on 25 March. It went surprisingly well. The indunas had instructions, or so it seemed, to sue for peace at any price. They had brought 316 of the stolen horses with them and promised a return of the rest of the plunder. 'Our King,' they pleaded, 'has now become like a child; alarmed and driven by the emigrants from his capital—which was always viewed by us impregnable; he is now living as a fugitive in caves and inaccessible rocks; acknowledges the emigrants as conquerors, and expects to receive from them the conditions they think proper to exact.' While the truth of this is doubtful, the indunas appeared to be in earnest.

Recognising that they had the upper hand, the Boers took full advantage of the situation. The conditions they laid down were stringent. Not only did they demand the return of all their arms and equipment, but insisted that 19,000 head of cattle be handed over as compensation for their losses. Their claim to the land ceded to Piet Retief was also to be upheld. From then on the Tugela was to act as a boundary between them and the Zulu; any of Dingane's subjects entering Natal without a pass would be shot. To all this the indunas, under the watchful eye of Captain Jervis, agreed.

Once the agreement had been reached—or rather dictated—the indunas were presented with snuff and beads, given three days' rations, and sent to report to Dingane. Pretorius returned immediately to Pietermaritzburg. Well pleased with his efforts, Captain Jervis sent an optimistic report of the proceedings to the Governor of the Cape. 'Not,' he concluded, 'that I really expect, nor do the

Boers, that the Zulus will fulfill the contract, nor will they be required to do so; because I am confident that many of the most influential farmers will forgo their losses for peace, and induce others to do the same.' He was soon to discover how wrong he was.

Not only did the Boers expect to be paid in full, but they became increasingly impatient when their demands were not met. They suspected, quite rightly, that Dingane was merely playing for time. It seems that, having been thwarted in his attempt to have the Boers expelled from Natal, the Zulu King had decided to change his tactics. He made no attempt to deliver the promised cattle and, in the middle of April, three of his spies were discovered on the outskirts of Pietermaritzburg. They had been sent, one of them confessed, to find out whether the Boers had dispersed as a result of the peace conference. The implications of their mission seemed all too obvious. 'Surely,' sighed one of the trekkers, 'this will shew that Dingaan is not to be trusted, and that his peace is a pretext to get the farmers separated.'

If Dingane really had such hopes, he was quickly disillusioned. Pretorius was in no mood to be put off with empty promises; he wanted action. Assembling a strong commando, he marched to the Tugela, went into laager, and sent a deputation to inform Dingane that he was waiting for the cattle to be handed over. His envoys reached the new Zulu capital towards the end of May.

Once again Dingane tried to delay matters. Battered and bloodied as he was, he could not bring himself to part with his most cherished possession—his splendid, much envied, herds—without angling for a concession. Backed by the faithful Dambusa, he put up a fine show of righteous indignation. The Boers, he complained, had looted his former capital—he was particularly incensed at the loss of some copper wire—and plundered his herds after the battle of the White Mfolozi; if he was expected to compensate the trekkers, then the trekkers should likewise return his property. Ingenious as was this argument, it carried no weight with the Boer envoys, who were already casting eager eyes over the teeming royal herds. They made it clear that they were determined to have every pound of animal flesh due to them; there was to be no possibility of compromise.

With Pretorius in laager at the Tugela, Dingane knew better than to push things too far. He quickly abandoned his tantrum, put on a brave face, and appeared to give in gracefully. On 7 June he duly handed over 1300 head of cattle, some 400 to 500 sheep, 52 guns and 43 saddles and bridles.

This, of course, was simply the return of the property stolen from the trekkers. The 19,000 head of cattle which the Boers demanded as compensation was still outstanding. Pretorius let it be known that he would accept ivory as payment for part of this debt, but that was his only concession. Come what may, Dingane would have to honour the treaty made by his indunas; only then could there be talk of a lasting peace.

[3]

At the beginning of December 1839 *De Ware Afrikaan*, a Dutch language newspaper in Cape Town, published an alarming report from the trekkers in Natal. It concerned Dingane's brother Mpande (or Panda as he was known) who was said to have crossed the Tugela with a large following and, on 'various plausible pretences', was advancing towards Pietermaritzburg. *De Ware Afrikaan* considered this an ominous development.

'Even if it is true that Dingaan and his brother have quarrelled,' warned the editor, 'we do not consider that either of them is on that account to be trusted. It seems that Panda, at one time, went so far as to demand leave to incorporate his people amongst the Emigrants —a request which, had it been granted, would have been only a prelude to a nightly massacre ... If the Boers act wisely they will rely solely upon themselves, and repose no confidence in a people so treacherous as the Zoolus.'

But Cape Town was a long way from Pietermaritzburg and news travelled slowly. By the time this report was published, the trekkers had little doubt that Mpande's intentions were friendly and that his arrival in Natal was not a threat, but a blessing. For Mpande had indeed deserted his brother to ally himself with the Boers. His defection was to play no small part in the final overthrow of Dingane.

Fat, amiable, and seemingly incompetent, Mpande was, like Shaka and Dingane, a son of Senzangakhona. His mother had been Senzangakhona's ninth wife and, in 1839, he was about forty years old and much married. Apart from his reputation as a weakling, little nor nothing is known of his childhood. As a young man, Mpande had served as a warrior in Shaka's army and he owed his continued existence to an indolence which had earned him Dingane's contempt. He admitted this. Explaining why Dingane had spared him after Shaka's death, he said: 'I had not influence enough, and could do no harm.'

The sacking of Durban had first drawn widespread attention to Mpande. As the nominal commander of the marauding impis, he had been given credit for the campaign. Once Dingane had been put to flight, he had been recognised as a possible saviour of the crumbling Zulu nation. More and more warriors had flocked to his kraal until, it is said, his fighting force rivalled that of Dingane. This might have been an exaggeration, but there can be no doubt that Mpande's influence was growing as Dingane's was declining; it only required a quarrel between the two brothers to create a fatal division in the Zulu army.

Such a quarrel was, perhaps, inevitable. Lethargic Mpande might have been, but he was not entirely without ambition. Nor could he have had any illusions about the dangers he courted by allowing himself to be seen as a possible rival to his brother. One or other of them would have to go. Mpande was astute enough to act before he could be acted against.

For details of the actual rift, one has only Mpande's word, but what he says seems feasible enough. It seems that Dingane, in an effort to restore his waning influence, decided to attack his old enemies, the Swazi. Not only was this intended as a show of strength but it was hoped that, if successful, it would result in the capture of sufficient cattle to satisfy the Boers without depleting the Zulu herds. But it did not work out like that. The last time Dingane had attacked the Swazi his impis had been supported by John Cane's armed force; now Cane was dead and the Zulu army was by no means what it had once been. After a brisk encounter in Swazi territory, Ndlela's force was sent reeling back across the Pongola river, hopelessly defeated.

Maddened by this further humiliation, Dingane immediately cast about for a scapegoat. He had not far to look. Mpande was made to measure. Dingane could now add to his suspicions of his brother's growing importance by accusing him of treachery. At the outset of the Swazi campaign, Mpande had been ordered to send reinforcements to assist Ndlela. This order had apparently been ignored. No warriors had arrived from Mpande's kraal and their failure to turn up was said to have contributed to the Zulu defeat. But Mpande was to deny that he had deliberately disobeyed his brother. He claimed that he had despatched a regiment to emGungundlovu but, for some reason or other, his warriors had been unable to locate the new capital and had returned home.

If Mpande expected Dingane to swallow this extremely lame excuse, he was sadly mistaken. Shortly after the defeated Ndlela returned to Zululand, messengers arrived at Mpande's kraal demanding an explanation for his disloyalty. Why, they wanted to know, had he not sent his warriors? Was he intending to join the white men? He was given little time to reply. A few days later, more messengers arrived with specific instructions: Mpande was to move his people and cattle to an area in northern Zululand and to visit Dingane and beg forgiveness. Wisely, Mpande refused to budge. 'Why,' he declared, 'should I allow myself to be murdered by a villain, or take flight with him?'

It says much for Mpande's increased power that Dingane made no attempt to attack his rebellious brother. As he must have realised, he had little hope of asserting his authority by force. When eventually Ndlela arrived at Mpande's kraal he came, not with a punitive expedition, but at the head of a diplomatic mission. As Dingane's head induna, he made a pathetic appeal to Mpande's followers to rally to the King's cause. 'Why,' he asked, 'don't you rise and proceed onward, or do you wait for Panda? If you wait for him, I can tell you that within a short time one of Dingaan's commandos will surround him; don't you clearly see that he has turned his face towards the whites?' This ultimatum had little effect. A few of the more nervous warriors agreed to join Ndlela but the majority sided firmly with Mpande.

But neither Mpande nor his people were confident enough to sit out their defiance. Knowing that Dingane would now be forced to take some sort of action, they decided to escape while the going was good. In the middle of September they rounded up their cattle, crossed the Tugela, and sent word of their arrival to Pieter-maritzburg.

That the arrival of this army of refugees caused considerable alarm in Natal is not surprising. For not only had the Zulu blatantly violated the peace treaty by crossing the Tugela, but it seemed highly unlikely that their intentions were as friendly as they pretended. Pretorius, in fact, was all for mounting a commando to drive Mpande back before he could start any trouble. He had every reason to regard this sudden appearance of Dingane's brother as just another Zulu subterfuge.

Over the past few months there had been a great deal of shilly-shallying on the part of the Zulu King. After handing over the Boers' stolen cattle in June, he had made no effort to pay off the rest of his debt. Nor, it seemed, did he intend to. His only attempt at negotiating a settlement had been in August when he was expected to deliver the promised cattle. Hopeful as this had seemed at the time, the Boers had been quickly disillusioned when it was discovered that Dingane's 'emissaries' were merely two of his menial servants—'a *beer brewer* and a *gardener*'. Furious at this thinly veiled insult, Pretorius had again threatened to invade Zululand. By the time Mpande arrived his patience was wearing thin; he was in no mood to put up with any more of Dingane's tricks.

But what if there was no trick? What if Mpande was sincere and had indeed revolted against his brother? If Zululand was on the brink of civil war, then the Boers would do well to make an ally of Mpande. A rival claimant to the Zulu throne was well worth cultivating. In this way it might be possible to overthrow Dingane and establish a new, friendly regime. It was a chance which Pretorius decided to take. At the beginning of October, Mpande and some of his leading indunas were summoned to Pietermaritzburg to explain themselves to the Volksraad.

The hearing took place on 15 October. Mpande, fat and flabby as he was, made a tremendous impression. In that ample person were combined two extremely effective attributes: majesty and charm. His bearing was superbly regal, his smile disarmingly wide. He was a man of imposing presence, a man who inspired trust. Even the more suspicious of the trekkers appear to have warmed to him.

Answering the Boers through an interpreter, he was only too ready to denounce Dingane. His brother, he claimed, was a blood-thirsty tyrant, a usurper who had murdered 'the whole royal family' and had spared him only because he was thought to have 'the heart of a woman'. Now things were different. Now Dingane was determined to kill him; this was why he sought the protection of the whites. If the Boers would grant his people land in Natal, he promised to be their friend and act as they wished him to act.

He did not consider himself, at that time, strong enough to fight Dingane; but, he said, 'if the people receive information of peace, they certainly will come to me in crowds'. Asked how many regiments Dingane had, he admitted that he was not sure; he had heard that over half the Zulu force had been killed in the recent Swazi campaign but he thought that Dingane could call on many more. At the Boers' request, he promised to send spies into Zululand to ascertain the strength of his brother's army.

More or less satisfied that Mpande was telling the truth, the Volksraad agreed to grant the refugees land. They were willing, they said, to recognise Mpande as the Zulu leader and, so long as he remained faithful, they would regard him as their ally.

The irony of this interview seems to have passed unnoticed. Only a matter of months earlier, the Boers had been seeking permission to settle in Natal; now it was they who were granting permission to the Zulu to live in their former territory. Jacob had been a prophet indeed.

This reversal of roles certainly did not dismay Mpande. He was only too ready to acknowledge his gratitude. 'My heart,' he told the Volksraad, 'is now full of joy, as I see that you deal with me in so good and kind a manner.'

A few days later a Boer delegation visited Mpande's newly built kraal and installed him as 'Reigning Prince of the Emigrant Zoolas.' This was to be his title until the overthrow of Dingane allowed him to assume full sovereignty. And it was secretly agreed that, once Mpande became sovereign, he would take over Dingane's debts, repay the promised cattle, and grant the Boers a great tract of land. This would be more land than Dingane or Shaka had ever been willing to cede—land stretching along the coast of Zululand as far as St Lucia Bay. Mpande, it was made clear, would be a tame king or no king at all.

The installation ceremony was a grand affair, attended by Mpande's assembled warriors and accompanied by much feasting and dancing. Yet, somehow, throughout the festivities, Mpande, dressed in a bright blue cloak presented to him by the Boers, looked dejected. He was made even more unhappy, or so it seemed, when a group of warriors, in a frenzy of excitement, summarily clubbed to death one of his recently appointed indunas.

'Why,' he cried, 'have you committed such an act in the presence of the white people? What must they think of me, as I have a few minutes since promised not to allow such cruelties; where shall I find friends and protectors in future when I shall again be compelled to flee?'

Well may he have asked. It was later rumoured that he had ordered the execution himself. It was said that he needed to demonstrate his newly acquired power by ordering the death of the induna, allowing himself to be smeared with his victim's blood and then eating the dead man's roasted heart 'as if to strengthen his body and double his heart'. Not everyone believed this; but the fact remains that the induna was killed and Mpande appeared to be unhappy. Whichever way one looked at it, the new reign could hardly be said to have started auspiciously.

[4]

In December 1839 the British troops at Port Natal were ordered back to the Cape. Captain Henry Jervis was apparently well satisfied with his peace-keeping mission. Before sailing, on Christmas Eve, Jervis sent the trekkers a cheery farewell message. He wished them every happiness and expressed the hope that they might 'cultivate those beautiful regions in quiet and prosperity, ever regardful of the rights of the inhabitants, whose country you have adopted and whose home you have made your own'.

Three weeks later, on 15 January 1840, Andries Pretorius set out to invade Zululand, determined to crush Dingane once and for all.

How far the timing of Pretorius's invasion was influenced by the departure of the British is a matter for speculation. No doubt he was pleased enough to be given a free hand. No doubt the farewell salvo fired by the Boers at Port Natal as the British departed did sound, as one observer remarked, more like 'good riddance' than bon voyage. All the same, Pretorius had fully intended moving against the fugitive King whether the British left or not. From his point of view, he had no option. Dingane's equivocal behaviour had made it imperative that he act and act swiftly.

'Of all the fine promises Dingaan has made,' wrote one of the trekkers in January 1840, 'not one has yet been fulfilled. Only a few Elephants' teeth and an inconsiderable number of cattle have been forwarded during the whole time, with no other motive than to gain time to escape with the bulk of his plunder.' There could be no question of the Boers allowing this to happen.

Dingane was well aware of what was in store for him. His spies had been as active as ever; he knew all about the alliance between Mpande and the trekkers; he knew that time was running out. Once news reached him that the British had left, he appears to have panicked. He immediately sent Dambusa and a minor induna named Khambazana to Pietermaritzburg with 200 head of hand-picked cattle and instructions to plead for peace. 'Go,' he said, 'speak as if I were speaking, and succeed in your errand.'

But there was scant hope of Dambusa succeeding. Things had gone too far; the gesture was made too late. Convinced that this was yet another of the King's ruses, the Volksraad arrested the two indunas, raised their demand for cattle to 40,000 and ordered the mobilisation of a commando. Appeals for help were sent to Boers scattered throughout, and beyond, Natal. Once it was known that these reinforcements were mustering, Pretorius started out from Pietermaritzburg.

That the Volksraad should have distrusted Dambusa is not surprising. When they had interrogated him, he had made no effort to defend himself. His main concern had been to justify Dingane's conduct; he spoke, it was said, too much in his master's favour and not enough in his own. Moreover, he had had Mpande to contend with. Usually so mild and amiable, Mpande had become positively hysterical in testifying against Dambusa. He had risen in a fury and accused Dingane's indunas of being responsible for every treachery committed by the King. Ndlela and Dambusa, he said, were behind every plot, every betrayal, every massacre, that had occurred at emGungundlovu. They had wanted to kill him in the same way that they had killed thousands of innocent men, women and children. So impassioned did he become, that even the Boers were astonished. 'If Panda had been permitted,' one of them gasped, 'he would have taken summary vengeance on Dambusa.'

For all that, Pretorius was wary of Mpande. There was always the chance that his anger, like his defection, was all part of a plot to lull the Boers' suspicions and lure them into yet another trap. It was a chance Pretorius could not afford to take. He decided to keep his new Zulu allies at a safe distance. When the commando set out, Mpande's army was placed under the command of his brilliant general Nongalaza (who had earlier defeated John Cane's expedition and sacked Durban) and ordered to march on a parallel route. Mpande was to be carefully watched and regarded as a hostage. By thus dividing his force, Pretorius not only safeguarded himself from possible treachery but ensured that any attack by Dingane would be fought on two fronts. His experiences in Natal had taught him many lessons.

The commando moved slowly towards Zululand, halting frequently and being joined from time to time by parties of Boers from outlying camps. There was no longer any urgency about the campaign. Most of the men treated the expedition as little more than a hunting trip. They joked about the cattle they would capture, the spoils they would share, the prisoners they would take back as servants. They were confident of success. By the time Pretorius was ready to enter Zululand, he could count on an effective fighting force of 400 men. Accompanied by an equal number of African servants, his fifty wagons splashed purposefully across the Tugela.

Once they had entered Dingane's territory they were joined by rebel clan leaders. The Zulu might not, as Mpande had predicted, have flocked to the invaders 'in crowds' but they came in sufficient numbers to boost the Boers' morale. They came dressed and armed for battle. They stamped out their war-dances and sang Pretorius's praises. 'Dingaan's greatness,' they chanted, 'will soon disappear as snow before the sun; and then we shall live in peace under the protection of the white men.'

On seeing Dambusa, who was being hauled along naked and in chains, they screamed abuse at him. They called him the murderer of Retief, the killer of women and children, and demanded his death. It was all very impressive. But still Pretorius kept his head. He accepted the rebels as allies, but packed them off to swell Nongalaza's ranks.

Cautious as Pretorius undoubtedly was, not everyone admired his efficiency. Adulphe Delegorgue, a visiting Frenchman who had joined the expedition out of curiosity, had some scathing things to say about the way in which the campaign was conducted. He admitted that the Boers were the best wagoners in the world, but deplored their lack of discipline. The fact that any man was free to disobey an order, or even refuse to fight, astonished him. He was alarmed at the way in which the convoy of wagons was spread out, unprepared for an emergency, and thought it madness that men were allowed to idle about the camp instead of being sent on patrol. The Commandant-General, he declared, 'had his own system of tactics which was to have no tactics at all'.

The Boers puzzled Delegorgue. He found them an odd mixture of piety and callousness. It was difficult for him to reconcile the hymn singing and Bible reading of the older men with the horseplay and coarse jokes of the youngsters. There seemed a strange dichotomy in men who could rise from their long and earnest prayers and gloat over the barbaric treatment meted out to their enemies.

Nowhere were these contradictions more in evidence than when the commando reached Blood River where, at the site of the battle laager, the sun-bleached bones of Zulu warriors were still to be seen, scattered in the long grass. The Boers described the battle to Delegorgue and told him of the rout which had followed. There had been wounded warriors, they said, who had tried to escape by hiding in the river, submerging themselves until, like hippos, only their noses were above the water. 'But,' says Delegorgue, 'as soon as the trick was discovered, the little river was inspected ... soon its semi-stagnant waters were tinged with red: all the fugitives were shot without mercy by the Boers, who made a joke of this easy destruction.'

That the Boers had ample reason for revenge, Delegorgue freely admitted. They had endured much, their women and children had suffered worse cruelties. Could bitter men be expected to act impartially? Nevertheless, the Zulu were savages and the Boers made much of wielding the sword of the Lord. The ways of Christians in Africa were difficult to fathom.

Even more shocking, in Delegorgue's opinion, was Pretorius's disregard for the rules of war. While the Frenchman was prepared to excuse acts committed in the heat of battle, he had nothing but contempt for the Boers' interpretation of justice. And in a particular case his criticism, despite his obvious prejudice, was well warranted.

At Blood River, Pretorius decided to hold a council of war. Dambusa and his companion, Khambazana, were put on trial—if such it can be called. There were judges and a prosecutor but no defending counsel; the court reminded Delegorgue of 'a revolutionary tribunal in the days of the terror'.

Mpande and the rebel chieftains were summoned to give evidence. Again Mpande lashed out at Dambusa; again he accused the indunas of being behind all Dingane's 'deeds of blood'; again he quivered with anger. Dambusa listened to him unmoved. Naked and fettered, the induna faced his accusers with a dignity that shamed them all, black and white. He denied nothing. He was Dingane's servant and as such he refused to beg for pardon at the white man's court. He declared himself ready to die, but pleaded for the life of Khambazana who, he argued, was innocent and did not deserve to die. But Mpande would not hear of any lives being spared and Mpande's word decided the fate of both prisoners. The two men were sentenced to death.

Dambusa remained loyal to Dingane to the end. When Pretorius, somewhat unctuously, called upon him to acknowledge the white men's God, to throw himself on the mercy of 'the Master on high, the Dispense of eternal punishment', he was scornful. He said he knew only one master—Dingane; if any other master existed, then that master would surely reward him for remaining faithful to his King. Dambusa required no sermons on fidelity.

The two indunas were executed a few hours later. Dambusa's last request was that he be shot by men, not boys. It was granted. Manacled to Khambazana, he faced the firing squad as calmly as he had faced his judges. The first volley killed Khambazana outright. Dambusa fell, badly wounded, but 'rose, stood firm, and presented a full front to the fire' until he dropped to the second round of bullets.

'These men,' mused the watching Delegorgue, 'know how to die.'

But had Dambusa deserved death? Was this the just reward of an envoy who had come under a flag of truce? Delegorgue thought not. Others agreed with him. When this shameful act became known, Pretorius was harshly criticised. Whatever Dambusa's sins, he should have been granted safe conduct on a mission of peace.

And it is doubtful whether Dambusa was the monster that
Mpande made him out to be. His greatest offences had been committed in trying to save Dingane from his follies. Had the King
listened to his indunas earlier, he would not have been driven to
expel the whites by treachery. Loyalty such as Dambusa displayed
is not a characteristic of monsters.

It is doubtful whether Dingane knew of his induna's loyalty. As
far as is known, the King was on the run. For days the commando
had been receiving vague reports of his movements. Nongalaza,
who, with Mpande's army had reached the White Mfolozi, sent
word to say that he had sighted a division of the Zulu army which
had been ordered to hold off the invaders while Dingane escaped
with a smaller force. But it seems that flight was not easy. Rebellion
was rife in Zululand and the King had found his path blocked by
hostile tribes. At one stage he had hoped to join up with Mzilikazi,
but this plan had had to be abandoned. It was thought that, as the
least of many evils, he would be forced to retreat into Swaziland.
In the meantime he was said to be hiding in a cave close to the new
emGungundlovu. This, at least, is what the spies reported.

Then, on the very day of Dambusa's execution, definite news had
reached the Boer camp. Nongalaza had marched further north and
reported that a battle with Dingane's defending force, under Ndlela,
was imminent. The commando immediately resumed its march and
Pretorius sent word to Nongalaza that he was on his way. But the
Boers were too late. The following morning one of their patrols met
a messenger from the north who told them that the battle had been
fought. Ndlela's impis had been defeated, great herds of cattle
captured, and the King had fled across the Pongola river into
Swaziland.

Details of this, the last of Ndlela's unsuccessful battles, are
scrappy. The opposing forces are said to have been evenly matched
and the slaughter on both sides was fearsome. In the final count it
was estimated that over 2000 had been killed and an equal number
wounded. The outcome was decided, not by Nongalaza's superior
tactics, but by rebellion in his enemy's ranks. When the battle was
at its height, one of the three regiments commanded by Ndlela
rose and joined the invading army, forcing their former comrades to
retreat. Ndela, now hopelessly outnumbered, escaped across the
Pongola to join Dingane.

Pretorius kept up the chase for over a week. He marched through pouring rain and heavy mists, but encountered only odd parties of Zulu hiding in the bush or in caves. These fugitives offered little or no resistance. Delegorgue was forced to modify his opinion of the Boers when he saw the magnanimity with which all who surrendered were treated. On arriving at the Pongola the commando gave up. They were told that Dingane had crossed the river five days earlier with some of his wives, a few cattle herds, and not more than one hundred armed men. Satisfied that the Zulu King had been put out of action, and worried by an outbreak of horse-sickness, Pretorius turned homeward. Nongalaza was left to patrol the river banks. After a few days of futile watching, he was given permission to travel south to join the commando at the Black Mfolozi. An important ceremony was about to take place.

To all intents and purposes, Dingane's troubled reign was over. Therefore, on 10 February 1840, his successor, Mpande, was formally installed as King by the Boer Commandant. All things considered, it was a curious proceeding. There was very little pomp and even less enthusiasm to mark the occasion. Watched by the commando and an assembly of warriors, Pretorius simply mounted a huge boulder, turned to Mpande and announced: 'I now appoint you to be King of the Zulu race that remains. . . . Maintain peace with our people as long as you live. Then I give you as a concession— for it is my territory, conquered by my weapons—the kingdom of Zululand.'

These were strange words with which to greet a new Zulu ruler, but the new Zulu ruler accepted them meekly. Mpande promised to do all that was asked of him, to remain faithful to the white men and the white men's government 'Should any power attack you,' he said in reply, 'I will on being apprised of it order my whole force to your assistance, and which shall, for your sake, if required, be sacrificed to a man.' The Boers then fired a salvo of twenty-two guns.

Not only had Dingane fled, but the spirit of Shaka had now been cast out.

A few days later Pretorius hoisted the flag of the Boer Republic and spelt out the precise terms of peace in an official proclamation. They were harsh. The territorial boundary was pushed back from the Tugela to the Black Mfolozi; the Boers laid claim to the entire sea coast of southern Zululand to, and including, St Lucia Bay. It was far more than had ever before been sought by the white men. In two years the trekkers had, at great cost, confounded their enemies and seized the better part of Shaka's once impregnable empire. The Zulu King was now their vassal.

Leaving Mpande to his impoverished kingdom, the commando rode back to Pietermaritzburg. With them they took some 1000 orphaned Zulu children as 'apprentices' and an estimated 36,000 head of cattle. They were hailed on their return as the *Beestekommando*, the Cattle Commando.

Dingane did not survive long in exile. Shorn of all semblance of power, he could command neither respect nor allegiance. What little influence he might have had was destroyed when, in a fit of vindictive passion, he ordered the execution of the one man who might have helped him—Ndlela. Of all Dingane's treacherous acts this was perhaps the most monstrous. His attacks on the whites could be explained, if not excused, by his fear of losing his kingdom, but nothing can justify the murder of his defeated, yet loyal, commander. By this act he forfeited what little sympathy he might otherwise have claimed.

It is possible also that, by killing Ndlela, the King sealed his own fate. For now he was alone. He could no longer call upon the advice and protection of his indunas. He had to rely entirely on his own wits and these, as soon became apparent, proved hopelessly inadequate.

Hunted in an alien territory, Dingane was easy prey for his enemies. They were not long finding him. Sometime in March 1840 he was assassinated. How he died and who killed him has never been satisfactorily explained. His death, like his early life, is largely a matter of legend.

One story, believed for years, told of how he was captured by the Swazi King and subjected to ghastly torture. First, it was said, he was pricked skin deep with a sharp assegai from head to foot. The next day he was bitten by dogs. And on the third day he was told to look on the sunrise for the last time and his eyes were bored out. By sunset he was dead 'for he had had neither food nor water for three days'. Another version has it that he was decapitated and his head taken to Pretorius. But such tales owe more to imagination than fact. A milder, but more feasible account—that he was stabbed to death by the Nyawo tribe, possibly assisted by Swazi warriors—appears nearer the truth and is generally accepted.

The sad thing is that nobody much cares. Unlike Shaka, Dingane left no heroic tradition behind him. He is acknowledged as an important Zulu King and as such his praises are sung on great occasions, but his memory is not revered.

'The betrayal of Piet Retief by King Dingane,' said a modern Zulu statesman, 'has never been forgotten by some Whites—but they forget that Dingane is not exactly our public hero.'

Let that be his epitaph.

PART THREE

DOWNFALL

THE RAPE OF ZULULAND

DINGANE'S DEATH MARKED, in a way, the beginning of the end of the Zulu Kingdom. The monarchy was to last for many years, but it was no longer the independent, all-conquering, unassailable monarchy established by Shaka. From now on the Zulu kings reigned in the shadow of their white neighbours and that shadow was constantly shifting and always threatening.

The first important shift in white overlordship came when the British replaced the Boers in Natal. Pretorius's proudly proclaimed trekker republic of Natalia did not survive for long. The seeds of its destruction were, to a large extent, sown in the circumstances of its foundation. For the trekkers were not only poor and divided among themselves, but their philosophy of racial exclusiveness made it impossible for them to administer the enormous, heterogeneous territory under the peaceful conditions they had envisaged when they left the Cape Colony.

The rulings of the Volksraad reserved citizenship of the new republic to persons of European descent who were born in the Cape Colony and were Dutch-speaking. Other Europeans—or 'uitlanders' as they were known—were suspected of divided loyalties and had to produce a certificate of good conduct before they were accepted as land-owning citizens. Non-whites had no rights in the settled parts and were allowed to live there only as servants. Such conditions pleased no one except the trekkers; even they found it increasingly difficult to cope with the many problems they had thus created.

One of the most telling accusations levelled at Shaka was that he had uprooted the indigenous tribes of the areas he had conquered and driven them from their hereditary lands. Time and again the white settlers had justified their desire to depose the Zulu kings by claiming that only then would the rightful owners of the de-populated regions be able to return and live in peace under a

civilised administration. This, it was said, would relieve the
dangerous pressure on the crowded frontier districts. It is hardly
surprising, therefore, that, once peace appeared to be established,
the displaced tribes did return to claim their homelands. They came
in increasing numbers, only to find that the white men wanted
them no more than had Shaka.

Attempts by the Boers to control this growing influx with a
system of pass-laws and the segregation of 'redundant natives'
(those not needed as servants and labourers) merely emphasised the
instability of the new republic. All the old problems of land encroachment and cattle raids, which the trekkers had experienced on
the eastern frontier of the Cape Colony, began to make themselves
felt. There was nothing new out of that part of Africa. It was, in
fact, the customary Boer reprisals after a serious cattle raid which
brought things to a head.

In December 1840, a commando under Pretorius, assisted by
African allies, set out on a punitive expedition against suspected
cattle raiders in southern Natal. They attacked a local chieftain
living near Mpondoland, killing between thirty and forty people
and making off with some 3000 head of cattle and seventeen child-
apprentices. Faku, the Mpondo chief, alarmed at this upheaval in
his vicinity, felt threatened. He appealed to the Governor of the
Cape for protection. The rights and wrongs of this Boer incursion
were to be hotly debated, but there can be no doubt that it decided
the long-term fate of the Natalia republic.

The British authorities, already disturbed by the campaigns of
the *Wenkommando* and the *Beestekommando*, were far from happy
at the prospects of further trouble in the frontier districts. When the
Boers requested recognition of their republic it was refused. In
May 1842, the Governor of the Cape ordered the reoccupation of
Port Natal. The Boers put up a spirited defence at Durban but,
after an initial success, they were forced to yield to superior numbers
and accept the inevitable. Once again, after so much hardship and
suffering, they were claimed as British subjects.

It was more than the majority of them could bear. They began to
pack up and leave Natal, settling in the areas to the west and north
of Zululand; areas which later became known as the Orange Free
State and the Transvaal. Disillusioned and resentful, their departure
was slow but unavoidable: there was, after all, little chance of their

settling down under British rule. By the end of 1847 very few Boers were living in Natal.

Natal was annexed by the British and administered as a district of the Cape Colony, under a Lieutenant-Governor. Pretorius's sweeping seizure of southern Zululand was nullified, Mpande was no longer considered a vassal, and the Tugela and Buffalo rivers were recognised as the boundaries between the Zulu and British administrations. The Cape authorities did, however, take the precaution of safeguarding the eastern sea route by laying claim to St Lucia Bay.

Mpande's kingdom, supposedly independent as it now was, compared very unfavourably with the dominions of Shaka and Dingane. With the British in Natal and the Boers settling in the Transvaal to the north, expansion was no longer possible. The Zulu King's authority was severely circumscribed. But this does not appear to have worried Mpande unduly. During his lifetime he had seen the small Zulu clan develop into a mighty nation, feared and respected by all neighbouring tribes, and if his influence was not as far-reaching as that of his half-brothers, his role was still an important one: he wielded a power far greater than his father, Senzangakhona, ever dreamt of possessing. The Zulu sovereign was still someone to be reckoned with.

For several years Zululand was relatively peaceful. Mpande established his great kraal close to the White Mfolozi river and his personal life followed the pattern set by Dingane in happier years. Mpande was, in fact, not unlike Dingane in many ways. Fat, pleasure loving and somewhat irresolute, he took full advantage of the trappings of royalty. Once more the royal kraal became the centre for all important Zulu festivals; for dances, initiations and ritual celebrations. And if Mpande did not fully share Dingane's love of bizarre dress, he was every bit as dedicated to his royal harem: in his lifetime he sired at least 23 sons as well as a number of daughters.

Largely free from the threat of external aggression, he was nevertheless forced, during the early years of his reign, to deal with internal threats to his sovereignty. In this he proved no less ruthless than his predecessors. When, in 1842, he suspected that Aldin Grout—the American missionary who had returned to Zululand two years earlier—was gaining too much influence, he sent his warriors to attack Grout's Zulu followers and destroy the kraals around the mission station. The following year he took the precaution of ridding himself of a possible claimant to his throne by murdering his younger brother Gqugqu—the only other surviving son of Senzangakhona—and his entire family. The massacre was particularly gruesome and resulted in one of Mpande's aunts, Mawa, taking fright and fleeing to Natal with thousands of Gqugqu's adherents. For many years 'The Crossing of Mawa' was remembered as a sensational event in Zulu history.

Although Mpande was no more of a warrior than Dingane had been, his existence as King still depended on his maintaining the military system initiated by Shaka. Young men had to be enrolled in regiments and opportunities had to be found for them to wash their spears in battle. This presented Mpande with an even greater problem than Dingane had faced in similar circumstances. Apart from minor local disturbances, battles were now exceedingly difficult to come by. There could be no question of Mpande repeating his brother's folly of attacking the well-armed whites and, with Mzilikazi out of the way, his chances of staging a full-scale war against blacks were slim indeed. All the same, he continued to recruit young warriors until—within a decade of his assuming power—he is said to have had nominal command of an army far larger than Shaka had ever fielded.

An opportunity for initiating some of the newly formed Zulu impis arose in 1848. The Hlubi clan, under their leader Langalibele, were accused of plundering the royal herds on the Pongola river and Mpande was able to send a punitive expedition to deal with them. The campaign was successful but all too short. Some of the cattle were recovered and the entire Hlubi clan was easily driven from Zululand and forced to settle in Natal. It provided the Zulu warriors with a battle of sorts, but this was hardly what Mpande was looking for. A more formidable foe was required.

The only place in which such a foe could be found was Swaziland, on the north-eastern border of the Zulu kingdom. Things being what they were, Mpande had little alternative but to launch an attack across the Pongola. He did so without apparent provocation. The Swazi and the Zulu were hereditary enemies and this, in itself, was sufficient reason for the Zulu attack in 1853. The blooding of spears could be delayed no longer. The untried impis were becoming restless and, equally important, Mpande's eldest son, Cetshwayo, was now in his middle twenties: it was imperative that he prove himself as a fighter and a commander. Open candidature for the Zulu throne entailed military fitness.

The first campaign against the Swazi was something of a fiasco. Learning of the Zulu approach, the enemy immediately scattered and hid themselves in caves and the dense bush. There was very little fighting and only a few cattle were captured. This simply was not good enough. In 1854 a second attack was planned. By this time the Swazi were on the alert and lost no time in sending most of their cattle into Boer territory before the Zulu impis appeared. But they were unable to escape themselves. Once again they took to the hills and the bush, but the Zulu smoked them out of the caves and flushed them out of the thickets. Out in the open they were encircled, forced to defend themselves and decisively defeated.

The hero of the campaign was undoubtedly Cetshwayo. Given the opportunity to distinguish himself, Mpande's son proved a worthy Zulu prince. His courage in taking on a whole pack of Swazi warriors single handed, killing several and putting the rest to flight, was reminiscent of the young Shaka. It did not pass unremarked.

Cetshwayo needed all the glory he could gather. For the mere fact that he was Mpande's eldest son by no means ensured his right to the Zulu throne. Zulu custom decreed that the heir apparent should be the son of the King's Great Wife—the wife chosen for dynastic reasons, and for whom a large price in cattle was paid—or, failing that, the son nominated by the King. As Mpande had never taken a Great Wife and was known to favour a younger son named Mbuyazi, Cetshwayo's position as heir was far from secure. Much depended on the popular support he could command.

Had Mpande been more resolute, things might have been different. Torn between the influence which Mbuyazi's mother wielded over him and Cetshwayo's growing popularity, he refused to commit himself by naming his heir. The King's indecisiveness resulted in factions developing around his two sons. It soon became evident that the succession would be decided by a trial of strength. Even so, Mpande remained aloof. When appealed to by his indunas, all he said was: 'Two bulls cannot live together in the same kraal.'

The clash between the two bulls took place at Ndondakusuka, near the Tugela, in December 1856. After a series of provocative

incidents, Cetshwayo led his followers—known as the Usutu—
against Mbuyazi's much smaller force. He won an undisputed
victory. It was, in fact, not so much a battle as a massacre—one of
the worst to occur in Zululand's blood-stained history. Mbuyazi
and his followers, including women and children, were trapped
between the charging Usutu impis and the flooded Tugela. Those
who escaped slaughter on shore were stampeded into the river,
where they were either drowned or were seized by crocodiles. For
weeks afterwards the coast of Natal was littered with the bodies of
those swept out to sea from the Tugela mouth. In just over an hour's
savage fighting, Cetshwayo's Usutu killed some 23,000 men, women
and children, including Mbuyazi and five of Mpande's other sons.
From that time on the corpse strewn battle site was known as
Mathambo—Place of Bones.

Cetshwayo was now recognised as the most powerful personality
in Zululand. Still Mpande refused to nominate him as his heir.
Formal nomination had, however, become superfluous. Having
dealt successfully with Mbuyazi, Cetshwayo had no hesitation in
ridding himself of further threats. An attempt by Mpande to
cultivate yet another son, Mthonga, was quickly frustrated. Cetshwayo sent a body of warriors to destroy the new favourite's kraal.
Mthonga and his brother only escaped with their lives by fleeing
Zululand. There could no longer be any doubt as to who would be
the next Zulu King.

Indeed, during the last years of his father's reign, Cetshwayo was
widely accepted, both as the heir apparent and as the effective Zulu
ruler. The ageing Mpande, whose interest in kingship had always
been more self-indulgent than zealous, knew better than to oppose
his strong-willed son indefinitely. Essentially a man of peace, Mpande
was content to remain in the background and leave decision-making
to Cetshwayo.

Further acknowledgement of Cetshwayo's status came in 1861.
Theophilus Shepstone, Secretary for Native Affairs in Natal,
arrived at Mpande's kraal and offered to recognise the Zulu heir
apparent on behalf of the British Government. His offer was
accepted, but not without reservations. Why, asked some, should it
be necessary for Natal to sanction Cetshwayo's right to the throne?
Was not Zululand supposed to be independent? By what right was
this British official interfering? Nor did Shepstone help matters

when, in his final speech, he instructed Cetshwayo to keep the peace and warned him that further injustices would not be tolerated. Who, indeed, was Shepstone to issue such orders? The shadow of the white man was very much in evidence.

Mpande lived for another eleven years. He was well into his seventies when he died in October 1872. His later years had been spent in idleness. He had become so gross that, unable to walk, he was pushed about in a small cart by two servants. Yet the old man commanded widespread respect and, at the time of his death, his country was enjoying a semblance of peace such as it had not known for many years. His subjects remembered him with affection.

Mpande was buried with all the ceremonial due to a great king. He was the last of Senzangakhona's sons and the only one to die a natural death after reaching maturity. That, in itself, was no mean achievement.

[2]

Cetshwayo (alternative spellings: Cetewayo, Cetywayo, Ketchwayo, Ketawayo) was in his mid-forties when he succeeded his father as Zulu King. He was, by any standards, a handsome man; tall and majestic, with strong, well defined features, penetrating eyes and the muscular build that distinguished all his family. Large boned and heavy thighed as he was, his active life had prevented him from becoming flabby and, unlike Mpande and Dingane, he fitted the role of warrior king to perfection. His commanding presence, intelligent expression, and natural dignity impressed all who met him. There was no mistaking the fact that, both in looks and in force of personality, Cetshwayo possessed all the qualities of the man he most admired—his remarkable uncle, Shaka.

Had things been different, this resemblance might well have gone beyond mere outward appearance. Brave, resolute and astute, Cetshwayo was eminently suited to the role of a powerful autocrat. He, far more than his immediate predecessors, was capable of building on the foundations laid by Shaka and leading his people to even greater heights. But, whatever his ambitions, his chances of becoming a nation maker were doomed from the outset. Hemmed in by his formidable white neighbours, his power was limited and his authority uncertain. He had inherited Shaka's position but lacked Shaka's opportunities for conquest and renown.

By the time Cetshwayo came to the throne, the colonisation of Natal was well under way. In 1870 the white population of the new colony was estimated to be some 18,000 men, women and children, most of whom came from Britain. More than half these new settlers lived in Durban and Pietermaritzburg; only in the north of Natal did the few remaining Boers outnumber the newcomers. As a result of this influx, Natal became, and remained, the most British of the South African colonies. This, of course, is what the early pioneers had schemed and struggled for, but when it came about only two of them witnessed the transformation.

In 1852 Henry Francis Fynn returned to Natal and died in Durban, under the British flag, nine years later. He had outlived Henry Ogle by seventeen months but had failed to match Ogle's record of residence. As far as is known, Ogle had never left Natal from the time he arrived there in 1824 with Lieutenant Farewell's expedition; by the time he died in Pietermaritzburg in February 1860 he could claim to be the colony's longest residing white inhabitant. But he could claim little more. He spent the last years of his life at his trading establishment near the Umkomaas river and appears to have obtained no other benefit from his pioneering struggles. Success, whether sought by white or black, was not easily come by in Natal.

Cetshwayo had to contend with others besides the British in Natal. Although the Boers had, for the most part, left Natal in the 1840s they had by no means disappeared from the Zulu King's orbit. Those who had trekked beyond the Drakensberg and the Vaal river to join their comrades had played a prominent part in founding two Boer republics—the Orange Free State and the South African Republic in the Transvaal—which were both recognised by Britain, in the early 1850s, as independent states. As the southern border of the Transvaal merged into the north-western regions of Zululand, there were continual disputes about the boundaries of the two territories. These disputes had started in Mpande's reign and were still very much alive when Cetshwayo became King. One way and another, the new Zulu sovereign had reason to be wary of his white neighbours.

And those neighbours were every bit as wary of him. The determined way in which Cetshwayo had established himself as King had not passed unnoticed. Both the British and the Boers recognised that they now had to reckon with a far more ambitious and powerful personality than the pliant Mpande. Almost from the time that Cetshwayo came to the throne, fears were expressed about his intentions. How long, it was asked, would this new warrior King allow his standing army to remain idle? Did he not pride himself on being another Shaka? Would he not be forced, sooner or later, to initiate his warriors by a 'washing of spears'? How could that ritual be observed, other than by an attack on the whites? One thing was certain: the military power of the Zulu nation under Cetshwayo was even greater than it had been in the days of Shaka. Dingane's incompetence and Mpande's passivity were things of the past.

Whether justified or not, fear of Cetshwayo mounted during the early years of his reign. Stories of the menace posed by the growing Zulu army were rife. It was reported that the young recruits were becoming more and more anxious for battle. Things had reached the stage, it was said, where the King would not be able to control his young hot-heads even if he wanted to—and few believed that he really wanted to. The colonists in Natal lived in constant dread of a Zulu invasion. The Transvaal Boers were equally apprehensive. That an excuse would be found for a confrontation with Cetshwayo was obvious.

Such an excuse was eventually manufactured by Sir Bartle Frere, the Governor of the Cape, who arrived in South Africa in March 1877. Frere's object, however, was not confined solely to the subjugation of the Zulu King. Cetshwayo, frightening as he appeared, was merely a pawn in a much larger game. Not for the first time, it was the complications of white politics which decided the fate of Zululand.

Some three years earlier, the British Colonial Secretary, Lord Carnarvon, had conceived the idea of federating the independent states of southern Africa. In this way he hoped to resolve the various conflicts which continued to plague the country and thus provide Britain with a stable base on the sea route to the East. Not surprisingly, the main obstacle to such a federation had been the dogged independence of the Boer republics. Having struggled manfully for years to escape the British, neither the Orange Free State nor the

Transvaal were willing to barter their freedom for a somewhat doubtful alliance. Carnarvon had therefore been obliged to change his tactics. Failing to win over the republics by diplomacy, he had embarked on a course of deliberate coercion. He had started with the Transvaal. Using the bankrupt, ill-organised state of the country as an excuse, he had sent a British agent (Theophilus Shepstone) into the Transvaal Republic to bring it under the protection of the British crown. It had been an audacious move but it had succeeded. What opposition there was to the annexation had been so scattered and confused that a promise of eventual self-government had been sufficient to throw it out of gear.

However, this was merely the first step in Carnarvon's federation plan. To coincide with the annexation of the Transvaal, he had appointed Sir Bartle Frere as Governor of the Cape. It was to be the new Governor's unhappy task to carry the federation a stage further.

As Frere saw it, there could be no hope of federating South Africa until the Zulu King had been brought to heel. Scare stories from Natal convinced him that Cetshwayo was a bloodthirsty monster who was intent on driving the white men from his borders. The King's sole ambition, Frere was told, was to 'emulate the sanguinary fame of his uncle Chaka . . . whose history is written in characters of blood'. That these stories had very little basis in fact seems to have bothered Frere not at all. He did not enquire into them too deeply. He had good reason not to. The possibility of a quarrel with the Zulu King involved far more than the future of Natal; there was reason to think that it would answer many of Frere's problems. Not least of these problems was the Boers' opposition to federation.

For, once the initial shock of the Transvaal annexation had sub-sided, resentment of continued British rule had spread throughout the former Boer republic. It was obvious that a gesture on the part of the British was needed to counteract the opposition. What better than the destruction of the Zulu military system? Not only would the subjugation of Cetshwayo free the Boers from the possibility of attack, but it would open up the north of Zululand to those farmers whose encroachments were already the subject of dispute. Every-thing, in fact, seemed to point to Zululand as the means of bolstering British prestige throughout South Africa and of winning support for the idea of federation under British protection.

Frere had every reason to think that Cetshwayo's downfall would be easily accomplished. On this point he had been reassured by the Lieutenant Governor of Natal, who wrote to him in July 1877 to say: 'If anything brings the Zulu King into collision with the English, his destruction will follow far sooner than he expects; because hatred and fear of him as a tyrant are daily increasing in the minds of the Zulu people.' It was all reminiscent of the earlier reports made about Shaka. Frere, like some before him, believed unquestioningly what he was told by those on the spot. He was soon to learn how mistaken such assumptions were.

An opportunity to bring things to the necessary climax was presented when Cetshwayo appeared to violate the border agreement he had made with the colony of Natal. In July, 1878, the unfaithful wives of two Zulu fled to Natal for protection. They were pursued by their husbands, captured, and taken back to Zululand to be put to death. When the Natal authorities demanded that the men who had invaded the colony be handed over to them for punishment, Cetshwayo made excuses for not doing so. A couple of months later a further affront to Colonial authority was felt when two Englishmen were detained by the Zulu for one and a half hours after they had accidently wandered into Zululand. Such incidents could hardly be described as Zulu aggression but they were seized upon by Sir Bartle Frere to colour the case he was building against Cetshwayo. After the abduction of the Zulu women he sent a report to the British Colonial Secretary which left little doubt as to his intentions. Unless the incident was 'apologised and atoned for,' he said, '. . . it will be necessary to send to the Zulu King an ultimatum which must put an end to pacific relations with our neighbours.'

The Ultimatum was delivered on the 11 December 1878. It was virtually a declaration of war. Its provisions, which had to be complied with in thirty days, set out to destroy the traditional Zulu way of life at a single stroke. It demanded that the Zulu army be disbanded immediately, that an end be brought to Shaka's system of military conscription (the system upon which the Zulu nation had been built) and it generally undermined the King's authority. It would have been impossible for Cetshwayo to carry out such radical reforms in so short a space of time even had he agreed that they were necessary. That he would not agree to them had been obvious from the start; to have done so would have been tantamount to abdication.

The thirty days' time limit expired on 11 January 1879, and

Sir Bartle Frere formally declared war. 'The British forces are crossing into Zululand to exact from Cetywayo reparations for violations of British territory . . .' he wrote in a Notification which was issued in both English and Zulu. 'The British Government has no quarrel with the Zulu people . . . When the war is finished the British Government will make the best arrangement in its power for the future good government of the Zulus in their own country, in peace and quietness, and will not permit the killing and oppression they have suffered from Cetywayo to continue.'

The purpose of this somewhat over-sanguine document was plain enough. The King, in whose person the Zulu nation was identified, was to be made the sole scapegoat. His powers were to be placed within the control of the British Government. With Cetshwayo out of the way it would be possible to implement the well tried 'native policy' of divide and rule—or so it was hoped. As it happened, it was not to be as simple as that. Zulu loyalty proved surprisingly strong and the plan met with a good deal of opposition from Cetshwayo's white supporters in Natal.

Cetshwayo was more fortunate in his white friends than had been his predecessors. The flickering flame of liberalism, which so often brightened the darker corners of South African history, had been dim indeed during the reign of Shaka and Dingane. For Cetshwayo, however, it shone in the person of John Colenso, the fiery, controversial Bishop of Natal. Bishop Colenso had arrived in Natal with his family in May 1855 and had immediately identified himself with the Zulu people. He had learnt their language, studied their customs and consistently championed their cause. A passionate man, of strong, independent views, he had clashed with his superiors and had been excommunicated from the Anglican Church for his unorthodox theological writings. But none of this had affected his devotion to his Zulu friends. To them he was Sobantu—the Father of the People. Throughout the troubled times ahead, Colenso and his family were to remain steadfast in their support of Cetshwayo. Unfortunately there was nothing they could do to prevent Sir Bartle Frere from having his war.

The Zulu War of 1879 is probably the best known, certainly the most written about, episode in Zulu history. The British army embarked upon the campaign with confidence, and were quite unprepared for its first, unprecedented disaster. At Isandhlwana, near the border of Zululand, the Zulu army launched a surprise attack on an encampment of soldiers under the command of Lord Chelmsford, the British Commander-in-Chief. The result was one of the most devastating massacres in the annals of British colonial warfare. Chelmsford himself was away on a reconnaissance expedition when the attack took place; he returned late that evening to find the camp obliterated.

While the Commander-in-Chief was groping in the darkness amid the debris of the Isandhlwana camp, another desperate battle was being fought a few miles away. At a Swedish mission station, near the crossing of the Buffalo river known as Rorke's Drift, a small band of British soldiers, huddled behind a makeshift barricade of mealie bags and biscuit boxes, were courageously holding a huge Zulu impi at bay. The bitter struggle, lit by the flames from the blazing mission hospital, raged throughout the night and ended at four o'clock the following morning. As the sun rose that day, all that remained of the Zulu impi were three to four hundred dead bodies heaped about the barricades. The little garrison had lost fifteen men killed and twelve wounded. Later, eleven Victoria Crosses were distributed among the heroic defenders of Rorke's Drift—the greatest number that had ever been awarded for a single action of the British army.

When details of the two battles reached England, Lord Chelmsford came under heavy fire from military critics. Much of this criticism has since been shown to have been unfair, but there can be no doubt that the catastrophic defeat at Isandhlwana stunned the British public. The Zulu King was no longer seen as a colourful monster in the wilds of Africa, but as a foe to be respected and feared.

The next engagement of any significance took place two months later at Kambula in the north of Zululand. Here, on 29 March, British troops repulsed a large Zulu force, taking toll of almost 2000 warriors. Spectacular as was this victory, it was by no means decisive. British optimism was short-lived. Two months later, while Chelmsford was reorganising his forces for a more determined onslaught, there came another disaster. The Prince Imperial of France, who had arrived in Zululand as a non-combatant, had been allowed to accompany a scouting party and had been killed in a skirmish after the rest of his troop had deserted him. Rarely had British military prestige sunk so low. Not everyone was able to share the detachment of the British Prime Minister, Benjamin Disraeli, who coolly observed: 'A very remarkable people, the Zulus: they defeat our Generals; they convert our Bishops; they have settled the fate of a great European dynasty.'

Criticism of Chelmsford's handling of the war mounted to such a pitch that it was decided to send out Sir Garnet Wolseley to replace him as Commander-in-Chief. Already smarting under a great deal of abuse, Chelmsford was determined not to return home under such humiliating circumstances. Spurred into decisive action, he pushed his troops on to Cetshwayo's royal kraal at Ulundi, near the White Mfolozi river. Here, on 4 July, the Zulu army was finally defeated.

[3]

True to the tradition established by Shaka in his later years, and firmly adhered to by Dingane, Cetshwayo had taken no part in the fighting. He was no longer a young man and, as King, his life was considered sacred. Unlike Dingane, he had proved his courage in earlier days and it was more important that he be safeguarded as a focal point for Zulu loyalty. Nevertheless he had played no small part in directing the movements of his impis. Throughout the war he had maintained constant contact with his commanders.

There is substantial evidence to show that Cetshwayo was genuinely bewildered by the invasion of Zululand. He had not sought a war and repeatedly sent messengers to negotiate a truce with the British authorities. All his peaceful overtures had, for one reason or another, been spurned. His last attempts to come to terms with Lord Chelmsford were made shortly before the battle of Ulundi. When these failed, he was forced to flee. He escaped from the royal kraal as the British troops were advancing for the final attack.

Surprisingly, no immediate attempt was made to pursue the King. Chelmsford having, in his own opinion, vindicated himself by bringing the war to a successful conclusion, lost no time in telegraphing his resignation and began preparing to leave South

Africa. He met his replacement, Sir Garnet Wolseley, on his way to Durban. It was now Wolseley's task to arrange a peace settlement.

Once he had established his headquarters at Ulundi at the beginning of August, Wolseley began searching for Cetshwayo. It was not easy. The local tribesmen, despite predictions to the contrary, proved stubbornly loyal. They refused to give the slightest hint as to the King's whereabouts. 'We were treated the same at every kraal,' reported one of the searchers. 'I had been a long time in Zululand, I knew the people and their habits, and, although I believed they would be true to their King, I never expected such devotion. Nothing would move them. Neither the loss of their cattle, the fear of death, nor the offerings of large bribes, would make them false to their King.' Obviously the stories of Cetshwayo's cruel despotism and oppression had been greatly exaggerated. But then such exaggerations were nothing new. How, one wonders, would a similar hunt for Shaka—that other 'hated monster'—have fared?

For all that, there was little hope of Cetshwayo evading capture. Wolseley's patrols were scouring the country. They finally caught up with the King at a small, secluded kraal in the Ngome forest. The kraal was surrounded and Cetshwayo, after first inviting his pursuers to shoot him, surrendered without a struggle. Utterly exhausted, the insides of his thighs chafed raw with continual walking and running, the last Zulu King emerged from the hut in which he had been hiding with tremendous, yet distressing, dignity. 'It was pitiful,' admitted one of his captors, 'to see this once great man as he was on that day.'

Cetshwayo was escorted to the coast and there, at Port Durnford, was transferred to a ship, the *Natal*, which conveyed him to Cape Town. With the King safely out of the way, Wolseley set about the thankless task of arranging the pacification of Zululand. On 1 September 1879, he summoned the principal Zulu chiefs to a meeting at Ulundi. The purpose of the meeting was to introduce the so-called settlement terms. Speaking through an interpreter, Wolseley opened the proceedings with an harangue on the misdeeds of Cetshwayo. The King, he told the chiefs, had broken his coronation promises and had therefore been deprived of his kingdom. He had been sent into exile and was never to return. The Zulu people had not been responsible for their King's actions and the English Queen had no intention of depriving them of their country or of annexing any portion of it. Instead, Zululand was to be divided into thirteen separate districts. Over each district a chief would be appointed to rule with justice and mercy. Certain customs which offended the British sense of justice were to be abolished and a British Resident would be installed to see that the commands of the Imperial Government were obeyed.

His harangue over, Wolseley proceeded to nominate the chiefs who had been chosen to rule the thirteen districts. Whoever was responsible for proposing the chiefs named by Wolseley could hardly have made a worse selection. Not only did the list show contemptuous disregard for the established Zulu hierarchy, but it paved the way for the worst type of office seekers. Prominent among these was John Dunn, an ambitious white adventurer who owed his position as a Zulu chief to Cetshwayo. Having shamelessly deserted the ex-King during the war, he was now rewarded for his treachery by being granted the largest of the thirteen districts. Disloyalty to Cetshwayo, in fact, appeared to rank high as a qualification for the new appointments, and his sworn enemies—such as the turn-coat chief, Zibhebhu—were included among those who benefited from the Wolseley settlement.

Sedition, however, proved a bad basis for the future stability of Zululand. No sooner had the British troops left the country than the new rulers were at each others' throats. Completely disregarding their installation promises, the more powerful of the chiefs embarked on a systematic plundering of their weaker neighbours. The era of 'justice and mercy' which was supposed to have followed the overthrow of Cetshwayo was ushered in by faction fighting, looting and kraal burning. To make matters worse, the British Resident was powerless to enforce the Government decrees. With only a handful of African irregulars at his disposal, it was impossible for him to police the territory, let alone control it. The war, in many ways, had left Zululand a greater threat to the peace of South Africa than it had ever been under the rule of Cetshwayo.

The continual Zulu disturbances did much to put paid to Lord Carnarvon's federation scheme. Far from teaching the Boers to appreciate the benefits of British protection, the recent war had left them astounded at British military ineptitude. From their own experiences of African warfare they were convinced that they could have handled the affair much better. Their demands for the independence of the Transvaal became more insistent, more determined. In Zululand, also, there was strong opposition to the settlement terms. Cetshwayo's followers, the Usutu, rallied to the exiled King's cause and began agitating for his return. No less vigorous was the fight put up by the King's European supporters. Hardly had Cetshwayo been imprisoned at Cape Town before the redoubtable Bishop Colenso launched a campaign aimed at securing his release and reinstatement as King. The British authorities were soon made to realise that dethroning the Zulu monarch had merely increased their difficulties.

On arriving at the Cape, Cetshwayo, dressed in an ill-fitting suit and a tall black hat, found himself the centre of attention. As the first of the fearsome Zulu Kings to arrive in a South African town, he was regarded more as a curiosity than as a defeated enemy. Somewhat to his amusement, the crowds that gathered to watch him being taken to Cape Town's old castle, proved surprisingly amiable and cheered his carriage on its way. Such friendliness was less apparent in the grim dungeons of the castle where, cooped up with some of his wives and attendants, he spent the first months of exile. Mercifully this close confinement was not permanent. The arrival of a new Cape Governor, Sir Hercules Robinson, in January 1881, resulted in the King being moved to Oude Molen, a dilapidated farm on the outskirts of Cape Town. Here his life, though far from comfortable, was made considerably easier; he could take long walks, receive visitors and maintain contact with his friends. As a further privilege, he was provided with a European interpreter.

There was no lack of visitors to Oude Molen. English travellers calling at the Cape were only too anxious to catch a glimpse of 'the ignorant and bloodthirsty despot' who had defied the British army. Expecting Frere's monster, they were, for the most part, completely disarmed by Cetshwayo's calm, jovial good nature. The King, for his part, never missed an opportunity to plead his cause. Among his more important visitors were the two sons of the Prince of Wales, Prince Eddy and Prince George (later King George V) who were touring the world in the H.M.S. *Bacchante*. After exchanging photographs with the young princes, Cetshwayo urged them to bring his plight to the notice of their grandmother, Queen Victoria.

The result of this meeting is uncertain but a visit from another of Queen Victoria's relations, Prince Louis of Battenberg, undoubtedly proved beneficial. When Prince Louis called on the Zulu King at the beginning of 1881, he was accompanied by a young woman journalist, Lady Florence Dixie, who was immediately captivated by the royal prisoner. Next to the faithful Colensos, Lady Florence was to become Cetshwayo's most convinced and passionate champion.

The youngest daughter of the 8th Marquis of Queensberry, Lady Florence Dixie was, in many ways, a remarkable woman. She had already startled London society by embarking on a big game hunting expedition in Patagonia and returning with a pet jaguar which, to the alarm of her neighbours, she paraded about on a leash. She had arrived in South Africa hoping to add to her bizarre reputation. The injustice of Cetshwayo's imprisonment provided her with just what she was looking for. After visiting Zululand and meeting Bishop Colenso, she returned to England determined to work for the King's restoration. Her support, although sometimes ill-directed, did much to publicise Cetshwayo's misfortunes.

As a member of an influential family and a staunch Tory, Lady Florence had important connections. She exploited them all. Not only did she make direct appeals for help to her friend the Prince of Wales and various Members of Parliament, but, primed by the Colensos, she bombarded the press, both in England and South Africa, with letters and articles detailing Zulu grievances. There was not an aspect of Zulu history that she was not prepared to defend. The British public, she insisted, had been badly misled by false reports from Zululand over the years and many of the charges levelled at Cetshwayo's predecessors—including those of mass murder—needed to be seen in perspective.

'Can the blackest deeds of even Chaka and Dingaan,' she asked, 'be drawn as a parallel with the terrible annihilation of human life not so very long ago in Christian Europe—7000 victims burnt alive for witchcraft at Treves, 600 by a Bishop of Bamberg, 800 in one year in the Bishopric of Wurtzburg, 1000 in the province of Como, 400 at once at Toulouse, 500 in three months at Geneva, 48 at Constance, 80 at the little town of Valry in Savoy, 70 in Sweden? . . . Did not Luther say, "I would have no compassion on these witches; I would burn them all"? If the influence of civilisation and

Christianity worked such deeds, how dare we raise such a hue-and-cry over the deaths of a few evil-doers who suffered punishment according to the laws and customs of Zululand?'

If somewhat over-simplified, it was a point worth making. Had she waited a little longer she would have been able to draw an even more striking parallel from Africa itself. It has been estimated that, at the turn of the century, some three million Africans died in the Congo as a result of the activities inspired by King Leopold II of the Belgians. Could civilised Europe really afford to point an accusing finger?

The campaign Lady Florence waged on Cetshwayo's behalf eventually paid off. In the middle of 1882, it was arranged for the King to visit England to discuss his position with officials at the Colonial Office. He arrived at Plymouth on board the s.s. *Arab* on 5 August and was immediately taken to London where lodgings were provided for him in Melbury Road, Kensington.

From the moment of Cetshwayo's arrival in England he was dogged by newspaper reporters and crowds of sightseers. His every word, his every move was reported in detail. What he ate, what he wore, how he slept, were all listed for the public's benefit. Every day the pavement outside his house was crowded with people trying to catch a glimpse of him. The road was constantly jammed with carriages. In vain did he protest about being followed about by the gaping crowds. 'I like the scenes I have to visit well enough,' he confessed to a friend, 'but I do not care to be made a show of; if English people have never seen a black man before I am sorry. I am not a wild beast, I did not come here to be looked at.'

The programme mapped out for him was full and exhausting. Apart from a few days when he was laid up with a cold, he followed it out to the letter. He was received at Marlborough House by the Prince and Princess of Wales, with whom he exchanged walking-sticks. He went to Osborne to visit the Queen. Later Victoria presented him with an inscribed silver mug and a photograph of herself; in return he sat for a portrait of himself in national costume, painted by the Queen's artist, Carl Sohn. Reproductions of this portrait were soon to be seen in every stationer's shop window in London; in it Cetshwayo looked, says one report, 'like a fat, black edition of Henry VIII'. He was taken over Woolwich Arsenal where—to impress him with Britain's might—he was shown how big guns were manufactured. When a 35-ton gun was fired for his benefit, he roared with laughter at the frightened starts of his attendants but remained perfectly unmoved himself. He did admit later, however, that after this visit he felt as if he had grown up in a day. 'I shall have a great deal to report to my nation when I return,' he said, 'for which I shall hardly be able to find words.'

Of greater significance were the three interviews he had with Lord Kimberley, Secretary of State for the Colonies. The upshot of these interviews was that his return to Zululand was assured on certain conditions. He must disband the Zulu army. He must agree to a British Resident acting as his adviser. He must observe the boundaries laid down by the British authorities. He must agree to a portion of his country, to be defined later, being allocated to those Zulu who did not wish to live under his rule. To all these conditions, except the last, the King agreed. When he protested against part of his country being taken from him, Kimberley advised him to wait and see how much was lopped off before refusing to agree to the division. Reluctantly, and mistakenly, Cetshwayo accepted this advice.

On the voyage home it was noticed that the King was extremely quiet and preoccupied. He had good reason to be. The division of Zululand was to lead to continual strife and his eventual downfall.

Under terms worked out in Cape Town, Cetshwayo lost half his former kingdom, including some of the best cattle country. To ensure a balance of power, Zululand was divided roughly into three parts. The northern part was allotted to the King's arch-enemy Zibhebhu; the southern part became a 'Zulu reserve' administered by a British Resident; and Cetshwayo was left to rule the truncated central part. When these terms were announced the King was appalled. He considered, not without reason, that he had been deceived by the promises made to him in London. But, other than registering a strong protest, there was nothing he could do. Faced with acceptance of the terms or permanent exile, he had no option but to sign the Cape Town agreement.

On 10 January 1883, after an absence of almost four years, Cetshwayo again set foot on Zulu soil. He landed from H.M.S. *Briton* at Port Durnford. His homecoming ushered in a period of fierce faction fighting. The bitterness that had built up in the divided country during his exile immediately became apparent. His own followers, the Usutu, now sought to settle a number of old scores. There was nothing the King could do to restrain them. With limited authority and no effective army, his power to control events was minimal. The British Government, having appointed Henry Francis Fynn's son (also named Henry Francis) as Cetshwayo's resident adviser, refused to intervene and the King's enemies were more or less given a free hand. Zibhebhu, the main target for Usutu hostility, was quick to seize his opportunity.

A crisis was reached in March 1883 when Zibhebhu turned on Cetshwayo's undisciplined followers and dealt the King a crippling blow. In a day-long battle, over 4000 Usutu were killed. There was a further clash in July. This time Zibhebhu routed the King's forces completely. The new royal kraal at Ulundi was attacked and burnt and Cetshwayo, wounded in the thigh, was forced to flee to the Nkandla forest in the British controlled reserve. He remained in hiding until October when his adviser, Henry Francis Fynn, sought him out and took him to Eshowe, the administrative centre of the reserve. Here, for the time being, he was placed under the supervision of the British Resident, Melmoth Osborn.

Zululand was now in a state of chaos. Zibhebhu was on the rampage and there seemed no way of restoring order. Fearing another attack, Cetshwayo refused to return to his territory. By remaining in the reserve, he became the focus for further disruption. Much as the Natal authorities wanted the King out of the way, they were reluctant either to exile him, or to use force to reinstate him. Appeals to the British Colonial Office only added to the confusion. The problem of pacifying divided Zululand seemed insuperable.

It was a problem which Cetshwayo did not live to see resolved. Less than four months after arriving at Eshowe, and while his fate was still in the balance, the King died.

In the afternoon of 8 February 1884, Melmoth Osborn received a message saying that Cetshwayo was seriously ill. Calling his senior medical officer, Dr Harvey Scott, Osborn immediately went to the nearby Gqikazi kraal in which the King was housed. On arriving there they discovered Cetshwayo stretched on his back in a hut: his body was cold and he had obviously been dead for some hours. Scott wanted to perform an autopsy but was prevented from doing so by the King's relatives. They adamantly refused to allow him to tamper with the body. In the circumstances the doctor could only make a rough diagnosis. He certified the death as being caused by a fatty disease of the heart.

That Cetshwayo died from heart disease remained the official verdict, but this verdict was not accepted by the King's followers. It has since been argued that there was no evidence to show, or even to suggest, that Cetshwayo suffered from a faulty heart. On the morning of his death he had appeared well, had been for a walk, and had shown no signs of illness until midday, when he had eaten some meat. The meat, it is said, had not been supplied by his own people. Shortly after his meal the King had been seized by severe convulsions; he had died almost immediately. His relatives, not surprisingly, were convinced that he had been poisoned. Nothing could shake this conviction. The belief that Cetshwayo was murdered by Zibhebhu's agents persists to this day.

Cetshwayo was the last of his family with any real claim to the Zulu sovereignty. He is usually regarded as the last Zulu King. His son, Dinuzulu, inherited little more than his father's misfortunes.

[4]

The story of the Zulu kings is largely a story of territorial conflicts. From the very outset, the fortunes of the Zulu dynasty were inextricably linked with a struggle for land.

By disrupting the age-old pattern of tribal settlements, exterminating his enemies and laying waste the surrounding country, Shaka founded a kingdom unique in the history of southern Africa. Never before had a tribal leader attempted such conquests. Shaka's claim to supremacy owed as much to territorial aggrandisement as it did to military superiority. So long as the Zulu kingdom remained intact, the dominance of the Zulu kings was assured. Obvious as this might appear, its significance needs to be appreciated. That land could represent power (rather than acting as grazing for cattle, the traditional symbol of wealth) was a revolutionary concept in tribal politics. It accounted not only for the rise of the Zulu nation, but for its eventual downfall: a downfall which was heralded by the coming of the first white men.

Within weeks of landing in Natal, Lieutenant Farewell had talked

Shaka into ceding him land. From that time on, a succession of land-hungry traders, trekkers and colonists had sought—by intrigue, by persuasion, by negotiation and, all else failing, by outright aggression—to encroach on the Zulu kings' domain. Their encroachments had resulted in numerous acts of betrayal, belligerence and bloodshed. Countless thousands, black and white, had died in the never-ending quest for land.

It would be easy to take a fashionable view and denounce the white pioneers of Natal as unprincipled opportunists. With little difficulty they could be depicted as avaricious intruders whose sole desire was to grab what they could at the expense of the country's black inhabitants. Such a judgement would, in a way, do something to balance the often repeated condemnations of the Zulu kings as unfeeling and inhuman monsters. Guilt, it might well be argued, should not be assessed entirely from one side. While this is true enough, it hardly makes for understanding. The fact is that the accusations against both black and white rely more on emotion than on reason.

Those who have condemned the Zulu kings have done so by measuring them against standards which the kings neither recognised nor understood. It is all very well to say, as is sometimes said, that there is such a thing as common humanity and that the kings, in their cruelty towards their subjects, lacked basic human impulses. All human impulses are conditioned by knowledge and experience and the Zulu kings were no different from other rulers who have justified their actions by appealing to an accepted code of ethics. However horrifying certain Zulu practices might have appeared to outsiders, those practices were recognised as conforming to tradition by the Zulu people. One might not admire every aspect of Zulu tradition but one must acknowledge that it existed. The Zulu kings could not do otherwise than act as Zulu kings.

In the same way it would be ridiculous to judge the white men by extraordinary standards. One must accept them also as average products of their times and circumstances. That many of the pioneers were self-seeking is undeniable. But is this a cause for pious horror? Are not most men, when it comes down to it, self-seeking? One might wish them to be different, but one must accept that they are not. Presented with the remotest chance of making a fortune or of finding happiness in a new life, how many men would not choose to be rich and happy? Such were the motivations of the majority of the white pioneers. They were neither the noble crusaders that they are often made out to be, nor were they the sinister hypocrites that they might be made to appear. For the most part they were ordinary men, behaving as ordinary men—with all their faults and virtues— in a dangerous and complex situation.

But, whether one is prepared to praise or blame, it is impossible to ignore the inexorable march of events. For the Zulu nation it spelt disaster. The process which Lieutenant Farewell started, by obtaining land from Shaka, was irreversible. As more and more white men arrived in Natal, so did the clamour for land intensify. Tension between white and black heightened and, as might have been foreseen, mutual suspicion led to continual conflict. Given the power-structure in southern Africa, there could have been only one solution to such a struggle. It is astonishing that this solution was not arrived at sooner. As it happened, it was not until three years after the death of the last Zulu king that the 'Zulu problem' was finally resolved: even then settlement was reached in a round-about way.

Cetshwayo's eldest son, Dinuzulu, was sixteen or thereabouts when his father died. A hefty, self-confident lad, he was said to be 'the image of his father and . . . fully alive to his position for he trod the earth as if he owned it'. But not everyone was willing to agree that he owned the earth, or even that part of it once ruled over by Cetshwayo. Although Dinuzulu was backed by his father's more important indunas, there were others who denied his right of suc- cession. Among these were the Natal authorities who steadfastly refused to acknowledge him as Cetshwayo's heir. The uncertainty of Dinuzulu's position added to the many problems which faced his advisers.

Not the least of these problems was, of course, the threat posed by the ever-hostile Zibhebhu. Until Zibhebhu was effectively removed from the scene, there was little point in Dinuzulu taking up the battered Zulu crown. But to get rid of Zibhebhu would not be easy. It required greater strength than Dinuzulu and his advisers could muster. No help could be expected from the British. Only too thankful to have Cetshwayo out of the way, they had no inten- tion of encouraging his son. If Dinuzulu was to assert his claim to Zulu leadership, he would have to look elsewhere for support. As things turned out, he did not have far to look. Indeed, the hoped-for assistance came looking for him.

Three years earlier, in 1881, the Boers of the Transvaal had reclaimed their independence. In a short, skilfully fought campaign, they had expelled the British from their country, hoisted their republican flag and declared their right to self-government. Gratifying as this was, it had not satisfied the land-hunger of all the Boers. There were still some burgers in the south-east Transvaal who looked longingly at the disputed Zulu territory beyond their borders. The news of Cetshwayo's death gave them new hope. Even before the King's death there had been talk of an alliance between the Boers and the Usutu; now the Boers felt free to offer their support to Dinuzulu. Their offer was accepted.

On Wednesday, 21 May 1883—three months after his father's death—Dinuzulu knelt on a wagon before some 9000 Zulu warriors while four Boers anointed him with castor oil, placed their hands on his head, and declared him to be the rightful Zulu King. The ceremony was makeshift but expensive. Two days later the Boers presented their bill. In return for their protection and assistance against Dinuzulu's enemies, they were to be awarded an unspecified amount of land in north-western Zululand in which they could establish an independent New Republic. Details of this land grant were to be set out later.

True to their promise, the Boers lost no time in dealing with Dinuzulu's principal enemy, Zibhebhu. At the beginning of June, a Boer force of just over one hundred men, invaded Zibhebhu's territory at the head of the Usutu army and scored a quick and decisive victory. The defeated Zibhebhu, like Cetshwayo before him, was forced to seek refuge in the southern reserve.

Then came the reckoning. When the Boers claimed their reward, the price they demanded was far in excess of anything that Dinuzulu and his advisers had envisaged. Under the terms of an agreement, signed on 16 August, some 3,000,000 acres were given over to the New Republic, while the rest of Zululand was placed under Boer supervision. Not only had Dinuzulu lost most of his father's territory but he, like Mpande, had become a vassal of the Boers. History in Zululand had a way of repeating itself.

It is doubtful whether Dinuzulu realised the full implications of the agreement he signed. Certainly he could not have foreseen its far-reaching consequences. In effect, he had not only surrendered his own rights but had sealed the fate of the Zulu nation. 'The majority of our people,' said one of his grandsons in 1973, 'are landless as a result of the mistake of that young man.'

Throughout 1885 Boer settlers poured into Zululand, measuring out farms, uprooting established clans and forcing tribesmen into service as labourers. They came not in the small numbers anticipated by Dinuzulu, but in their hundreds. The promise of free land acted as a magnate for adventurers throughout the Transvaal. Whatever might be said in defence of the earlier Natal pioneers, nothing can exonerate the cynical, land-grabbing opportunists who now invaded Zululand. Their actions were not sanctioned by the Transvaal Government, nor did the majority of them have the flimsy excuse of claiming a just reward for supporting Dinuzulu. Only a hundred odd men had taken part in the campaign against Zibhebhu, but for this assistance eight hundred farms were claimed. As the agreement signed by Dinuzulu had merely specified the *amount* of land to be granted, without stipulating the boundaries of that land, the newcomers began to spread across the country at an alarming rate. Soon it looked as if all Zululand would be overrun.

At the beginning of 1886, the Usutu leaders made desperate appeals for help to the Natal authorities. They claimed that the Boers were exceeding the terms of their agreement and robbing them of their traditional homeland. The British, already apprehensive about the activities of German speculators, who were seeking to purchase a huge slice of coastal Zululand, decided to intervene. At first the Boers strongly objected to any suggestion of interference but eventually, realising that by co-operating with the British they could obtain official recognition of their demands, they sent a delegation to Pietermaritzburg.

Thus was the fate of Zululand settled. As a result of negotiations with the Governor of Natal, the Boers agreed to drop their claim of suzerainty over the Zulu nation and to accept definite boundaries for their New Republic. The rest of the country was taken over, in May 1887, as a British Protectorate.

Neither Dinuzulu nor his advisers had intended this to happen. But there was little they could do about it. When Dinuzulu attempted to reassert his authority, he was firmly put in his place. 'The Queen,' he was told, 'now rules in Zululand and no one else.'

Despairingly he again sought help from his former allies in the New Republic. His overtures were ignored. Unable to reconcile himself to his loss of independence, he continued to defy the rulings of the Natal authorities. The last straw came when, at the beginning of 1888, Zibhebhu was reinstated in his former territory. An inevitable clash between the Usutu and Zibhebhu's followers resulted in a warrant being issued for Dinuzulu's arrest. There were further clashes when the British attempted to serve this warrant and Dinuzulu was forced to seek refuge in the Transvaal. For three months he evaded capture but finally gave himself up. He was tried and sentenced to ten years' imprisonment on the island of St Helena.

Although his father's old champion, Bishop Colenso, had died in 1883, Dinuzulu's cause was fervently upheld by the Colenso family. The Bishop's eldest daughter, Harriet, was tireless in her efforts to obtain justice for Dinuzulu. During his exile she visited him on St Helena. She continued to write pamphlets attacking British policy in Zululand and was partly responsible for a slight reduction of Dinuzulu's sentence. He was allowed to return to Zululand in January 1898. His exile had been meaningless. 'During that time,' it was reported, 'Dinuzulu learned to wear European clothing, to speak a very little English, and to play the air of the National Anthem with one finger on the piano. It may be doubted whether he picked up anything else.' But he was to need much more.

Settled again in Zululand, Dinuzulu was first provided with a house in Eshowe and then allowed to return to his Usutu kraal. Nominally employed as a 'government induna', he was also recognised as a district chieftain. To his own people, however, he remained the Zulu King. Whatever the white men might decree, Dinuzulu was Cetshwayo's son and as such he fostered, and commanded, the allegiance of the Usutu. His influence went far beyond that permitted to him by the British. In fact, it was this aura of sovereignty which led to his final downfall.

In 1897, while Dinuzulu was in exile, Britain had granted direct control of Zululand to the Natal Government. Four years later, as might have been expected, Zululand was opened to European settlement. To meet the expense of the developing territory, Natal imposed a poll tax of £1 on all adult males, white and black. This tax was bitterly resented by the Africans who, earning an average of £5 a year, objected to paying the same as affluent Europeans. So

great did this resentment become that when, in 1906, a petty chieftain named Bambatha refused to pay the tax, his defiance
boomeranged and sparked off a serious rebellion. This, the last Zulu
rising, resulted in the deaths of nearly 4000 Africans and 30 whites.
A further 4000 Africans were eventually arrested and sentenced to
lashings. Many of them were reported to have had their backs cut
to ribbons. Thus was peace restored.

Although Dinuzulu had taken no active part in the rebellion, he
was strongly suspected of having inspired it. Personifying, as he did,
all the mystique of his powerful forbears, he could not escape suspicion. He was known to have sheltered Bambatha's wife and
children; many of those arrested had repeatedly implicated him.
The truth of these accusations, however, was to be heatedly
contested.

At the end of 1907, Dinuzulu was apprehended on twenty-three
charges of high treason. Once again the indomitable Harriet
Colenso rallied to his support. A brilliant Cape attorney, W. P.
Schreiner, was engaged to conduct his defence. After a somewhat
questionable trial, Dinuzulu was convicted on only three counts. He
was fined £100 and sentenced to four years' imprisonment for
harbouring rebels.

After serving part of his sentence at Newcastle in Natal, Dinuzulu
was released in 1910 on the orders of the sympathetic General Louis
Botha, who had recently become the first Prime Minister of the
Union of South Africa. Convinced of Dinuzulu's innocence, Botha
arranged for him to be sent to a farm near Middleburg in the
Transvaal and to be granted an allowance of £500 a year. He was
forbidden, however, to return to Zululand.

Grossly overweight and suffering from dropsy, Dinuzulu died,
after a severe haemorrhage, on 18 October 1913. He was forty-five.
His last expressed wish, it is said, was to be buried with his ancestors
in Zululand. It was granted.

At an impressive ceremony near the royal kraal, Dinuzulu was
buried in the presence of thousands of his followers. Replying to an
address by a Government official, one of the indunas spoke for the
entire Zulu assembly. 'You White people,' he said, 'are a nation of
great inconsistencies. We fought against you in Cetshwayo's day.
We were overcome, and we gave you our allegiance. We thought
there would be peace, but truly your service is hard. Dinuzulu

never fought you, but you arrested him. Cetshwayo is dead and buried. His son, whose death you have caused, lies here today. Let the feud cease.'

It has been said of Dinuzulu that he was 'cunning and fickle and appealed for help to the Boers and the British in turn'. But when one considers how much of his life was spent as a pawn in the white men's politics, this is hardly surprising. Cunning he might have been but, as the results showed, he was no match for his devious opponents. In the end they won, not he.

Dinuzulu died less than a hundred years after the first white pioneers had set foot in Natal. It had been a period of tremendous upheaval: starting with the white men deferentially begging favours from the all-powerful Zulu monarch and ending with an un-acknowledged King battling to reclaim his hereditary authority. No one was more aware of this tragic turn of events than Dinuzulu. This had been made abundantly clear when, shortly after the British annexation of Zululand, he had pleaded for recognition of his descent from Shaka, Dingane, Mpande and Cetshwayo.

'Dinuzulu must know,' the Governor of Natal had said, 'and all Zulus must know that the rule of the House of Shaka is a thing of the past. It is dead. It is like water spilt on the ground . . .'

More than water had been spilt on the ground.

REFERENCES

Abbreviations of principal sources.

C.A.   *Cape Archives, Cape Town. Colonial Office and Government House files.*

P.R.O.   *Public Record Office, London. Colonial Office files.*

Bird   *The Annals of Natal 1495–1845 (2 vols), edited by John Bird. Davis, Pietermaritzburg, 1888.*

Chase   *The Natal Papers (in 2 parts), edited by J. C. Chase. Godlonton, Grahamstown, 1843.*

Fynn   *The Diary of Henry Francis Fynn. Shuter & Shooter, Pietermaritzburg, 1969.*

Isaacs   *Travels and Adventures in Eastern Africa by Nathaniel Isaacs. Struik (reprint in one volume), Cape Town, 1970.*

Gardiner *Narrative of a Journey to the Zoolu Country by A. F. Gardiner. William Crofts, London, 1836.*

Cory   *The Diary of the Rev. Francis Owen, edited by G. E. Cory Van Riebeeck Society, Cape Town, 1926.*

S.A.C.A. *South African Commercial Advertiser.*

PART ONE

Chapter One

p.3   'would have been the glory . . .'; Colenso: *Ten Weeks*, p.5.
p.5   'Kaffirs have an unaccountable . . .'; Quoted: Fynn: p.182.
      'excellent and trustworthy . . .'; Ibid.
p.6   'a composition of cunning . . .'; W. F. Owen: *Narrative*, p.72.
      'aboriginal inhabitants'; Ibid, p.71.
      'At this time . . .'; Ibid.
      'To the southwards . . .'; Ibid, p.79.
p.7   'a tremendous motion . . .'; Ibid, p.82.
      'without altering . . .'; Ibid.
p.8   'For the purpose . . .'; C.A.: G.H. 118/839.
p.9   'In respect to society . . .'; Thompson: *Travels* vol 2, p.189.
p.11 'amiable and enterprising . . .'; Steedman: *Wanderings* vol 1, p.271.
      'uninhabited but abounding . . .'; C.A.: G.H. 1/8 No 605.
      'Mr King . . . the opportunity . . .'; S.A.C.A. 31 January 1829.

p.12   'The aspect of the whole . . .'; Pringle: *Narrative*, p.7.
'I was fully expecting . . .'; C.A.: G.H. 118/839.
p.13   'It then blowing . . .'; Ibid.
p.14   'an idea that Gold . . .'; Ibid.
'The Harbour though small . . .'; Ibid.
p.15   'When we became . . .'; Ibid.

Chapter Two

p.17   'My intentions are . . .'; C.A.: G.H. 28/10.
p.18   'I hope Your Lordship . . .'; Ibid.
'H.E. begs that . . .'; Ibid.
'Mr F. G. Farewell is represented . . .'; C.A.: G.H. 23/7.
p.19   'a handsome percentage . . .'; Fynn: p.56.
p.21   'This he was determined . . .'; Ibid, p.59.
p.22   'My enquiries as to . . .'; Ibid, pp.60/61.
p.24   'My life evidently . . .'; Ibid, p.63.
p.25   'The most exaggerated . . .'; Ibid, p.66.
p.28   'Cleanliness was a . . .'; Ibid, p.70.
'We saw large parties . . .'; Ibid.
p.31   'Farewell there is Shaka'; Ibid, p.72.

Chapter Three

p.33   'satisfying the ideas . . .'; Fynn: p.295.
p.34   'a masculine and savage . . .'; Isaacs: p.161.
p.37   'Though the lateness . . .'; Omer-Cooper: *Zulu Aftermath*, pp.11/12.
p.40   'The idea of Godongwana . . .'; Fynn: p.6.
'He learned the strength . . .'; Bird: vol 1, p.163.
p.41   'In either version . . .'; Thompson: *Oxford History*, vol 1, p.334.
(Professor Thompson discusses the dual theories—the trade theory of Professor Monica Wilson and the population theory of Professor Max Gluckman—concerning the rise of Dingiswayo in full. I am greatly indebted to his enlightening arguments on this aspect of Nguni society.)
p.46   'His regal, dignified bearing . . .'; Ritter: *Shaka Zulu*, p.55.
p.47   'sent orders to the slayers . . .'; Ibid, p.67.
p.50   'Knowing the spot . . .'; Fynn: p.15.
p.53   'By next dawn . . .'; Ritter: *Shaka Zulu*, pp.164/5.
p.54   'He was the senior . . .'; Thompson: *Oxford History* vol 1, p.345.

Chapter Four

p.59   'It was a most exciting . . .'; Fynn: p.73.
'found out Chaka's . . .'; Isaacs: p.277.
'The king found him . . .'; Ibid.
p.60   'he was the greatest . . .'; Fynn: p.74.
'It seemed to produce . . .'; Ibid.

p.61 'Are you then ...'; Ibid, pp.76/77.
'I will have you sent ...'; Ibid.
p.62 'far superior to those Shaka ...'; Fynn: p.77.
p.64 'the consequences of this ...'; Ibid, p.79.
p.68 'Some were put to death ...'; Ibid, p.85.
p.69 For details of Farewell's grant see: Ibid, pp.87/88.
p.71 'Moreover he wanted ...'; Ibid, p.93.
p.72 'a quantity of staves ...'; *Cape Government Gazette*, 4 June 1825.
p.73 Lieutenant Hawes's report; Ibid.
'very much distressed ...'; Isaacs: p.*xxx*.

Chapter Five

p.75 'prevailed upon some respectable ...' and 'a stated salary ...';
see: Lieutenant Farewell's letter to S.A.C.A. 31 January 1829.
p.76 'I should not my Lord ...'; C.A.: G.H. 1/8 No 583.
p.77 'I readily embraced ...'; Isaacs: p.*xxix*.
'the civilities ...' and 'I was too young ...'; Ibid, p.*xxviii*.
p.78 'effect the recovery ...'; Ibid, p.*xxx*.
'I will not pretend ...'; S.A.C.A. 31 January 1829.
'grant him stores ...'; C.A.: C.O. 293/1317.
p.79 'We began rapidly ...'; Isaacs: p.3.
p.81 'Here I was destined ...'; Ibid, p.15.
'formed the design ...'; S.A.C.A. 31 January 1829.
'near the anchorage ...'; C.A.: G.H. 1/8 No 583.
'a practical shipwright ...'; Isaacs: p.16.
p.82 'the many vicissitudes ...'; Isaacs: p.18.
p.83 'old friend ...' and 'The meeting ...'; Ibid, p.21.
'I have every reason ...'; S.A.C.A. 31 January 1829.
p.85 'cast off his stern ...' and 'We could scarcely ...' and 'His dress
consists ...'; S.A.C.A. 11 July 1826.
p.86 'Indeed nothing pleases ...'; Quoted: Kirby *Andrew Smith*, p.62.
p.87 'Jacob the interpreter ...'; Fynn: p.121.
'I frequently saw some ...'; Quoted: Kirby *Andrew Smith*, p.61.
p.88 'our vessel had sustained ...'; S.A.C.A. 11 July 1826.
'I requested permission ...'; C.A.: C.O. 293/21.
p.89 'There now remains ...'; Ibid.
'If there is a person ...'; C.A.: C.O. 235/262.

Chapter Six

p.91 'on the king's business'; Isaacs: p.32.
p.92 'took the criminals ...'; Ibid, p.36.
p.94 'Several of the people ...'; Ibid, p.50.
'for the sake of ...'; Ibid, p.51.
p.95
p.96 Report of the *Helicon*; *Cape Government Gazette*; 24 April 1826.

368 REFERENCES

p.96 'The Crew of my wrecked . . .'; C.A.: C.O. 293/138.
p.97 'The following interesting . . .' and 'History perhaps . . .'; S.A.C.A. 11 July 1826.
p.98 'Of this establishment . . .'; Ibid.
p.99 'a sorry figure . . .' and 'We had our little . . .'; Isaacs: pp.69/70.
p.100 'Powder was scarce . . .'; Fynn: p.122.
p.101 'too much like an old . . .'; Isaacs: p.66.
'very friendly and most . . .'; Quoted: Kirby *Andrew Smith*, p.66.
p.102 'This urged the Zulus . . .'; Fynn: p.126.
p.104 'a pretty woman . . .'; Isaacs: p.71.
'determined to seize her . . .'; *Times of Natal* 14 December 1892.
p.105 'a number of his boys . . .' and 'Father kill them . . .'; Isaacs: p.72.
'He began taking . . .'; Ibid, p.73.

Chapter Seven

p.106 'To enter into the merits . . .'; Isaacs: p.75.
p.107 'to oppose me . . .' and 'I shall merely . . .'; S.A.C.A. 31 January 1829.
p.108 'deserted my employ . . .'; Ibid.
p.109 'I was most happy . . .'; S.A.C.A. 2 May 1829.
p.110 'evinced great pleasure . . .'; Isaacs: p.77.
'Mr King had likewise . . .'; S.A.C.A. 31 January 1829.
p.111 'with an exclusive right . . .'; Isaacs: p.85.
p.112 'Fortunately for all . . .'; Ibid, p.87.
'Something must be . . .' and 'To go to war . . .'; Ibid, p.88.
p.114 'Yes they could . . .'; Ibid, p.89.
p.115 'at this particular . . .' and 'In Thee . . .'; Ibid, p.92.
p.117 'roots and medicines . . .' and 'could not . . .'; Ibid, p.94.
p.119 'I cannot but conceive . . .'; Ibid, p.103.
p.120 '*Maye ngo Mama!*'; Fynn: p.133.
p.121 'No further orders . . .'; Ibid.
p.122 'But there were nations . . .'; Ibid, p.139.

Chapter Eight

p.124 'bring back immense . . .'; Fynn: p.143.
p.125 'Chaka's principal residence . . .'; Bird: vol 1, p.94.
'friend James Saunders . . .' and 'free and exclusive . . .'; Ibid.
'evinced more friendship . . .'; Isaacs: p.117.
p.127
p.128 Cloete's interviews with Sotobe; Ibid, pp.120/123.
p.129 'insignificant display . . .'; Isaacs: p.123.
p.130 'For the first time . . .'; Fynn: p.143.
'I told him . . .' and 'Black people . . .'; Ibid, p.145.
p.131 'He accordingly sent messengers . . .'; Fynn: pp.146/147.
p.132 'The misery already . . .'; Thompson: *Travels* vol 1, pp.174/5.
'The terrible Chaka . . .'; Quoted: S.A.C.A. 21 January 1829.

p.133
p.136   Dundas's report; P.R.O. C.O. 48/125.

p.134   'circulated in the Colony . . .'; Fynn: p.148.
         'It was a very shrewd . . .'; Ibid, p.149.

p.135   'The valour and enterprise . . .'; Quoted: Rivet-Carnac: *Hawk's Eye*,
         p.72.

p.136   'I have reason to believe . . .'; C.A.: G.H. 23/8 p.378.
         'Mr Jas King . . .'; Ibid.

p.138   'The Officer whom I sent . . .'; C.A.: G.H. 23/8, p.370.

p.139   'The messenger from Chaka . . .'; Ibid, p.378.
         'Mr Farewell's party . . .'; Isaacs: p.126.

p.140   'broke into a thousand . . .'; Ibid, p.128.

p.141   'that Capt King was . . .'; S.A.C.A. 31 December 1829.
         'the extraordinary violence . . .'; Isaacs: p.134.

p.142   'Oh Nat, what a pity . . .'; Ibid, p.135.
         'Mr Isaacs being in attendance . . .'; S.A.C.A. 17 January 1829.

p.143   'I set off . . .'; S.A.C.A. 31 January 1829.

Chapter Nine

p.146   'sent a force of about . . .'; C.A.: G.H. 23/9, pp.39–47.
         'had been long . . .'; Fynn: p.156.

p.147   'Dead bodies . . .'; Ibid.

p.148   'You shall never see . . .'; S.A.C.A. 31 December 1828.
         'What is the matter . . .'; Ibid.
         'As soon as I go . . .'; Fynn: p.31.

p.151   'Shaka wanted to know . . .'; Ibid, p.147.

p.152   'Mr Isaacs was very . . .'; S.A.C.A. 24 January 1829.

p.152
p.153   Sir Lowry Cole's report; C.A.: G.H. 23/9, pp.39–47.

p.154   'The frightful stories . . .'; S.A.C.A. 15 November 1828.
         'Chaka conceives   '; Ibid

p.157   'I am not aware that history . . .'; Isaacs: p.151.
         'my readers to draw . . .'; Ibid.

p.158   'somewhat incredible . . .'; Ibid, p.*xxiii*.
         'Make them out as bloodthirsty . . .'; *Africana Notes & News*, June
         1968, p.67.
         'to re-write the whole . . .'; Fynn: p.*xiii*.

p.159   'On one occasion . . .'; Fynn: p.28.
         'revenging their injuries . . .'; Ibid, p.134.

p.160   'When once he had . . .'; Isaacs: p.156.

p.163   'The nations, Shaka . . .'; Vilakazi: *Zulu Horizons*, p.66.

PART TWO

Chapter Ten

p.167   'It is believed . . .'; S.A.C.A. 27 December 1828.

p.169 'only as warriors . . .'; Fynn: p.159.
p.170 'Ngwadi alone . . .'; Ibid, p.160.
'would not wait long . . .'; Ibid.
p.171 'The different tribes . . .'; Isaacs: p.173.
p.172 'liberality and kindness'; Fynn: p.162.
p.173 'We got all . . .'; Isaacs: p.144.
'make themselves comfortable'; Ibid.
p.174 'the princes' and 'This popularity . . .'; Ibid, p.161.
'valued companion . . .'; Ibid, p.162.
p.175 'to the mission . . .'; C.A.: G.H. 23/9, pp.39–47.
'for the perusal . . .'; Isaacs: p.163.
p.176 Sir Lowry Cole's report; C.A.: G.H. 23/9, pp.39–47.
p.177 'Chaka, according to all . . .'; S.A.C.A. 27 December 1828.
'I imagine . . .'; Ibid, 31 January 1829.
'the presence of a lieutenant . . .'; C.A.: G.H. 1/15, p.665.
p.179 'The Qwabes' boldly . . .'; Fynn: p.166.
'entering into terms . . .'; Ibid, pp.167/8.

Chapter Eleven

p.182 'Frank had lately . . .'; Bain: *Journals*, p.83.
'a little of some . . .'; Ibid, pp.96/97.
'I was afterwards . . .'; Ibid, p.108.
p.183 'a state of consternation . . .'; Ibid, p.123.
p.185 'was forced to kill . . .'; Kirby: *Andrew Smith*, p.51.
'had been exceedingly . . .'; Isaacs: p.161.
p.186 'like a distant . . .'; Gardiner: p.28.
p.187 'This house . . .'; Ibid, pp.200/201.
'It is death to cough . . .'; Kirby: *Andrew Smith*, pp. 92/93.
p.188 'The King's eyes . . .'; Gardiner: pp.36/37.
p.189 'Tall, corpulent and . . .'; Ibid, p.57.
'To a bystander . . .'; Ibid.
'He has massacred . . .'; Fynn: p.174.
p.190 'Where are your . . .'; Bryant: *Olden Times*, p.145.
p.191 'liberal offer . . .'; Isaacs: p.167.
p.193 'with great liberality . . .'; Isaacs: p.174.
'Whatever I can collect . . .'; Ibid.
p.194 'He displayed extraordinary . . .'; Ibid, p.179.
Interviews with Dingane; Ibid, pp.176/181.
'a quantity of muskets . . .'; C.A.: G.H. 23/9.
p.195 Isaacs's reply; *Grahamstown Journal*, 15 June 1832.

Chapter Twelve

p.197 'they gave a solemn . . .'; C.A.: G.H. 26/19, p.6.
'Far from manifesting . . .'; Isaacs: p.192.

p.198 'They are the wives . . .' and 'They killed one . . .' and 'She started . . .';
Isaacs: pp.182/183.

p.200 'The information which I . . .'; C.A.: G.H. 26/19, p.4.

p.201 'a most desirable . . .'; S.A.C.A. 5 February 1831.
'I will not be long . . .'; Kirby: *Andrew Smith*, p.72.
'To my surprise . . .'; Isaacs: p.260.

p.202 'These with other decorations . . .'; Isaacs: p.262.
'I am angry with . . .'; Ibid, p.263.

p.204 'I am waiting a short . . .'; Fynn: p.194.
'It consisted of beads . . .'; Ibid, p.195.

p.205 'the terror of the . . .'; Ibid, p.197.
'I declared the whole . . .'; Ibid.

p.206 'I made no inquiry . . .'; Ibid, p.199.
'Let us fall in . . .'; Ibid.
'Rather than deceive . . .'; Ibid, p.200.

p.207 'Please come and meet . . .'; S.A.C.A. 12 September 1852.
'I was on the point . . .'; Fynn: p.205.
'a violent noise . . .'; Ibid, p.206.

p.208 'All that we succeeded . . .'; Ibid.

Chapter Thirteen

p.209 'I have given up . . .'; Isaacs: p.178.

p.211 'a man capable . . .'; Harris: *The Wild Sports of Southern Africa*, p.101.
'His appearance is rather . . .'; Kotze: *Letters of American Missionaries*,
p.130.

p.212 'the good old fashioned . . .'; Bryant: *Olden Times*, p.429.

p.213 'There is nothing firm . . .'; Isaacs: p.219.
'I seize this opportunity . . .'; S.A.C.A. 10 September 1831.

p.214 'once more in . . .' and 'We received . . .'; *Grahamstown Journal*,
6 January 1832.
'Tell the Governor . . .' and 'I did better . . .'; Ibid, 30 March 1832.

p.215 'I see now the . . .'; Ibid.

p.216 'embarrassing' and 'to ascertain . . .'; C.A.: G.H. 23/2, p.360–61.
'that one white man after . . .'; Kotze: *Letters of American Missionaries*,
p.98–99.

p.218 'getting Natal settled . . .'; *Africana Notes and News*, June 1968, p.67.

p.219 'So long as they abstain . . .'; Isaacs: p.289.

p.220 'I know him to be . . .' and 'had married . . .'; *Africana Notes and News*,
June 1968, pp.68/69.

Chapter Fourteen

p.222 'with several Kaffer women'; Kirby: *Andrew Smith*, p.32.

p.223 'It is no uncommon thing . . .'; Ibid, p.86.
'The men die from it . . .'; Ibid, p.47.
'Almighty, I have never . . .'; Ibid, p.169.

p.224 'If a military party . . .'; Ibid, p.171.

p.225   'on the subject of a military . . .'; S.A.C.A. 25 January 1834.
        'Christianity and civilisation'; Ibid.
p.226   'why they did not come . . .'; *Grahamstown Journal*, 12 December 1832.
p.227   'How must this appear . . .'; Ibid, 30 March 1832.
p.229   'a permanent establishment . . .'; Kirby: *Andrew Smith*, p.163.
p.236   'Dingane has been told . . .'; *Grahamstown Journal*, 30 March 1832.

Chapter Fifteen

p.238   'There is the beast . . .'; Gardiner: p.30.
p.241   'Hitherto I had . . .'; Ibid, p.34.
p.242   'Dingarn with all . . .'; Ibid, p.42.
p.244   'I told him that I hoped . . .'; Ibid, p.71.
p.245   'that they might appear . . .'; Ibid, p.81.
p.246   'Ah! they shall not . . .'; Ibid, p.121.
        'I observed here . . .'; Ibid, p.127.
p.247   'appeared deep in . . .' and 'Now you must . . .'; Ibid, p.137.
p.248   'Poor creatures . . .'; Ibid, p.152.
        'He appeared in high . . .'; Ibid, p.160.
p.249   'They are all to be . . .'; Ibid, p.163.
        '*Their bonds must* . . .' and 'Inhuman wretch . . .'; Ibid, p.166.
p.250   'The fact is these three . . .'; Ibid, p.186.

Chapter Sixteen

p.251   'Full well do I . . .'; Gardiner: p.222.
        'Most gladly would . . .'; Ibid, pp.208–9.
p.253   'Chief of the . . .' and 'Great chief . . .'; Ibid, pp.213/14.
        'such civil authorities . . .'; Ibid, p.222.
p.254   'I rejoice to hear . . .'; Ibid, pp.394–5.
p.255   'an elephant chair . . .'; Mackeurtan: *Cradle Days*, p.187.
        'country three moons . . .'; Bird: vol 1, p.201.
        'Maritime Zoolahs . . .'; Kotze: *Letters of American Missionaries*, p.9.
p.256   'We found at Natal . . .'; *Quarterly Bulletin of South African Library*,
        June 1957, p.131.
        'He examined minutely . . .'; Bird: vol 1, p.203.
p.257   'If you succeed . . .'; Kotze: *Letters of American Missionaries*, p.99.
p.259   'I will not be killed . . .'; Bird: vol 1, p.378.
        'boy to cast balls . . .'; Ibid, p.195.
p.260   'most cruel and utterly . . .'; Ibid, p.322.
p.261   'the unanimity that . . .'; Ibid.
        'the bones of his . . .'; Mackeurtan: *Cradle Days*, p.197.
        'firm attitude'; Bird: vol 1, p.322.
p.262   'in the course of . . .'; Ibid, p.314.
p.263   'fervour and eloquence . . .'; Cory: p.19.
p.264   'punish any act . . .'; Bird: vol 1, p.321.
        'If desolating . . .'; Ibid, p.323.

p.265 'I trust I shall . . .'; Cory: p.19.
'Dingarn has promised . . .'; Ibid.
p.266 'It is on top of . . .'; Ibid, p.32.
p.267 'an apter scholar . . .'; Ibid, p.47.
'opposed to missionaries' and 'angry with . . .'; Kotze: *Letters of American Missionaries*, p.218.

Chapter Seventeen

p.269 'central event . . .'; Walker: *Great Trek*, p.1.
p.271 'We will not molest . . .'; Quoted: Ibid, p.105.
p.273 'Early in the morning . . .'; Kotze: *Letters of American Missionaries*, p.154.
'made our field . . .'; Ibid, p.169.
p.274 'The conviction that we . . .'; Bird: vol 1, p.326.
p.275 'fortified against . . .'; Bryant: *Olden Times*, p.436.
'were only a few . . .'; Cory: p.44.
p.276 'It was to purchase . . .'; Cory: p.59.
'You do not know . . .'; Bird: vol 1, p.364.
'We are as hard . . .'; Cory: p.62.
p.277 'With the request . . .'; Smit: Diary, p.184.
'You must prove this . . .'; Bird: vol 1, p.368.
p.278 'I will speak to Mr . . .'; Cory: p.64.
'to understand a Kaffir . . .'; Ibid, p.157.
p.279 'From God's great . . .'; Chase: pp.132–137.
(The letter is headed Port Natal but dated 8/11/1837—the day before Retief left emGungundlovu)
p.281 'It is not without apprehension . . .'; Cory: p.93.
p.282 'He had merely said . . .'; Ibid, p.65.
p.283 'the whole communication . . .'; Ibid, p.101.
p.284 'I am not without . . .'; Ibid, p.85.
p.285 'his master that he was not . . .'; Ibid, p.105.
p.286 'amazing influence'; Ibid.
'Know all Men by this . . .'; Bird: vol 1, p.366.
p.287 'You will see that . . .'; Jane Williams's statement in Moodie: *History of Battles*, vol 1, p.426.
'They said he was good . . .'; Cory: p.108.
'The papers were . . .'; Kotze: *Letters of American Missionaries*, p.234.
p.288 'We are sure . . .'; Bird: vol 1, p.380.
p.288 The description of the attack on the Boers and the subsequent massacre
p.289 ignores the fanciful versions given later and is based on that given by William Wood, the nearest one can get to an eye-witness. See Bird: vol 1, p.381 and Chase: part 1 p.7.

Chapter Eighteen

p.290 'covered with perspiration'; Jane Williams in Moodie: *History of Battles*, vol 1, p.426.

p.290 'They are taking the . . .'; Ibid, p.427.
p.291 'If I had understood . . .'; Ibid.
'I began to tremble . . .'; Cory: p.107.
'made an indiscribable . . .'; Kotze: *Letters of American Missionaries*, p.224.
p.292 'We will go . . .'; William Wood in Bird: vol 1, p.381.
'They are (I cannot . . .'; Cory: p.108.
p.294 'At once I suspected . . .'; Ibid, p.176.
p.295 'On the table . . .' and 'Father's come . . .'; Ibid, p.176.
'I cannot tell . . .' and 'I must tell . . .'; Ibid, p.176/177.
p.297 'I composed my mind . . .'; Cory: p.115.
'God is now . . .'; Ibid, p.120.
p.298 'plunder and revenge'; Ibid, p.124.
'The wild beast . . .'; Ibid, p.126.
p.299 'There is no king . . .'; Ibid, p.130.
p.302 'The tumultuous cries . . .'; Ibid, p.133.
p.303 'scarcely anything left . . .'; Ibid, p.138.
'It is with deep . . .'; Ibid, p.137.
p.304 'Tears of gratitude . . .'; Chase: part 2, p.22.
p.305 'This man has been . . .'; Quoted: Meintjes: *Voortrekkers*, p.131.
p.306 'colonization or annexure'; Chase: p.52.
'The Lord in His . . .'; Bird: vol 1, p.245.
p.307 'Of that fight . . .'; Ibid, p.375.
p.308 'like pumpkins . . .'; Ibid, p.246

Chapter Nineteen

p.310 'The sight of them . . .'; Chase: part 2, p.71.
p.314 'A large pleasant . . .'; Ibid, p.90.
'To ask us to . . .'; Ibid, p.74.
p.315 'I am on the brink . . .' and 'I have never . . .'; Bird: vol 1, p.517.
p.316 'When Dingaan makes . . .'; Chase: part 2, p.89.
'Our King has now . . .'; Ibid, p.91.
'Not that I really . . .'; Bird: vol 1, p.518.
p.317 'Surely this will show . . .'; Ibid, pp.97–98.
p.318 'Even if it is true . . .'; *De Ware Afrikaan*, 3 December 1839.
p.319 'I had not enough . . .'; Chase: part 1, p.106.
p.320 'Why should I allow . . .'; Ibid, p.105.
'Why don't you rise . . .'; Ibid.
p.321 '*a beer brewer* . . .'; Ibid, p.102.
'the whole royal . . .'; Ibid, p.106.
p.322 'the heart of a woman . . .'; Bird: vol 1, p.553.
'if the people receive . . .'; Chase: p.106.
'My heart is now . . .'; Ibid.
'Reigning Prince . . .'; Ibid, p.108.
p.323 'Why have you . . .'; Ibid, p.109.
'As if to strengthen . . .'; Bird: vol 1, p.568.

p.323 'cultivate the beautiful . . .'; Quoted: Mackeurtan *Cradle Days*, p.255.

p.324 'Of all the fine . . .'; *De Ware Afrikaan*, 25 February 1840.
'Go he said . . .'; Bird: vol 1, p.564.

p.325 'If Panda had been . . .'; *De Ware Afrikaan*, 25 February 1840.
'Dingaan's greatness . . .'; Chase: part 1, p.121.

p.326 'had his own system . . .'; Bird: vol 1, p.564.
'But as soon as . . .'; Ibid, pp.566–567.

p.327 Damdusa's trial and death; Bird: vol 1, pp.569–571.

p.329 'I now appoint you . . .'; Ibid, p.376.
'Should any power . . .'; Chase: part 1, p.126.

p.330 'for he had neither . . .'; Bird: vol 1, p.376.

p.331 'The betrayal of Piet Retief . . .'; Chief Gatsha Buthelezi quoted in *The Cape Argus*, 15 January 1972.

PART THREE

Chapter Twenty

p.339 'Two bulls cannot . . .'; Quoted: Binns: *The Last Zulu King*, p.36.

p.344 'emulate the sanguinary . . .'; Quoted: Dixie: *Defence of Zululand*, p.33.

p.345 'If anything brings . . .'; Ibid, p.75.
'apologised and atoned . . .'; Ibid, p.44.

p.348 'A very remarkable . . .'; *Cambridge History of the British Empire*, vol viii, p.478.

p.349 'We were treated . . .'; *Cape Times*, 11 September 1879.
'It was pitiful . . .'; Quoted: Binns: *Last Zulu King*, p.173.

p.351 'the ignorant and bloodthirsty'; Dixie: *Defence of Zululand*, p.53.

p.352 'Can the blackest . . .'; Ibid, p.29.

p.353 'I like the scenes . . .'; *Natal Mercury*, 10 October 1882.
'like a fat, black . . .'; Ibid, 25 September 1882.

p.354 'I shall have a great deal . . .'; Colenso: *Ruin of Zululand*, vol 2, p.72.

p.358 'the image of his father . . .'; Ibid, p.339.

p.360 'The majority of our people . . .'; Chief Gatsha Buthelezi. Quoted in *Cape Times*, 5 May 1973.
'The Queen now rules . . .'; Quoted: Binns: Dinuzulu, p.113.

p.361 'During that time . . .'; *South Africa*, 25 October 1913.

p.362 'You white people . . .'; Ibid.

p.363 'cunning and fickle . . .'; *Dictionary of South African Biography*, vol 1, Dinuzulu.
'Dinuzulu must know . . .'; Quoted: Binns: Dinuzulu, p.113.

SELECT BIBLIOGRAPHY

(For unpublished sources see Reference Notes)

Becker, Peter. *Path of Blood*, Longmans, London 1962
—— *Rule of Fear*, Longmans, London 1964
Binns, C. T. *The Last Zulu King*, Longmans, London 1963
—— *Dinuzulu*, Longmans, London 1968
Bird, John. *The Annals of Natal, 1495-1845* (2 vols), Davis, Pietermaritzburg 1888
Booth, A. R. (ed.) *Journal of the Rev. George Champion*, Cape Town 1967.
Brooks, Edgar & C. de B. Webb. *A History of Natal*, University of Natal Press 1965
Bryant, A. T. *Olden Times in Zululand and Natal*, Longmans, London 1929
—— *The Zulu People*, Shuter & Shooter, Pietermaritzburg 1949
Bulpin, T. V. *Natal and the Zulu Country*, Books of Africa, Cape Town 1966
Cambridge History of the British Empire, Vol. VIII
Chase, J. C. *The Natal Papers*, Godlonton, Grahamstown 1843
Colenso, Frances E. *The Ruin of Zululand* (2 vols), Ridgeway, London 1884
Colenso, John. *Ten Weeks in Natal*, Cambridge 1855
Cory, G. E. (ed.) *The Diary of the Rev. Francis Owen*, Van Riebeeck Society, Cape Town 1926
Cowley, Cecil. *Kwa Zulu: Queen Mkabi's Story*, Struik, Cape Town 1966
Cox, G. W. *The Life of John William Colenso*, Ridgeway, London 1888
Dictionary of South African Biography, Vol. 1 (1968), Vol. 2 (1972)
Dixie, Lady Florence. *A Defence of Zululand and its King*, Chatto, London 1882
—— *In the Land of Misfortune*, Bentley, London 1882
Furneaux, Rupert. *The Zulu War*, Weidenfeld & Nicolson, London 1963
Fynn, Henry Francis (edited by James Stuart and D. Mck. Malcolm) *The Diary of Henry Francis Fynn*, Shuter & Shooter, Pietermaritzburg 1969
Gardiner, Allen. *Narrative of a Journey to the Zoolu Country*, William Crofts, London 1836
Gibson, J. Y. *The Story of the Zulus*, Davis, Pietermaritzburg 1903
Harris, W. C. *The Wild Sports of Southern Africa*, London 1841
Hattersley, A. F. *Portrait of a Colony: The Story of Natal*, Cambridge 1940
Holden, W. C. *History of the Colony of Natal, South Africa*, A. Heylin, London 1855
Isaacs, Nathaniel (edited by L. Herrman) *Travels and Adventures in Eastern Africa*, Struik (Reprint), Cape Town 1970 (originally published: Churton, London 1836)
Kay, Rev. S. *Travels and Researches in Caffraria*, London 1833

Kiewiet, C. W. de. *The Imperial Factor in South Africa*, Cambridge 1937
Kirby, Percival (ed.) *Andrew Smith and Natal*, Van Riebeeck Society, Cape Town 1955
Kotze, D. J. *Letters of the American Missionaries 1835–1838*, Van Riebeeck Society, Cape Town 1950
Krige, Eileen. *The Social System of the Zulus*, Longmans, London 1936
Lister, Margaret (ed.) *Journals of Andrew Geddes Bain*, Van Riebeeck Society, Cape Town 1949
Lugg, H. C. *Historic Natal and Zululand*, Shuter & Shooter, Pietermaritzburg 1949
Mackeurtan, Graham. *The Cradle Days of Natal*, Grigg (Reprint), Durban 1972 (originally published: Longmans, 1930)
Marquard, Leo. *The Story of South Africa*, Faber, London 1963
Marsh, John. *A Memoir of Allen F. Gardiner*, Nisbet, London 1857
Martineau, J. *Life and Letters of Sir Bartle Frere*, Murray, London 1895
Meintjes, Johannes. *The Voortrekkers*, Cassell, London 1973
Millar, A. K. *Plantagenet in South Africa*, O.U.P., 1965
Mitford, Bertram. *Through the Zulu Country*, K. Paul Trench, London 1883
Mofolo, Thomas. *Chaka*, O.U.P., 1931
Moodie, D. C. F. *The History of the Battles of the British, the Boers and the Zulus etc in Southern Africa* (2 vols), Murray & St Leger, Cape Town 1888
Morris, Donald R. *The Washing of the Spears*, Cape, London 1966
Omer-Cooper, J. D. *The Zulu Aftermath*, Longmans, London 1966
Owen, W. F. *Narrative of Voyages*, London 1833
Oxford History of South Africa (2 vols), edited by M. Wilson & L. Thompson
Page, Jesse. *Captain Allen Gardiner*, Pickering & Inglis, London 1897
Pringle, Thomas. *Narrative of a Residence in South Africa* (Reprint), Struik, Cape Town 1966
Ransford, O. *The Great Trek*, Murray, London 1972
Rees, Wyn (ed.) *Colenso Letters from Natal*, Shuter & Shooter, Pietermaritzburg 1958
Ritter, E. A. *Shaka Zulu*, Panther, London 1958
Rivett-Carnac, Dorothy. *Hawks Eye*, Timmins, Cape Town 1966
Roberts, Brian. *Ladies in the Veld*, Murray, London 1965
Samuelson, R. C. *Long, Long Ago*, Knox, Durban 1929
Selby, John, *Shaka's Heirs*, Allen & Unwin, London 1971
Smit, Erasmus (translated by W. G. A. Mears) *The Diary of Erasmus Smit*, Struik, Cape Town 1972
Smith, Edwin. *Life and Times of Daniel Lindley*, Epworth Press, London 1949
Soga, J. H. *South-eastern Bantu*, Witwatersrand University Press, 1930
Stuart, J. *A History of the Zulu Rebellion, 1906*, Macmillan, London 1913
Steedman, A. *Wanderings in Southern Africa* (2 vols), Longmans, London 1835
Thompson, George (edited by V. S. Forbes) *Travels and Adventures in Southern Africa* (2 vols), Van Riebeeck Society, Cape Town 1967
Troup, Freda. *South Africa: An Historical Introduction*, Eyre Methuen, London 1972
Tomasson, W. H. *Transvaal and Zululand*, Remington, London 1881

Vilakazi, B. W. *Zulu Horizons*, Timmins, Cape Town 1962
Vulliamy, C. E. *Outlanders*, Cape, London 1938
Walker, E. A. *History of South Africa*, Longmans, London 1957
—— *The Great Trek*, A. & C. Black, London 1934
Walker, Oliver, *Proud Zulu*, Werner Laurie, London 1949
Watt, Elizabeth, *Febana*, Peter Davies, London 1962
Wilson, Helen. *The Two Scapegoats*, Davis, Pietermaritzburg 1914
Wood, W. *Dingaan, King of the Zoolahs*, Collard, Cape Town 1840
Worsfold, Basil. *Sir Bartle Frere*, Butterworth, London 1923

Periodicals and Newspapers
Africana Notes and News, Quarterly Bulletin of the South African Library, South African Commercial Advertiser, Grahamstown Journal, Times of Natal, Natal Mercury, Cape Times, Cape Argus, Cape Government Gazette, De Ware Afrikaan.

INDEX